W9-BZO-575

# INSIDERS'GUIDE® to
# Florida Keys &
# Key West

### SEVENTEENTH EDITION

## JULIET DYAL GRAY

## Globe
## Pequot

GUILFORD, CONNECTICUT

All the information in this guidebook is subject to change. We recommend that you call ahead to obtain current information before traveling.

# Globe Pequot

An imprint of Rowman & Littlefield
Insiders' Guide is a registered trademark of Rowman & Littlefield.

Distributed by NATIONAL BOOK NETWORK

Copyright © 2015 Rowman & Littlefield
Maps: Design Maps Inc. © Rowman & Littlefield

British Library Cataloguing in Publication Information Available

ISSN 1529-174X
ISBN 978-1-4930-0148-4 (paperback)
ISBN 978-1-4930-1554-2 (e-book)

∞™ The paper used in this publication meets the minimum requirements of American National Standard for Information Sciences—Permanence of Paper for Printed Library Materials, ANSI/NISO Z39.48-1992.

# Contents

## Directory of Maps

# About the Author

Juliet Dyal Gray is a native Floridian who writes about the Florida Keys for many national publications, including *Delta Sky* magazine. She is also an editor of *Key West Magazine*. Her writing career has taken her on many journeys, including snorkeling around the islands of the Galapagos and on safari in South Africa. In addition to writing, Juliet produces theater at the Key West Theater and is a co-founder of both the nonprofit Performing Arts Project (performing artsproject.com) and On the Rock Productions (ontherockkeywest.com). Juliet writes from her home in Key West, Florida.

# Acknowledgments

I am extremely grateful to the amazing people in the Florida Keys, which I am proud to call home. My eternal thanks goes to my Key West friends for their support, especially Liz Love, Mike Marrero, Elizabeth Miller, and Anne Walters. I am also grateful for the support of my parents, Jake and Kay Dyal, my husband, Christian Gray, and my siblings, Caroline and Jake Dyal. As I continue to live and work in the Florida Keys, I am also truly thankful to be a permanent *Insider* in paradise.—JDG

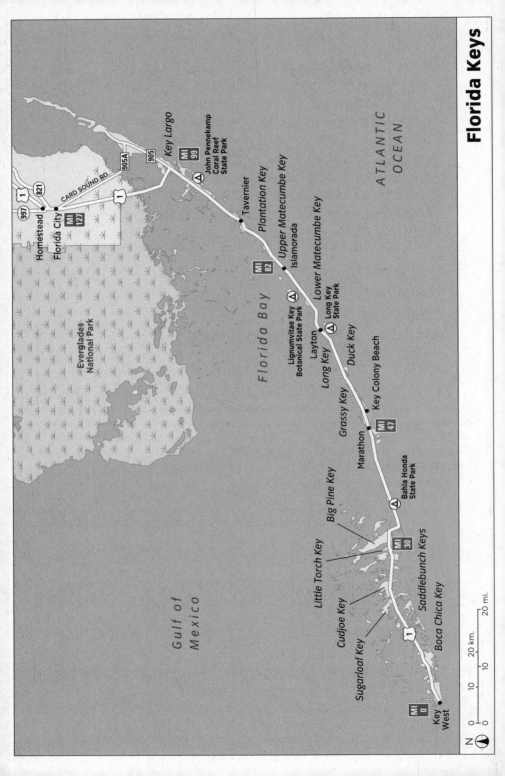

**Florida Keys**

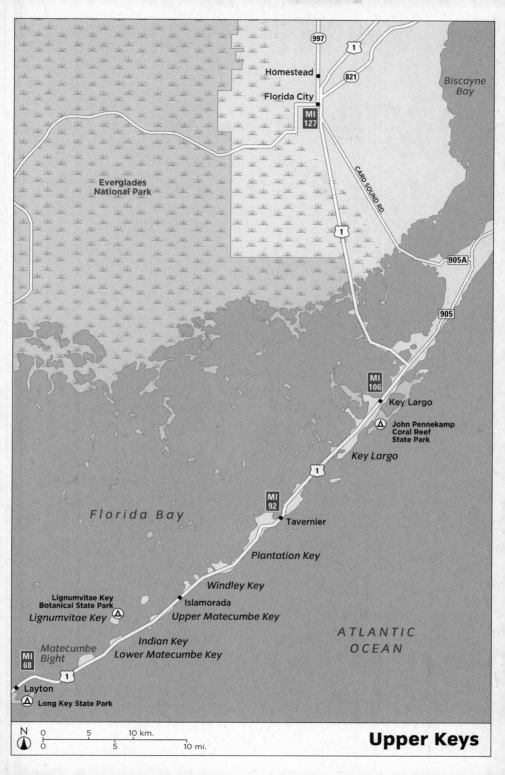

# Upper Keys

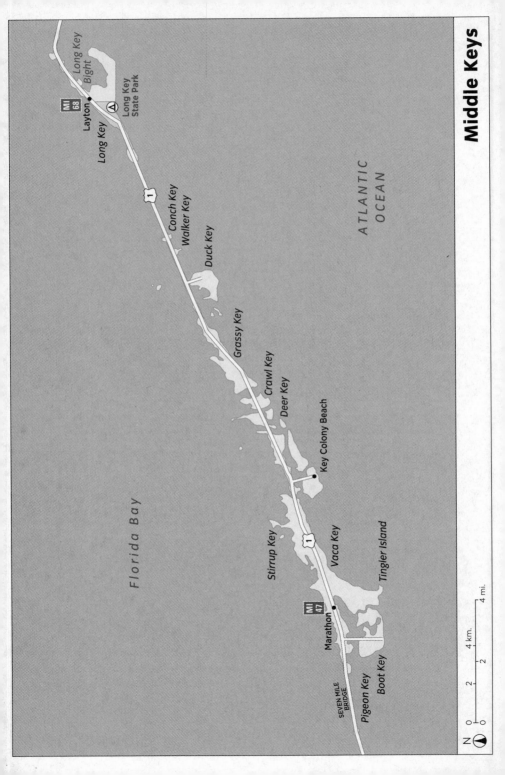

**Middle Keys**

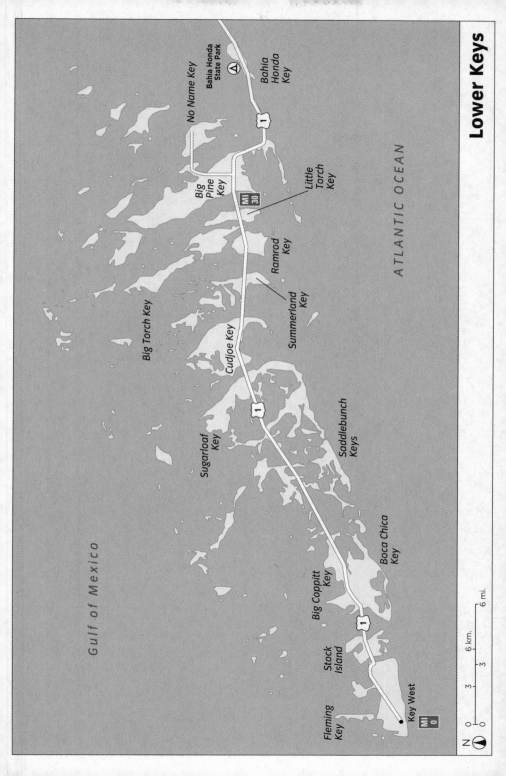

**Lower Keys**

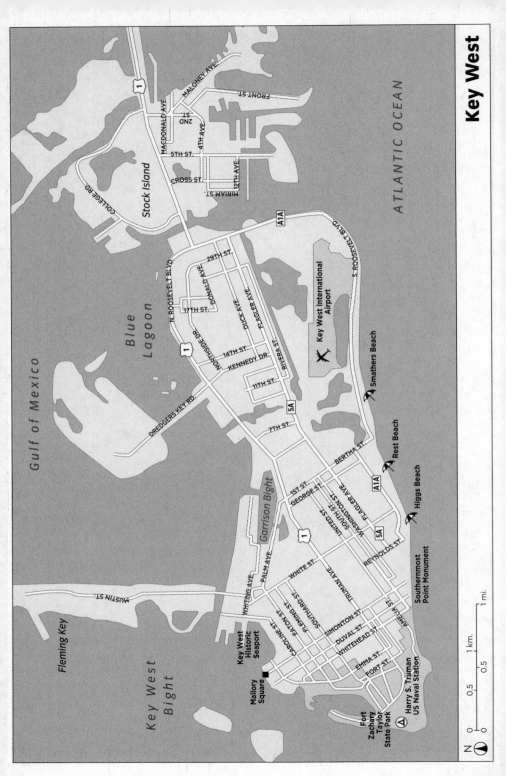

# Key West

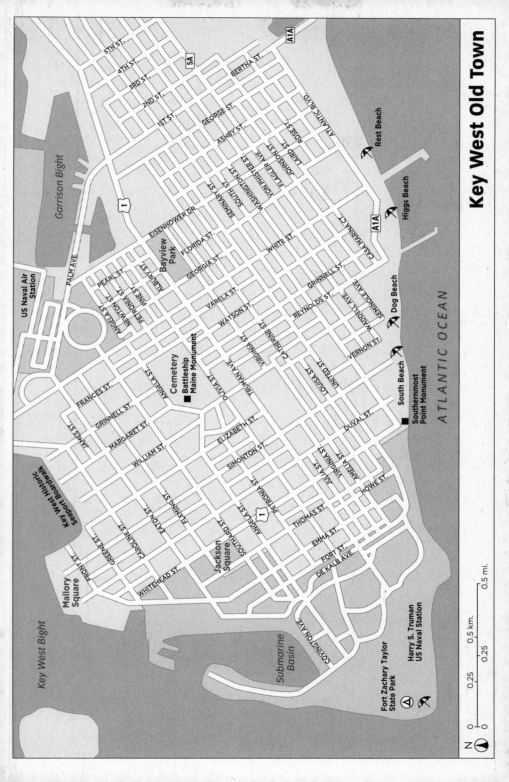

# Key West Old Town

# How to Use This Book

Here at the southernmost tip of the continental US, the serpentine Overseas Highway fuses many of our 800-plus islands with ligaments of vaulted bridges and concrete connective tissue.

Ours is a marriage of land and sea. To merely introduce you to the topside society of the Florida Keys would neglect the flamboyant and fascinating communities living below. This guide lifts the curtain, bringing the many facets of our watery stage to life. We treat you to our unique geology and colorful history. We introduce you to the flora and fauna of the habitats of our tropical ecosystem. We take you where you may have never been before—fishing, diving, and boating in our waters.

We'll help you sate your appetite with listings of restaurants, seafood markets, and specialty food shops. We'll show you where the action is with the rundown on attractions, recreation sites, festivals and special events, and nightlife of the Keys. We'll offer myriad alternatives for you to rest your weary head: hotels, motels, inns, guesthouses, and condos; campgrounds; even resort marinas and anchoring-out spots for your motor or sailing yacht. Landlubber or seafarer, everything you need to know is in the *Insiders' Guide to Florida Keys & Key West*.

To navigate this book, begin with the assumption you are traveling "down the Keys"—that is, from Key Largo to Key West. We have organized our information alphabetically traveling down from the Upper Keys through to Key West. Most addresses are indicated by mile marker. Mile markers are those small green signs with white numbers you'll see posted at the sides of the Overseas Highway (US 1). We have designated mile-marker addresses as either oceanside (on your left as you travel down the Keys) or bayside (on your right as you go toward Key West). At Key West, which is MM 0, locations are stated using street names.

Most chapters have several parts. A general preface to the subject matter acquaints you with aspects of the topics common to all areas of the Florida Keys. This is followed by specifics for the Upper Keys (MM 106 on Key Largo to MM 70 on Long Key), Middle Keys (MM 70 to MM 39 on Ohio Key), Lower Keys (MM 39 to Stock Island), and finally Key West, the entrance to which is actually about MM 5 on Stock Island, although mile-marker appellations are not used in Key West.

Throughout all the chapters we have sprinkled Insiders' Tips (indicated by an **i** ), extracted from those in the know (with a little arm-twisting). You'll find enlightening Close-ups chock-full of information on everything from where to find the best food festivals to details about our amazing and rich history. And just so you will be sure to understand the language, we have included a glossary of Keys-speak. You'll also find listings accompanied by the ★ symbol—these are our top picks for attractions, restaurants, accommodations, and everything in between that you shouldn't miss while you're in the area. You want the best this region has to offer? Go with our Insiders' Choice. Moving to the Florida Keys or already live here? Be sure to check out the back of the book, where you will find the **Living Here** appendix that offers sections on relocation, real estate, education, health care, and media.

You hold in your hand a passport to the Florida Keys. We help you hit the road, explore the sea, and speak the language of the natives. Locals call this Paradise. You can judge for yourself.

# History

The saga of the Keys, like the livelihoods of its inhabitants, tethers itself first, foremost, and forever to the sea. Our fragile strand of coral beads, which arcs southwest from the US mainland to within 100 miles of Cuba, has been for eons at the mercy of the elements. Nature determined, more than humans ever did, the course of our history. That is, until one man accomplished what natural forces could not: He connected the islands to each other and to the mainland US.

We will chronicle the Florida Keys, therefore, as a man-made triptych, highlighting the eras before, during, and after Henry Flagler's Florida East Coast Railroad Extension refashioned the subsequent history of the region.

## The Gulf Stream: Treasure Highway

Long before the Overseas Highway became the main road of the Florida Keys, another highway controlled the islands' destiny: the great, blue river-in-the-Atlantic—the Gulf Stream. (The warm water of the Gulf Stream, the temperature of which varies greatly from surrounding waters, flows in a northerly direction between the Keys and Cuba, up the northeast coast of the US, and then turns toward the east where it crosses the Atlantic Ocean to the European continent.) Conquistadores, explorers, and adventurers capitalized on the pulsing clockwise current (2 to 4 knots) to carry them swiftly back to Europe, where they unloaded the harvested riches of the New World at the feet of greedy monarchs.

The Spanish were the first to send their treasure-laden ships on this precarious route past our island chain, which is protected from the ocean's fury by a barrier coral reef (see the Diving & Snorkeling chapter). The Gulf Stream, which is not a definitive channel, winds an uneven course about 45 miles wide just outside the reef. Bad weather or bad judgment dashed the hopes, dreams, and cargo of hundreds of ships against this unforgiving coral graveyard.

It was the Native Americans who initially took advantage of this unexpected shipwrecked bounty, but salvaging became big business in the Keys with the arrival of the Bahamian Conchs (pronounced konk). The passing ships inspired piracy from many nations, particularly the English, who lurked in the cuts and channels between the islands waiting to raid the ships' caches of gold and silver.

The Native Americans learned the ways of the Europeans, trading with the Spanish in Havana by means of large oceangoing canoes, pirating English ships, and free-diving to salvage the cargo of their wrecked vessels. The white man's diseases, however, greatly reduced Native American numbers. In 1763

Spain gave Florida to England in exchange for Cuba. At this time the last of the indigenous Native American families fled to Havana, fearing retribution for the cruelty they had heaped upon the British sailors found dashed upon the reef and stranded.

## Key West

A time-honored story persists that warring tribes of mainland Seminoles and island Calusas had one final battle on the southernmost island of our chain of keys. Spanish conquistadores purportedly found the island strewn with bleached bones of the Native Americans and called the key Cayo Hueso (pronounced KY-o WAY-so), or "island of bones." Bahamian settlers pronounced the Spanish name as Key West.

Settled long before the other keys in the chain, Key West was very much a maritime frontier town by the 1820s, booming with sea-driven industries. Ships sailing out of Key West Harbor set across the Florida Straits to Havana, their holds filled with the fish, sea turtles, and sponges harvested along the length of the Keys. A lively fishing trade with Cuba continued into the 1870s. The melting pot of Key West included seamen from many cultures: African-American Bahamians, West Indian African Americans, Spanish Cubans, and white Bahamians of English descent.

Key West was incorporated in 1828. Within 10 years it was the largest and wealthiest city in the territory of Florida, even though it could be reached only by ship, a geographic fact of life that continued until Henry Flagler's Florida East Coast Railroad Extension was finished in 1912. But it was the very waters isolating Key West from the rest of the world that contributed to its wealth.

## Piracy

When the US gained possession of Florida and the Florida Keys in 1821, the island of Key West took on a strategic importance as a US naval base. Lieutenant Matthew Perry, who was assigned to secure the island for the US, deemed Key West a safe, convenient, and extensive harbor. It became the base of operations to fight the piracy that ravaged the trading vessels traveling the Gulf Stream superhighway and those heading through the Gulf of Mexico to New Orleans. English, French, and Dutch buccaneers had threatened the Spanish treasure galleons in the 18th century. In the early days of the 1800s, Spanish pirates, based mainly in Cuba, hid among the islands of the Keys and preyed on all nations, especially the US. Using schooners with centerboards that drew only 4 to 5 feet of water, the pirate ships dipped in and out of the shallow cuts and channels to avoid capture.

In 1830 Commander David Porter was sent to Key West to head up an antipiracy fleet and wipe out the sea-jacking from the region. Commandeering barge-style vessels equipped with oars, Porter and his crews were able to follow

> **i** In 1898 the battleship USS *Maine* sailed from Key West Harbor to Havana Harbor in Cuba, where the ship exploded and sank. The ship's gun-sight hood is located at the Florida Keys Historical Military Memorial at Mallory Square in Key West. Crewmen from the disaster are buried in the Key West Cemetery, and the investigation took place in the Key West Custom House.

the sea dogs into the shallow waters and overtake them. After 1830 the area was safe from banditry once again.

### The Wrecking Industry

Whereas the Gulf Stream was once the sea highway carrying Spanish treasure galleons back to Europe, in the 18th and 19th centuries the route was traversed in the opposite direction. Trading vessels sailed from New England ports to the French and British islands of the West Indies and the Antilles, hugging the shoreward edge of the Gulf Stream so as not to have to run against its strong northerly currents. They often ran aground on the reef, giving birth to a lucrative wrecking industry that salvaged silks, satins, lace, leather, crystal, china, silver, furniture, wine, whiskey, and more.

After the US took possession of Florida in 1821, Key West became an official wrecking and salvage station for the federal government, which sought to regulate and cash in on the lucrative trade that until this time was going to Nassau or Havana. Salvage masters had to get a license from a district court judge, proving that they and their salvage vessels were free of fraud. By 1854 wrecking was a widely practiced profession in the Keys. Fleets of schooners patrolled the Keys from Biscayne to the Dry Tortugas. First they would assist the shipwrecked sailors, then try to save the ship (there was no Coast Guard in those days).

Unlike early unregulated times, the wreckers couldn't just lay claim to the ship's cargo for themselves. They were paid off in shares of the bounty. During peak wrecking years, 1850 to 1860, nearly one ship per week hit the reefs, some with cargo valued in the millions of dollars.

Although by 1826 some of the reefs along the length of the Keys were marked by lighthouses or lightships, most remained treacherous and claimed many cargoes, particularly in the Upper Keys where the Gulf Stream meanders close to the reef. The construction of additional lighthouses along the reef in the mid-1800s improved navigation to the point that the wrecking industry gradually faded away by the end of the 19th century.

## Sponging

Sponging developed quickly in the Keys after the area became part of the US, maturing into a commercially important industry by 1850.

Sponge harvesting initially was accomplished from a dinghy: One man sculled while the other looked through a glass-bottomed bucket. The spotter held a long pole with a small, three-pronged rake on one end used to impale the sponge and bring it into the boat. Onshore the sponges were laid on the ground to dry in the sun so that the living animal within would dehydrate and die. The sponges then were soaked for a week and pounded on a rock or beaten with a stick to remove a blackish covering. Cleaned of weeds, washed, and hung to dry in bunches, the sponges were displayed for sale.

Cubans, Greeks, and Conchs harvested the sponges as fast and furiously as they could, with little regard for how the supply would be maintained, and it inevitably began to diminish. The Greeks began diving into deeper waters for the sponges, much in demand on the world market by 1900, and eventually moved to Florida's west coast at Tarpon Springs, where the sponging was more bountiful.

By 1940 a blight had wiped out all but about 10 percent of the Keys' sponge population. Although sponges again grow in our waters, commercial sponging is no longer a viable industry, as synthetic sponges have absorbed the market.

## Cigar-Making

Cuba, closer to Key West than Miami is, has always played a role in the historical evolution of the Keys. Cuban fishermen long frequented the bountiful Keys waters, and in the 19th century Cuban émigrés brought new life and new industry to Key West. William H. Wall built a small cigar factory in the 1830s on Key West's Front Street, but it was not until a year after the Cuban Revolution of 1868, when a prominent Cuban by the name of Señor Vicente Martínez Ybor moved his cigar-making factory to Key West from Havana, that the new era of cigar manufacturing began in earnest.

E. H. Gato and a dozen or so other cigar-making companies followed Martínez Ybor, and an influx of Cuban immigrant cigar workers "washed ashore," joining the melting pot in Key West. Tobacco arrived in bales from Havana, and production grew until factories numbered 161, catapulting Key West to the rank of cigar-making capital of the US. Though the manufacturers moved their businesses to Key West to escape Cuban tariffs and the cigarmakers' union, the unions reestablished themselves in Key West by 1879, and troubles began anew.

The industry continued to flourish in Key West until its peak in 1890, when the city of Tampa offered the cigar manufacturers lower taxes if they would move to the Gulf Coast swamplands, an area now called Ybor City. With this incentive, the cigar-making industry left the Keys, but many of the Cuban people stayed, creating a steady Latin influence on Key West that has endured to this day.

**The Salt Industry**
Early settlers of Key West and Duck Key manufactured sea salt beginning in the 1830s, using natural salt-pond basins on both islands. Salt was essential for preserving food in those days because there was no refrigeration, and Key West became the largest supplier of the nation's salt. Capricious weather often flooded the salt ponds with freshwater, ruining the salty "crop." By 1876 the salt industry no longer existed in the Keys on a national level. The destructive forces of repeated hurricanes made the industry economically infeasible. Today, artisanal salt farmers still exist and sell to specialty stores throughout the Florida Keys.

**Homesteading the Keys**
Bahamians also homesteaded in the keys in the early 19th century, settling in small family groups to farm the thin soil. Familiar with cultivating the unique land of limestone islands, the Bahamians worked at farming pineapples, key limes, and sapodillas, called "sours and dillies."

Many believe Indian Key was the first real settlement in the Upper Keys. By 1834 it had docks, a post office, shops, and a mansion belonging to the island's owner, Jacob Housman. It became the governmental seat of Dade County for a time, but attacks from mainland Native Americans proved an insurmountable problem for this little key. Through the ensuing decades, Bahamian farmers

i Key West was once the largest manufacturer of cigars in the United States. In 1915 Key West had 29 cigar factories, employing 2,100 workers, who hand-rolled 62,415,000 stogies from imported Cuban tobacco.

homesteaded on Key Vaca, Upper Matecumbe, Newport (Key Largo), Tavernier, and Planter. By 1891 the area that is now Harry Harris Park in Key Largo had a post office, school, church, and five farms (see the Recreation chapter).

The census on any of these keys varied widely over the course of the century, and little is known as to why. For instance, Key Vaca had 200 settlers in 1840, according to Dr. Perrine of Indian Key, but by 1866 a US census revealed an unexplained population of zero for Key Vaca.

## FLAGLER'S FOLLY: THE FLORIDA EAST COAST RAILROAD EXTENSION

The dream of one man changed the isolation of the Florida Keys for all time. Native New Yorker Henry Flagler, born in 1830 and educated only to the eighth grade, established the Standard Oil Company with John D. Rockefeller in 1870 and became a wealthy, well-respected businessman. In 1885 he purchased a short-line railroad between Jacksonville and St. Augustine and began extending the rails southward toward Miami, then only a small settlement.

Flagler's vision of his railroad project went beyond Miami, however. He wanted to connect the mainland with the deep port of Key West, a booming city of more than 10,000 people, in anticipation of the growing shipping commerce he thought would be generated by the opening of the Panama Canal in the early years of the 20th century.

By 1904 the railroad extended to Homestead, at the gateway to the Keys. The year 1905 saw the commencement of what many perceived as an old man's folly: a railroad constructed across 128 miles of rock islands and open water, under the most nonidyllic conditions imaginable, by men and materials that had to be imported from throughout the world. Steamships brought fabricated steel from Pennsylvania, and cement from Germany and Belgium was used to create concrete supports below the waterline. Cement for above-water concrete came from New York State, sand and gravel from the Chesapeake, crushed rock from the Hudson Valley, timbers and pilings from Florida and Georgia, and provisions from Chicago. Barges carried freshwater from Miami to the construction sites. Nothing was indigenous to the Keys except the mosquitoes and the sand flies.

By 1908 the first segment, from Homestead to Marathon, was completed, and Marathon became a boomtown. Ships brought their cargoes of Cuban pineapples and limes here, where they were loaded onto railway cars and sent north. (The railroad turnaround was at the current site of Knight's Key campground.) Railroad workers used Pigeon Key as a base for further railway construction.

The 7-mile "water gap" between Marathon and Bahia Honda took some engineering prowess to overcome, and the completion of the project was severely hampered by several devastating hurricanes in 1909 and 1910. But on January 22, 1912, Henry Flagler—by then age 82—finally rode his dream from Homestead to Key West. He traveled across 42 stretches of sea, more than 17 miles of concrete viaducts and concrete-and-steel bridges, and more than 20 miles of filled causeways, ultimately traversing 128 miles from island to island to the fruition of his vision. He entered Key West that day a hero. He died the following year, probably never knowing that his flight of fancy changed the course of the Florida Keys forever.

Flagler's railroad, called the Key West Extension, made Key West America's largest deepwater port on the Atlantic Coast south of Norfolk, Virginia. Trade with the Caribbean increased, and Key West flourished for 23 years, recovering from the loss of the sponge and cigar industries. The Florida East Coast Railroad Company completed construction of Key West's first official tourist hotel, the Casa Marina, in 1921. La Concha was built in 1928.

In 1923 Monroe County appropriated funds to construct a road paralleling the railroad. The bumpy rock road crossed Card Sound with a long area of fill and a wooden bridge. A half-dozen humpback bridges crossed the creeks and cuts on Key Largo. Extending the length of Key Largo, the road continued across Plantation Key, Windley Key, and Upper Matecumbe. At the southern end of our island chain, a narrow, 32-mile road connected Key West with No Name Key off Big Pine Key. By 1930 a car ferry service provided the waterway link between the two sections of roadway, which traversed what we now call the Upper and Lower Keys.

By 1934 the failing economy prompted the Federal Emergency Relief Administration to step in, and it commenced development and promotion of Key West as a magnet for increased tourism in the Keys.

To that end, developers began building bridges to connect the Middle Keys to each other and to the two sections of finished roadway. A "bonus army" of World War I veterans was employed to accomplish this momentous task. However, in 1935 Mother Nature reasserted her authority and once again charted the destiny of our islands. On Labor Day what today we would call a Category Five hurricane hit the Upper and Middle Keys, destroying much of Flagler's railroad. Hundreds of lives were lost when the 17-foot storm surge hit the crew working on a bridge at Islamorada.

> **i** In 1885 a trolley line, the Key West Street Car Association, was established in Key West. The open-sided wooden cars had four benches and were pulled by two mules. In 1898 the Key West Electric Company bought the line and ran 10-bench cars that operated on existing broad-gauge tracks using power from a double-wired overhead system.

Because of mismanagement and lack of foreign freight heading northward from Cuban and Caribbean ports, the railroad was already in receivership. The railroad chose not to rebuild, citing financial difficulties. By this time it had become cheaper to haul cargo by truck than by train. The county's Overseas Road and Toll Commission purchased the right-of-way from the Florida East Coast Railroad and converted the single-track railway trestles, which remained intact after the hurricane, into two-lane bridges for automobiles. The highway from Homestead to Key West opened for traffic in 1938.

The 100th anniversary of Henry Flagler's railroad was celebrated in 2012. The website flaglerkeys100.com offers a historical time line, photos, and videos about the ill-fated Florida Keys Over-Sea Railroad.

## EPILOGUE

In the late 1930s the US Navy, stationed in Key West, began construction of an 18-inch pipeline that carried freshwater from wells in Homestead to Key West. The naval presence in Key West grew with the beginning of World War II, when antisubmarine patrols began surveillance of surrounding waters. The navy also improved the highway to better accommodate the transfer of supplies for its military installation. The Card Sound Road was bypassed. The new road, which followed the old railroad bed, now is known as the "Stretch." By 1942 the Keys enjoyed freshwater and electricity service, and the Overseas Highway (US 1) officially opened in 1944, ushering in a new era of development that continues to this day.

After World War II the Florida Keys became more and more popular as a sportfishing destination, and fishing camps dotted the shores from the Upper Keys to Key West. Still a rather remote, primitive spot to visit, the Keys nevertheless continued to evolve into a desirable tourist terminus, and Key West burgeoned as a port of call. Also contributing to Key West's rebirth was the discovery of pink gold: shrimp. Fishermen who had caught a shark in the waters between Key West and the Dry Tortugas found the fish's stomach filled with large pink shrimp. This led to the discovery of a bountiful shrimping area off the Tortugas, and the Key West "pinks" shrimping industry was spawned in the Florida Keys. It is still a viable occupation as far up the Keys as Marathon.

From 1978 to 1983 the old rail-bed conversion bridges were retired. Modern concrete structures, some four lanes wide, now span our waters. Many of the old bridges have been recycled as fishing piers, but others still stand, abandoned and obsolete alongside their successors, crumbling reminders of the Keys' not-so-distant past.

By the 1980s the Florida Keys had emerged as a tourist-driven economy. Tourism remains the major industry of the Keys today, with the water-based attractions of Key West topping the list of most popular destinations.

# Welcome to the Florida Keys

To be in the Florida Keys is to become one with nature, for the Keys offer unparalleled opportunities to be in direct daily contact with her substantial bounty. You'll know what we mean the moment you crest the first of the 42 bridges now spanning our islands and feel the vast power of the surrounding seas. Gaze down on our string of coral pearls from the air and you'll see that the Keys look insignificant juxtaposed against the encompassing Atlantic Ocean and Gulf of Mexico.

## HABITATS OF THE FLORIDA KEYS

The word *tropical* generally refers to plants and animals living in the latitudes between the Tropic of Cancer in the Northern Hemisphere and the Tropic of Capricorn in the Southern Hemisphere. The Florida Keys are somewhat north of the Tropic of Cancer, but the warming influence of the nearby Gulf Stream assures us the benefits of a tropical climate.

Our natural flora grows nowhere else in North America, and the combination of our eight interrelated habitats and the creatures dwelling therein is truly unique.

### The Land

#### Hardwood Hammocks
The vegetation of the Florida Keys is more common to the tropical Caribbean Basin than to the adjoining temperate areas of mainland Florida. Found throughout the Keys, West Indian tropical hardwood hammocks nurture highly diverse communities of rare flora and fauna—more than 200 species—some found nowhere else in the US. The hammocks (originally an Indian word meaning "shady place") also shelter a variety of endangered species. The largest contiguous hammock in the continental US is on North Key Largo. Known as the Dagny Johnson Key Largo Hammock Botanical State Park, it encompasses 2,700 acres. A dense understory of plants, shrubs, and vines adapts to the shady conditions on the hammock floor. Wildflowers must reach for the sky under the shady foliage top hat of the hammock, often turning into creeping vines. The Key Largo wood rat, an endangered species that looks more like a big-eared Disney mouse than a London sewer rat, joins the key raccoon, the Key Largo

cotton mouse, opossums, gray squirrels, and an assortment of migratory birds amid the flora of the hammocks.

## Pinelands

The pinelands in the Lower Florida Keys differ from the vast forests you may have seen in other areas of the US. Adapting to growing conditions with limited freshwater, the tall, spindly trees are small in girth and sparsely foliated. Primarily found on Big Pine Key, these South Florida slash pines mingle with an understory of silver palms and brittle thatch palms, both of which are rare outside the Keys and protected under the Preservation of Native Flora of Florida Act. Among the 7,500 protected acres in the Lower Keys, other pinelands grace No Name Key, Little Pine Key, Cudjoe Key, Sugarloaf Key, and Summerland Key.

The most famous pineland resident in the Lower Keys is undoubtedly the key deer, a subspecies of the Virginia white-tailed deer, found nowhere else in the world. These tiny deer, each about the size of a large dog, attempt to coexist with human inhabitants who have taken over much of the unpreserved woodlands of the Lower Keys. However, the diminutive animals frequently venture out of the woods and onto the Overseas Highway, where they are often struck and killed by vehicles. For that reason, speed limits through Big Pine Key are reduced (45 mph daylight, 35 mph nighttime) and strictly enforced by law enforcement officials.

## The Shoreline

### Mangrove Habitats

Called the island builders, mangroves comprise the predominant shoreline plant community of the Florida Keys, protecting the landmass from erosion. Able to establish itself on the coral underwater bedrock or in the sand, the mangrove's root structure traps, holds, and stabilizes sediments. Over time the infant mangrove habitats establish small islets such as those you'll see peppering Florida Bay and the oceanside nearshore waters. Mangrove habitats bordering the Keys filter upland runoff, maintaining the water quality of our seas.

Important as a breeding ground and nursery for juvenile spiny lobster, pink shrimp, snook, mullet, tarpon, and mangrove snappers, the mangroves also shelter these sea creatures from their predators. (See the Diving & Snorkeling and Fishing chapters for more on the fascinating underwater creatures living here.) Great rookeries of wading birds and shorebirds roost and nest on the canopy of broad leaves that shelter the mangrove habitats, creating a virtual aviary in every uninhabited islet.

### Sand Beach Habitats

Most of the islands of the Florida Keys have a limestone rock shoreline, but Long Key, Bahia Honda Key, and small portions of the shoreline of Lower Matecumbe have beaches of sand consisting not of quartz but of tiny fossils. These minuscule remains of calcareous, lime-secreting marine plants and animals are broken down by wave action upon the sea bottom. Only keys that have a break in the offshore reef line or are near a deep tidal channel receive enough sediment to build a natural beach. Fronted in most cases by beds of sea grass, the Keys' beaches always have a "weed line" onshore made up of remnants of turtle grass, manatee grass, or sargassum weed washed up with the tide.

> **i** Cuba is closer to Key West than Miami is. Cuba sits roughly 90 miles off the southern tip of Key West, while Miami is 130 miles north of "the Rock."

## The Sea

### Sea-Grass Habitats

In the shallow nearshore waters of the ocean and Florida Bay, sediments build up on the limestone bedrock sea bottom, supporting a variety of sea grasses that perform an integral function in our tropical ecosystem. Sea grasses grow entirely underwater, one of the few flowering plants to do so. Most prevalent of the sea grasses in the Florida Keys are the sweeping meadows of turtle grass, which have interlocking root systems that burrow as deep as 5 feet into the sediment. The wide, flat blades, often more than 12 inches long, break the force of the waves and slow current velocity.

The turtle grass traps marine sediments and silt carried in and out on the tides, allowing them to settle to the bottom. This natural filtration system

---

### Sunset Views

Mallory Square in Key West isn't the only public place to view our world-famous sunsets. Many oceangoing vessels offer sunset cruises, and if you are a land lover, head up the Keys. On Big Pine Key, Bahia Honda State Park on the beach offers an unobstructed scenic view. Head on up to Marathon and stop at the entrance to the old Seven Mile Bridge for the nightly celebration where gazers can see the Florida Straits and the Atlantic Ocean.

clarifies the water and enhances coral growth in the nearby reef habitat. The sunken pastures of turtle grass and the less abundant shoal grass and manatee grass, which have rounded leaves and weaker root systems, become very dense, providing food and shelter for marine life at all levels of the food chain (see the Fishing chapter for more on the species dwelling within).

More than 80 species of resident and migratory coastal birds forage the sea grasses, feeding on fish and invertebrates of the habitat.

### Hardbottom Habitats

Wave action and tidal currents sweep the limestone bedrock of the nearshore sea-bottom habitats nearly clean, permitting no sediment buildup. Algae, sponges, gorgonian corals, and stony corals attach themselves directly to the bedrock. Snapping shrimp often make their homes within the sponges; they make a popping sound with their large snapping claw to repel predators. More seaward of the nearshore waters, colonies of soft corals dominate the underwater hardbottom landscape. A feathery fairyland blooms like a backstage theater costume room.

Tentacled anemones also call the hardbottom habitat home and peacefully coexist with conchs and tulip snails, the spiral-striped, spindle-shaped mollusks. The much-sought-after stone crabs and juvenile spiny lobsters try to stay out of sight here (see the Diving & Snorkeling chapter). Boat wakes, anchor damage, and collection of sea creatures by divers and snorkelers threaten the hardbottom habitats.

### Coral Reef

Extending 200 miles, from Fowey Rocks near Miami to the Dry Tortugas, our living coral reef habitat—the only one in the continental US—is a national treasure. The reef plays host to an unbelievable assortment of marine creatures, fish, and vegetation (see the Diving & Snorkeling and Fishing chapters). The coral reef habitat, together with the mangrove and sea-grass habitats, is the breeding ground for 70 percent of the commercial fishing industry's catch.

This wave-resistant barrier, which protects the sea-grass meadows from erosion and heavy sedimentation, is particularly beautiful off the Upper Keys. The landmass of Key Largo shields the coral habitat from changing water temperatures and sediments that emanate from Florida Bay through the tidal channels of the Middle and Lower Keys. Though it rigidly protects the shoreline of the Florida Keys from tropical storms, the coral reef itself is a fragile habitat. Field studies have indicated some coral die-off and the sometimes-fatal bleaching or discoloration of the corals in select areas of the Keys' barrier reef. Excessive nutrients in the water due to land-based pollution will degrade water quality and foster the growth of algal blooms, which screen the sunlight, robbing the coral of the oxygen that is necessary for healthy development.

Humans constitute one of the reef's most destructive threats. Anchor damage, boat groundings, and snorkelers and divers touching, collecting, or stepping on the delicate organisms can cause injury and certain death to the reef. See Protectors of Paradise in this chapter for more information on how you can help preserve and protect our reefs while still enjoying them.

### Bare-Mud- & Bare-Sand-Bottom Habitats

Along the barrier reef, skeletons of reef plants and animals form areas of open, bare-sand sea bottom, inhabited by species of algae, sea urchins, snails, clams, and worms that serve as the food train for visiting starfish, conch, and finfish. Similar belts or patches of bare-mud-bottom habitats, both oceanside and in Florida Bay, support a like assemblage of marine creatures. Joining this group are burrowing shrimp, whose tunneled dwellings leave telltale mounds in the mud.

## Our Wildlife

Nowhere will you be more aware of our unique ecosystem than when you are experiencing the Florida Keys in a small dinghy, canoe, sea kayak, or shallow-draft skiff equipped with a push pole and tranquilly gliding through our shallow, mangrove-lined inshore waters in search of sightings of indigenous birds and aquatic creatures. Though the dedication to spotting feathered friends may be referred to as "birding" or "bird-watching" in some areas of the country, here in the Keys another arena of fascinating marine creatures presents itself in the shallow waters of our flats. You can easily explore on your own without a guide, or you can sign up for a guided eco-tour (see the Recreation chapter).

Hundreds of virgin mangrove islets sprinkle the inshore waters of the inhabited Keys, often serving as giant rookeries for shorebirds and wading birds that are attracted to the abundant chow wagon beneath the surface of the water. Look to our Recreation chapter for information on renting a kayak, canoe, or small skiff. See the Attractions chapter for descriptions of the wildlife refuges of the Florida Keys, many of which encompass myriad outlands. Read on for a primer of the most frequently encountered species in our tropical ecosystem.

### Nature's Aviary

When exploring around the mangrove islets in search of wild birdlife, be sensitive to the presence of nesting birds. Do not anchor within 200 feet of an island, and keep noise to a minimum so as not to frighten the birds. If you do happen to flush a bird from its nest, move away from the nest area so that the bird will swiftly return to guard its young. Here are several species you can expect to spot:

- Brown Pelican: You'll see these cute, personality-packed fish-beggars everywhere, especially hanging out at fishing marinas. Look for them on their favorite gravity-defying perches atop mangroves or feathery Australian pines.

- American White Pelican: These winter visitors to the Florida Keys (they are frequently spotted in Montana in the summer months) live together in flocks in the uninhabited wild of the backcountry keys. The white pelicans, far from the panhandling ways of the browns, are cooperative feeders, congregating as a team on the water's surface and herding fish into an ever-narrowing circle where the group will dine. Look for white pelicans at Little Arsnicker or Sandy Keys in the Upper Keys backcountry.

- Cormorant: Cormorants by the thousands inhabit rookeries in the mangroves of the unpeopled islands. Like the lesser-seen anhinga, or water turkey (more prevalent in the Everglades), the cormorant's plumage becomes waterlogged, which facilitates diving and swimming skills in its endless search for fish. You'll often see the birds perched on poles and buoy markers, wings outstretched in a drying maneuver. Cormorants swim with only their necks and heads visible above the water.

- Snowy Egret & Great Egret: Both snowy and great egrets thrive in the Florida Keys. Distinguished from their cousins, the great white herons, which also grace the shorelines of the Keys, the white egrets have black legs with yellow feet and black bills. Though both egrets display magnificent white plumage, the snowy egret is about half the size of the great egret.

- Great White Heron: Found only in the tropical ecosystem, this large white heron, more than 4 feet tall, is not as fearful of humans as other species, and is often seen in backyards and other inhabited areas. You'll be able to tell a great white heron from a great egret because the heron has long yellow legs and a yellow beak. Herons and egrets build their lofty stick nests atop the mangroves of remote rookery keys.

- Roseate Spoonbill: A rare sighting in the Florida Keys, the roseate spoonbill, or pink curlew, is more common in the upper Florida Bay near Flamingo in Everglades National Park. The roseate spoonbill moves its large spatulate bill from side to side underwater in the shallows, searching for minnows and small aquatic creatures. This distinctive bird is known for its pink body accented by an orange tail, a bare greenish head, bright red shoulder and chest patches, and a black-ringed neck.

- White Ibis: Common in the Florida Keys, the white-plumed ibis bears black-tipped wings, most apparent when spread in flight, a distinctive scarlet, down-curved bill, and red legs. You'll often see young ibises, which are brown, in a flock of their white brethren, searching for aquatic insects, crabs, shrimp, and small snakes.

- Osprey: The high platform-topped poles you may see along the Overseas Highway have been erected for the osprey, which builds its bulky nest atop, laying three eggs out of harm's way each breeding season. Resembling a bald eagle, the osprey can be distinguished by a black streak behind each eye.

- Magnificent Frigatebird: The graceful, effortless flight of the frigatebird, or man-o'-war bird, often heralds fish below, for this coastal forager is constantly on the lookout for finned pleasures. Having a wingspan greater than 7 feet, the frigatebird inflates its throat sac and floats on air currents, its deeply forked, scissorlike tail a distinctive sight.

- American Bald Eagle: Once endangered nearly to the point of extinction, American bald eagles have made a recovery all across the US due to preservation efforts. Look for the bald eagle's distinctive white head and tail high in the mangroves of uninhabited keys in Florida Bay, where they build their nests.

### Nature's Aquarium

As you pass through the shallow sea-grass, mud, sand, and hardbottom habitats surrounding mangrove areas of our uninhabited keys, you may observe life below the surface of the water. Be sure to wear polarized sunglasses and proceed in a shallow-draft craft.

Starfish: Commonly adorning the sandy bottom areas or sea-grass meadows of the shallow waters are cushion sea stars, often referred to as "starfish." These heavy-bodied, orange-brown creatures with five thick, starlike arms don't look alive, but they are.

Loggerhead Sponge: The most common sponge you will see from your small skiff or while snorkeling in these waters is the loggerhead sponge, a barrel-shape sponge easily identified by the dark holes in its upper surface.

Stingray: This unusual creature, shaped like a diamond or disk, often lies motionless on the ocean bottom, partially buried in the sand. The ray has eyes and breathing holes on its topside, with its mouth positioned on the underside to feed off the seafloor.

Horseshoe Crab: You'll quickly spot the distinctive spikelike tail and smooth, horseshoe-shaped body shell of this 300-million-year-old species as the crab forages the sea-grass habitat for algal organisms.

Sea Turtle: Keep a close lookout for the small head of the giant sea turtle as it pops out of the water for a breath of air. Loggerhead sea turtles can remain submerged for as long as three hours. Green turtles, once commonplace here but overharvested for use in soup, for steaks, in cosmetic oils, and for leather, are rarely encountered today.

Manatee: On a lucky day, you may catch a rare glimpse of the timid West Indian manatee, or sea cow, a docile aquatic mammal that likes to graze on the turtle-grass flats. The brownish-gray manatee has armlike flippers, a broad, spoonlike tail, and an adorable wrinkled face. It can grow up to 15 feet long, weighing in at nearly a ton. Protected as an endangered species, the manatee often rolls on the water's surface for air and cannot swim rapidly enough to avoid collision with oncoming boaters, a constant source of peril (see the Boating chapter for regulatory information).

Bottlenose Dolphin: A more-frequent sight on any water-based excursion is that of bottlenose dolphins. Seen in free-swimming pods in open waters, the graceful dolphins undulate through the waves with rhythmic regularity, and they are sometimes curious enough to approach your boat.

Fish of the Flats: Alert attention to underwater movements in the sea grass of the flats may net you a sighting of a baby black-tip or bonnethead shark, a nurse shark, barracuda, bonefish, and more. See The Flats section of the Fishing chapter for descriptions of the finned treasures lurking beneath the shallows.

## WEATHER & CLIMATE

The mild tropical climate of the Florida Keys has no equal in the US. In fact, neither frost, nor ice, nor sleet, nor snow ever visits our islands.

### Temperature

The proximity of the Keys to the Gulf Stream in the Straits of Florida and the tempering effects of the Gulf of Mexico dictate that average winter temperatures vary little more than 14 degrees from those of the summer months. Average year-round temperature is about 75 degrees, and southeasterly trade winds and fresh sea breezes keep summer temperatures from ever reaching the triple-digit inferno experienced by the Florida mainland.

### Rainfall

The Florida Keys experience two seasons: wet and dry. From November through April, the sun shines abundantly and less than 25 percent of the year's precipitation falls, usually associated with a cold front in the dead of winter. May through October is the rainy season, when nearly three-quarters of our annual

> **i** The long blue line that divides part of the new Stretch from Florida City to Key Largo is not just any "blue line." Famed artist Wyland (a resident of Islamorada; see the Entertainment chapter) was asked by the Florida Department of Transportation to choose a color for this otherwise-dull 3-foot-high line of concrete. He chose "Belize Blue" from his personal color book and explained that it represented the color of the Florida Keys.

rainfall occurs during brief daily showers or thunderstorms. But these percentages are deceiving; our climate is really quite dry. Average rainfall in the winter is less than 2 inches a month; summer months see closer to 4 to 5 inches of rain.

### Hurricanes

While the Keys typically have an idyllic climate, hurricanes have always been a key ingredient in our tropical mix. The potentially deadly weather systems move westerly off the African coast during hurricane season (officially June 1 to Nov 30, but most prevalent in Aug and Sept) and generally turn north near the Lesser Antilles, often heading our way.

Visitors to the Florida Keys during hurricane season should heed official warnings to evacuate our islands in the event of a potential hurricane. Because we have only one main artery linking our islands to the mainland (the Overseas Highway), it takes 22 to 26 hours of crawling, bumper-to-bumper traffic to clear residents and visitors out of the Florida Keys. Officials warn that storm-watching during a hurricane is not a diversion to be considered here. A sizable hurricane will cut off all services in the Keys along with communications to the outside world.

## PROTECTORS OF PARADISE

The natural wonders that make up the Florida Keys have good friends in the following organizations, which oversee efforts to protect the region's environment as best they can.

**NATIONAL MARINE SANCTUARY,** (305) 809-4700; floridakeys.noaa .gov. The Florida Keys National Marine Sanctuary encompasses 2,800 square nautical miles, incorporating within its boundaries all of the Florida Keys, including the Marquesas Keys, the Dry Tortugas, and surrounding waters. Ecologists hope that the access restrictions and activity regulations in select areas of the Florida Keys National Marine Sanctuary will help protect sensitive

# Close-up

## Sunrise, Sunset

In the Florida Keys we justifiably lay claim to the most spectacular sun awak-
enings and finales in the universe. Anglers rise early enough to witness the
brilliant fireball burn its way out of the ocean. Divers relish the midday sun's
intense rays, which light up the ocean waters like a torch, illuminating the
colorful corals below. Sunbathers lie prone on pool decks and man-made
beaches, soaking in the solar rays, storing up some much-needed vitamin D.

But our sunsets take center stage in the twilight hours. Both visitors and
residents jockey for an unobstructed vantage point from which to watch the
smoldering orange ball ooze into the sea. Flotillas of small boats drift anchor-
less in the gulf waters. Travelers pull their autos off the Overseas Highway and
stand at the water's edge, their awestruck attention riveted on the setting sun.
Key West even has a daily sunset celebration ceremony at Mallory Square,
complete with fire-eaters, jugglers, and Keys buskers of every shape and
description.

areas of the ecosystem. Furthermore, professionals feel that, with minimal
human contact, areas of high ecological importance will evolve naturally and
those areas representing a variety of habitats will be sustained. This zoning program is monitored for revision every five years (see the Boating chapter for
more information on specific regulations and restrictions).

**THE NATURE CONSERVANCY, nature.org.** The Nature Conservancy
established the Florida Reef Resilience Program to develop strategies for coping
with climate change and to improve the health of our fragile coral reefs. This
program includes a coral restoration project, which, in addition to research,
establishes underwater nurseries to help grow coral. As of this writing, approximately 50,000 coral colonies exist in eight in-water coral nurseries, with more
on the way in the coming years.

**REEF RELIEF, 631 Greene St., Key West, FL 33040; (305) 294-3100; reef
relief.org.** Reef Relief, a Key West–based nonprofit membership organization,
works toward the preservation and protection of the coral reef habitat of the
Florida Keys. The group's first project was to install more than 100 mooring
buoys, which, when used properly, eliminate anchor damage at the reef. The
Florida Keys National Marine Sanctuary maintains the mooring buoys.

Another part of Reef Relief's mission is public awareness and education regarding the living coral reef habitat. To this end, the organization sponsors numerous cleanup campaigns that attract hundreds of volunteers. They comb shorelines and out-islands and dive the reef, collecting trash and storm-driven debris.

**TURTLE HOSPITAL,** 2396 Overseas Hwy., Marathon, FL 33050; (305) 743-2552; turtlehospital.org. Located near mile marker 48.5 Bayside, in Marathon, is the famed Turtle Hospital, a nonprofit turtle rapid-care center and recovery room. Local veterinarians volunteer their time, often performing complicated turtle surgery on fibropapilloma tumors, impactions, and shell fractures caused by hit-and-run boating injuries. After surgery, the turtles are moved to the recovery room, some in outdoor tanks and the rest in the property's original saltwater pool.

More than 5,000 schoolchildren visit the Turtle Hospital every year, learning about the fascinating reptilian order, Chelonia. The general public visits, too. The Turtle Hospital offers a guided educational experience seven days a week. The tour requires reservations and, since this is a working hospital, cancellations occur due to turtle emergencies and/or weather.

# Getting Here, Getting Around

You are headed for the Florida Keys. Whether you travel by land, by sea, or by air, you must conform to some strict, uncompromising standards that you might not be aware of.

First, remove your socks. You won't need them here. Don your shorts and flip flops. They are *de rigueur*. Slip on those shades. How else can you see? And take off your watch. The pace is slower here—you're on Keys time now.

Things really are different here. Our single main street stretches 126 miles—from Florida City to Key West—and dead-ends at the sea. Our 42 bridges span the kissing waters of the Atlantic Ocean and the Gulf of Mexico, from Key Largo to Key West. And our Keys communities resound as distinctively as the ivories of a piano. So come on down. We're playing your song.

## BY AIR

### Commercial Flights

**KEY WEST INTERNATIONAL AIRPORT, 3491 S. Roosevelt Blvd., Key West, FL 33040; (305) 296-5439; keywestinternationalairport.com.** Key West is the Florida destination of choice for thousands of visitors each year, and the Key West International Airport has doubled in size to accommodate them, undergoing a $31 million renovation to expand to 50,000 square feet. There are now two security screening lines and two baggage-claim carousels, in addition to two locations of the Conch Flyer, the airport restaurant/lounge. One is located before security, and the other next to the gates.

The pre-security Conch Flyer location has loads of pictures and memorabilia of Key West history. The bar stools are designed with propellers as legs to support the seats. The food is really great, too, and available in both locations.

If you are meeting a flight, short-term metered parking is available. You may also park in the long-term lot. Weekly rates are available.

Alamo, Avis, Budget, Dollar, Enterprise, Hertz, National, Thrifty, and Tropical rental cars are available at the airport terminal; Alamo and Enterprise are just a courtesy call away (see listings in our Rental Cars section in this chapter). Whenever possible, make reservations for your vehicle in advance. Taxis stand by in front of the airport awaiting each flight, and many hotels offer complimentary shuttle service.

## Directions to the Keys

Directions from Miami International Airport via Florida's Turnpike:
Take LeJeune Road south to Highway 836 West to Florida's Turnpike South,
Homestead. Continue on Florida's Turnpike until it ends in Florida City at
US 1. Continue south on US 1 to the Keys.

Flights into and out of Key West are provided by the following airlines:

- American Airlines, (800) 433-7300; aa.com

- Delta Air Lines, (800) 221-1212; delta.com

- Silver Airways, (800) 881-4999; silverairways.com

- US Airways, (800) 428-4322; usairways.com

**MIAMI INTERNATIONAL AIRPORT, 2100 NW 42nd Ave., Miami, FL
33126; (305) 876-7000; miami-airport.com.** An international airport offering
flights on most major airline carriers, Miami International Airport is accessible
from either I-95 or Florida's Turnpike via Highway 836 and LeJeune Road.
You can rent a car (see the listing in this chapter for contact information) and
drive the distance to the Keys. Miami to Key Largo is approximately 60 miles;
to Islamorada, 80 miles; to Marathon, 115 miles; to Big Pine, 130 miles; to
Key West, 160 miles.

i A Russian-made 1972 Antonov AN-24 Air Cubana
was hijacked from Havana in 2003 and flown to Key
West by architect Adermis Wilson Gonzalez, with
32 passengers aboard. Purchased by someone at
auction, then left in airport storage for years, the plane
is now used as a permanent training tool for airport
emergency crews.

**FORT LAUDERDALE–HOLLYWOOD INTERNATIONAL AIRPORT,
100 Terminal Dr., Fort Lauderdale, FL 33315; (866) 435-9355; broward.org/
airport.** Smaller than Miami International, this airport off I-595 offers fewer
flight options but is hassle-free when compared to Miami. To drive to the Keys
from Fort Lauderdale–Hollywood International Airport, exit the airport and

follow the signs for I-595 West. Take I-595 to the Florida Turnpike and follow the signs for the Florida Keys. Driving from Fort Lauderdale–Hollywood International Airport will add about 45 more minutes to your total trip.

### Private & Charter Aircraft

**AIR KEY WEST, 3491 S. Roosevelt Blvd. (at Key West International Airport), Key West, FL 33040; (305) 923-4033; airkeywest.com.** Fully certified, licensed, bonded, and insured as an FAA air carrier, Air Key West can take you to other US cities, the Bahamas, or the Caribbean. This aircraft charter service offers affordable rates and professional, reliable service.

**MARATHON JET CENTER, MM 52 Bayside, Marathon, FL 33050; (305) 743-1995; marathonjetcenter.com.** Located at the west end of Florida Keys Marathon Airport, Marathon Jet Center is a flight-based operation that caters to general aviation and light aircraft. Marathon Jet Center offers aircraft charter for rent in and out of the Florida Keys.

## BY SEA

Visit the Florida Keys as the pirates and buccaneers did before you: by sea. Navigate your motor or sailing craft through the Intracoastal Waterway, which extends from Miami through Card Sound and Barnes Sound and down the length of the Keys in the Florida Bay / Gulf of Mexico. Or parallel the oceanside shores following Hawk Channel, a well-marked route protected by the reef.

For complete information on arriving and vacationing on the water, see our Cruising chapter.

**KEY WEST EXPRESS, 100 Grinnell St., Key West, FL 33040; (888) 539-2628; seakeywestexpress.com.** Key West Express is a fun alternative for traveling to and from Key West for visits to Fort Myers and Marco Island. Operating the only high-speed ferry service to these points, you can stay for a few hours or a couple of days in these locations. Departures and arrivals vary per season.

## BY LAND

The Overseas Highway tethers our islands to the mainland like one long anchor line. Addresses along this common main street are issued by mile markers, designated as MM. Commencing with MM 127 in Florida City and culminating with MM 0 in Key West, small green markers with white numbers are posted every mile. Here in the Keys everything is grounded by a mile marker, and you'll note that we orient most of the addresses we give in this book by mile marker.

As you head toward Key West, mile-marker numbers descend in order. Anyplace on the right side of the road bordering Florida Bay or the Gulf of Mexico is referred to as "bayside." The opposite side of the road, bordering the Atlantic Ocean, is therefore called "oceanside." So addresses on the Overseas Highway will usually be referred to by both mile-marker number and a bayside or oceanside distinction.

Key West, the southernmost point in the continental US, slumbers closer to Havana than it does to Miami—when it sleeps, that is, which is not all that often. In Keys-speak, this is where the action is.

Although more than 25,000 people make Key West their home, this island still retains a small-town charm. The quaint Old Town area remains essentially a charming, foliage-canopied grid of streets lined with gingerbread-trimmed frame structures that evoke a succession of bygone eras. The Midtown area is predominantly residential. New Town takes in the shopping centers and fast-food and hotel chains along N. Roosevelt Boulevard on the gulf side and across the island to the airport and beaches along S. Roosevelt Boulevard on the Atlantic side.

Old Town is anchored by Duval Street, which has been dubbed "the longest street in the world" because it runs from the Atlantic to the Gulf of Mexico. It is actually only a little more than a mile long. Although finding your way around Key West is not difficult, the narrow, often one-way streets—combined with a proliferation of tourist-driven rental cars and scooters in peak seasons—can make driving around this island both frustrating and time-consuming. Old Town is best explored on foot or by bicycle.

Key West provides public bus service and several other unique modes of transportation, which we describe in this chapter.

## Rental Cars

Public transportation in the Keys is practically nil. You really need a car to get around, unless you are staying strictly in Key West. Most rental car agencies are at the airports in Fort Lauderdale, Miami, or Key West. Some pick up and deliver vehicles. Reserve your automobile before you arrive in the Keys—availability in peak seasons is often limited—at one of the following agencies:

**ALAMO RENT A CAR,** 2516 N. Roosevelt Blvd., Key West, FL 33040; (888) 826-6893; alamo.com

**AVIS RENT A CAR,** 3491 S. Roosevelt Blvd. (at Key West International Airport), Key West, FL 33040; (305) 296-8744 or (800) 831-2847; avis.com

**BUDGET,** 3491 S. Roosevelt Blvd. (at Key West International Airport), Key West, FL 33040; (305) 294-8868 or (800) 527-0700; budget.com

# Close-up

## Glossary

**backcountry:** shallow sea-grass meadows and mangrove islet waters of Florida Bay.

**bayside:** anything on the opposite coast from the Atlantic; for instance, Florida Bay in the Upper Keys, the Gulf of Mexico in the Middle and Lower Keys.

**bight:** a body of water bounded by a bend or curve in the shore; several are found in Key West.

**blue water:** deep, offshore waters of the Atlantic Ocean.

**bubba:** slang for best friend, buddy.

**chickee:** an open-sided, thatched-roof hut commonly found near the water's edge that is used as shelter from the sun.

**coconut telegraph:** local gossip about any subject, person, place, or thing.

**Conch (pronounced "konk"):** a descendant of the original Bahamians who settled the Keys; a person born in the Florida Keys.

**conch:** meat of a marine mollusk used in chowder and fritters; once a staple in the diet of early Conchs and Keys-dwelling Native Americans, now an endangered species that may not be harvested in the Keys.

**conch cruiser:** a bicycle that is painted and decorated with outrageous artwork and embellishments.

**con leche:** this is the fuel that keeps the locals humming: hot coffee with steamed milk and sugar.

GETTING HERE, GETTING AROUND

**DOLLAR RENT A CAR,** 3491 S. Roosevelt Blvd. (at Key West International Airport), Key West, FL 33040; (305) 296-9921 or (800) 800-4000; dollar.com

**ENTERPRISE RENT-A-CAR,** 2516 N. Roosevelt Blvd., Key West, FL 33040; (305) 292-0220 or (800) 736-8222; enterprise.com

**HERTZ RENT A CAR,** 3491 S. Roosevelt Blvd. (at Key West International Airport), Key West, FL 33040; (305) 294-1039 or (800) 654-3131; hertz .com

**Duval crawl:** the notorious barhopping Key West scene from one end of Duval Street to the other.

**Fat Albert:** two large, white blimps tethered on Cudjoe Key (MM 23) that the US government uses to track aircraft, boat traffic (especially for drug enforcement), and weather by radar.

**flats:** shallow, nearshore waters of the Atlantic.

**freshwater Conch:** a person who has lived in the Florida Keys for at least seven years.

**hammock:** an elevated piece of bedrock covered with a hardwood tropical forest; also a woven lounger strung between two palm trees.

**Keys disease:** the party life in the Keys, which has a tendency to have a lengthy duration; starting early in the day to late at night, drinks and other vices can be a 24/7 lifestyle.

**mile marker, or MM:** the green-and-white signs along US 1 that mark miles, in descending order, from Florida City (MM 127) to Key West (MM 0).

**no-see-ums:** tiny, biting insects with a hot, painful, stinging bite.

**oceanside:** anything on the Atlantic coast of the Keys.

**puddle jumpers:** small commercial planes that fly in and out of the Key West airport and carry passengers to major airport hubs.

**the Rock:** slang for the Florida Keys, usually uttered by locals heading for the mainland: "I need to get off the Rock."

**the Stretch:** the "stretch" of highway (US 1) that leads into and out of the Keys, from MM 123 near Florida City to MM 105 in Key Largo.

**NATIONAL RENTAL CAR,** 2516 N. Roosevelt Blvd., Key West, FL 33040; (877) 222-9075; nationalcar.com

**THRIFTY CAR RENTAL,** 3491 S. Roosevelt Blvd. (at Key West International Airport), Key West, FL 33040; (305) 294-8644 or (877) 283-0898; thrifty.com

**TROPICAL RENTALS,** 1300 Duval St., Key West, FL 33040; (305) 294-8136; tropicalrentacar.com

## Taxi Service

If you don't have your own automobile or haven't rented a car for the duration of your visit, you may find yourself in need of ground transportation within the Keys. Be aware that the fare could get pricey (sometimes approaching the cost of a daily rental vehicle), especially if you are traveling any distance. But if you need a lift, try one of these:

### Upper Keys
**Mom's Taxi,** (305) 451-9700 or (305) 852-6000

### Middle Keys (Marathon)
**Dave's Island Taxi,** (305) 731-9022
**Friendly Cab Company,** (305) 289-5454
**On Time Taxi,** (305) 289-5656

### Lower Keys
**Big Pine Taxi Service,** (305) 872-2662
**Courtesy Taxi and Delivery Service,** (305) 872-9314
**Sunset Taxi,** (305) 872-4233

### Other Key West Taxis
**Five 6's Cab Company,** who have "gone green" with hybrids, (305) 296-6666, keywesttaxi.com
**Friendly Cab Company,** (305) 295-5555

## Airport Limousine & Shuttle Service

In the event you are stranded without transportation to either of the mainland airports, alternative transport is available. These companies offer a variety of services, often also catering to private groups and functions. The following are dependable options in the Florida Keys: Keys Shuttle (305-289-9997 or 888-765-9997; keysshuttle.com) and Sea the Keys (305-896-7013; keywest daytrip.com).

i Everyone has heard of the Blue Ridge Parkway, Route 66, and the Las Vegas Strip. They have each been designated as one of America's Byways, according to the National Scenic Byways Program, with 150 such roads in 46 states. Now, US 1 has officially become one of America's Byways. Visit byways.org for more information.

## Bus Service

**CITY OF KEY WEST DEPARTMENT OF TRANSPORTATION,** 627 Palm Ave., Key West, FL 33040; (305) 293-6426; keywestcity.com. Public-transport city buses circle the island of Key West several times a day along color-coded routes. Signs at all of the bus stops sport colored dots to indicate the routes they serve. Remember that this is an island where the buses traverse in a great big circle. You simply cannot get lost if you stay on a particular bus, since it will eventually return to the stop where you boarded it. For more information, call the Key West Department of Transportation (KWDOT).

A complete timetable and route map is available from KWDOT. "BOB" is the Bikes on Buses program. This allows customers to take their bicycles on the bus at no additional cost by securing them onto a bike rack attached to the front of the bus.

**GREYHOUND BUS LINES,** Miami International Airport, Miami, FL 33126; Key West International Airport, Key West, FL 33040; (800) 231-2222; greyhound.com. Greyhound bridges the gap in mass ground transit from Key West to Miami and beyond. Buses depart Miami International Airport for the Key West depot, which is housed in the Adam Arnold Annex at the airport, usually twice a day, 7 days a week. The trip will take 4 hours, 30 minutes from Key West to Miami International. Fares to and from Miami International Airport depend on embarking and disembarking sites. Greyhound schedules and fares are subject to change. Be sure to confirm your specific travel arrangements when purchasing tickets.

**DADE-MONROE EXPRESS,** (305) 770-3131; miamidade.gov/transit. Miami-Dade Transit (MDT) provides bus service from Florida City to the city of Marathon at MM 50. The route designation is #301. Stops are Key Largo MM 98, Tavernier MM 87, and Islamorada MM 74.

**LOWER KEYS SHUTTLE,** (305) 809-3910; kwtransit.com. Lower Keys Shuttle operates between Key West and Marathon, connecting with the Dade-Monroe Express in the City of Marathon at MM 50. This provides the link between Key West and Florida City.

## Alternative Key West Transportation

**CITYVIEW TROLLEY,** 330 Elizabeth St., Key West, FL 33040; (305) 294-0644; cityviewtrolleys.com. Experience Key West and learn about its rich history from the comfortable seating of this hop-on/hop-off open-air trolley service. There are 9 stops on the route, including Mallory Square, La Concha, the White Street Pier, the Southernmost Point, and the Hemingway Home. The first tour begins at 9:30 a.m., with the last reboard at 4:30 p.m., and trolleys run at a 30-minute frequency. Tickets for adults are about $20 and children (4–12) are about $10. Children under 4 ride free.

★**CONCH TOUR TRAIN, 303 Front St., Key West, FL 33040; (305) 294-5161 or (800) 868-7482; conchtourtrain.com.** Take a train ride around Key West and travel through time as you learn about this historic city. Enjoy open-air seating with a personal narrative from the driver of the train. Departing every 30 minutes, the tour lasts 1.5 hours and there is only one stop toward the end of the ride. Adult tickets run about $30; kids 12 and under ride free. Buying tickets online will save you about 10 percent. *Note:* The Conch Trains that you see chugging around town are bona fide touring vehicles; you cannot get on and off a Conch Train at will. See our Attractions chapter for further information on this and other tours.

**OLD TOWN TROLLEY TOURS OF KEY WEST, 3840 N. Roosevelt Blvd., Key West, FL 33040; (305) 395-4958 or (800) 213-2474; historictours .com/keywest.** Listen to a narrative of historic Key West on this continuous-loop tour, learning as you go. Although this transportation option is promoted and sold as a 90-minute tour, with over 100 points of interest, you can hop on and off the trolley as many times per day as you wish. It's one hassle-free way to shop, dine, or take in the myriad attractions Key West has to offer.

You can pick up the trolley at Mallory Square beginning at 9 a.m. daily. The trolley disembarks at 12 different stops, including Mallory Square, Historic Key West Seaport, Crowne Plaza La Concha, and the Southernmost Point. Trolleys stop at each location every 30 minutes.

> **i** The Florida Keys have sights fit for a queen! In 1991 Queen Elizabeth II and Prince Philip spent a weekend cruising the Florida Keys on board their ship, the HMY *Britannia*. In Key West they toured Fort Jefferson National Monument at the Dry Tortugas.

Cost of the trolley tour is about $30 per day for adults and teens; children age 12 and younger ride free. Buying tickets online will save you about 10 percent.

## Bicycles, Mopeds, Scooters, & Electric Cars

Key West is the perfect place to explore by bicycle, moped, scooter, or electric car. The egg-shaped electric cars are eerily quiet and understandably slow. They seat two or four, have no doors, and top out at 25 mph, making them ideal for an island where the speed limits never go above 35. Many places rent a choice of electric cars, mopeds, scooters, or bicycles by the hour, day, overnight, or week (see our Recreation chapter for information on bicycle rentals).

Some companies consider a daily rental to be 24 hours; others cap the day at 8 hours. Inquire when you call. Some rental agencies even have double scooters that seat two; it is illegal to carry a passenger on any other kind. The following Key West companies rent a full range of vehicles, and most of them offer complimentary pickup and drop-off:

- **A & M Rentals,** 523 Truman Ave., or 513 South St., Key West, FL 33040; (305) 896-1921; amscooterskeywest.com.

- **Adventure Rentals,** 617 Front St., Key West, FL 33040; (305) 293-8883; keywest-scooter.com

- **Moped Hospital,** 601 Truman Ave., Key West, FL 33040; (866) 296-1625; mopedhospital.com

- **Pirate Scooter Rentals,** 401 Southard St., Key West, FL 33040; (305) 295-0000; piratescooterrentals.com

- **Sunshine Rentals,** 1910 N. Roosevelt Blvd., Key West, FL 33040; (305) 414-2976; sunshinescootersinc.com

- **Tropical Rentals,** 1300 Duval St., Key West, FL 33040; (305) 294-8136

**PARADISE PEDICAB, 401 Southard St., Key West, FL 33040; (305) 292-0077.** Take a tour of Key West the slow and easy way—in a pedicab. These bicycle-powered vehicles are a great way to feel the warm breeze on your face and breathe in the tropical air as your cyclist narrates the sights. Just make sure you agree on the price before you start your journey.

### Foot Power

Strolling Key West is a great way to work off the pounds you'll be packing on by grazing the tempting kiosks, juice bars, ice-cream shops, restaurants, and, of course, bars of Key West. The sidewalk-lined streets in Old Town often front little-known lanes where unusual shops or galleries hide beneath ancient foliage. You'll miss these—and much of the mystery and charm of this southernmost city—if you don't get out of your car and walk a bit.

## Are We Almost There?

Driving in the Keys takes time and patience. Speed limits are strictly enforced, and in some areas, 45 mph is as fast as the law allows. Here are approximate drive times from various locations (please note that times may vary due to weather and road conditions):

| | |
|---|---|
| Miami to Big Pine Key | 2.5 hours |
| Key West to West Palm Beach | 5 hours |
| Key West to Miami | 3.5 hours |
| Marathon to Orlando | 7 hours |
| Key West to Fort Lauderdale | 4 hours |
| Key West to Naples | 5.5 hours |

**And for you road warriors:**

| | |
|---|---|
| Key West to Anchorage, Alaska (4,020 miles) | 81 hours |

## Key West Parking

Parking is plentiful and free of charge in the Keys, until you visit Key West. Ask any Key West local if there's a downside to living in the southernmost city, and he or she will almost always complain about parking. There are simply too many cars in Old Town Key West, and too few places to put them. And because the permanent population of this tiny island keeps growing, and most visitors either arrive by car or rent a vehicle when they get here, the parking problem isn't going away anytime soon.

Patrons of the shops and restaurants in Duval Square (1075 Duval St.) will find free parking available in an adjacent lot accessed from Simonton Street. Free parking for patrons of some Duval Street restaurants, shops, and bars may also be available in designated lots off either Whitehead or Simonton Streets, both of which run parallel to Duval. Metered curbside parking is, of course, available on several downtown streets, including Duval, Whitehead, and Simonton, as well as along most of the streets that intersect them. Special curbside parking areas are designated for scooters and mopeds; do not leave vehicles on the sidewalk.

Here's how parking in residential Old Town works: Curbside spots along many Old Town streets have been ruled off with white paint and marked with the large white letters spelling out residential parking. In order to park your vehicle in one of these spots, your car must display either a Monroe County license plate or a residential parking permit (available from the City of Key West with proof of residence).

If you park in one of the residential parking spaces and your car does not show the proper proof of residence, you may return to find it gone. Your illegally parked vehicle will likely have been towed to the city's impound lot on Stock Island. If you want to be right in the thick of things, you will either have to feed a meter or pay to park in a lot. The city is now equipped with machines on parts of Duval and Southard Streets that allow you to pay for hours at a time via credit card and place the receipt on your dashboard, thus eliminating the need for coins. The traditional meters still exist as well. Meter maids (and men) regularly patrol the streets of Key West at all hours, and tickets are liberally distributed. All-day parking is available for more reasonable prices at several privately owned lots on either side of Duval Street; watch for the lot attendants holding cardboard signs. You might also consider one of the convenient parking facilities described below.

**KEY WEST BIGHT PARKING LOT, Corner of Caroline and Margaret Streets; (305) 809-3864.** Located adjacent to the attractions at Key West Historic Seaport, this open-air lot offers full-day parking for a maximum of about $16.25. If you just need to run a quick errand, you can park here for an hourly charge. The fully automated lot is accessible 24 hours to cars, motorcycles, and scooters only; no RVs, trailers, or buses permitted.

**MALLORY SQUARE PARKING LOT, Corner of Wall and Front Streets.** This parking lot is convenient to all the west-end attractions and the sunset celebration. Through the years, however, it has been reduced in size to accommodate the enlarged and improved Mallory Square, so parking space is limited. Rates run about $4 per hour, day and night, or $32 for 24 hours. The lot is open from 8 a.m. until midnight. Cars, motorcycles, small trucks, and vans are welcome; campers, RVs, buses, and trailers are not.

**OLD TOWN PARKING GARAGE, Key West Park N' Ride, 301 Grinnell St., Key West, FL 33040; keywestcity.com.** The Old Town Parking Garage offers you the chance to find one of 250 covered parking spaces at a reasonable rate anytime, day or night. Cars, small trucks, and motorcycles are welcome here. For about a $13 fee, you can park and then ride one of the shuttles several blocks to the downtown area. If your stay will be long-term, choose the monthly rate of about $99 plus tax.

# Accommodations

In this chapter we escort you through some of the Florida Keys' more outstanding facilities. Our selections are based on attributes of rooms, service, location, property, and overall ambience.

## Location & Amenities

Like our Conchs (those of us born in the Keys) and Keys characters (those of us who were not), accommodations in the Florida Keys are highly individualistic. Most are situated on the Florida Bay, the Gulf of Mexico, or the Atlantic Ocean. We commonly refer to the Atlantic as "oceanside." For simplicity's sake in this chapter, we refer to the bayside and gulfside as "bayside."

Oceanside accommodations offer exotic sunrises and proximity to dive sites, oceanside flats, and blue-water locations for sportfishing. Water access is generally deeper on the oceanside than in the bay, affording boaters and sailors more options. Bayside lodgings can boast of our spectacular Keys sunsets, which sink into the placid skinny waters of the gulf like a meltdown of molten lava. Some hotels, motels, resorts, and inns sit alongside inland canals or marina basins, and many of our waterfront facilities are accessible by boat.

Whether the accommodations are bayside, oceanside, large, small, or somewhere in between, all of our guest properties exude a casual, barefoot ambience. To one degree or another, all bestow the uninterrupted escape for which the Florida Keys have always been known.

### Ecotourism in the Keys

Ecotourism is on everyone's mind. More and more companies are "going green" worldwide, and this includes properties in the Florida Keys. Meeting the criteria means purchasing renewable energy, recycling, installation of low-flow showerheads, energy-efficient lighting and appliances, upgrading air-conditioning filters, using environmentally friendly cleaning products, and, in the case of the Hyatt, using natural woods for room furnishings. In addition to the entire Southernmost Hotel Collection, more than 680 resorts in Florida have completed the Florida Department of Environmental Protection's Certified Green Lodging Program, and are designated as such. For a complete list of designated properties in the Keys, visit floridagreenlodging.org. To learn more about companies that are going green in the Keys, visit keysglee.com.

## Rate Information

Rate structures for Keys lodgings vary nearly as much as the accommodations themselves, but you can draw a few generalizations. Rates fluctuate by season and depend largely upon the size of the accommodation and its proximity to the water.

High season (Dec through Apr) supports the highest rates. High-season rates usually prevail during sport lobster season at the end of July (a near holiday in the Keys; see the Diving & Snorkeling chapter), Fantasy Fest in October (our southernmost decadent version of Mardi Gras; see our Annual Events chapter), and most national holiday weekends. You must make reservations well in advance of your visit during any of these times. Many facilities fully book available accommodations one year in advance for the high season and the holidays.

A second season commences in May and continues through the summer months, attracting vacationers seeking to escape the steamy heat of the rest of Florida and the Deep South. Rates during this period are generally slightly less than those in the high season.

Low season is September, bringing a savings of about 20 percent off high-season rates. Just keep in mind that a lot of the local businesses and restaurants close in the month of September for vacation.

In all cases, rates are quoted for the high season. Prices are figured on a double-occupancy average rate per night. Villas, efficiencies, and condominium units, which generally establish rates per unit rather than per person, will be quoted as such. And even though these units traditionally are rented by the week, we have computed our code on an average daily rate so that you can compare apples with apples.

It is not uncommon to find accommodations that run the gamut of several price-code categories all at the same place. The code will indicate if you can expect a range of space and pocketbook possibilities.

### *Price Code*

Price codes are high-season rates figured without additional fees, such as room service and parking, and without the 12.5 percent room tax.

| | |
|---|---|
| $ | Less than $120 |
| $$ | $120 to $200 |
| $$$ | $200 to $300 |
| $$$$ | $300 and higher |

## THE FLORIDA KEYS

### *Upper Keys*

At the top of the Keys, Key Largo, home of John Pennekamp Coral Reef State Park, bustles with an energetic crowd of divers and snorkelers in all seasons.

The orientation here is definitely geared toward the underwater treasures of the coral reef that lies just 4 miles offshore. Many motels and resorts in this area offer diving and snorkeling packages.

The settlement of Tavernier snuggles between Key Largo and Islamorada. This quiet area is known for its historic qualities. Dubbed the Sportfishing Capital of the World, Islamorada stretches from Plantation Key at MM 90 to Lower Matecumbe Key at MM 73. This village of islands, incorporated in 1998, is renowned for its contingent of talented game-fishing guides (see the Fishing chapter) and prestigious fishing tournaments.

The Upper Keys pulsates with tiki bars and watering holes as well as an array of fine restaurants (see the Restaurants chapter) and activities for families and sports enthusiasts alike (see the Attractions chapter).

**AMARA CAY, MM 80, Oceanside, 80001 Overseas Hwy., Islamorada, FL 33036; (305) 664-0073; theislamoradaresort.com. $$$.** At this newly opened resort, guests enjoy a heated pool and spa, a tiki bar, and a palm-laden, sandy sunning area. There is also a private seawall beach with hammocks, thatched huts and pier, as well as a complete selection of water sports on the premises, including snorkeling and diving excursions, parasailing, and fishing charters. Many guest rooms and suites have furnished balconies overlooking the ocean. For dining, grab a table at Otremare Italian restaurant, which is open for breakfast and dinner, and serves traditional Italian cuisine with a tropical twist. For lunch or dinner, try the American cuisine poolside at Sparrows Rum Bar.

**AMY SLATE'S AMORAY DIVE RESORT, MM 104.2 Bayside, 10425 Overseas Hwy., Key Largo, FL 33037; (305) 451-3595 or (800) 426-6729; amoray.com; $$.** An eclectic collection of plantation-style villas springs to life daily as scuba enthusiasts rustle about, eager to embark on the resort's 45-foot *Amoray Diver* for the half-hour ride to John Pennekamp Coral Reef State Park (see the Diving & Snorkeling chapter). Varying in size, amenities, and price, the rooms range from the standard motel variety to small apartments with full kitchens. Dive-and-Stay Packages are available and include the cost of diving, room accommodations, tanks, and weights. Amenities available to all guests include free Wi-Fi, the use of the pool, kayaks, barbecue grills, and all snorkeling equipment.

**ATLANTIC BAY RESORT, MM 92.5 Bayside, 160 Sterling Rd., Tavernier, FL 33070; (305) 852-5248 or (866) 937-5650; atlanticbayresort.com; $$$.** Atlantic Bay Resort enjoys 3 acres of prime bayfront property, planted with palms and bougainvillea, and featuring a large beach area peppered with chaise lounges and barbecue grills, Adirondack beach chairs, and hammocks. Unique to this property is a special feature of Florida Bay called the "deep hole," where depths drop dramatically to 20 feet right offshore. A coral rock ledge shelters lobsters, starfish, sergeant major fish, mangrove snappers, and parrotfish, making for dynamic snorkeling. The Atlantic Bay Resort offers 19 efficiencies, cottages, or suites for up to 4 people, all with full kitchens and free Wi-Fi. Boat dockage and use of the boat ramp are available to guests at no extra charge. Guests also enjoy complimentary use of kayaks and paddleboards.

**AZUL DEL MAR, MM 104.3 Bayside, 104300 Overseas Hwy., Key Largo, FL 33037; (305) 451-0337; azulhotels.us;  $$$–$$$$.** The sprawling lawn that flows to the private beach that rolls into the Gulf of Mexico sets the mood at this adults-only property. Rooms feature soft beds with down comforters; sleek kitchens with microwaves, fridges, mini-dishwashers, and coffeemakers; and TVs, CD players, and DVD players to watch movies from their in-house library. Aveda products are located in the bath, as well as plush bath and beach towels, and coffee and tea packets are offered in-room to guests as well. There is no formal dining area at Azul, but gas grills are available for guests, and there are many fine restaurants in the vicinity.

**BAYSIDE INN KEY LARGO, MM 99.5 Bayside, 99490 Overseas Hwy., Key Largo, FL 33037; (305) 451-4450 or (800) 242-5229; baysidekeylargo .com; $$–$$$.** Located on beautiful Florida Bay in the heart of Key Largo, this locally owned location is an ideal getaway. Fifty-six bright, tropical-themed guest rooms overlook the bay. One-bedroom Waterfront Suites feature a full kitchen, living room with a king-size Murphy bed, dining room, private bathroom, bedroom with a king-size bed, pull-out queen couch, and a private balcony overlooking the pool, beach, and sunsets. Bay View Rooms offer a full waterfront view, surrounded by tropical gardens and palm trees. Each room has a king-size bed with beach, waterfront, and sunset views, and a small refrigerator and microwave. In addition to the rooms, there is also a fitness center and a fabulous heated pool that overlooks Florida Bay.

**BREEZY PALMS RESORT, MM 80 Oceanside, 80015 Overseas Hwy., Islamorada, FL 33036; (305) 664-2361 or (877) 412-7339; breezypalms.com; $–$$$.** Quaint coral buildings with turquoise doors and screened porches mark Breezy Palms Resort, a cozy place nestled on 320 feet of oceanfront. The brightly wallpapered motel rooms, efficiencies, apartments, and cottages are clean and spacious, featuring rattan furniture and colorful island floral prints. Coconut palms pepper the property, which sits directly on the Atlantic Ocean and sports a sandy beach as well as a swimming pool. A brick barbecue, picnic table, shuffleboard, and volleyball net add to the amenities; dockage is available for an additional fee. No straight inboards or personal watercraft, such as Jet Skis or WaveRunners, are permitted. Breezy Palms is accessible by boat.

**CALOOSA COVE RESORT,** MM 73.8 Oceanside, 73801 Overseas Hwy., Islamorada, FL 33036; (305) 664-8811 or (888) 297-3208; caloosacove .com; $$$. This condominium complex, sitting on a 10-acre parcel of prime oceanfront property, offers 30 spacious, light, and bright efficiencies and one-bedroom suites. A covered deck that looks directly at the Atlantic fronts every unit. Caloosa Cove's large irregularly shaped heated pool, surrounded by extensive decking and thatched-palm huts, sits directly on the ocean's edge, affording endless vistas of the beyond. The grounds encompassing the coral-laden exterior of Caloosa Cove burgeon with mature tropical plantings. Activities and amenities on condo premises include shuffleboard and basketball courts, a barbecue area, lighted tennis courts, a full-service marina, fishing charters, and boat and bicycle rentals. The nearby Safari Lounge serves your choice of cocktails.

**CASA MORADA,** MM 82.2 Bayside, 136 Madeira Rd., Islamorada, FL 33036; (305) 664-0044 or (888) 881-3030; casamorada.com; $$$–$$$$. Tucked on the shores of Florida Bay, out of the fray of US 1 on a residential street, this all-suites hotel exudes the charm of a Caribbean villa. The 16 suites, each unique, have private terraces or semiprivate gardens overlooking the water and are decorated with a mixture of wrought-iron and mahogany furniture, which was exclusively created for Casa Morada. Cross a small, circa-1950 bridge to a private island and you'll find a sandy playground with a pool, secluded cabana, and terrace with breakfast, lunch, and beverage service. Continental breakfast is complimentary, as is Wi-Fi, the use of bikes, kayaks, paddleboards, and snorkel equipment, and the yoga classes held on Sat and Sun.

★**CHEECA LODGE & SPA,** MM 82 Oceanside, 81801 Overseas Hwy., Islamorada, FL 33036; (305) 664-4651 or (800) 327-2888; cheeca.com; $$$$. Majestically sprawling amid 27 manicured, tropical acres with more than 1,200 feet of beachfront, Cheeca Lodge & Spa creates a vacation enclave with all 214 spacious guest rooms and suites sporting tropical themes and colors. Many rooms have balconies that overlook the ocean or across the grounds of the resort, and some units have screened porches. There is also a 5,700-square-foot luxury spa on-site and an overflowing cache of recreational options: a saltwater lagoon for easy on-site snorkeling, an oceanfront pier replete with complimentary fishing equipment, a Jack Nicklaus–designed 9-hole par 3 golf course, nature trails, water sports, adult and family pools, as well as kayaking, bicycling, and windsurfing.

**CHESAPEAKE BEACH RESORT,** MM 83.4 Oceanside, 83409 Overseas Hwy., Islamorada, FL 33036; (305) 664-4662 or (800) 338-3395; chesapeake-resort.com; $$$–$$$$. The elegant Chesapeake Beach Resort hugs the Atlantic on 6.5 acres of lushly landscaped grounds. This pristine 3-story,

65-unit resort is home to 13 villas, 44 guest rooms, and 8 suites. The Chesapeake sports 2 heated pools, a hot tub, tennis courts, an outdoor gym, as well as a 700-foot sunning beach and a saltwater lagoon used for parking boats. A boat ramp and boat dockage are provided. Suites and villas offer full kitchens and have balconies or screened porches. Fishing, snorkeling, diving, and parasailing excursions, as well as sunset cruises, can be booked nearby. Free Wi-Fi and the use of kayaks, Hobie cats, bicycles, and paddleboats are included in your stay.

**CORAL BAY RESORT, MM 75.6 Bayside, 75690 Overseas Hwy., Islamorada, FL 33036; (305) 664-5568; thecoralbayresort.com; $$$$.** Coral Bay Resort's motel rooms, efficiencies, cottages, apartments, and villa suites are white-trimmed, pastel pink, air-conditioned Conch-style dwellings. The fresh interiors sparkle with light furniture, pastel fabrics, and tile floors. You'll enjoy Coral Bay's fresh water heated pool as well as the sandy beach on the Gulf of Mexico. Fishing and snorkeling in the 14-foot-deep saltwater tidal pool are excellent. The pier itself has built-in seating and a fish-cleaning station. Guests can dock their own vessels for free or use the resort's paddleboat for exploration. Waters beyond the dock are illuminated at night, so the seaside fun doesn't have to end at sunset.

**COURTYARD KEY LARGO, MM 99.7 Oceanside, 99751 Overseas Hwy., Key Largo, FL 33037; (305) 451-3939 or (800) 731-9092; marriott.com; $$$.** The Courtyard's recently renovated 91 rooms have all the amenities you would expect from a Marriott hotel: The spacious rooms all feature complimentary Wi-Fi, a mini refrigerator, and private balcony. The hotel wraps around a small, private, heated, kidney-shaped swimming pool and also has a whirlpool on the grounds. In addition, the fitness room houses treadmills, ellipticals, and free weights. And if you are looking to enjoy your days out on the water, boating, sailing, scuba diving, and snorkeling are all activities that are available on-property.

**DOVE CREEK LODGE, MM 94.5, Oceanside, 147 Seaside Ave., Key Largo, FL 33037; (305) 852-6200 or (800) 401-0057; dovecreeklodge.com; $$$.** This 21-bedroom boutique retreat offers oceanfront, ocean-view, and garden-view rooms. A complimentary continental breakfast is served daily in the lobby, and the oceanfront pool and hot tub are heated year-round. The property sits right next door to one of the best seafood establishments in the Keys, Snapper's Waterfront Restaurant (see Restaurants chapter), where they say: "Our seafood is so fresh we have to change the menu daily 'cause we don't know what's coming in off the boats." You can arrive by land or sea for your stay. Dove Creek Lodge offers family and wedding packages and group rates. No pets or smoking allowed.

**HAMPTON INN AT MANATEE BAY,** MM 102 Bayside, 102400 Overseas Hwy., Key Largo, FL 33037; (305) 451-1400; hamptoninnkeylargo.com; $$$. Not far from John Pennekamp Coral Reef State Park, Dolphin Cove, Theater of the Sea, Florida City Outlet Mall, and Everglades National Park, you will discover Key Largo's Hampton Inn. There are 100 rooms, decorated with a quiet tropical coolness, each offering flat-screen TVs, free Wi-Fi, a refrigerator, microwave, coffeemaker, and wet bar. Each guest room has either a private balcony or patio that opens directly to the heated pool, beach, or surrounding tropical gardens. Pets are welcome at the Hampton Inn.

**HILTON KEY LARGO RESORT,** MM 97 Bayside, 97000 Overseas Hwy., Key Largo, FL 33037; (305) 852-5553 or (800) 871-3437; keylargoresort .com; $$$. This luxury resort lounges on 12.5 acres in a lush hardwood forest along the Gulf of Mexico. Accommodations are comfortable, with nature trails, a private beach, exciting water sports, sportfishing, 2 heated pools (family and adult), fitness/sauna/whirlpool facilities, 2 outdoor lighted tennis courts, 3 restaurants, and room service. All 190 rooms and suites have modern tropical decor. The on-site Splashes Pool Bar has grab-and-go food for lunch and dinner, Treetops Bar & Grille offers dining with a Mediterranean and Caribbean twist for breakfast and dinner, and the Waves Beach Bar is the best place to enjoy lunch or an afternoon cocktail.

**HOLIDAY INN KEY LARGO RESORT AND MARINA,** MM 99.7 Oceanside, 99701 Overseas Hwy., Key Largo, FL 33037; (305) 451-2121 or (800) 843-5397; holidayinnkeylargo.com; $$$. Rooms at the Holiday Inn face lush tropical gardens or the harbor, and the colorful accents in each room reflect the flora that flourishes outside. Palm trees, frangipani, and bougainvillea weave a foliage trail between the hot tub and 2 heated freshwater pools, one of which is embellished with a tropical waterfall. There is a fitness center on-site as well as a Jacuzzi for your post-workout recovery. Bogie's Cafe offers breakfast, lunch, and dinner, and the Tiki Bar serves light fare all day while live music percolates poolside on most weekend evenings.

**JULES' UNDERSEA LODGE,** MM 103.2 Oceanside, 51 Shoreline Dr., Key Largo, FL 33037; (305) 451-2353; jul.com; $$. For a unique experience, Jules' Undersea Lodge has to be near the top of the list. You actually dive 21 feet beneath the surface of the sea to enter the lodge. The only underwater hotel in the world, this lodge is located under the surface of a tropical mangrove in the Emerald Lagoon. The cottage-size building has hot showers, a well-stocked kitchen (with refrigerator and microwave), books, music, and even pizza delivery. As you snuggle in your bed, you can view the sea life that appears at the windows of this aquatic habitat. To get into Jules' Undersea Lodge, you must be a certified scuba diver.

**KONA KAI RESORT,** MM 97.8 Bayside, 97802 Overseas Hwy., Key Largo, FL 33037; (305) 852-7200 or (800) 365-7829; konakairesort.com; $$$$. Toward the southern end of Key Largo sits this adults-only gem with intimate, cottage-style suites and guest rooms. Tropical fruits in season, such as the guava and star fruit, grow throughout the gardens of this 2-acre property. There is a heated freshwater swimming pool and a hot tub accented by a magnificent circular staircase and paver-stone deck. Lounge chairs, picnic tables, and barbecue grills sit close to Kona Kai's white-sand beach, which is guarded by a stone alligator. You'll be able to snorkel, swim, or fish off a platform at the end of a dock, and a paddleboat, kayak, and other water "toys" are available free of charge.

**KON-TIKI RESORT,** MM 81.2 Bayside, 81200 Overseas Hwy., Islamorada, FL 33606; (305) 664-4702; kontiki-resort.com; $$–$$$. Kon-Tiki's pebbled walkways, private patios, and cottages consistently attract anglers and families alike. The resort's quiet, U-shaped property boasts a shuffleboard court, pier, private beach on Florida Bay, park benches, a heated freshwater pool, and grill and picnic areas. The primary attraction here, though, is the saltwater pond stocked with all sorts of tropical fish. Guests are invited to don snorkel and mask and take an underwater look-see. Accommodations feature bright, clean, and comfortable motel units, fully equipped efficiencies, and one-bedroom apartments, most of which have private patios or screened porches.

★**LA SIESTA RESORT & MARINA,** MM 80.2 Oceanside, 80241 Overseas Hwy., Islamorada, FL 33606; (305) 664-2132 or (877) 278-0369; lasiestaresort.com; $$. Tucked away amid the palm trees and the tropical foliage, you'll find La Siesta Resort & Marina. There are a few options for lodging on the property, including one-, two-, and three-bedroom cottages and suites. The Insider tip here is to request cottage 101. Cottage 101 has a navy-and-white nautical theme replete with white wainscoting and framed photos of fishing expeditions from yesteryear hanging on the walls, as well as a personal patio with a view of the marina and ocean beyond. And then there is the best amenity of all: your own personal hammock under the palm trees. Sure, there are water sports and a heated pool on-site as well, but the hammock beckons. How can you resist?

**LOOKOUT LODGE RESORT,** MM 87.7 Bayside, 87770 Overseas Hwy., Islamorada, FL 33036; (305) 852-9915 or (800) 870-1772; lookoutlodge .com; $$$. Lookout Lodge is a clean, modestly priced, pet-friendly motel of Spanish-influenced architecture. The resort's rooms and suites feature decidedly 1960s decor and amenities. All suites have kitchenettes, tile floors and baths, and ceiling fans. A limited number of pet-friendly rooms (small pets only) are available. Steps lead from the resort's raised man-made beach to the private lagoon for swimming and snorkeling. The property features gas grills, picnic tables, and lounge chairs, but no swimming pool. Dock space, available for an additional fee, is limited and must be reserved in advance.

**MARINA DEL MAR RESORT AND MARINA, MM 100 Oceanside, 527 Caribbean Dr., Key Largo, FL 33037; (305) 451-4107; marinadelmarkey largo.com; $$$.** The pet-friendly Marina Del Mar Resort and Marina, on a quiet, dead-end street along an ocean-fed canal and boat basin, draws an active boating, fishing, and diving crowd. The 76 rooms are bright and modern, with tile floors, ceiling fans, white wicker furnishings, and bold tropical accents, and feature king-size beds or 2 double beds. A complimentary continental breakfast is offered daily, and restaurants and attractions are nearby. The hotel also offers complimentary Wi-Fi and parking and maintains 2 tennis courts, a small fitness room, and a heated swimming pool with a brick sundeck and hot tub.

**MARINER'S RESORT VILLAS & MARINA, MM 98 Oceanside, 97501 Overseas Hwy., Key Largo, FL 33037; (305) 853-5000; keyscaribbean.com; $$$.** This gated resort on 16 lush acres brimming with coconut palms, bougainvillea, and mangrove trees amid the beautiful townhomes and villas, allows guests the comforts of a private residence with all the amenities of a resort. Classic Caribbean color schemes, along with a 43-slip marina, give you the feeling of being on an island. On the premises are 2 pools—one of which is a 7,800-square-foot, oceanfront lagoon-styled pool that has 2 zero-entries—a Jacuzzi, clubhouse, fitness center, 2 tennis courts, a professional dive shop, and just about any kind of water sport you can imagine.

**MARRIOTT KEY LARGO BAY BEACH RESORT, MM 103.8 Bayside, 103800 Overseas Hwy., Key Largo, FL 33037; (305) 453-0000 or (888) 236-2427; marriottkeylargo.com; $$$.** Bayside sunset views and a prime location near John Pennekamp Coral Reef State Park are only two of a multitude of pluses at the Marriott Key Largo Bay Beach Resort. The resort offers on-site dining and bar options in addition to a 24-hour fitness center and a day spa that has treatments indoors as well as private, open-air tiki huts for outdoor massage options. Pirate Island Divers provides on-premises water sports ranging from diving, snorkeling, parasailing, and glass-bottomed boat excursions to boat and personal watercraft rentals. Fishing charters can be booked through the hotel as well. Boat dockage is available for guests' vessels at no extra charge.

★**THE MOORINGS VILLAGE & SPA, MM 81.5 Oceanside, 123 Beach Rd., Islamorada, FL 33036; (305) 664-4708; themooringsvillage.com; $$$$.** Eighteen cottages and homes are sprinkled among 18 acres of this former coconut plantation. Hammocks laze between majestic palms; winding, floral-draped trails emit the essence of gardenia; and kayaks and paddleboards dot the 1,100-foot white-sand beach. Citrus trees, teak lounge chairs with cushions, and hammocks are scattered about the lush bougainvillea-bedecked grounds. Guests enjoy use of paddleboards, kayaks, bicycles, an 82-foot heated lap pool, and a tennis court. Spa services are also available, as well as daily yoga classes. Pristine and private, the Moorings Village rates as one of the best-kept secrets in the Keys.

**OCEAN HOUSE, MM 82.9 Oceanside, 82885 Overseas Hwy., Islamorada, FL 33036; (305) 664-4844 or (866) 540-5520; oceanhousefloridakeys.com; $$$.** This adults-only boutique resort features eight suites, replete with ocean views, a private beach, and lush tropical gardens. On the expertly manicured grounds, you'll also find a saltwater swimming pool, an oceanfront spa pool, beachside firepit, and private poolside cabanas. Each tropically named suite features a private outdoor terrace, a full-size refrigerator, coffeemaker, microwave, flat-screen TV, and free Wi-Fi. There is a daily complimentary continental breakfast, and the use of bicycles, paddleboards, and snorkeling equipment are all included in your stay. Unwind with an in-room spa treatment or book a fishing charter through the on-site concierge. However you choose to spend your days at this Islamorada gem, your stay at the Ocean House will not disappoint.

**OCEAN POINTE SUITES, MM 92.5 Oceanside, 500 Burton Dr., Key Largo, FL 33070; (305) 853-3000 or (800) 882-9464; opsuites.com; $$$.** Directly on the Atlantic Ocean, this tropical, contemporary, 3-story, all-suite stilt condominium complex offers 160 units with private balconies with either ocean or mangrove views. Just outside your door are nature walks, a private beach, a large heated swimming pool, barbecue grills, picnic areas, beach volleyball courts, and lighted tennis courts. The 60-acre property also has a playground, a boat ramp capable of handling watercrafts up to 28 feet, and a marina. If you feel like a bite, head for the Waterfront Cafe for breakfast, lunch, an afternoon snack, or a light dinner. Kayak rentals also are available.

**PELICAN COVE RESORT AND MARINA, MM 84.5 Oceanside, 84457 Overseas Hwy., Islamorada, FL 33036; (305) 664-4435 or (800) 445-4690; pelicancovehotel.com; $$$.** Perched beside the Atlantic Ocean, Pelican Cove Resort—constructed in concrete with a tin roof and Bahamian shutters—ensures a balcony and ocean view from almost every one of its 63 rooms. Behind the recently renovated resort, steps connect the raised man-made beach to the ocean, where waters can run about 30 feet deep. A swimming pool with sundeck, outdoor cabana bar and cafe, poolside hot tub, and volleyball net all front the beach. Watersports, including sailing, windsurfing, kayaking, snorkeling, and scuba diving, are all complimentary, and the resort can set you up with fee-based fishing guides and eco-tours.

**THE PELICAN KEY LARGO COTTAGES ON THE BAY,** MM 99.34 Bayside, 99340 Overseas Hwy., Key Largo, FL 33037; (305) 451-3576 or (877) 451-3576; hungrypelican.com; $$. Murals of manatees, pelicans, roseate spoonbills, and egrets decorate the outside walls of the 1-story "old Keys" buildings at the Pelican, which are linked by masses of bougainvillea. Each of the 23 rooms is air-conditioned and has a small refrigerator, TV and DVD player, private bathroom with a shower, tile floors, and Internet access. Some also have kitchens, and there is a coin-operated laundry facility available as well. The daily continental breakfast is complimentary, as is the use of the resort's kayaks. You'll be able to swim or snorkel between the Pelican's 2 fishing piers. The property also sports a large thatched hut for lounging, and barbecue pits are scattered about.

**SUNSET COVE BEACH RESORT,** MM 99.5 Bayside, 99360 Overseas Hwy., Key Largo, FL 33036; (305) 451-0705 or (877) 451-0705; sunsetcovebeachresort.com; $. There is much character to be found at Sunset Cove: Dinosaurs and zebra sculptures dot the landscape, and all the pet-friendly units are individually decorated, most still sporting 1950s and '60s decor and furnishings. The cottages also have full kitchens. Each unit showcases wall murals of exotic flora and fauna, painted by area artists. Down at the waterfront, you'll enjoy oversize rattan swinging chairs that are hung under the tiki huts and free use of kayaks. Sunset Cove does not have a swimming pool, but there is beach access. Guests enjoy a free continental breakfast.

**TARPON FLATS INN & MARINA,** MM 103.5 Oceanside, 29 Shoreland Dr., Key Largo, FL 33037; (305) 453-1313 or (866) 546-0000; tarponflatsinn.com; $$$. Standing on the banks of Largo Sound, this 3-story B&B offers modern accommodations with a Caribbean flair. A fishing camp in the 1960s and '70s, the resort comes complete with its own beach. British Colonial mahogany furniture is the decor in suites and rooms. The verandas off the rooms frame fabulous views of Largo Sound and the surrounding state parks. The resort's marina can accommodate your boat or charter one for some of the best fishing and fun in the Keys. Fishing not your thing? The inn can arrange snorkel and dive trips, or you can just go along for the ride and take some dazzling photos to show folks back home.

**TOPSIDER RESORT,** MM 75.5 Bayside, 75500 Overseas Hwy., Islamorada, FL 33036; (305) 664-8031 or (800) 262-9874; topsiderresort.com; $$. The 20 octagonal, elevated time-share villas at Topsider Resort flank a wooden boardwalk that marches from the secluded parking lot to the crystalline waters of the Gulf of Mexico. Each features 2 bedrooms, 2 baths, a dining area, living room, full kitchen, and a washer and dryer. The units are identical in layout and updated on a rotating basis. Be sure to inquire as to when your unit was last renovated before booking. Guests at Topsider Resort enjoy an elevated heated pool and spa, a tennis court, children's swings and slides, grills, picnic tables, and bayfront wooden lounges for sunning on the sandy lagoonside beach. Minimum stay here is 3 nights, but most guests opt for a week's sabbatical.

**WHITE GATE COURT,** MM 76 Bayside, 76010 Overseas Hwy., Islamorada, FL 33036; (305) 664-4136 or (800) 645-4283; whitegatecourt .com; $–$$. The 7 private 1940s-era restored villas and bungalows at the pet-friendly White Gate Court are situated on 3 acres abutting the placid Gulf of Mexico. Spacious interiors feature fully equipped kitchens and sparkling bathrooms. All units have covered porches and outdoor tables and chairs, and some even feature rope hammocks. Lounge chairs pepper a 200-foot white-sand beach where guests enjoy swimming and snorkeling in the sandy-bottom gulf. White Gate Court does not have a pool but does offer free use of bicycles and kayaks. A finger dock stretches into the water for fishing, and tiki torches and barbecue grills are available for an evening cookout.

> **i** The Monroe County Tourist Development Council can help you find the perfect spot to rest your head as well as help you plan your entire Florida Keys vacation. Call them toll-free at (800) 352-5397 or visit fla-keys.com.

## Middle Keys

The Middle Keys stretch from the Long Key Bridge to the Seven Mile Bridge. Long, Conch, Duck, and Grassy Keys lead the way to the string of bridge-connected islands known as the incorporated city of Marathon.

Basing your accommodations in the Middle Keys offers some distinct advantages. The barrier reef sheltering the prolific fishing waters of the Atlantic supports a plethora of marine life and harbors a number of primo shipwrecks for divers (see the Diving & Snorkeling chapter). Fishing in the Middle Keys rivals that of the famed Islamorada, a well-kept secret. From flats to backcountry, blue water to bridges, you won't hear too many tales of the "one that got away" here (see the Fishing chapter).

Marathon currently offers one golf course, the nine-hole Key Colony Beach public course.

The Dolphin Research Center on Grassy Key is a must-do regardless of where your accommodations might be. And in Marathon, Crane Point Museum and Nature Center will captivate the whole family, as will historic Pigeon Key, at the end of a length of the old Seven Mile Bridge accessed at MM

47 (see the Attractions chapter). Sombrero Beach in Marathon, a very nice man-made public beach, provides endless ocean vistas to all.

Like the rest of the Keys, this whole area is packed with recreational water options, from party fishing boats and glass-bottomed reef excursions to personal watercraft and sea kayak rentals (see the Recreation chapter).

The pace is less tiki-bar frenetic here than in the Upper Keys. The sidewalk rolls up at a relatively early hour. But this area will appeal to families with children, as well as serious anglers and divers who, after a day on or under the water, relish a relaxing dinner at one of the many top-notch restaurants.

**BANANA BAY RESORT & MARINA,** MM 49.5 Bayside, 4590 Overseas Hwy., Marathon, FL 33050; (305) 743-3500; bananabay.com; $$–$$$. This dazzling 10-acre plantation-style resort with 61 rooms located on Florida Bay is a popular Marathon destination. The grounds are ancient: gnarled trunks of massive royal poinciana trees, 20-foot traveler's palms, and mature bird-of-paradise plants. And don't miss the bananas, 15 varieties tucked between towering scheffleras and gumbo-limbos, papayas, and staggering banyan trees. Don't let this quiet island charm fool you. There is plenty to do here besides lounging by the freshwater swimming pool or soaking in the outdoor whirlpool. Banana Bay offers an on-premises playland: tennis, sea kayaking, sailboarding, or rentals of personal watercraft, sailboats, and more. Banana Bay also offers popular island wedding packages, including a choice of romantic settings for the ceremony.

**BAY VIEW INN MOTEL AND MARINA,** MM 63 Bayside, 3 North Conch Ave., Conch Key, FL 33050; (305) 289-1525 or (800) 289-2055; bayviewinn .com; $–$$. Located in the heart of Conch Key, with views of the Gulf of Mexico, the brightly colored Bay View Inn Motel and Marina is a quiet retreat from the busy crowds of larger resorts. The nonsmoking inn offers free Wi-Fi, boat dockage, a freshwater swimming pool, and a variety of rooms, efficiencies, and family suites. Some of the efficiencies and rooms are situated at the waterfront on the marina and have individual grills for that daily catch or late-night dining. The Bay View can arrange for golf and tennis games, Jet Ski, kayak, and boat rentals, so you are sure to enjoy the great outdoors during your stay.

**THE BLACKFIN RESORT & MARINA,** MM 49.5 Bayside, 4650 Overseas Hwy., Marathon, FL 33050; (305) 743-2393 or (800) 548-5397; black finresort.com; $–$$$. The 35-unit pet-friendly Blackfin Resort and Marina sits on 4.5 acres abutting the Gulf of Mexico. Room types include single, double, efficencies, and small and large apartments. The grounds are peppered with poinciana, gumbo-limbo, strangler fig trees, and curving coconut palms. Stone paths wind through gardens of tropical flora. On a remote point of land at the end of the marina marked by a miniature lighthouse, guests enjoy a 600-foot, man-made, sandy beach sprinkled with lounge chairs, picnic tables, barbecue grills, and a thatched hut. A freshwater pool overlooks the gulf. The placid waters of the gulf shelter a potpourri of tropical fish, a virtual aquarium for anglers and snorkelers. Kayak rentals are available on-site.

**BONEFISH RESORT,** MM 58 Oceanside, 58070 Overseas Hwy., Marathon, FL 33050; (305) 743-7107 or (800) 274-9949; bonefishresort.com; $$. Family owned and operated, Bonefish Resort is one of those little gems reflecting old Florida Keys. This true motel is a "happy camper" resting among coconut palms, banana trees, hibiscus flowers, and tropical gardens. Open the hand-painted door to your efficiency or room and step into a bright, fun space. The deluxe efficiency has a full kitchen, private deck/patio, and barbecue grill, while the efficiency offers a full kitchen and outdoor area. Guest rooms have a double bed and furnishings to suit. Walk the white-sand beach and come back for a swim in the pool or enjoy the picnic area.

**COCO PLUM BEACH AND TENNIS CLUB,** MM 54.5 Oceanside, 109 Coco Plum Dr., Marathon, FL 33050; (305) 743-0240 or (800) 228-1587; cocoplum.com; $$$$. Hidden among more than 50 varieties of palm trees and other tropical plantings, this pod of 20 3-story raised homes bestows a true island ambience. Coco Plum Beach and Tennis Club has planted a fruit-and-spice park that sports banana trees, citrus, and key lime trees. Lounge by the swimming pool, or pop into one of the blue cabanas sprinkled about the sandy beach area. The hot tub awaits your tired muscles after a few hours of spirited tennis or beach volleyball. Or just fold yourself into one of the many secluded hammocks and take a snooze. Reservations for 7 nights are preferred, but 3- to 6-night stays are available, space permitting.

**CONCH KEY COTTAGES,** MM 62.3 Oceanside, 62250 Overseas Hwy., Marathon, FL 33050; (305) 289-1377 or (800) 330-1577; conchkeycottages .com; $$$. The individual Conch Key Cottages are as unique as the tropical flora and fauna for which they're named. Accommodations range from a 5-bedroom, 5-bath, fully furnished oceanfront home, to a 1-bedroom, 1-bath, fully furnished private garden cottage. A small swimming pool sits amid towering palms, and several varieties of bananas hang at the ready for guest consumption. Conch Key Cottages maintains a boat ramp where guests may dock their vessels at no extra charge. In addition, the Wi-Fi, continental breakfast, and use of kayaks are all complimentary. There is also an on-site concierge service that can set you up with anything from in-room spa treatments to dive, snorkel, or fishing trips.

**CONTINENTAL INN,** MM 53.8 Oceanside, 1121 W. Ocean Dr., Key Colony Beach, FL 33051; (305) 289-0101 or (800) 443-7352; marathonresort

.com; $$–$$$. Don your mask, fins, and snorkel, because a small, rocky formation at the edge of Continental Inn's beach supports an aquarium of marine life. Located on the coveted sandy stretch of Key Colony Beach, this condominium resort, with its white-stone balustrade, looks faintly Mediterranean. Gulls and terns dart about the oceanfront huts as guests drink in the limitless vistas of the Atlantic. These individually owned, simply decorated, one- and two-bedroom condos flank a large, heated swimming pool. You can play the links at the nearby public golf course, head for the tennis courts, or take your kids to a nice playground (see the Recreation chapter). No boats or trailers are allowed.

**CORAL LAGOON RESORT & MARINA,** MM 53.5 Oceanside, 12399 Overseas Hwy., Marathon, FL 33050; (866) 904-1234; corallagoonresort .com; $$$. These 25 Key West–style villas and detached marina homes with white picket fences and wooden shutters sit on 6 acres next to the full-service Boat House Marina (see the Boating chapter). The 2-story homes offer an open floor plan with 3 bedrooms, 2.5 baths, luxury interiors with peaceful tropical colors, a full kitchen, washer and dryer, and wonderful water views from the first- and second-floor private porches. There is a heated pool on the property as well. The resort rents these homes daily, weekly, or monthly, and allows easy access to the Atlantic Ocean for excellent blue-water offshore fishing and the Gulf of Mexico for thrilling backcountry wreck fishing and boating.

**GULF VIEW WATERFRONT RESORT,** MM 58.7 Bayside, 58743 Overseas Hwy., Marathon, FL 33050; (305) 289-1414 or (877) 289-0111; gulf viewwaterfrontresort.com; $–$$. This small, pet-friendly private resort hosts 11-unit accommodations that include guest rooms with refrigerators and microwaves as well as one- and two-bedroom apartments with full-size kitchens. Numerous birds, tortoises, and iguanas can be found residing on the property, as well as a lovely freshwater heated pool, boat ramp, dock, and even a putting green for the land lovers. Swing low in a hammock or sit under one of the tiki huts and gaze out over hundreds of palm trees surrounded by beautiful tropical vegetation. Bicycles are available for rent, and complimentary kayaks, canoes, and paddleboats are just begging to be used in the clear blue Keys waters.

**THE HAMMOCKS AT MARATHON,** MM 48.2 Bayside, 1688 Overseas Hwy., Marathon, FL 33050; (305) 743-9009 or (800) 456-0009; bluegreen rentals.com; $$$. Perched in lush tropical foliage, the Hammocks at Marathon hosts parrotfish, tarpon, and lobster in the clear waters of their lagoon, while egrets, pelicans, and herons populate the mangroves. Palm trees and tiki huts dot the landscape, which also features a pool and hot tub. Lodging options include studios (without kitchens); 1 bedroom, 1 bath, and kitchen; or 2 bedrooms, 1.5 baths, and kitchen. On the property, Barnacle Barney's Tiki Bar & Grill overlooks the marina, with a full bar and menu. Barney's also celebrates the famous Florida Keys sunsets with the firing of a cannon as the sun sizzles into the cool gulf waters.

**HAWK'S CAY RESORT AND MARINA,** MM 61 Oceanside, 61 Hawks Cay Blvd., Duck Key, FL 33050; (305) 743-7000 or (888) 395-5539; hawks cay.com; $$$$. Hawk's Cay's rambling 60-acre Caribbean-style resort resides on one of the five islands of Duck Key. Accommodations range from rooms in the main building to private 3-bedroom vacation rentals. Unique to this Keys property is the saltwater lagoon, belted by a man-made, sandy beach. You can also observe the ongoing dolphin discovery program at the Dolphin Connection (see the Attractions chapter); sign up for fishing, parasailing, sailing, or sea kayaking; play tennis; work out at the Indies Club recreation and fitness center; treat yourself to spa services at the Calm Waters Spa, and then dine in one of the two popular restaurants on the premises.

**KEY COLONY BEACH MOTEL,** MM 54 Oceanside, 441 E. Ocean Dr., Key Colony Beach, FL 33050; (305) 289-0411; kcbmotel.com; $. Sitting proudly beside the ocean in Key Colony Beach—often called "condo row"—the modest Key Colony Beach Motel provides simply furnished rooms, each featuring 2 double beds, a refrigerator, and an excellent location. A lovely, palm-lined, sandy beach fronts this 2-story white motel, which also has a heated freshwater swimming pool. All you need here is a towel, some sunscreen, and a good book.

**LIME TREE BAY RESORT,** MM 68.5 Oceanside, 68500 Overseas Hwy., Long Key, FL 33001; (305) 664-4740 or (800) 723-4519; limetreebay resort.com; $$$. Located on the "island" of Long Key among 100 palm trees, the Lime Tree Bay Resort is a true gem. In addition to the idyllic location, the property also contains a pool that sits right on the water's edge, and tiki huts, hammocks, and barbecue areas all dot the property. Take a swim in one of the 2 pools, snorkel right off the beach, or take out a complimentary sea kayak. Each of the rooms and suites features free Wi-Fi and handsome tropical furnishings, like Mexican-tile flooring and paddle ceiling fans. This beautiful resort has received a Superior Small Lodging Award and offers different packages throughout the year, so be sure to ask if they are running any specials.

**RAINBOW BEND RESORT,** MM 58 Oceanside, 57884 Overseas Hwy., Grassy Key, FL 33050; (305) 289-1505 or (888) 929-1505; rainbowbend .com; $$$. Stretched across 2.5 acres of palm-speckled oceanfront beach, Rainbow Bend presents a mixed bag of sleeping rooms, efficiencies, and suites, and each day of your stay entitles you to 4 free boating hours. Use of canoes, kayaks, and paddleboats is also complimentary. Relax on the beach, or if freshwater appeals to you, dip into the large pool and hot tub that edge the property. A long, wooden pier extends into the shallow ocean waters for fishing or docking your own small watercraft for the duration of your stay. The Hideaway Cafe, which overlooks the beach, offers lunch and dinner (see our Restaurants chapter). A complimentary breakfast is served here each morning.

**THE REEF RESORT, MM 50.5 Bayside, 6800 Overseas Hwy., Marathon, FL 33050; (305) 743-7900; reefatmarathon.com; $$.** These 22 octagonal villas, suspended on stilts, provide a luxurious Keys getaway. Lushly landscaped grounds on 6 acres, surrounding the 2 tennis courts, belie the fact that the Reef Resort borders the Overseas Highway. Bicycles, canoes, paddleboats, and rowboats are available at no extra charge for guests who can tear themselves away from the swimming pool. There is also free Wi-Fi. Picnic tables, grills, and thatched huts on the waterfront inspire a cookout at sunset. The Reef Resort's marina offers dockage for your boat of 25 feet or less (5-foot draft at low tide). Rentals are available for the week or the month.

**SEA ISLE CONDOMINIUMS, MM 53.8 Oceanside, 1101 W. Ocean Dr., Key Colony Beach, FL 33050; (305) 743-0173 or (877) 743-0173; seaisle condos.com; $$.** The sandy beach and ocean views distinguish this 24-unit condo resort. Three tri-level white buildings, one behind the other, line Sea Isle's narrow strip of Key Colony Beach. Built in the late 1960s and individually owned and decorated, the furnishings of these spacious two-bedroom, two-bath apartments swing widely among styles of ensuing decades. Nevertheless, all necessities for a sun- and fun-filled vacation are provided: a heated swimming pool, gas grills, picnic tables, lounge chairs, and thatched huts. Stroll down Key Colony's "condo row" to the public golf course and tennis courts, or head into Marathon for a selection of boating, fishing, and diving activities (see the chapters devoted to those subjects).

**SOMBRERO RESORT & MARINA, MM 50 Oceanside, 19 Sombrero Blvd., Marathon, FL 33050; (305) 289-7662 or (800) 433-8660; sombrero resortmarina.com; $$.** The Sombrero Resort flanks Boot Key Harbor and an adjoining inland canal, and offers 41 rooms and 26 villas with all the amenities of a resort. Though not on the ocean, this destination resort allows you to be within steps of all the action, yet bathed in a laid-back and relaxing atmosphere. A keystone deck surrounds the large swimming pool, complete with a tiki bar that offers live music every Fri and Sat night. You'll be able to improve your tennis on one of the 4 courts, get your daily workouts in the exercise room, and use the complimentary Wi-Fi to stay connected to the outside world.

**TRANQUILITY BAY BEACHFRONT HOTEL & RESORT,** MM 48.5 Bayside, 2600 Overseas Hwy., Marathon, FL 33050; (305) 289-0888 or (866) 643-5397; tranquilitybay.com; $$$$. Built on 12 acres overlooking the aquamarine Gulf of Mexico, Tranquility Bay hosts magnificent palm trees that shade the sand dunes, where sea oats sway in warm breezes and a 2.5-acre white-sand beach sparkles in the sunlight. The beach houses offer a choice of 2 or 3 bedrooms, and the 16 luxury single-level Tropical Garden Guestrooms provide intimate accommodations. Part of your stay should include dinner at the Butterfly Café, which serves fresh Florida seafood. And be sure and catch a sunset by one of the three pools or at TJ's Tiki Bar, which is perched right on the beach.

**TROPICAL COTTAGES,** MM 50.5 Bayside, 243 61st St., Marathon, FL 33050; (305) 743-6048; tropicalcottages.net; $–$$$. Built in 1952, this enchanting hideaway caters to honeymooners, weddings, reunions, and small groups. The pet-friendly Tropical Cottages are adjacent to the Florida Keys Land and Sea Trust, which offers kayak trails that make for quiet exploring of backcountry and calm waters. (Don't forget to put snorkeling on your list as well.) The staff can arrange bicycle and kayak rentals, snorkeling tours, fishing trips, and even airplane or helicopter rides. Complimentary Wi-Fi is included with your stay, and they have recently added a tiki bar to the property, at which you can find live music most weekends.

**WHITE SANDS INN,** MM 57.6 Oceanside, 57622 Overseas Hwy., Marathon, FL 33050; (305) 743-5285; whitesandsinn.com; $$. Hugging a prime piece of direct ocean frontage on Grassy Key, the pale-pink-and-white White Sands Inn houses 7 one-room units, a Tree Top Terrace suite, and the Sunrise Beach House, a 3-unit house at ocean's edge that enjoys sweeping vistas of the Atlantic and a heated swimming pool. The inn rests amid towering coconut palms at water's edge, where sparkling white sand forms a natural sandy beach that you can walk along for miles at low tide. Grills are available, and a large picnic table rests under a thatched hut. A long, curved pier stretches out into the ocean, where kayaks, a rowboat, and a paddleboat are docked for free usage by guests.

> **i** If you are not staying at one of the large resort properties in the Keys, no big deal! Their restaurants and bars still offer an excellent atmosphere for socializing. Typically, establishments have casual eats at an outside bar, and in many cases reservations are not necessary.

**YELLOWTAIL INN,** MM 58 Oceanside, 58162 Overseas Hwy., Grassy Key, FL 33050; (305) 743-8400 or (800) 605-7475; yellowtailinn.com; $$$. The quaint Yellowtail Inn is charming, and its ocean-view efficiencies, cottages, and private oceanfront suites are reminiscent of old Keys style. All of the accommodations are decorated in Keys tropical-casual, with the light and airy colors of carefree sunny days. On the lovely grounds, located on unspoiled Grassy Key, you will find a small heated freshwater swimming pool, fishing pier, small private beach, and barbecue grills. Kayaks, paddleboats, fishing and snorkeling gear, and bicycles are all available for rent on the property. There is also a coin laundry facility on the grounds. Nearby attractions include the Dolphin Research Center, Pigeon Key, fishing charters, and sunset sails.

## Lower Keys

The Lower Keys, sleepier and less densely populated than the Middle or Upper Keys, distinguish themselves with acres and acres of shallow-water turtle-grass flats and copious uninhabited mangrove out-islands. The Lower Keys are surrounded by the Great White Heron National Wildlife Refuge, a large area in the Gulf of Mexico encompassing tiny keys from East Bahia Honda Key to the Content Keys to Cayo Agua and the Bay Keys. Big Pine Key is the home of the National Key Deer Refuge, a preserved area of wilderness sheltering our diminutive key deer.

Fishing is outstanding here, though ocean access is more limited. The Lower Keys can also boast of the Looe Key National Marine Sanctuary, one of the best snorkeling and diving reefs in the world. (See the Welcome to the Florida Keys and Diving & Snorkeling chapters for details.)

Accommodations are scattered throughout the Lower Keys, where campgrounds tend to dominate. (See the Campgrounds chapter if you'd like to camp in the area.) Most of the accommodations here started as fishing camps decades ago and have been updated to varying degrees. Several wonderful bed-and-breakfast inns are tucked away on a little-known oceanfront road, offering seclusion, privacy, and limitless vistas of the sea.

Crowning the assets of Lower Keys accommodations is Little Palm Island, a premier resort that rules in a class by itself. Whatever your lodging choice in the sanctuaries of the Lower Keys, your proximity to Key West more than makes up for any tourist attractions or nightlife that may be lacking here.

**BARNACLE BED & BREAKFAST,** 1557 Long Beach Dr., Big Pine Key, FL 33043; (305) 872-3298 or (800) 465-9100; thebarnacle.net; $$. Barnacle Bed & Breakfast resides on a serene stretch of beach that extends out into the Atlantic. Constructed as 3 rotated, star-shaped levels, the Barnacle houses a foliage-filled atrium that serves as the location for the complimentary breakfast buffet. Comfortably furnished with ceiling fans, a sofa, TV, table, and chairs, the atrium also serves as a common room. Guests enjoy use of kayaks, bicycles, snorkeling gear, and barbecue grills. Children younger than age 16 are not permitted. Finding Long Beach Road is a little tricky: Turn left at Big Pine Fishing Lodge, MM 33, oceanside, and proceed about 2 miles.

**DEER RUN BED & BREAKFAST, MM 33 Oceanside, Long Beach Dr., Big Pine Key, FL 33043; (305) 872-2015; deerrunfloridabb.com; $$.** The diminutive key deer really do have the run of this B&B, as they stroll the grounds like boarded guests. Staying at Deer Run is akin to vacationing in a nature preserve, and the care for animals is not limited to the outdoors. The food at Deer Run is vegan and is prepared without the use of any animal products or by-products. Deer Run's Florida Cracker–style home overlooks a peaceful beach, only 50 feet beyond a raised hot tub that fronts a productive bonefish flat. Deer Run caters to adults; children under the age of 18 are not permitted.

**LITTLE PALM ISLAND RESORT & SPA, MM 28.5 Oceanside, Little Torch Key, FL 33042; (305) 515-4004 or (800) 343-8567; littlepalmisland .com; $$$$.** Little Palm is an exquisite resort encapsulated on its own island, 3 miles offshore from Little Torch Key. TVs, telephones, and alarm clocks are banned from the rooms, and the unhurried pace encourages serious lounging beside the free-form pool, atop the crystal sand beach, enveloped in a two-person hammock, or in the meditative Zen garden secreted away deep within the 5.5 acres of island. If you are looking for a more active vacation, fishing and diving trips as well as day sailers, kayaks, canoes, a Hobie Cat, and snorkeling and fishing equipment are available. Children younger than age 16 are not permitted.

**OLD WOODEN BRIDGE GUEST COTTAGES AND MARINA, MM 30.5 Bayside, 1791 Bogie Dr., Big Pine Key, FL 33043; (305) 872-2241; old woodenbridge.com; $$.** In operation since the 1950s, the Old Wooden Bridge is tucked away at the foot of the bridge that connects Big Pine Key to No Name Key. (The bridge was wooden when the camp was built, but it has since been replaced with a concrete structure.) The Old Wooden Bridge Guest Cottages and Marina sits on Bogie Channel, where you can access both the Gulf of Mexico and the Atlantic Ocean. There is nothing fancy or pretentious about this place. There are 14 one- and two-bedroom cottages, as well as campsites, a pool, and picnic and barbecue areas where key deer roam free.

**PARMER'S RESORT, MM 28.5 Bayside, 565 Barry Ave., Little Torch Key, FL 33042; (305) 872-2157; parmersresort.com; $$.** Originally a fishing camp in the 1930s, Parmer's Resort offers 43 units in 13 buildings sprinkled over the 5-acre property in a homey 1960s style that differ widely in both size and amenities. Small, medium, and large motel rooms; standard and small efficiencies; cottages; and one- and two-bedroom apartments are all clean and simple. The property fronts Big Pine Channel, but there is no beach. A free-form swimming pool anchors the center of the property. But you can always stoke up the barbie, because Parmer's loans small gas grills to cook your catch of the day. A complimentary continental breakfast is served daily.

## Key West

This diverse, charming, historic city is considered one of the nation's top travel destinations. Key West's accommodations range from the comfort of a standard motel room to the luxury of a private suite in a historic inn. In this section, we escort you through a variety of facilities. Our selections are based on attributes of rooms, service, location, and overall ambience. All properties have air-conditioning, cable TV, and telephones unless stated otherwise.

### Motels

**BEST WESTERN HIBISCUS MOTEL, 1313 Simonton St., Key West, FL 33040; (305) 294-3763 or (800) 780-7234; bestwestern.com; $$$.** As Best Westerns go, this independently owned affiliate is small and understated. It is also one of only a few chains or franchises within Key West's historic Old Town. Of concrete-block construction, the Hibiscus has 61 units, including standard rooms and 5 one-bedroom efficiencies. Standard rooms are relatively large, with 2 queen-size beds, while efficiencies offer separate bedrooms and kitchens. Decor is bright and clean and features wood furnishings and carpeting. All units overlook either the motel's heated swimming pool and hot tub or the street and a variety of palms. Breakfast, parking, and Wi-Fi are all included.

**BLUE MARLIN MOTEL, 1320 Simonton St., Key West, FL 33040; (305) 294-2585 or (800) 523-1698; bluemarlinmotel.com; $$–$$$.** With its heated swimming pool and off-street parking, the Blue Marlin is a good choice for families who want to be near the action. The 57 rooms at this 2-story, cement-block structure—all of which overlook the pool—are clean, bright, and spacious. The best thing about the Blue Marlin, perhaps, is its location. It's tucked just a block off Duval Street on the Atlantic side of the island, and the Southernmost Point and South Beach are about 3 blocks away. There's no restaurant on the premises, but several reasonably priced eateries and a convenience store are located nearby.

### Hotels

**LA CONCHA HOTEL & SPA, 430 Duval St., Key West, FL 33040; (305) 296-2991 or (877) 270-1393; laconchakeywest.com; $$$$.** Not only is La Concha the tallest building on the island of Key West, but it's also situated in the center of busy Duval Street. Originally opened in 1926, La Concha's 150 guest rooms and 10 suites are furnished with a mix of vintage-inspired design and modern touches. Free Wi-Fi is included, and a Starbucks is located on the street level of the building. The spacious pool, set amid lush island foliage, features a multilevel sundeck and a tiki bar. The seventh floor houses the spa's luxury suites, which not only offer a bird's-eye perspective on downtown Key West, but are also one of the best places in town to view the sunset.

**THE INN AT KEY WEST,** 3420 N. Roosevelt Blvd., Key West, FL 33040; (305) 294-5541 or (800) 330-5541; theinnatkeywest.com; $$$. The Inn at Key West is located along N. Roosevelt Boulevard just 3 miles from Duval Street. The 106 rooms are decorated with tropical furnishings and include free Wi-Fi, and some offer private balconies where you can take in a wandering breeze from the Gulf of Mexico. On the premises is the largest tropical freshwater pool in Key West. Creatively landscaped foliage and vegetation surround a lively full-service tiki bar. The Inn at Key West houses the casual open-air Hammock's Cafe, which serves breakfast and lunch. Concierge services are also available for booking everything from sightseeing tours to sports activities.

**ORCHID KEY INN,** 1004 Duval St., Key West, FL 33040; (305) 296-9915 or (800) 845-8384; orchidkey.com; $$$. Built in the 1950s and tucked between old Conch houses and storefronts, the owners have brought this 24-room property back to life in a big way. Massive renovations have been made while maintaining the original footprint. The pool has a dramatic sunning shelf, and the hot tub features a tiled wall with a purple orchid mosaic and a rain waterfall. Near the pool is a bar where guests are served drinks in the afternoon and evening and a continental breakfast in the morning. This property is centrally located for all activities in Old Town Key West, so you can walk or ride bikes to restaurants, shops, and activities.

**PEGASUS INTERNATIONAL HOTEL,** 501 Southard St. (corner of Duval), Key West, FL 33040; (305) 294-9323 or (800) 397-8148; pegasus keywest.com; $$. Located on a busy corner in the heart of downtown Key West, Pegasus International Hotel offers 30 rooms with various bedding combinations, including 2 double beds, a queen-size bed, or a king-size bed. Rates are reasonable, especially considering the hotel's prime location, which is within easy walking distance of Mallory Square and the restaurants and bars on lower Duval Street, plus the fact that parking, Wi-Fi, and breakfast are all free. Amenities here also include a rooftop swimming pool, hot tub, and sundeck, all located on the second floor and all overlooking bustling Duval Street.

**PELICAN LANDING RESORT & MARINA,** 915 Eisenhower Dr., Key West, FL 33040; (305) 296-0500; pelicanlandingkeywest.com; $–$$$. The inconspicuous gulfside Pelican Landing is a 15-unit condominium and marina complex on Garrison Bight. Guests are offered a choice of standard rooms, suites, and penthouses (the latter accommodating up to 14 guests). All suites have balconies overlooking the marina, and all accommodations have washer-dryers. Pelican Landing's heated swimming pool is surrounded by a sundeck, and gas barbecue grills and a fish-cleaning station are available for guests. The marina offers 15 boat slips accommodating vessels up to 35 feet with a 12-foot beam. All guests have off-street parking. Charter fishing boats are just across the dock.

**SOUTHERNMOST HOTEL IN THE USA,** 1319 Duval St., Key West, FL 33040; (305) 296-6577 or (800) 354-4455; **southernmostresorts.com;** **$$$.** Gingerbread architectural detail and native flora come together at Southernmost Hotel. Situated just across from Southernmost on the Beach, Southernmost Hotel's 6 buildings with 118 recently renovated rooms available are surrounded by ample parking and are trimmed with exotic plants, flowers, and trees. One of the hotel's 2 swimming pools sits in the center of the parking lot, concealed by lush greenery and a wall. The courtyard features the main pool, surrounded by decking, and a hot tub. The on-property Pineapple Bar serves a limited lunch menu. Scooter and bicycle rentals and concierge services are available.

**SOUTHERNMOST ON THE BEACH,** 508 South St., Key West, FL 33040; (305) 296-6577 or (800) 354-4455; **southernmostresorts.com;** **$$$$.** So you want to stay at a gorgeous property right on the beach? Then book your reservation at the Southernmost on the Beach. This recently renovated 124-room lodging offers rooms and suites with ocean views or partial ocean views, a private beach, oceanfront pool, Shores bar, and hammocks on the West Lawn. The private pier is a great place to catch a front-row seat to the Atlantic Ocean's spectacular sunrises and early winter sunsets. Have lunch or wine and dine at the Southernmost Beach Cafe. Duval Street is just a block away, but once at this lovely resort, you will think you are on a deserted island.

**TRUMAN HOTEL,** 611 Truman Ave., Key West, FL 33040; (305) 296-6700 or (866) 487-8626; **trumanhotel.com;** **$$.** If you like the convenience of your hotel being within walking distance of all the major attractions, including Duval Street, then book your stay at the Truman Hotel. The rooms and suites have all been recently redone. The spectacular baths contain glass-tile walls, mahogany vanities, and glass sinks that "float" atop marble surfaces and flow perfectly with the cool blues, browns, and creams in the rooms. An open courtyard with tables and chairs for reading or sunning is very inviting. The pool, replete with relaxing underwater jets, is surrounded by palm trees and lounge chairs and is the perfect place to unwind before cocktail hour. Harry and Bess would approve!

*Full-Service Resorts*

**CASA MARINA RESORT AND BEACH CLUB,** 1500 Reynolds St., Key West, FL 33040; (305) 296-3535 or (888) 679-5490; casamarinaresort.com; $$$$. This beautiful property is a Florida Keys fairy tale, a legend that has hosted the likes of baseball great Lou Gehrig, actress Rita Hayworth, and President Harry Truman. Sleek guest rooms, suites, and public areas; 2 pools; private cabanas; and a private water walkway to the Atlantic Ocean await guests. The Sun-Sun restaurant and bar is located between the beach and pool area for a romantic breakfast, lunch, or dinner. All that combined with the Casa Marina's location on the largest private beach in Key West, minutes from Old Town and Duval Street and 3 minutes from Key West International Airport, makes this laid-back, elegant hotel an ideal choice.

**HYATT KEY WEST RESORT AND SPA,** 601 Front St., Key West, FL 33040; (305) 809-1234 or (888) 591-1234; keywest.hyatt.com. $$$$. Fronting the Gulf of Mexico, the 5-story Hyatt Key West is a 3-building, 118-unit complex of luxurious rooms that overlook the city, pool, or Gulf of Mexico. The Hyatt has an outdoor swimming pool and hot tub, 2 dive boats, a charter fishing boat, and a 68-foot sailing yacht for afternoon snorkeling and early-evening sunset sails. There is also the Jala Spa to soothe and pamper guests in addition to an on-site fitness center. Water sports and scooter and bike rentals are available, and the hotel has a small private beach. The poolside Blue Mojito Pool Bar and Grill is a great place to enjoy the sunset.

**KEY WEST MARRIOTT BEACHSIDE HOTEL,** 3841 N. Roosevelt Blvd., Key West, FL 33040; (305) 296-8100 or (866) 679-5490; beachsidekeywest .com. $$$-$$$$. Proudly standing sentinel at the entrance to Key West on Roosevelt Boulevard is the Beachside Marriott. Elegance abounds here, but still with a Key West charm about the property. The 5,600-square-foot ballroom can handle any event, and there is a heated pool on the grounds flanked by lush tropical foliage, rooftop sundecks, and a small beach for midnight strolls. Head to the Blue Bar by the pool for casual afternoon refreshments. Then in the evening, glide indoors to the swank Tavern N Town restaurant set with white tablecloths, for classic dishes of foie gras and grilled duck. You get the picture!

**★THE MARQUESA HOTEL,** 600 Fleming St., Key West, FL 33040; (305) 292-1919 or (800) 869-4631; marquesa.com; $$$$. This cluster of homes dates from the 1880s. Each standard room, deluxe room, junior suite, standard suite, and terrace suite is furnished with an eclectic collection of antique English and West Indian reproductions that evoke the ambience of an exquisite English plantation. Accommodations are spacious, with oversize marble baths. Many rooms feature French doors and private porches overlooking

2 pools and the garden. At the east end of the garden, brick steps accented by a fountain lead to a newer building of complementary architecture. Breakfast (available for a nominal fee) includes a feast of baked goods fresh from the oven of the highly praised Cafe Marquesa (see the Restaurants chapter).

**OCEAN KEY RESORT AND SPA,** Zero Duval St., Key West, FL 33040; (305) 296-7701 or (800) 328-9815; oceankey.com; $$$$. From their rooms and balconies, Ocean Key guests can see the ocean, our famous sunsets, and the offbeat Mallory Square entertainers. On the premises are the Sunset Pier, which has a full bar, waterfront dining, and live entertainment nightly; the Hot Tin Roof restaurant (see our Restaurants chapter); the poolside Liquid Lounge bar, only open to resort guests; a fitness center; and a marina with fishing, snorkeling, dive charter boats, and a glass-bottomed tour boat. Ocean Key offers its tranquil SpaTerre for its guests. This serene escape is a 2,550-square-foot Indonesian-inspired spa with numerous treatments available, from manicures to massage therapies.

**PARROT KEY HOTEL & RESORT,** 2801 N. Roosevelt Blvd., Key West, FL 33040; (305) 809-2200 or (888) 665-6368; parrotkeyresort.com; $$. This lush property, located on the Gulf of Mexico in New Town, has extremely large (by Key West standards) rooms and suites, 4 pools, and on-site water sports and fitness center. Each room in Parrot Key is decorated in a seaside cottage motif with original Florida Keys art for accents. Tropical landscaping hides you away, with lush gardens and sunbathing terraces surrounding two sides of the resort. Dine poolside or grab a cocktail at the tiki bar and restaurant at Café Blue. There is also complimentary Wi-Fi as well as a free shuttle to Smathers Beach, located on the other side of the island.

**PIER HOUSE RESORT & SPA,** 1 Duval St., Key West, FL 33040; (305) 296-4600 or (800) 723-2791; pierhouse.com; $$$–$$$$. For more than 40 years, the Pier House has offered luxury lodging in Key West with views of the beautiful Key West Harbor, the pool, or of sunbathers along a portion of the resort's private beach. Lush tropical foliage and brick paving surround the swimming pool and outdoor hot tub. The Pier House is also host to a full-service spa that offers fitness facilities, facials, massages, a hair salon, and manicures and pedicures. Room service is available, and a concierge will arrange for additional needs. The hotel also features a restaurant called HarbourView Cafe and the Chart Room Bar. Off-street parking is abundant.

**THE REACH RESORT,** 1435 Simonton St., Key West, FL 33040; (888) 318-4316; reachresort.com; $$$$. The Reach Resort offers miles of ocean water to view and a glistening white-sand beach with the sound of rolling waves. Rooms and suites overlook the Atlantic Ocean, the pool, or Old Town

Key West, and are furnished with sunny lemon-colored walls and terra-cotta-tiled floors with Caribbean artistic touches and private balconies. The resort has an outdoor swimming pool, hot tub, and full water-sports concession for rafts, parasailing, personal watercraft rentals, and more, right on the beach. Their Spencer's by the Sea restaurant, known for its amazing steak dinners (see our Restaurants chapter), sits on the first floor with stunning ocean views and breakfast, lunch, or dinner dining inside and out.

**SHERATON SUITES KEY WEST,** 2001 S. Roosevelt Blvd., Key West, FL 33040; (305) 292-9800 or (800) 325-3535; sheratonkeywest.com; $$$–$$$$. Situated across the street from Smathers Beach, the brightly colored 3-story, pet-friendly Sheraton is an all-suite facility built around an expansive concrete sundeck and a swimming pool. The roomy suites are decorated in relaxing tropical colors and furnished in colorful wicker. The Coral Crab Café offers breakfast, lunch, and dinner. Sheraton Suites offers guests complimentary shuttle service to and from the airport as well as transportation to Mallory Square (see the Attractions chapter). The staff at the guest activities desk will assist you in planning fishing and diving excursions, restaurant bookings, and more. On the premises are a hot tub, fitness center, off-street parking, and a gift shop.

**SUNSET KEY GUEST COTTAGES, A WESTIN RESORT,** boat dock to island is at 245 Front St., Key West, FL 33040; (305) 292-5300 or (866) 837-4249; sunsetkeycottages.com, $$$$. The guest cottages at Sunset Key are tucked away on a private island directly across the harbor from the Westin hotel. Access is strictly by private launch, which operates throughout the day and night between Sunset Key and the Westin marina. Located amid swaying palms and lush flowering hibiscus, the cottages offer beachfront, ocean, or garden views. In addition to a white-sand beach, the island features a freshwater pool, hot tub, 2 tennis courts, a health club, and a full-service gourmet restaurant and bar, Latitudes (see the Restaurants chapter), which is the perfect place to view the amazing Key West sunset.

**THE WESTIN KEY WEST RESORT & MARINA,** 245 Front St., Key West, FL 33040; (305) 294-4000 or (866) 716-8108; westinkeywestresort.com; $$$$. The bayfront Westin was designed so that all rooms provide views of the pool, the bay, or the marina and its surrounding waters. Guests here also are provided launch service to a relatively secluded beach at Sunset Key. The 2 buildings that make up the Westin have 178 rooms. The 3-story building overlooks the marina; the other, a 4-story structure, sits adjacent to Mallory Square. Situated in historic Old Town near the old Custom House, the Westin and its grounds are surrounded by brick walkways. On the premises are a swimming pool, hot tub, and sundeck area; fitness facilities; a restaurant offering indoor and outdoor dining; and a sunset deck and lounge.

### B&Bs, Inns & Guesthouses

Key West's Conch-style mansions and captains' and cigar-makers' homes date from the 1800s, and many have been marvelously restored to accommodate a thriving tourist industry. Close to 100 intimate hideaways are tucked along the streets, avenues, and lanes of Key West's Old Town, and these charming, romantic inns, bed-and-breakfasts, and guesthouses provide a sense of history, tranquility, and intimacy within the active city.

You'll find few waterfront or water-view guesthouse accommodations. Rather, rooms enjoy tranquil garden views or views of the ever-changing, active streetfront. Key West welcomes diversity, and some guesthouses cater primarily or exclusively to gay travelers. Others are considered all-welcome or gay-friendly. In a separate section at the end of this chapter, we highlight primarily and exclusively gay retreats, many of which maintain clothing-optional policies. In fact, a few seemingly conservative guesthouses and inns on the island have begun to incorporate a clothing-optional policy; therefore, it is always a good idea to call ahead and check with the property before finalizing your reservation. Rooms do have a maximum capacity. Inquire about this and all other details when you call to make reservations.

As a general rule, guesthouses are for adults only. If a particular property welcomes children, we'll tell you. Otherwise, you may assume that you should either leave the kids at home or look elsewhere in this chapter for kid-friendly accommodations.

**ALMOND TREE INN,** 512 Truman Ave., Key West, FL 33040; (305) 296-5415 or (800) 311-4292; almondtreeinn.com; $$$. The Almond Tree Inn sits at the historic crossroads of Truman Avenue and Duval Street in Old Town Key West. A tranquil waterfall is on the lush, tropically landscaped property, and sundecks surround the pool. Private, off-street parking assures convenience away from the well-traveled Old Town location. A complimentary continental breakfast is served daily, the Wi-Fi is free, and complimentary beer and wine are offered each afternoon underneath the pavilion. Some of the 22 rooms are King Suites, with a king-size bed and a Tempur-Pedic sleeper sofa, while others are Queen Suites, offering 2 queen-size beds and a Tempur-Pedic sleeper sofa.

**AMBROSIA HOUSE,** 622 Fleming St., Key West, FL 33040; (305) 296-9838; ambrosiakeywest.com. $$$. This delightful B&B compound offers spacious, tropical-themed rooms, two-room suites, two-story townhomes, and a two-bedroom, two-bath cottage. The buildings are surrounded by lush tropical landscaping and clear, cool ponds. Located in the heart of Old Town Key West, just 1.5 blocks off Duval, Ambrosia is convenient to shopping, restaurants, and nightlife. The units all have private baths and entrances (most with French doors) that open onto intimate outdoor spaces, including private verandas, pools, patios, and luscious gardens accented with fountains and sculptures. Free Wi-Fi is included in your stay, and children are welcome, as are pets.

**ANDREWS INN & GARDEN COTTAGES,** 223 Eanes Ln., Key West, FL 33040; (305) 294-7730 or (888) 263-7393; andrewsinn.com; $$–$$$. This tiny inn is practically in Hemingway's backyard. You'll find it tucked behind his former house—the only thing that separates the two is a brick wall—on a shaded narrow lane. Just outside your door, you'll find a lush tropical garden and comfortable lounge chairs situated around a cool, refreshing pool. Andrews Inn offers complimentary mimosas and continental breakfast each morning and cocktails by the pool every afternoon. We should warn you about the neighbors: A representative from that gang of six-toed cats that resides next door at the Hemingway Home is likely to wander over to say hello.

**THE ARTIST HOUSE,** 534 Eaton St., Key West, FL 33040; (305) 296-3977 or (800) 582-7882; artisthousekeywest.com; $$$. With the addition of guest suites a block away from the original property, the Artist House now offers accommodations at two levels—in a charming Victorian mansion and in modern villas. The one you choose is a matter of personal taste. The Artist House Guest Villas are exceptionally bright and roomy, and each of the 6 suites has been recently renovated and includes a fully equipped kitchen. The 3 rooms in the house have been renovated as well. Private sundecks and a heated swimming pool round out the amenities. Children age 5 and older are permitted.

**AUTHORS OF KEY WEST GUESTHOUSE,** 725 White St., Key West, FL 33040; (305) 294-7381 or (800) 898-6909; authorskeywest.com; $$. Each room in this private 3-building compound is named for one of Key West's legendary authors, like Ernest Hemingway and Tennessee Williams. The main 2-story, 8-room house is lined with lush tropical foliage and offers a 2-sided sundeck. Two poolside Conch houses, built around the turn of the 20th century, are also available for rent; both have small private porches. Rooms within the main house are equally diverse, offering views of the street, the sundeck, or the gardens. The inn provides off-street parking, and bicycles are available for rent. Pets are not permitted. Note that the entrance to Authors is on Petronia Street.

**AZUL KEY WEST,** 907 Truman Ave., Key West, FL 33040; (305) 296-5152; azulkeywest.com; $$$–$$$$. This graceful Queen Anne mansion, built for wealthy cigar baron Walter James Lightbourn, was completed in 1903. In 1992 it was transformed into a hotel, and in 2007, the home was beautifully restored to its current charming splendor. Listed on the National Register of Historic Places, Azul Key West offers guests stylized bedrooms with flat-screen TVs, Wi-Fi, and a shimmering pool. Each room opens onto a deck, veranda, balcony, or the sparkling swimming pool. There are six queen and five king rooms, each with a private entrance and en suite bathroom. Breakfast fare is a "Tropical Continental" featuring fruit, yogurt, and cereal.

**THE BANYAN RESORT, 323 Whitehead St., Key West, FL 33040; (305) 296-7786 or (866) 371-9222; thebanyanresort.com; $$–$$$.** The Banyan Resort is a collection of 8 beautifully preserved and refurbished Conch-style homes, some of which are listed on the National Register of Historic Places. One of these buildings formerly served as a cigar factory. Each bright and airy suite in this tropical, historic resort includes a full kitchen and free Wi-Fi. Floor plans range from fully equipped studios to one- and two-bedroom suites. All accommodations have French doors leading to private patios and verandas that overlook gardens filled with jasmine, frangipani, rare orchids, and two magnificent 200-year-old banyan trees. Limited off-street parking is available at an additional charge.

**BLUE PARROT INN, 916 Elizabeth St., Key West, FL 33040; (305) 296-0033 or (800) 231-2473; blueparrotinn.com; $–$$.** Built in 1884 with wood pegs that are more hurricane-friendly than nails, the Blue Parrot Inn offers 9 guest units. The only blue parrot in residence here is a stuffed one; however, the cats you'll see wandering the grounds are very much alive. A heated swimming pool surrounded by extensive decking sets the scene for a leisurely continental breakfast consisting of fresh fruit, bagels, English muffins, and home-baked quiche or fruit breads served every morning. The atmosphere at the Blue Parrot is friendly and intimate. Guests must be at least 16 years of age, and no pets are allowed.

**CASA 325, 325 Duval St., Key West, FL 33040; (305) 292-0011 or (866) 227-2325; casa325.com; $$–$$$.** Casa 325 offers spacious suites, lofts, and studios in a vintage Victorian building that has been recently restored and decorated in a tropical island theme. Located right on Duval Street, but still managing to feel secluded, the suites feature queen-size beds, kitchenettes with refrigerators, microwaves, wet bars, and ceiling fans. A center courtyard showcases gardens and a swimming pool on this quaint property. The on-site concierge service can book practically any activity on the island, from parasailing to kayaking through the mangroves. The location is on the lower end of Duval Street, right in the middle of numerous bars, restaurants, and attractions.

**CHELSEA HOUSE POOL & GARDENS, 709 Truman Ave., Key West, FL 33040; (305) 294-5229 or (800) 549-4430; historickeywestinns.com; $$–$$$.** The Chelsea House actually includes two former estate properties, both in the Victorian, Queen Anne architectural style: the Peter H. Hanlon house, built in 1905, and the George L. Lowe house, erected in 1891. They stand on an acre of tropical gardens, which includes a large, heated pool and many comfortable lounging areas. Chelsea House was named for a resident cat in the 1970s (a British shorthair named Chelsea). Continuing the English tradition, a few guest rooms at Chelsea House are pet-friendly. All guest rooms provide a private bath with shower and cable TV. Free Wi-Fi is available in the courtyard.

**THE CONCH HOUSE HERITAGE INN,** 625 Truman Ave., Key West, FL 33040; (305) 293-0020 or (800) 207-5806; conchhouse.com; $$–$$$. Since the 1800s this historic 2-story estate has been passed down from generation to generation. The current owners are Sam Holland Jr. and his mother, Francine Delaney Holland. She is the great-granddaughter of Cuban émigré Carlos Recio, a close friend of Cuban revolutionary José Martí. The inn is listed on the National Register of Historic Places and combines Old World decor with modern amenities. The 10 bedrooms in the main house feature high ceilings, wooden shutters, wraparound porches, and picket fences. A poolside cottage offers 3 guest rooms decorated with Caribbean prints and wicker. Children older than age 12 are permitted at the inn.

**CUBAN CLUB SUITES, $$$$; LA CASA DE LUCES, $–$$$; DOUGLAS HOUSE, $–$$$$; douglashouse.com;** 419 and 422 Amelia St., Key West, FL 33040; (305) 294-5269 or (800) 833-0372. Cuban Club Suites, La Casa de Luces, and Douglas House Guest Rooms share guest check-in and lobby facilities on Amelia Street, but Cuban Club Suites is actually in a separate building at 1102 Duval Street. Cuban Club's 2-story luxury suites are condominiums occupying second and third floors above boutiques that are open to the public. La Casa de Luces offers 8 units ranging from 2 small rooms sharing a bath to large garden suites. Douglas House is a collection of 6 Victorian homes, each house containing 2 to 5 spacious units, for a combined total of 15. Within the Douglas House compound are 2 swimming pools and a hot tub surrounded by gardens.

**CURRY MANSION INN,** 511 Caroline St., Key West, FL 33040; (305) 294-5349 or (800) 253-3466; currymansion.com; $$. This 22-room mansion built by Florida's first millionaire family is today a museum, housing a selection of turn-of-the-20th-century furnishings and memorabilia. It is also the centerpiece for a guesthouse that is consistently rated among the best in Key West. Guests at the Curry Mansion Inn do not actually stay in the mansion; they do, however, have full access to it. Guest accommodations consist instead of 28 rooms adjacent to the mansion, most of which open onto a pool. A complimentary breakfast buffet is offered poolside each morning; complimentary cocktails are served daily in the late afternoon.

**CYPRESS HOUSE,** 601 Caroline St., Key West, FL 33040; (305) 294-6969 or (800) 549-4430; cypresshousekw.com; $$$–$$$$. This former estate property includes two Classic Bahamian Conch-style houses and one Grand Conch Mansion, dating from 1888 and 1895. The pine and cypress used in the 1800s for construction did not require a protective coat of paint, and the main building continues that tradition today. The 40-foot heated lap pool surrounded by lush, tropical gardens on the grounds of this 100-year-old mansion is among the largest at any of Key West's inns. Porches on the first and second floor are accessible to guests. A complimentary breakfast buffet is served poolside, as is a nightly cocktail hour with beer, wine, and snacks.

**DUVAL HOUSE, 815 Duval St., Key West, FL 33040; (305) 294-1666 or (305) 294-1667; duvalhousekeywest.com; $$–$$$.** This 2-story inn may be set on busy Duval Street, but its pigeon plums, banyans, and hibiscus successfully guard it from intrusion. Lounge poolside amid traveler's palms and light jazz music, linger on a shady hammock, or chat with others in the gazebo. In the 1880s, Duval House was inhabited by cigar-makers. Today the 28 standard and deluxe rooms and apartments are furnished with English antiques, white wicker, and French doors. All are air-conditioned, and all except the 2 apartments and 2 front rooms look out onto the gardens.

**EDEN HOUSE, 1015 Fleming St., Key West, FL 33040; (305) 296-6868 or (800) 533-5397; edenhouse.com; $–$$$$.** For years Eden House was known as a hangout for writers, intellectuals, and Europeans. Over the past few years, owner Mike Eden has added several enhancements. Constructed of wood and concrete, the facility categorizes units by luxury rooms and efficiencies; private rooms and efficiencies with bath or shower; semiprivate rooms with shared baths; and European rooms with double or twin-size beds, a sink, and a bath and shower in the hall. Many units have French doors leading to porches and decks near the center of the facility, where gardens surround a swimming pool, hot tub, and gazebo. Be sure to check out the sundeck and hammock areas.

**THE FRANCES STREET BOTTLE INN, 535 Frances St., Key West, FL 33040; (305) 294-8530 or (800) 294-8530; bottleinn.com; $–$$$.** Tucked away in a quiet residential neighborhood on the edge of Old Town, this charming pet-friendly inn takes its name from the owner's collection of antique bottles and cobalt-blue glassware displayed in every window and along several interior shelves. The atmosphere here is quiet and intimate. Each of the Bottle Inn's guest rooms has a private bath and air-conditioning. White wicker chairs line a gracious porch across the front of the house, and in the lush tropical gardens, a complimentary continental breakfast is served each morning under the poinciana trees.

**★THE GARDENS HOTEL, 526 Angela St., Key West, FL 33040; (305) 294-2661 or (800) 526-2664; gardenshotel.com; $$$–$$$$.** In 1930, the late Key West resident Peggy Mills began collecting various species of orchids from Japan, Bali, and other exotic parts of the world. As neighboring homes were placed on the market, Mills would purchase and level them, adding to her garden until it encompassed a full city block. The gardens have been restored to much of their original splendor, gaining the attention of botanists worldwide. A complex of 5 guesthouses and a carriage house, the hotel offers 17 units set around a tiki bar, swimming pool, hot tub, fountain, and a winding path of bougainvillea, orange, jasmine, palm, mango, breadfruit trees, and more.

★HERON HOUSE, 512 Simonton St., Key West, FL 33040; (305) 294-9227 or (888) 861-9066; heronhouse.com; $$$. HERON HOUSE COURT, 412 Frances St., Key West, FL 33040; (305) 296-4719 or (800) 932-9119; heronhousecourt.com; $$$. Centered on a 35-foot swimming pool decorated with a mosaic of a heron, and a Chicago brick patio and sundeck, many of the 23 rooms at the Heron House feature unique woodwork and stained glass created by local artists. Platform-style oak beds are handcrafted, and most of the accommodations have French doors leading to private porches or balconies overlooking the gardens. The Heron House also has a sister property known as Heron House Court, which is similarly styled and resides in an early-20th-century building that is listed on the National Register of Historic Places. There is a heated outdoor pool and hot tub on the property, and guests enjoy complimentary continental breakfast and beer and wine during happy hour on the weekends.

ISLAND CITY HOUSE HOTEL, 411 William St., Key West, FL 33040; (305) 294-5702 or (800) 634-8230; islandcityhouse.com; $$–$$$$. At Island City House, two 1880s homes and a cypress-wood house designed to resemble a cigar factory encompass an enclave lined with brick walkways and lush tropical gardens. Wood decking surrounds the hot tub and swimming pool, and antique iron benches and bistro-style tables are set around a fountain and fishpond in the courtyard. Island City House itself is a Conch-style mansion with 12 suites. The Arch House maintains 6 suites; 4 are studios and 2 are two-bedroom suites. At the Cigar House, built on a cistern and the former site of a cigar factory, spacious suites feature French doors leading to private patios and decks. Children are permitted.

THE KEY WEST BED & BREAKFAST—THE POPULAR HOUSE, 415 William St., Key West, FL 33040; (305) 296-7274 or (800) 438-6155; keywestbandb.com; $–$$. This home, known as the William Russell House, was built in 1898 by shipbuilders who were skilled in crafting structures able to weather any storm. The 9 guest rooms and suites, some with shared baths, others with private baths and decks, feature a mix of bright colors, elegant Victorian furnishings, exposed Dade County pine, and 13-foot ceilings. The Third-Floor Front (TFF) room is noted for its 5-foot arched French window, which provides a view of the sunset above the city's rooftops and trees. There are no TVs on the property, but there is a Jacuzzi and sauna available.

★LA MER HOTEL AND DEWEY HOUSE, 504 and 506 South St., Key West, FL 33040; (305) 296-6577 or (800) 354-4455; southernmostresorts

.com; $$$$. La Mer Hotel and Dewey House are Key West's only oceanfront B&Bs. The two properties are connected by tropical green gardens with swaying palm trees, a fountain, a dipping pool, and loads of romantic charm. La Mer is a turn-of-the-20th-century Conch house, and each room is elegantly decorated with private balconies or patios. The Dewey House was once home to John Dewey, educator and philosopher, and remained a private residence until 1997. While here, you will be treated to a deluxe continental breakfast and afternoon tea served with fresh fruit and cheese. Guests must be 18 years of age, and no pets are permitted. Both properties feature privileges to Southernmost Hotel and Southernmost on the Beach.

**LIGHTHOUSE COURT,** 902 Whitehead St., Key West, FL 33040; (305) 294-9588 or (877) 249-9588; historickeywestinns.com; $$$. Covering half a city block in Old Town, Lighthouse Court is a historic compound of 10 Conch houses dating from 1890 to 1920 located directly next door to the Lighthouse Museum, across the street from the Hemingway Home, and a block away from Duval Street. The half-acre grounds offer charming brick paths dotted with tree swings and hammocks. Chaise lounges and a sundeck beckon you out of the heat of the tropical sun. If you really want to embody the aura of old Key West, reserve the Hemingway Suite: The 1,000-square-foot penthouse overlooks his Key West home and has views of the lighthouse from the living room, sundeck, and bedroom.

**THE MERMAID AND THE ALLIGATOR,** 729 Truman Ave., Key West, FL 33040; (305) 294-1894 or (800) 773-1894; kwmermaid.com; $$–$$$. This charming and inviting 1904 Victorian home is located an easy 3-block walk from Duval Street in the enclave known as the heart of Key West's historic district. Wi-Fi is included; a full complimentary breakfast is served poolside, and in the evening guests can enjoy a complimentary glass of wine or lemonade at the Outdoor Pavilion. There is a heated plunge pool with benches and whirlpool jets on the property. Among the bonuses of staying at the Mermaid and the Alligator is the resident pooch, Caya, a friendly jet-black flat-coated retriever who will welcome you and put a smile on your face.

**OLD TOWN MANOR,** 511 Eaton St., Key West, FL 33040; (305) 292-2170; oldtownmanor.com; $$–$$$$. Built in 1886 in Greek Revival style, Old Town Manor is home to 2 significant buildings: a 3-story home, and a carriage house that at one time served as a dry goods store. This pet-friendly property was one of Key West's first ornamental gardens, and today the century-old palms with cascading orchids still stand. The gardens also host 2 fishpond fountains, rare flowering and fruit trees, as well as a Brazilian jacaranda tree with blue bell-shaped flowers. Located just steps off Duval Street, in the hub of Old

Town, the place is delightfully furnished, using the practice of feng shui with touches in keeping with the history of the past.

**THE PALMS HOTEL, 820 White St., Key West, FL 33040; (305) 294-3146 or (800) 558-9374; palmshotelkeywest.com; $$.** The main Conch-style house with its wraparound porches was built in 1889. It features Caribbean influences and is listed on the National Register of Historic Places. All 20 rooms are painted in pastels and furnished with wicker and Caribbean-style decor; rooms in the main house have separate access to the porch. Private entrances, private baths, and ceiling fans are standard. There is a full-service poolside tiki bar, and the large heated swimming pool is open around the clock. The Palms has a small parking lot on the street directly behind the hotel; on-street parking is also available. Children and pets are permitted.

**THE PARADISE INN, 819 Simonton St., Key West, FL 33040; (305) 293-8007 or (800) 888-9648; theparadiseinn.com; $$$–$$$$.** Bahamian-style houses and cigar-makers' cottages are home to the 15 suites and 3 cottages of the Paradise Inn. Painted white with Caribbean-blue Bahamian shutters, all units have high ceilings, large marble baths, natural oak flooring, and unique window dressings that combine stagecoach and handkerchief valances with wood mini-blinds. French doors lead to outdoor porches in all but one cottage, and the interior decor features distressed pine, botanical prints, and pale shades of tan. The inn's diverse garden features Barbados cherry and avocado trees and bromeliads. Even the pool and hot tub, separated by a lily pond, evoke luxury.

**PILOT HOUSE GUESTHOUSE, 414 Simonton St., Key West, FL 33040; (305) 293-6600 or (800) 648-3780; pilothousekeywest.com; $–$$.** This 100-plus-year-old Conch-style home provides rooms and suites that mix antique furnishings with functional pieces. Frangipani and royal poinciana trees thrive in the yard, and a gumbo-limbo grows through the roof of what is known as this facility's spa building. Set along the brick-patio backyard is a Spanish-style stucco cabana building that offers 6 suites. Passageways rather than doors create privacy for each area of these suites, and all entrances face the swimming pool. The backyard swimming pool is larger than most in Key West, and an in-ground spa is sheltered from the sun by a tin roof with lattice. Both are clothing-optional.

**ROSE LANE VILLAS, 522–524 Rose Ln., Key West, FL 33040; (305) 292-2170 or (800) 294-2170; roselanevillas.com; $$–$$$$.** The Rose Lane Villas are actually in a treasure of a home built in 1886 for Dr. William Warren. This charming oasis greets you when you step onto the front porch, and the cheery wicker furniture beckons you to stay and rest a spell. Steps from Duval Street, you'll feel a million miles away from it all in the seclusion of Rose Lane Villas. All one-, two-, and three-bedroom villas have kitchens complete with full refrigerators and all essentials. If you just want to read a book or nap, outside by the in-ground pool is the perfect spot to catch a few rays.

★**SANTA MARIA SUITES RESORT**, 1401 Simonton St., Key West, FL 33040; (305) 600-5165 or (866) 726-8259; santamariasuites.com; $$$$. An island unto itself, steps away from vivacious Duval Street and the Atlantic Ocean, you'll discover Santa Maria Suites Resort. The 35 luxurious two-bedroom, two-bath suites with glass-front balconies overlook a sensual pool surrounded by exotic tropical greenery. All suites have state-of-the-art kitchens with wine chillers, flat-screen TVs, Wi-Fi, washer and dryer, housekeeping, and private parking. Put on those red-soled Louboutins and pop that bottle of Cristal—the modern and chic Santa Maria Suites Resort is one to savor. The resort also houses the chic sushi restaurant Ambrosia (see the Restaurants chapter).

**SIMONTON COURT**, 320 Simonton St., Key West, FL 33040; (800) 944-2687; simontoncourt.com; $$$. Situated on 2 acres of property that once boasted a cigar factory, Simonton Court is a private compound consisting of the 2-story Inn as well as a Manor House, Townhouse Suites, The Mansion, 6 cottages, and 4 pools. Within the Inn are 9 old Key West–style rooms featuring high ceilings and heavily shuttered windows. The Manor House suite offers a spacious two-bedroom complex with a full kitchen and private outdoor pool. Simonton Court's 2-story Townhouse Suites are extremely plush, decorated in Grand Floribbean–style antiques. Simonton Court's tropically landscaped gardens, antique brick pathways, and swimming pools all come aglow at night, with lighting emphasizing all the right places.

**SOUTHERNMOST POINT GUEST HOUSE**, 1327 Duval St., Key West, FL 33040; (305) 294-0715; southernmostpoint.com; $–$$$. The Southernmost Point Guest House, across from the Southernmost House, is a showy, 3-story, Conch-style mansion built in 1885 for E. H. Gato Jr., son of Key West's first cigar manufacturer. The home is notable for its wraparound porches and private balconies, some of which afford partial ocean or garden views. Rooms come in varying sizes, but all have private entrances, private baths, and ceiling fans. All guests are given a key to the hot tub (large enough for 12 people). Lounge chairs are provided amid the guesthouse's tropical gardens of banana, coconut palm, breadfruit, and mango trees.

**SPEAKEASY INN**, 1117 Duval St., Key West, FL 33040; (305) 296-2680; speakeasyinn.com; $$$. The Speakeasy, a turn-of-the-20th-century inn, offers spacious rooms in its main Duval Street house plus 3 spacious suites in a back-alley building along Amelia Street. The original building was the home of Raul Vasquez, a cigar selector at the Gato cigar factory whose true passion was rum-running between Key West and Cuba. The newer building, built as a residence for the owner's stepdaughter, offers what is referred to as the Gallery Suite, considered to be the best offering in the house. This and other rooms at the Speakeasy also offer private tiled baths, refrigerators, wet bars, and ceiling fans.

**TRAVELERS PALM INN AND GUESTHOUSES**, 815 Catherine St., Key West, FL 33040; (305) 304-1751; travelerspalm.com; $$$$. The recently renovated Travelers Palm consists of 3 cottages that are completely eco-friendly. Owners Roxanne Fleszar and Michel Appellis met on the property in 1996 and eventually purchased it in 2000. The extensive renovations garnered them a Certificate of Excellence from the Historic Florida Keys Foundation. Captain's Quarters is the largest and most modern of the cottages and can accommodate up to 4 people. This two-bedroom, two-bath cottage also features a full kitchen, living room, and dining room with a front porch and side decks that contain a gas grill. All the cottages have access to the on-site solar-heated pool replete with a stone waterfall.

**WEATHERSTATION INN**, 57 Front St., Key West, FL 33040; (305) 294-7277 or (800) 815-2707; weatherstationinn.com; $$–$$$. The Weatherstation Inn is located just 2 blocks off bustling Duval Street, but you would never know it. Rarely does any sound intrude. This 2-story, 8-room guesthouse sits on the grounds of the Old Navy Yard inside the gated Truman Annex compound, just down the street from Harry Truman's Little White House. The beach at Fort Zachary Taylor is a short walk away (see the Attractions chapter). With its glistening hardwood floors and elegant island furnishings, the inn calls to mind the plantation homes of the British and Dutch West Indies. The balconies and decks overlook lush tropical landscaping, and amenities include a heated pool, concierge service, and free parking.

**WESTWINDS INN**, 914 Eaton St., Key West, FL 33040; (305) 296-4440 or (800) 788-4150; westwindskeywest.com, $$. This complex encompasses a 2-story New England–style home, 2-story Conch houses, and poolside cottages. Room decor is wicker throughout, with queen-size beds in suites, private entrances to the cottages and Conch houses, and some furnished private and shared porches. Suites include one-bedroom cottage and Conch units with kitchenettes, and kitchenless accommodations that sleep several guests. In back of the compound, brick walkways wind through gardens of hibiscus, bromeliads, and other flowers and shrubs, and a mini waterfall. There are two large pools on the property, one of which includes a jet spa.

★**WICKER GUEST HOUSE**, 913 Duval St., Key West, FL 33040; 305-296-4275 or (800) 880-4275; wickerguesthouse.com; $$. Located right on Duval Street, the Wicker Guest House is actually a complex of 6 meticulously restored houses that spans an entire block. The rooms surround the lush oasis of the sundeck and sparkling heated pool, which is surrounded by swaying coconut palms, hibiscus, fragrant frangipani, avocado, key lime, Spanish lime, and Ackee trees, and their famous night-blooming jasmine. There is also a comfy guest lounge area right next to the pool. Accommodations include rooms and suites, some with kitchens or kitchenettes, private porches or balconies, and all with private baths.

## Pet-Friendly Accommodations

Household pets are members of the family, but traveling with them can create a dilemma. Here in the Florida Keys, which is one of the pet-loving capitals of the world, you will find properties that welcome one and all. In the Upper Keys, that's Lookout Lodge Resort, Marina del Mar, and White Gate Court. In the Middle Keys, try Blackfin Resort, Gulf View Waterfront Resort, and Tropical Cottages. In Key West, consider the Chelsea House Pool & Gardens, Francis Street Bottle Inn, Old Town Manor, Sheraton Suites, and Rose Lane Villas. Visit petfriendly.com or bringfido.com for more listings.

### Gay Guesthouses

**ALEXANDER'S GUESTHOUSE,** 1118 Fleming St., Key West, FL 33040; (305) 294-9919 or (800) 654-9919; alexanderskeywest.com; $$$. The main 3-story building of Alexander's, a Conch-style design, was built around the turn of the past century and has since been renovated. Two additional 2-story Conch houses combine for a total of 17 guest rooms. This LGBT guesthouse, which attracts both gay men and women, is gay-owned and -operated. The rooms at Alexander's are relatively basic, equipped with queen-size beds. All rooms have private baths, and two share shower facilities. A highlight is the cobalt-blue-tiled swimming pool surrounded by lush tropical flora. An expanded continental breakfast is served by the pool each morning; signature cocktails are offered at the Pink Monkey Bar every evening.

**EQUATOR RESORT,** 818 Fleming St., Key West, FL 33040; (305) 294-7775 or (800) 278-4552; equatorresort.com; $$$. The building that houses this state-of-the-art, all-male resort looks as though it might have been around for a while, but it is new. It was simply designed to blend with the surrounding structures in this Old Town neighborhood. All 18 rooms are bright and spacious, and each features Mediterranean tile floors, in-room refrigerators, genuinely ample closets, and plenty of walking-around space. Common areas are equally well designed, with a clothing-optional pool, 8-man outdoor whirlpool, lush tropical gardens, a sundeck, and covered patio. A complimentary full breakfast is served daily and a complimentary cocktail hour takes place every evening.

# Restaurants

Take in the glorious sights in the Florida Keys, then treat your taste buds to a culinary holiday they will never forget. We are an island of restaurants offering stone crabs, yellowtail snapper, conch fritters, *ropa vieja,* and key lime pie. (For preparing your own fare, see the Specialty Foods, Cafes & Markets chapter.)

Enjoy the relaxed atmosphere of our restaurants, where even the most upscale dining carries a laid-back apparel code. Be it a roadside cafe or a resort dining room, you need dress no more formally than "Keys casual," typically an ensemble of shirt and shorts, shoes or sandals. Men may leave their sport jackets at home, and don't even think about bringing a suit to the Keys unless it is the swimming variety. The same code applies to women; we don't discriminate here. The occasional restaurant, such as Pierre's, or Little Palm Island, affords you the chance to dress up a bit more if you like—but the choice is yours.

The decor of a restaurant doesn't hold to the strict expectations of other parts of the country, either. You'll find that the most unassuming hole-in-the-wall cafe, diner, or bistro may serve the best food in town. Don't drive by. Some of our culinary treasures are hidden way off the beaten track. We'll help you find them.

## OVERVIEW

We have organized the restaurants of the Keys alphabetically by location. The type of cuisine served can be found in the description.

Free on-site parking is available at virtually all of our recommended establishments in the Upper, Middle, and Lower Keys. However, most restaurants in Key West do not have on-site parking. Most restaurants suggest that you make reservations, especially during the high season. Those that do not take reservations will be noted.

Many restaurants serve limited alcoholic beverages. You may infer that unless we specify that an establishment offers a full-service bar (usually the larger restaurants or resort facilities), only beer and wine will be served.

Accessibility varies greatly in restaurants throughout the Keys. While many of our establishments are at ground level, and some second-story locations within large resorts may have elevators, steps sometimes must be negotiated, and some bathrooms may be too tiny to accommodate a wheelchair. If this is of particular concern to you, be sure to call the restaurant to see exactly what arrangements might be made to fit your needs.

Unless otherwise specified, you may assume that our recommended restaurants are air-conditioned. Those that provide outdoor seating or accessibility to the sea will be highlighted. Children are generally welcome in Florida Keys restaurants. The odd exceptions or age restrictions will be stated.

The dollar-sign price code indicated in each restaurant listing will help you gauge the cost of your dining experience (see key below). Some of our restaurants include soup or a house salad with an entree; at others, entrees are strictly a la carte. Most of our restaurants accept major credit cards but rarely a personal check. If plastic is not acknowledged, we alert you in advance so that you won't be caught short of cash.

### Price Code
Our price-code rating reflects the cost of dinner entrees for two, without cocktails, appetizers, wine, dessert, tax, or tip.

| | |
|---|---|
| $ | Less than $25 |
| $$ | $25 to $40 |
| $$$ | $40 to $60 |
| $$$$ | More than $60 |

## DINING

### Upper Keys

★**ALABAMA JACK'S,** 58000 Card Sound Rd. (Oceanside), Homestead, FL 33030; (305) 248-8741; alabamajacks.com; Classic American & Southern; $. There are a couple of reasons why one would choose the back way into the Florida Keys. Card Sound Road, north of Key Largo, offers an incentive to take this scenic excursion. The traffic is not as heavy, the wildlife is more prolific, and you can eat at Alabama Jack's. No trip to the Florida Keys is complete without stopping at this Caribbean honky-tonk. Alabama Jack's is rated as having the best conch fritters and key lime pie by everyone who manages to find the place. It sits on the water, where you can feed the fish, check out the mangroves, and enjoy the friendly Keys attitude of the staff.

**ATLANTIC'S EDGE, NIKAI SUSHI, LIMONCELLO,** Cheeca Lodge & Spa, MM 82 Oceanside, 81801 Overseas Hwy., Islamorada, FL 33036; (305) 664-4651 or (800) 327-2888; cheeca.com; Contemporary American; $$$. The fine-dining room at Atlantic's Edge restaurant located in the Cheeca Lodge & Spa has panoramic vistas of the Atlantic Ocean, with seating indoors and out. Atlantic's Edge is open for breakfast, lunch, and dinner nightly, offering libations from a full bar. The Nikai Sushi restaurant features an abundance of fresh sushi options, from tartare to maki and vegetable rolls to specialty rolls. Nikai is open for lunch and dinner, with a selection of more than 35 Japanese sakis and wine. Limoncello is a family-friendly Italian restaurant with fresh pasta, hand-rolled pizzas, and entrees like chicken Parmesan.

**BAYSIDE GRILLE, MM 99.5 Bayside, 99530 Overseas Hwy., Key Largo, FL 33037; (305) 451-3380; keylargo-baysidegrill.com; Seafood; $$.** Perched on the very edge of Florida Bay, Bayside Grille commands one of the premier waterfront vistas in the Keys. Small, casual, and bistro-ish, the open-air Bayside Grille's layout of tables fronted by glass pocket doors enables all diners to take in the shimmering blue sea while dining. Seafood reigns here: the Keyribbean Style Jumbo Shrimp—wild-caught pink shrimp sautéed with fresh garlic, capers, and lime juice and served with coconut steamed rice and vegetables—is a favorite. But landlubbers will also find a good selection of entrees as well, like the Certified Angus, a 14-ounce hand-cut New York strip rubbed in their house seasoning, grilled, and topped with honeyed onions.

**★THE BEACH CAFÉ AT MORADA BAY, MM 81.6 Bayside, 81600 Overseas Hwy., Islamorada FL 33036; (305) 664-0604; moradabay.com; Contemporary American; $$.** The Beach Café at Morada Bay in Islamorada delivers a tapas-style selection of appetizers along with eclectic entrees. Pastel beach tables and low Adirondack-style chairs pepper a wide expanse of sandy beach that fronts the gentle waters of Florida Bay. Any of The Beach Café's fresh fish selections—all imaginatively prepared—will more than satisfy your taste for the sea. This is the perfect place to watch the sun set, as the restaurant perches at the edge of Florida Bay and musicians often stop by for a lively impromptu set. The Beach Café is open for lunch and dinner daily.

**THE BUZZARD'S ROOST, MM 106.5 Oceanside, 21 Garden Cove Dr., Key Largo, FL 33037; (305) 453-3746; buzzardsroostkeylargo.com; Seafood; $$.** "You hook it and we'll cook it," say the owners of this casual waterfront restaurant in Key Largo. You can also come by boat if you really want to have a waterfront experience. If the fishing wasn't that great on your outing, they offer some tasty menu items that will surely fill your tank. One of the best appetizers is the Corny Blue Crabcakes. This is blue crab meat blended with veggies and roasted corn, served with remoulade sauce. The catch of the day is prepared grilled, blackened, Jamaican jerked, broiled, fried, or sautéed in lemon butter and wine. Buzzard's Roost also serves delicious conch fritters, with key lime cocktail sauce.

**CHAD'S DELI AND BAKERY, MM 92.3 Bayside, 92330 Overseas Hwy., Tavernier, FL 33070; (305) 853-5566; chadsdeli.com; $.** At Chad's Deli, you can expect lots of good food at reasonable prices and quick service! That is not only a winning combo (just like some of their menu items), it is also what makes Chad's Deli and Bakery a success in the Upper Keys. The waitstaff is very friendly and knows all the regulars by name, which goes a long way in a small place like Tavernier and the Keys. Their specialties are four-way sandwiches, specialty pizzas (try the bacon cheeseburger pizza), calzones, pasta, and salads.

They also serve beer and wine to round out your meal. Chad's is open Tues through Sun for breakfast and daily for lunch and dinner.

**CRAIG'S RESTAURANT, MM 90.5 Bayside, 90154 Overseas Hwy., Tavernier, FL 33070; (305) 852-9424; craigsrestaurant.com; Classic American; $$.** Chef-owner Craig Belcher opened his namesake establishment in 1981 with his signature sandwich, which is billed as the "World Famous Super Fish Sandwich." A diner-style restaurant with an all-day menu, Craig's tries to please every palate, be it down-home or gourmet. The aforementioned fish sandwich consists of dolphin or catfish on grilled whole wheat bread with American cheese, tomatoes, and tartar sauce. For the landlubbers, a tasty steak sandwich and delicious French dip are also on offer. Open daily for breakfast, lunch, and dinner, Craig's does not accept reservations.

**DIGIORGIO'S CAFE LARGO, MM 99.5 Bayside, 99530 Overseas Hwy., Key Largo, FL 33037; (305) 451-4885; keylargo-cafelargo.com; Italian; $$.** This vibrant, third-generation-owned restaurant has been serving up home-style Italian specialties in the Upper Keys for more than 40 years. The DiGiorgio family offers everything Italian, from pasta to pizza, along with some local delicacies thrown in for good measure. A local favorite is the popular DiGiorgio's Eggplant—slices of fresh eggplant, lightly battered, baked with house-made marinara sauce and topped with melted mozzarella, and served with pasta. On the specialty cocktail front, try the Hemingway Cocktail, made with Ron Zacapa rum, lime juice, maraschino liqueur, and agave nectar, finished with a light froth and a spiced sugar rim. Cafe Largo has a full bar and extensive wine list, and is open daily at 4:30 p.m.

**DJ'S DINER AND COFFEE SHOP, MM 99.4 Oceanside, 99411 Overseas Hwy., Key Largo, FL 33037; (305) 451-2999; djsdiner.com; Classic American; $.** Established in 1958, DJ's regulars claim "they serve the best breakfast in town," so you'd best be hustling on over to get a table. Try the Keys Benedict: country ham steak, grilled tomatoes, poached eggs, and hollandaise sauce on a choice of English muffin or biscuits. DJ's serves daily lunch specials, too, like the highly praised blackened tuna Caesar wrap, but no dinners. So, get up early, have a *big* appetite, and enjoy this bright spot in the Upper Keys.

**THE FISH HOUSE AND THE FISH HOUSE ENCORE RESTAURANT & SUSHI BAR, MM 102.4 Oceanside, 102401 Overseas Hwy., Key Largo, FL 33037; (305) 451-0650; fishhouse.com; Seafood; $$.** The owners of the perennially popular Fish House have opened Encore, an upscale fine-dining restaurant that serves various selections of sushi, sashimi, and other fresh seafood items. From the baby grand piano to the long mahogany bar, the decor is elegant, but you do not need to be similarly attired to dine here. The Fish

House is more casual in design, with its Keys-centric fishing decor. You'll find plenty of fish on the menu in both locations, such as the wildly popular Fish Matecumbe, fresh catch (your choice of mahimahi, grouper, or yellowtail snapper) baked with tomatoes, shallots, basil, capers, olive oil, and lemon juice. The Fish House is open daily for lunch and dinner; no reservations accepted. Encore is open daily for dinner only, and reservations are recommended.

**GREEN TURTLE INN, MM 81.2 Oceanside, 81219 Overseas Hwy., Islamorada, FL 33036; (305) 664-2006; greenturtlekeys.com; Seafood; $$.** Sid and Roxie's Green Turtle Inn, which is actually a restaurant, welcomed an eager public in 1947. The location now showcases three businesses in harmony: the Green Turtle Inn, Sandy Moret's Florida Keys Outfitters (see the Fishing chapter), and the Wyland Art Gallery. At the Turtle, you can expect a "traditional Keys menu with flair." The "traditional" aspect features Keys lobster or the catch of the day; for the "flair," try turtle or conch chowder. The 50-seat restaurant with an open kitchen, full bar with tasting stations, catering, gourmet to go, and a Green Turtle Inn product line makes this a hot hangout in the Upper Keys. Breakfast, lunch, and dinner are served Tues through Sun.

**GUS' GRILLE, Marriott Key Largo Bay Beach Resort, MM 103.8 Bayside, 103800 Overseas Hwy., Key Largo, FL 33037; (305) 453-0000; marriottkeylargo.com; Seafood; $$.** This restaurant serves "Floribbean" dinner specialties such as pan-seared yellowtail snapper with garlic mashed potatoes, white wine caper sauce, and cilantro-tomato salsa. Unobstructed views of Florida Bay and the famous Keys sunset are available from virtually every seat in the house. Booths line the window walls of the light and airy dining room; outdoor patio dining is also available. Walk over the suspension bridge from Gus' Grille to Breezer's Bar and Grille for great drinks with luscious sunset views. Open daily for breakfast, lunch, and dinner, Gus' has wheelchair-accessible facilities and an elevator.

> *i* Planning a fun night out in the Upper or Middle Keys? Keyhopper Taxi and Transportation has you covered with their "Barhopper" services from Marathon to Key Largo. They also do one-day Key West trips and airport runs, but you must plan ahead and book in advance for all their services. Call (305) 393-0146 for more information.

RESTAURANTS

## The Lime of the Keys

Key lime fruit is very small (1 to 2 inches), round, and a greenish-yellow color at maturity. The tart juice extracted from the limes goes on and into almost everything edible, from fish and meats to salads, drinks, and, of course, desserts. Key limes were grown commercially in southern Florida and the Florida Keys until the 1926 hurricane wiped out the citrus crop. The trees were replaced with a Persian lime, and most remaining key lime trees were found in backyards in the Florida Keys. But commercial production of the key lime trees is once again happening on a small scale, and key limes do seem to be making a slight comeback as a Florida crop in recent years. Once you have tasted a true key lime, any other lime will pale in comparison.

**HARRIETTE'S, MM 95.7 Bayside, 95710 Overseas Hwy., Key Largo, FL 33037; (305) 852-8689; "We don't have a website, but we're working on that"; Classic American; $.** This popular roadside diner-style restaurant offers reasonably priced home-style meals in a simple setting. Tables and chairs surround counter dining; local arts and crafts on consignment provide the decor. Harriette's specialty? Ensuring that no guest leaves the restaurant hungry. Open for breakfast and lunch, Harriette's serves filling omelets, oversize homemade biscuits with sausage gravy, burgers, and hot and cold sandwiches. The restaurant caters primarily to a repeat local crowd, so lunch specials change daily. Look for comfort food at Harriette's: meat loaf, pork chops, stuffed peppers, roast pork, and chicken and dumplings. Open daily from 6 a.m. to 4 p.m. on weekdays and to 3 p.m. on the weekends. Reservations are not accepted.

**★HOBO'S CAFE, MM 101.7 Oceanside, 101691 Overseas Hwy., Key Largo, FL 33037; (305) 451-5888; hoboscafe.net; Classic American; $.** Keys casual is the norm here, with shirts and shoes the required dress, but if you have socks on, you are overdressed. Try the hot crabmeat and artichoke dip to start, then the fresh catch of the day served either blackened, coconut-crusted, pan-sautéed, stuffed with lump crab meat, Godfather-style (sautéed with fresh garlic and white wine, topped with tomato, oregano, and parsley, and served over spinach), or Palermo-style (baked and topped with sautéed onions, bell peppers, marinara, and melted provolone). Hobo's serves lunch and dinner daily. An Insiders' secret is out about one of the best locals' places in the Upper Keys.

**HOG HEAVEN SPORTS BAR & GRILL, MM 85.3 Oceanside, 85361 Overseas Hwy., Islamorada, FL 33036; (305) 664-9669; hogheavensportsbar .com; Seafood and Classic American; $.** The congenial outdoor saloon of Hog Heaven Sports Bar sits unassumingly on the waterfront. Watch televised sports on one of the 17 flat-screen TVs located throughout the property, talk with the many locals who frequent the place, or head to the point, where a private beach offers a secluded setting. Many great seafood and landlubber menu options abound, but if you are really ready to indulge, try the piggy platter appetizer: 3 fried shrimp, 3 chicken wings, 3 hogs in a blanket, 3 poppers, 5 onion rings, and a small order of curly fries. Hog Heaven is open daily for lunch and dinner, and offers live entertainment every weekend.

**ISLAMORADA FISH COMPANY AND MARKET,** MM 81.5 Bayside, 81532 Overseas Hwy., Islamorada, FL 33036; (305) 664-9271; restaurants .basspro.com; Seafood; $$. Islamorada Fish Company, primarily a seafood market that opens at 9 a.m. (see the Specialty Foods, Cafes & Markets chapter), also serves lunch and dinner daily until 10 p.m. Eat indoors at the Island Conch House Eatery or outside under umbrella tables that perch on a peninsula jutting into Florida Bay. Islamorada Fish Company's restaurant is so popular that it is not unusual to wait an hour or more for a table. But don't worry: The restaurant is attached to the World Wide Sportsman's cavernous sports emporium, so you can browse your wait away, look at the sunset, and wait for your name to be called.

**ISLAND GRILL,** MM 85.5 Oceanside, 85501 Overseas Hwy., Islamorada, FL 33036; (305) 664-8400; keysislandgrill.com; Seafood; $$$. If you are seated inside, ask for a table near the window, which is right along the canal facing Snake Creek. Outdoor tables are the best choice because you are actually on the dock area of the restaurant. Try the appetizer of spicy seared tuna nachos served over fried wontons with a seaweed salad amid ginger and sweet soy dressing. Entrees include Low Country shrimp and grits with jumbo shrimp, fresh sausage, two cheeses, and fresh marinara over stone-ground grits, as well as wasabi-crusted fresh catch of the day (mahimahi, yellowtail, or hogfish), lightly seared, then baked with a creamy wasabi sauce and Japanese bread crumbs. Open daily for breakfast, lunch, and dinner.

**JERSEY BOARDWALK PIZZA,** MM 88.8 Bayside, 20 High Point Rd., Tavernier, FL 33070; (305) 853-3800; jerseyboardwalkpizza.com; Italian; $. Boardwalk Pizza creates handmade pizza and bakes the pies in a stone-lined pizza oven. This is a small eatery that is big on taste. Locals rave about the crust, characterized as neither thick nor thin, but light, fluffy, and tender. You'll also find cheesesteaks, subs, calzones, and pasta here. Make sure to try the Philly cheesesteak served three ways: the traditional, with grilled onions and provolone cheese; the works, with grilled onions, green peppers, mushrooms, and provolone cheese; or the Californian, the traditional style topped with lettuce, tomato, and mayo. This pizzeria is open daily for lunch and dinner.

**KAIYO GRILL & SUSHI, MM 81.7 Oceanside, 81701 Overseas Hwy., Isla-morada, FL 33036; (305) 664-5556; kaiyokeys.com; Seafood; $$$.** Kaiyo's delightful blend of "Florida Asian" results in an exciting presentation of sushi and Keys-inspired dishes. Ones to try are the steamed ginger pork dumplings with sesame dipping sauce and the drunken scallops: diver scallops pan-seared in duck fat with bacon and caramelized onions in a seasonal beer reduction served with lobster-mashed potatoes and seasonal vegetables. And where did the restaurant's unusual name come from? In Japanese, *kai* means "small body of water" and *yo* means "large body of water." Kaiyo is open for lunch and dinner Mon through Sat. Reservations are recommended.

**KEY LARGO CONCH HOUSE, MM 100.2 Oceanside, 100211 Overseas Hwy., Key Largo, FL 33037; (305) 453-4844; keylargoconchhouse.com; $.** If you're a coffee connoisseur in Key Largo, you'll want to find your way to the Key Largo Conch House, which is located in a Conch-style house that sits on a lush wooded lot. Choose from among house-blend coffee, gourmet flavors of the day, and espresso drinks. If you prefer a cool drink, how about an iced coffee or a fruit smoothie made with a green-tea base? After making your choice, pick a seat on the wide porch and enjoy the free Wi-Fi in the fresh air. An extensive menu is also on offer for breakfast, lunch, and dinner, and their conch fritters are some of the best in the Keys. The Conch House is open seven days a week.

**LAZY DAYS RESTAURANT, MM 79.9 Oceanside, 79867 Overseas Hwy., Islamorada, FL 33036; (305) 664-5256; lazydaysrestaurant.com; Seafood; $$.** Lazy Days provides the ideal setting for kicking back, gazing over the sparkling blue Atlantic, and dining on a revolving selection of seafood offerings. The elevated plantation-style building with turquoise roof, French doors, and wraparound balcony perches directly on the shoreline of the ocean. Some of the menu favorites, such as cracked conch served fried or sautéed with tomatoes, scallions, Parmesan cheese, and key lime butter, or jumbo shrimp baked with crabmeat stuffing and topped with béarnaise sauce and key lime butter, are house standouts. Lazy Days serves lunch and dinner daily.

**LORELEI RESTAURANT & CABANA BAR, MM 82 Bayside, 96 Madeira Rd., Islamorada, FL 33036; (305) 664-2692; loreleicabanabar.com; Seafood; $.** The legend of Lorelei maintains that a nymph's sweet, lyrical singing lured sailors to shipwreck on a rock. Today's Lorelei lures you to a primo perch on the very edge of Florida Bay. The Cabana Bar breaks the day starting at 7 a.m., then serves a casual menu from 11 a.m. to 9 p.m., offering live entertainment nightly starting just before sunset. The seafood-inspired menu makes a gustatory decision a difficult task. Landlubbers are accommodated with steak, chicken, ribs, and pasta offerings, and there is even a vegan option on the menu. The Lorelei Restaurant is open daily for breakfast, lunch, and dinner.

**MARKER 88, MM 88 Bayside, 88000 Overseas Hwy., Islamorada, FL 33070; (305) 852-9315; marker88.info; Seafood; $$$.** Combining bayside ambience with innovative preparation of the Keys' freshest bounty, Marker 88 is a culinary landmark. Favorite dishes include sustainable seafood items like the onion-crusted mahimahi served with toasted onions and a white wine, key lime juice, and butter sauce. Marker 88 is surrounded by heavy tropical vegetation and rambling docks, and a deck laden with wooden outdoor tables and chairs provides the perfect setting for a predinner sunset toast or a starlit after-dinner drink. This boat-accessible restaurant maintains a full bar and is open daily for lunch and dinner. Reservations are recommended.

★**M.E.A.T. EATERY AND TAP ROOM, MM 88 Oceanside, 88005 Overseas Hwy., Islamorada, FL 33036; meateatery.com; Classic American; $.** Yes, meat is on the menu at this tiny eatery and taproom. And the burgers here are nothing short of divine. Go all the way with the Inside-Out Juicy Lucy Burger, a pimento-cheese-and-bacon-stuffed Angus burger topped with American cheese, lettuce, and tomato and served with house fries. Looking for something a little lighter? Try the Nancy Pants, a 5-ounce Angus burger served with cheese, lettuce, tomato, and house fries. Optional toppings include house-made pickled jalapeños or red onions, beer-battered onions, bacon, a sunnyside up egg, and more. In addition to craft and microbrewed beers, M.E.A.T. also has root beer on tap, as well as fresh-made ice cream and milkshakes.

**MRS. MAC'S KITCHEN, MM 99.4 Oceanside, 99336 Overseas Hwy., Key Largo, FL 33037; (305) 451-3722; mrsmacskitchen.com; Classic American; $.** If good home cooking is what you want and you're craving plenty of carbs, this is the place to satisfy all of the above. The house is bedecked with anti-quated license plates that only add to the tropical charm of this Key Largo legend. The menu is long, the sandwiches are hearty, the conch chowder is authentic, and the nightly specials will bring you back—to Mrs. Mac's! Try the Conch Salad: freshly ground conch mixed into a delicious Bahamian-style salad (that means spicy) and served over lettuce in a bowl with crackers alongside. Open Mon through Sat for breakfast, lunch, and dinner. Closed Sun.

**NUM THAI RESTAURANT & SUSHI BAR, MM 103.2 Bayside, 103200 Overseas Hwy., Key Largo, FL 33037; (305) 451-5955; Thai; $–$$.** If your taste for Asian food hovers around Thailand or Japan, Num Thai can offer you the best of both worlds: spicy Thai curries and noodle dishes, or sushi, sashimi, and traditional Japanese dishes. Japanese offerings include *temaki,* cone-shaped hand rolls; *hosomaki,* medium rolls cut into bite-size pieces; a wide assortment of sushi, by the piece or in dinner combos; and tempura. Or enjoy Thai satays; spicy beef salad; seafood, chicken, or beef curries; or volcano jumbo shrimp, grilled and fried with chili sauce. Num Thai is open for lunch Mon through Fri and dinner every day. American and Asian beers, wine, plum wine, and sake are all offered.

**OLD TAVERNIER RESTAURANT, MM** 90.3 Oceanside, 90311 Overseas Hwy., Tavernier, FL 33070; (305) 852-6012; oldtavernier.com; **Mediterranean; $$.** One of the Upper Keys' most popular establishments for more than 20 years, the Old Tavernier marries the Mediterranean and the Caribbean with a continental flair to create a singular cuisine. Try the seared yellowfin tuna served with wasabi, hoisin glaze, ginger, rice, and vegetables. Guests have the option of dining indoors—where white linen tablecloths are aglow with candles and watercolor sailboat scenes dot the walls—or outdoors on a balcony overlooking a narrow canal. Old Tavernier has a full bar and wine list, is open daily for dinner only, and is accessible by boat.

★**PIERRE'S LOUNGE AND RESTAURANT AT MORADA BAY, MM** 81.6 Bayside, 81600 Overseas Hwy., Islamorada, FL 33036; (305) 664-3225; pierres-restaurant.com; **Contemporary American; $$$.** Pierre's is the place to go for a romantic dining experience. Flickering candlelight greets you in the downstairs lounge area for predinner libations, and a covered porch welcomes you to sit and watch the famed Keys sunset. Walk up the sweeping curved staircase, and your dining adventure begins. The decor, tropically British colonial, is elegant yet casual. Dine indoors or out on the covered porch. The culinary stars shine with such signature dishes as local hogfish meuniere, served with a house-grown parsley and heirloom tomato salad, sautéed fingerling potatoes, French beans, and lemon juice. Pierre's is open every evening for dinner only.

**SEÑOR FRIJOLES, MM** 103.9 Bayside, 103900 Overseas Hwy., Key Largo, FL 33037; (305) 451-1592; senorfrijolesrestaurant.com; **Mexican; $.** Señor Frijoles sits on Florida Bay next to Sundowners and offers popular Tex-Mex fare, such as burritos, enchiladas, and quesadillas. But you'll also find some jazzed-up Conch Republic versions, such as grilled mahimahi or lobster fajitas and the cumin-encrusted mahi tacos, served with cabbage, housemade cotija cheese, citrus pico, and chipotle sour cream. Feeling parched? Señor Frijoles offers 9 different margaritas made with freshly squeezed lime juice, as well as many other tropical libations and Mexican beers with which you can toast the fabulous Keys sunset. Señor Frijoles is accessible by boat and open for lunch and dinner daily.

**SMUGGLER'S COVE RESORT AND MARINA, MM** 85.5 Bayside, Islamorada; (305) 664-5564; smugscove.com; **Classic American; $$.** If you want to find a good place to eat, ask a local. Smuggler's Cove, a locals' favorite in Islamorada, puts on no pretensions. What they do put on, however, is great pulled pork, and a burger that, among other entrees, draws raves. On the appetizer side, make sure to try the fresh guacamole. The menu is updated with new dishes regularly, and there are options for kids and vegetarians as well. In addition to the great food, Smuggler's Cove hosts nightly entertainment every day of the week. Smuggler's Cove is open 7 days a week for lunch and dinner and is boat-accessible.

**SNAPPER'S WATERFRONT RESTAURANT, MM 94.5 Oceanside, 139 Seaside Ave., Key Largo, FL 33037; (305) 852-5956; snapperskeylargo.com; Contemporary American; $$.** The best part of Snapper's is sitting out on the deck near the water overlooking Snapper's Marina—next to the food, that is. Sample some Applewood Smoked Bacon Wrapped Scallops, or the local favorite: Conch Fritters served with cocktail sauce. Snapper's offers an extensive selection of seafood as well as sandwiches, burgers, and many selections for landlubbers. There's a lot of action and a frenzied atmosphere, but it's worth the visit. Weekends feature live entertainment nightly in season. The restaurant serves lunch and dinner 7 days a week and brunch on Sun, and is accessible by boat. Reservations are accepted.

**SUNDOWNERS, MM 104 Bayside, 103900 Overseas Hwy., Key Largo, FL 33037; (305) 451-4502; sundownerskeylargo.com; Classic American; $$.** One of Key Largo's most popular places to enjoy the sunset, this open and airy—yet cozy and intimate—establishment overlooks the azure expanse of Blackwater Sound. Sundowners' Key Largo fish sandwich, jerk-seasoned fresh mahimahi topped with grilled onions and American cheese on a kaiser roll, wins raves. If you prefer a more elaborate meal, try the locals' favorite, whole yellowtail snapper—crispy fish dusted in cornmeal and fried, served with sweet Thai chili sauce. Gluten-free and vegetarian menus are also available. Sundowners offers a full bar and is open for lunch and dinner. Reservations are recommended. The restaurant is accessible by boat.

**TOWER OF PIZZA, MM 100.6 Bayside, 100600 Overseas Hwy., Key Largo, FL 33037; (305) 451-1461; towerofpizzakeylargo.com; Italian; $.** Antipasto, Greek salad, minestrone, and a plethora of great pasta dishes vie with fantastic pizza at Tower of Pizza. Sauces and dough here are homemade, as are the desserts, and cheeses are fresh. Locals particularly like the Sicilian-style pie, but you can build your own from a long list of tantalizing ingredients, or choose from the soups, salads, hot or cold subs, stromboli, calzones, or pasta entrees. Tower of Pizza offers free delivery services (including wine and beer), available between MM 94 to MM 107, and is open every day for lunch and dinner.

★**ZIGGIE AND MAD DOG'S, MM 83 Bayside, Islamorada; (305) 664-3391; ziggieandmaddogs.com; Contemporary American; $$.** Steaks, chops, and seafood are on the menu at this Keys landmark. Partners Randy Kassewitz and Miami Dolphins football player Jim "Mad Dog" Mandich turned this historic property (originally built in the 1930s) into a fine-dining establishment serving fantastic food like grilled duck breast served with warm lingonberry sauce, and baked jumbo shrimp with mango and crab stuffing. The wine list is extensive. And while the decor may have changed since the '30s, not to worry—the fish stories still abound in the chic bar area. (Be sure to ask the bartender about Al Capone playing cards in the back room.) Open daily for lunch and dinner; reservations recommended.

## Middle Keys

★ALMA, Hawk's Cay Resort, MM 61 Oceanside, 61 Hawk's Cay Blvd., Duck Key, FL 33050; (305) 743-7000; hawkscay.com; Mexican and Spanish; $$$. Alma is a Latino-themed restaurant with a relaxed, upscale vibe. Seating includes cozy, indoor banquettes or candlelit dining outside on the veranda. Start with oysters on the half shell served with shallot mignonette. Follow with the seafood paella: fresh Florida catch of the day, shrimp, lobster, mussels, Spanish chorizo sausage, Calasparra Spanish rice, fresh peas in a saffron and seafood broth with caper and piquillo aioli. Adjoining the restaurant is the Bar at Alma, at which you can savor drinks and try their outstanding tequila and rum collection. Mojitos, anyone? Alma is open daily for dinner only and is accessible by boat.

★BARRACUDA GRILL, MM 49.5 Bayside, 4290 Overseas Hwy., Marathon, FL 33050; (305) 743-3314; barracudagrillmarathon.com; Contemporary American; $$. The entrees showcase imaginative preparation and presentation at the Barracuda Grill, a small, lively bistro in the heart of Marathon. A daily changing menu of the chefs' creative interpretations rivals the old favorites, which include the veal chop and a mango snapper. Not your typical family restaurant, at Barracuda Mom and Dad can dine sumptuously and keep their kids happy, too. Barracuda Grill opens for dinner Mon through Sat at 6:25 p.m. and is cash-only. Reservations are not taken. This popular spot fills up quickly, especially in high season, so come early if you don't want to wait for a table.

**BURDINES WATERFRONT AND CHIKI TIKI BAR & GRILLE,** MM 47.5 Oceanside, 1200 Oceanview Ave., Marathon, FL 33050; (305) 743-5317; burdineswaterfront.com; Classic American; $. Burdines sits on a channel into Boot Key Harbor, and the view here is as good as the food. The Chiki Tiki Bar & Grille sits on the second floor, where you enjoy ocean breezes with a true Keys decor. The service is friendly and you are made to feel welcome and appreciated. The menu holds a bountiful selection, from fresh fish sandwiches to green chile cheeseburgers. If you order nothing else, be sure to get the fries;

they are hand-cut and served with their famous "fry dust." The Chiki Tiki Bar & Grille is open for lunch and dinner daily and is accessible by boat.

**BUTTERFLY CAFÉ, Tranquility Bay Beachfront Hotel & Resort, MM 48.5 Bayside, 2600 Overseas Hwy., Marathon, FL 33050; (305) 289-7177; tranquilitybay.com; Seafood; $$.** Housed in the main building of the lovely Tranquility Bay Beachfront Hotel & Resort (see the Accommodations chapter), this fine restaurant is truly "Keys casual" with a traditional flair. Its chic but casual design and open, airy, high ceilings flowing out onto a large veranda with breathtaking views of gulf sunsets only enhance the fare. The menu changes seasonally, but usually includes the Caribbean jerk chicken and the panko-crusted grouper, both of which are excellent choices. The Butterfly Café is open for dinner nightly. Gluten-free and children's menus are available, and reservations are required.

**CABANA BREEZES, 401 E. Ocean Dr., Key Colony Beach, FL 33051; (305) 743-4849; cabanabreezes.com; Contemporary American; $–$$.** Famous bandleader Guy Lombardo once owned this popular landmark back in the 1950s. Different names (the Colony House and the Shamrock) may have come and gone, but the outstanding food and service remain the same, keeping this eatery at the top of the locals' hit parade. Menu toppers range from beer-battered fish-and-chips and the grouper or mahimahi sandwich—grilled, fried, or blackened to perfection on a kaiser roll—to a 12-ounce New York strip steak topped with a black truffle butter sauce and served with fingerling potatoes and the house vegetable. Cabana Breezes is open daily for lunch and dinner.

**DOCKSIDE TROPICAL CAFÉ, MM 53 Oceanside, 35 Sombrero Rd., Sombrero Marina, Marathon, FL 33050; (305) 743-0000; docksidetropical cafe.com; Seafood and Classic American; $.** There are cold drinks and also good eats available here. Start with a local favorite, Smilin' Bob's Smoked Fish Dip, or the dirty chips, fresh kettle-cooked chips topped with blue cheese and bacon crumbles, green onions, and blue cheese dressing. Then follow with the blackened fish sandwich (your choice of mahimahi or grouper on a brioche), or Bob's Bitchen Big Bad Beach Burger. Dockside has a full bar with a fun cocktail menu—Dockside Rum Punch, anyone?—and is open for breakfast in season, and lunch and dinner daily, year-round.

**HIDEAWAY CAFE, Rainbow Bend Resort, MM 58 Oceanside, 57784 Overseas Hwy., Marathon, FL 33050; (305) 289-1554; hideawaycafe.com; Contemporary American; $$.** The only thing rivaling the direct ocean vistas at Hideaway Cafe is the cuisine. Sure to please the foodie in you, the Hideaway also will intrigue the diner who likes to pig out: The Hideaway Rib Steak is large enough to serve a family of four, and the seafood Wellington is a dream!

Other favorites include seafood crepes (a seafood combo rolled in a homemade crepe) topped with flamingo sauce (a tomato-flavored Alfredo sauce), and seafood puttanesca (shrimp, scallops, and shellfish in a spicy red sauce). Hideaway Cafe is open daily for lunch and dinner. Plan to drink in the view along with your libations. Reservations are recommended.

**THE HURRICANE, MM 49.5 Bayside, 4650 Overseas Hwy., Marathon, FL 33050; (305) 743-2220; hurricaneblues.com; Classic American; $.** The Hurricane has been Marathon's favorite place to eat, drink, and be merry for more than 50 years. Open-mic nights are held every Wed, and live bands usually play Thurs, Fri, and Sat night. Open every day of the week, the Hurricane is famous for their $5 lunches and late-night pizza. Try their original fried (grilled is available as well, for $1 more) mahimahi. Their prices simply can't be beat in the Florida Keys!

**THE ISLAND FISH COMPANY RESTAURANT & TIKI BAR, MM 54 Bayside, 12648 Overseas Hwy., Marathon, FL 33050; (305) 743-4191; islandfishco.com; Seafood; $$.** Perched on a narrow spit of land jutting out into the Gulf of Mexico, the Island Fish Company provides one of the most scenic sunset spots in the Middle Keys. Try the conch ceviche—unforgettable key lime–marinated pieces of tender conch with onions and peppers in a lime vinaigrette served with tortilla chips—or the Buffalo shrimp, flash-fried Key West pink shrimp tossed in hot pepper sauce and served with ranch dressing and a fried jalapeño pepper. The restaurant is open for breakfast, lunch, and dinner daily, and reservations are not accepted.

**KEY COLONY INN, MM 54 Oceanside, 700 W. Ocean Dr., Key Colony Beach, FL 33051; (305) 743-0100; kcinn.com; Italian; $$.** The Key Colony Inn is a favorite dining haunt of residents and visitors alike. Besides the varied menu selections of Italian-style pasta, veal, and chicken dishes, Key Colony offers innovative presentations of Florida Keys seafood, steaks, and interesting daily specials. If dinner conversation is important, request a corner table, which may be a bit quieter. Or if the weather is fine, and it usually is, sit outside on the covered veranda. The Key Colony Inn features a full-service bar and is open for lunch and dinner daily and for brunch on Sun from 11 a.m. to 2 p.m.

**KEYS FISHERIES MARKET & MARINA, MM 49 Bayside, 3502 Louisa St., Marathon, FL 33050; (305) 743-4353 or (866) 743-4353; keysfisheries .com; Seafood; $–$$.** For more than 40 years Keys Fisheries Market & Marina has been the Middle Keys' answer to the eat-the-seafood-right-off-the-boat dining experience. Though the place is rustic and informal, the fish doesn't get any fresher than this, because Keys Fisheries is just that: a working fishery and fish market (see the Specialty Foods, Cafes & Markets chapter). Your wisest choices here will be local Keys seafood—such as grouper, yellowtail snapper, or mahimahi—lobster bisque or chowder, Key West shrimp, and in season, the freshest stone crabs in Marathon, served hot or cold, cooked right off the boat. Keys Fisheries Market & Marina is open for lunch and dinner daily.

**LEIGH ANN'S COFFEE HOUSE, MM 51.5 Oceanside, 301 Sadowski Causeway, Key Colony Beach, FL 33051; (305) 743-2001 or (305) 743-6676; Classic American; $.** Homemade soups rival sandwiches on bagels, croissants, and sub rolls. For breakfast, try the French toast soufflé or the homemade biscuits with sausage gravy. And for lunch, the homemade chicken salad—made fresh daily, and served on your choice of bread along with a side of Italian pasta salad—is highly recommended. Specials are made in small batches to ensure freshness. Leigh Ann's serves beer and wine as well. Make sure to ask them about their Wine Club and monthly Wine Dinners. This is a happening place! Open for breakfast, lunch, and dinner Mon through Sat and until mid-afternoon on Sun.

**PANDA HOUSE, MM 50 Bayside, 5230 Overseas Hwy., Marathon, FL 33050; (305) 743-3417; pandahousechinese.com; Chinese; $.** One cannot live by Florida Keys seafood alone! Panda House has been serving Chinese cuisine in Marathon for more than 15 years, and the locals pack this place for the enormous all-you-can-eat lunch buffet. The menu boasts Szechuan, Hunan, and Cantonese cuisines. The friendly staff gets right to the business of making sure your plate is full and you do not leave hungry. It's an ideal spot for families and if you have a crowd to feed. Panda House is open daily and offers free delivery in Marathon.

**PORKY'S BAYSIDE, MM 47.5 Bayside, 1410 Overseas Hwy., Marathon, FL 33050; (305) 289-2065; porkysbaysidebbq.com; Classic American & Southern; $.** This open-air restaurant sits on the water in a picturesque setting, which is also home to Captain Pip's Marina & Hideaway, offering overnight accommodations, boat rentals, and sportfishing charters. Porky's is widely known for its barbecue and all-you-can-eat ribs special every Wed night, and the daily breakfast is not to be missed. Try the Porky's Smoked Pork Breakfast Sandwich: scrambled eggs, smoked pork, and veggies topped with melted pepper jack cheese on a roll and served with a side of home fries. Porky's serves breakfast, lunch, and dinner every day and has live music every night from 6:30 to 9 p.m. Reservations are accepted for large parties only.

**SEVEN MILE GRILL, MM 47.5 Oceanside, 1240 Overseas Hwy., Marathon, FL 33050; (305) 743-4481; 7-mile-grill.com; Seafood, Classic American, and Mediterranean; $.** You can't miss this watering hole, as it sits off US 1 at the beginning of the Seven Mile Bridge heading south to Key West, where it has been since 1954. When it opens in the morning, you see the many folks lining the bar to sip their favorite beverage and toast the local color that is the Florida Keys. New owners have breathed life into the menu. To wit, an entire section is devoted to Mediterranean food, Greek in particular, including gyros, souvlakis, and spanakopita. There is also a children's menu available, as well as wine and beer. Seven Mile Grill serves breakfast, lunch, and dinner daily.

**SUNSET GRILLE & RAW BAR,** MM 47 Oceanside, 7 Knights Key Blvd., Marathon, FL 33050; (305) 289-3588; sunsetgrille7milebridge.com; Seafood and Classic American; $. Located at the foot of the Seven Mile Bridge, the Sunset Grille & Raw Bar is a great place to grab a drink poolside or under the shade of their massive tiki hut. The expansive views of the famous bridge certainly make for one gorgeous sunset. The expansive menu includes specialty sandwiches like the Voodoo Grouper Sandwich (blackened gulf grouper topped with a mango/guava mayonnaise), numerous burgers and seafood baskets, and even signature sushi rolls, like the 7 Mile Roll: tempura shrimp, cream cheese, avocado, and jalapeño masago topped with tuna and spicy mayonnaise. Sunset Grille serves breakfast, lunch, and dinner daily.

## Lower Keys

★**BOBALU'S SOUTHERN CAFE,** MM 10 Bayside, 301 US Hwy. 1, Big Coppitt Key, FL 33040; (305) 296-1664; Classic American & Southern; $. The cuisine at Bobalu's is inexpensive, home-style, and hearty. The menu includes delicious house specialties like the crispy southern-fried chicken, which is homemade with a honey glaze, or the roast turkey with stuffing, which is Thanksgiving-inspired and served year-round. The local favorite is the New Haven–style pizza, a Neapolitan-style pie with a crispier crust. Key West's favorite native son, Jimmy Buffett, has been known to dine at the Big Coppitt location on occasion, and he even mentioned this place in his book, *Where Is Joe Merchant?* Bobalu's is open in Big Coppitt Tues through Sat for lunch and dinner.

**BOONDOCKS GRILLE & DRAFT HOUSE,** MM 27.5 Bayside, 27205 Overseas Hwy., Ramrod Key, FL 33042; (305) 872-4094; boondocks.us .com; Classic American; $$. Housing the largest miniature golf course in all of the Florida Keys, Boondocks is also home to a grill and draft house with an extensive menu. In addition to the daily happy hour special of 50 percent off all appetizers, Boondocks offers drink and other food specials every weekday. No matter when you go, you will find a celebratory atmosphere under the giant tiki hut that houses the restaurant and bar. They even have a Patio Pet Menu to ensure that Fido is as well fed as you are. Boondocks is open for lunch and dinner daily, and has live entertainment on most nights of the week.

**★LITTLE PALM ISLAND RESORT & SPA,** MM 28.5 Oceanside, 28500 Overseas Hwy., Little Torch Key, FL 33042; (305) 872-2551 or (800) 343-8567; littlepalmisland.com; Contemporary American; $$$$. Step into a fairy tale the moment you check in at the mainland substation on Little Torch Key to await your luxurious launch, the *Woodson,* that will spirit you to the island. As you arrive at the island's dock, you'll spot the Great House amid towering coconut palms. Classic European preparations fused with Floridian, Caribbean, and Pan-Asian flavors are the tantalizing offerings from the chef. Little Palm offers libations from a full-service bar and maintains an extensive wine list. A limited number of reservations are accepted from the general public for lunch and dinner daily. Children must be age 16 or older to dine at Little Palm Island.

**LOOE KEY TIKI BAR,** MM 27.5 Oceanside, 27340 Overseas Hwy., Ramrod Key, FL 33042; (305) 872-2215; looekeytikibar.com; Seafood and Classic American. This open-air tiki bar is where you will find many locals and ardent dive tourists alive and kicking in the Keys. Sandwiches and basket dinners accompany a fine sampling of good conversation from the patrons who frequent this no-pretense bar. Try the smoked fish dip served with olives, jalapeños, and crackers, and then follow it up with a Tiki burger or Fish Po Boy, fried fish with lettuce, tomato, and tangy po boy dressing. Taco and open-jam nights are hosted every Tues by Looe Key's Coral Rock Jam Band, and there is live music nightly.

**MANGROVE MAMA'S RESTAURANT,** MM 20 Bayside, 9991 Overseas Hwy., Sugarloaf Key, FL 33042; (305) 745-3030; mangrovemamasrestaurant .com; Seafood; $$. This brightly hued roadhouse offers a rustic garden in the back where you can dine amid the banana trees. The old chairs are painted in a barrage of drizzled primary colors; ceramic fish sculptures adorn the walls. Bright tropical tablecloths cover the simple tables, and painted buoys hang from the trees and rafters. Try the hogfish filets encrusted with plantains, served with Mama's banana rum sauce. The restaurant serves lunch and dinner daily and brunch on Sun. Indoor dining is air-conditioned. In addition to a full-service bar, Mangrove Mama's has an extensive wine list. Reservations are suggested for dinner.

**★NO NAME PUB,** MM 31 Bayside, 30813 Watson Blvd., Big Pine Key, FL 33043; (305) 872-9115; nonamepub.com; Classic American; $. No Name Pub is a funky establishment that is located off the beaten path. Turn west at the traffic light at MM 31 in Big Pine onto Key Deer Boulevard. Proceed to Watson Boulevard and take another right. At the fork in the road, bear right, heading toward No Name Key. Go across a bridge and past a residential subdivision. Just before the No Name Bridge across Bogie Channel, the pub will be on your left. The famous pizza at No Name is deep dish and arrives at your picnic table steaming hot. No Name Pub is open daily for lunch and dinner from 11 a.m. until 11 p.m.

★THE SQUARE GROUPER BAR AND GRILL, MM 22.6 Oceanside, 22658 Overseas Hwy., Cudjoe Key, FL 33042; (305) 745-8880; squaregrouper barandgrill.com; Contemporary American; $$. Located midway between Key West and Big Pine, this establishment serves memorable Keys cuisine. Conch and lobster fritters with Asian dipping sauce are a crowd-pleaser, and be sure to try the seared tuna with spicy pineapple sauce. The catch of the day is prepared in a different manner nightly. For dessert, try the key lime ice cream served with shortbread cookies. The Square Grouper is open for lunch and dinner Tues through Sat, but make sure to call in advance, as they have been known to close for a month or so during the slow summer season.

## Key West

A&B LOBSTER HOUSE, 700 Front St. (upstairs), Key West, FL 33040; (305) 294-5880; aandblobsterhouse.com; Seafood; $$. Situated beside the water at the foot of Front Street, A&B Lobster House, named for its original owners, Alonzo and Berlin, offers terrific views of the yachts moored at the Key West Historic Seaport. The signature dish of sautéed jumbo scallops served with braised shiitake mushrooms, asparagus, and a lemon-garlic butter sauce is not to be missed. Steaks and pasta dishes are also available. Dine inside or outside on the wraparound porch; in either case, reservations are suggested. After dinner, retire to Berlin's Bar to sample the fine selection of cigars and after-dinner drinks. A&B Lobster House is open daily for dinner; Berlin's Bar opens at 5:30 p.m. for predinner cocktails.

ABBONDANZA, 1208 Simonton St., Key West, FL 33040; (305) 292-1199; abbondanzakeywest.com; Italian; $. The specialty at this casual Italian eatery is pasta, of course, in a variety of shapes and with sauces that range from Alfredo to pomodoro. You'll also find such main dishes as chicken marsala and veal parmigiana, plus daily specials. The food is quite tasty, the atmosphere is comfortable, and you're sure to discover that the portions at this restaurant live up to its name, which is Italian for "plenty." There is a full bar, and the menu selections are more reasonably priced than some other Italian restaurants in town. Abbondanza is open daily for dinner. Reservations are accepted for larger groups only.

ALONZO'S OYSTER BAR, 700 Front St. (downstairs), Key West, FL 33040; (305) 294-5880; alonzosoysterbar.com; Seafood; $–$$. If you like oysters, Alonzo's is the place to go. You can order them up raw, on the half shell, baked, or batter-dipped and fried. Check the chalkboard daily to find out where the oysters are from and what kinds are available. This casual seaside eatery also serves freshly shucked clams, lobster, conch, mussels, and a variety of dishes made with the native shrimp known as Key West pinks. Alonzo's serves lunch and dinner 7 days a week, and during happy hour the entire right-hand side of the menu is half off. There's plenty of indoor and outdoor seating; reservations are not necessary. Free parking is available.

★**AMBROSIA JAPANESE RESTAURANT,** 1401 Simonton St., Key West, FL 33040; (305) 293-0304; Seafood; $$. Sake it to me! The sun rises brightly on this wildly popular Japanese restaurant. With a plethora of sushi and sakes, as well as great service, you will understand why it is a locals' top choice for sushi on the island. Diverse flavors and textures combined with outstanding sauces will beckon you for a return engagement. Try the duck tataki: duck breast marinated in sweet miso paste, sliced thin, served with yuzu paste and balsamic soy sauce. Don't forget to explore the drink menu, as Ambrosia offers a full bar. They will be happy to see you for lunch and dinner, both of which are served daily.

**ANTONIA'S RESTAURANT,** 615 Duval St., Key West, FL 33040; (305) 294-6565; antoniaskeywest.com; Italian; $$. Northern Italian cuisine stars at this Duval Street staple. Favorite dishes include the soufflé al Caprino—warm goat cheese soufflé served with pan-seared asparagus, baby green beans, carrots, Belgian endive, and roasted tomato vinaigrette; Fettuccine alla Checca—homemade fettuccine, homemade mozzarella cheese, fresh tomato, olive oil, and basil; Dentice del Giorno—yellowtail snapper served with potato puree, fresh vegetable and a choice of sauces, fresh roma tomato and black olive, meuniere with pine nuts or caper, anchovy and cream. Antonia's maintains an extensive Northern Italian and American wine list. The restaurant is open daily for lunch and dinner.

★**AZUR,** 425 Grinnell St., Key West, FL 33040; (305) 292-2987; azur keywest.com; Mediterranean; $$. Toss Greek, Italian, and Iberian cuisines in with a tropical setting and you get a Mediterranean mix called Azur. The menu changes seasonally, and highlights include a whole branzino fish, grilled and served with rosemary, garlic, cured tomatoes, kalamata olives, and Yukon potatoes. Desserts vary as well, but one standout is crème brûlée infused with lavender and topped with berries. Wine and beer are also on offer. Azur's best ingredient is the innovative talent of the two owners who create memorable dishes in this truly outstanding restaurant. Azur is open for breakfast, lunch, and dinner Mon through Sat and brunch on Sun.

★**BAD BOY BURRITO,** 1128 Simonton St., Key West, FL 33040; (305) 292-2697; badboyburrito.com; Contemporary American; $. Hands down, this is the locals' favorite lunch in Key West, be it by delivery or sitting on a bench outside the tiny establishment. Bad Boy starts with organic flour tortillas, adds basmati rice and rattlesnake beans, and the rest is up to you. Try the veggie approach and add sautéed mushrooms, tomatilla sauce, shaved cabbage, shredded cheese, grilled green onions, and avocado. Carnivore options include pork carnitas, duck, chicken, and seasoned ground Kobe beef. Bad Boy also has items on the menu that don't require you to create, like the Cayo Hueso Fish Tacos and Disco Duck Quesadilla. Bad Boy is open and delivers Mon through Sat from 11 a.m. to 10 p.m.

**BAGATELLE, 115 Duval St., Key West, FL 33040; (305) 296-6609; bagatelle keywest.com; Contemporary American; $$$.** Situated on two floors of a gracious old Key West home, Bagatelle serves fresh local ingredients with island inventiveness. Try the grilled 8-ounce lobster tail served with saffron mango risotto, grilled asparagus, and a roasted red pepper coulis. Wraparound balconies on both levels afford outdoor dining, or you may choose to dine indoors. Bagatelle is a premier spot from which to view the Fantasy Fest Parade (see the Annual Events chapter). Reservations for the evening of Fantasy Fest should be made well in advance of the event, even up to a year. Bagatelle serves breakfast, lunch, and dinner daily. Reservations are suggested.

**BANANA CAFE, 1215 Duval St., Key West, FL 33040; (305) 294-7227; bananacafekw.com; French; $$.** Settle into this quiet bistro and choose from more than 40 breakfast and lunch crepes. The thin, pancake-like crepes are stuffed with veggies, fish, and meat, and they are designated either sweet or savory. The most popular crepe among patrons is the ratatouille and grilled asparagus served with field greens, feta cheese, and a balsamic glaze. Dinner options also include such offerings as the sautéed yellowtail snapper served in a citrus beurre blanc sauce with cherry tomatoes, haricots verts, and gnocchi. Banana Cafe is open daily for breakfast, lunch, and dinner. Reservations are recommended, particularly on weekends.

**BENIHANA, 3591 S. Roosevelt Blvd., Key West, FL 33040; (305) 294-6400; benihana.com; Japanese; $$$–$$$$.** This famous restaurant chain is a contact sport when it comes to the ancient Japanese art of *teppanyaki* (literally translated, *teppan* is iron and *yaki* is grilled). I don't know the word for "performance" in Japanese, but as a patron of this restaurant, you get your money's worth. The menu is vast and appealing while your tableside chef performs his or her magic. A full bar is available, and a private Kimono Room can be reserved for those special occasions with 20 or more people. The view from the front of the building is the Atlantic Ocean, while inside you are serenaded by the knife blades chopping on the sizzling grill. Benihana is open for dinner nightly.

**BETTER THAN SEX DESSERT RESTAURANT,** 926 Simonton St., Key West, FL 33040; (305) 296-8102; betterthansexkw.com; Desserts; $. This romantic place will put you in the mood . . . for dessert. Vintage in music ('30s and '40s), flirtatious in atmosphere (flickering candlelight), and truly amazing in the dessert department, this restaurant serves *only* desserts along with wines and coffees. One such presentation is a Chocolate Cab, a wine goblet coated with lush chocolate then filled with wine. A standout is the chocolate cake, made with a hint of Young's Chocolate Stout Beer and tart dark chocolate frosting and served with Irish Cream ice cream and salted caramel. You will be smitten—after all, this is Key West!

**BIG JOHN'S PIZZA,** 1103 Key Plaza, Key West, FL 33040; (305) 293-9576; bigjohnspizzakw.com; Pizza; $. Big John's Pizza is an eatery located in a New Town shopping center where all the locals go to partake in pizza, pizza, and some more pizza. The couple who owns Big John's takes great pride not only in their food but also in their friendly and cheerful help. The menu offers homemade garlic knots, buffalo chicken salad, 20-inch pizzas, calzones, strombolis, and more. Big John's is open daily for lunch and dinner and offers free delivery anywhere in the city limits of Key West. A minimum order amount is needed for delivery beyond MM 2.

**BISTRO 245,** The Westin Key West Resort and Marina, 245 Front St., Key West, FL 33040; (305) 294-4000; westinkeywestresort.com; Contemporary American; $$$. Imagine, a Sunday-brunch buffet table that is 70 feet long—so long you can barely see the other end! Dine indoors or out with a panoramic view of the Gulf of Mexico, all the while indulging in great Florida Keys cuisine. Favorite menu items include the truffle-crusted grouper served with lobster hash, tomato lime butter, and haricots verts; and the herb-seared local mahi, served with tangerine butter, scallion potato cake, and grilled asparagus. Regular menu offerings for breakfast, lunch, and dinner Mon through Sat, and the enormous food fest is Sun only.

**BLACKFIN BISTRO,** 918 Duval St., Key West, FL 33040; (305) 509-7408; blackfinbistro.com; Contemporary American; $$. Stop into this classic bistro-style restaurant for a chance to relax and unwind after the sensory overload of Duval Street. You won't find loud, tropical artwork stuffed into every corner here. Instead, rest your eyes on the soothing island photography and fresh, clean lines of the cool bistro tables. And the food is just as lovely as the decor. From the yellowfin tuna burger to the grilled ahi tuna, one bite is all it will take to figure out why the locals keep coming back to Blackfin Bistro. Open for breakfast and lunch (both served 11 a.m.–5 p.m.) as well as dinner daily.

**BLUE HEAVEN,** 729 Thomas St., Key West, FL 33040; (305) 296-8666; blueheavenkw.com; Classic American; $$. Blue Heaven—at various times a bordello, a pool hall, a railroad water tower, a cockfighting arena, a boxing ring (frequented by Papa Hemingway himself), and an ice-cream parlor—is a popular restaurant in historic Bahama Village with a unique ambience. Roosters, hens, and chicks strut all around the picnic tables that fill the restaurant's backyard; so do the resident kitties. Jimmy Buffett's song "Blue Heaven Rendezvous" was inspired by this establishment, and Kenny Chesney confessed to Oprah that it is his favorite restaurant. Blue Heaven has a full bar and serves breakfast, lunch, and dinner daily. Reservations are accepted for parties of 10 or more.

**B.O.'S FISH WAGON,** 801 Caroline St., Key West, FL 33040; (305) 294-9272; bosfishwagon.com; Seafood; $$. Belly up to the counter and place your order for a fish sandwich, grilled or fried; add sides like fries or onion rings only if you're really hungry. The portions here are huge. The menu also features fish-and-chips, the ubiquitous conch fritters, burgers, and hot dogs. To quench your thirst, select from bottle or draft beer, wine by the glass (plastic, that is), sodas, or key limeade. The decor here can only be called Key West eclectic— fishing nets, lobster traps, a muffler shop sign, even an old pickup truck. B.O.'s is open for lunch and dinner Mon through Sat.

★**THE CAFE,** 509 Southard St., Key West, FL 33040; (305) 296-5515; thecafekw.com; Contemporary American; $. The Cafe serves mostly vegetarian and vegan food that is full of flavor and a big hit with the locals. Large portions and the fun staff cap off the experience. The walls are filled with local art that is also available for purchase. For lunch, try the falafel, served with bean salad or sweet potato fries for an extra fee. At dinnertime, start with cold peanut noodles to share—soba noodles with edamame, red peppers, peanuts, and black sesame seeds—and follow with the delicious blackened mahimahi served with roasted red potatoes, grilled asparagus, and mango-pineapple salsa.

**CAFE MARQUESA,** The Marquesa Hotel, 600 Fleming St., Key West, FL 33040; (305) 292-1244; cafemarquesa.com; Contemporary American; $$. Cafe Marquesa, situated in the historic Marquesa Hotel, remains a consistent winner in the Key West restaurant wars. Gracing the white linen tablecloths is an eclectic assortment of innovative dishes. The menu changes regularly, but specialties of the house have included conch and blue crab cake with creole tartar sauce and jicama slaw, peppercorn-dusted seared yellowfin tuna, feta-and-pine-nut-encrusted rack of lamb, and grilled marinated Key West shrimp. Reservations are highly recommended in all seasons. Cafe Marquesa serves dinner nightly.

**CAMILLE'S RESTAURANT,** 1202 Simonton St., Key West, FL 33040; (305) 296-4811; camilleskeywest.com; Classic American; $$. The reasonably priced menu at this eclectic local favorite features a wide array of breakfast, lunch, and dinner specials; it changes daily and nightly. A real crowd-pleaser is Paradise Pasta—Key West pink shrimp, lobster, asparagus, and red and yellow peppers in a garlic Alfredo sauce. Weekend breakfast at Camille's is a particular treat, offering pecan waffles, eggs Benedict, and a variety of omelets, including build-your-own egg-white omelets. And for lunch, the chicken salad sandwich is always a delicious choice. Liquor and wine are offered. Camille's is open daily for breakfast, lunch, dinner, and happy hour.

**CHICO'S CANTINA,** MM 4.5 Oceanside, 5231 Overseas Hwy., Stock Island, FL 33040; (305) 296-4714; chicoscantina.com; Mexican; $. Sit among giant cacti, Mexican tapestries, and a selection of south-of-the-border folk art at Chico's Cantina, a perennial favorite for Mexican cuisine. Complimentary salsa is prepared with fresh tomatoes, onions, and peppers. The sizzling fajitas—with a choice of vegetarian, chicken, beef, chicken-and-beef combo, shrimp, or shrimp-and-beef combo—are accompanied by fresh vegetables, cooked just until crispy. And the fish adobado, grilled in corn husks, packs just the right spicy zing. Daily specials usually highlight local seafood such as yellowtail snapper. Chico's is open daily and serves the same menu for both lunch and dinner. Beer and wine are served; takeout is available.

**CHINA GARDEN WEST,** 531 Fleming St., Key West, FL 33040; (305) 296-6177; chinagardenkeywest.com; Chinese; $. China Garden West offers your typical American version of Chinese fare, with chef's specials like pressed duck, subgum wonton, and sea-grass salad. They also have great combo platters offering Asian delights. The China Garden West in Searstown (3300 N. Roosevelt Blvd.; 305-296-5618) has the same menu. Both locations are open 7 days a week; takeout is offered, and free delivery is available with a minimum order of $10.

**THE COMMODORE WATERFRONT RESTAURANT,** 700 Front St., Key West, FL 33040; (305) 294-9191; commodorekeywest.com; Seafood; $$. Tables covered in white linen are surrounded by mahogany paneling, brick walls, and lush greenery. Ceiling fans gently whirl, and window walls look out onto the charming harbor of Key West Historic Seaport. Signature dishes abound. The Commodore Seafood Medley is lobster, shrimp, scallops, and mussels served in a light garlic sauce with vegetables, while the New York strip is first seared to seal in the juices, then broiled and served with your choice of béarnaise, Roquefort, or au jus sauce and a baked potato. The Commodore serves dinner nightly, and reservations are recommended. Free parking is available at A&B Marina.

**CONCH REPUBLIC SEAFOOD COMPANY,** 631 Greene St., Key West, FL 33040; (305) 294-4403; conchrepublicseafood.com; Seafood; $–$$. The menu here is heavy on seafood. Entrees include the local favorite jumbo shrimp stuffed with lump crabmeat, wrapped with bacon and served with mango salsa, island rice, and greens. The full-service bar boasts one of the best rum selections around—more than 80 varieties—along with 25 kinds of beer. Check out the 80-foot aquarium stocked with local seafood that is the centerpiece of the restaurant, and don't miss the 1,200-pound antique still that stands behind the bar in honor of the rumrunners of yesteryear. A full menu is available for lunch and dinner daily, and happy hour and live music are offered nightly.

**CROISSANTS DE FRANCE,** 816 Duval St., Key West, FL 33040; (305) 294-2624; croissantsdefrance.com; $. Viva les croissants—and your waistline! Seduction in broad daylight is what awaits you with their pastry selections, which are lovingly created by classically trained pastry chefs. This beloved tiny treasure also dishes up galettes (large, thin, buckwheat flour pancakes served with savory or sweet fillings), quiches, croissants, and sandwiches, like the hot roast beef on a baguette: top round roast beef with caramelized onions, Swiss cheese, lettuce, and au jus on a warm baguette. Croissants de France is open daily for breakfast and lunch.

★**CUBAN COFFEE QUEEN,** 284 Margaret St. and 5 Key Lime Square, Key West, FL 33040; (305) 292-4747; (305) 294-7787; cubancoffeequeen .com; $. With one location adjacent to the Historic Key West Seaport and the other conveniently placed in Old Town, the Cuban Coffee Queen has your Key West coffee needs covered. Both locations house a small takeout spot with limited outdoor seating offering fantastic coffee and breakfast and lunch staples. Order a Cortadito, a double Cuban espresso with cane sugar and topped with steamed milk. Then pair it with the Key Wester breakfast sandwich: two eggs, American cheese, and your choice of ham, bacon, sausage, or pork roll on pressed Cuban bread. Sandwiches, smoothies, and salads are also on offer. Cuban Coffee Queen is open for breakfast and lunch daily, serving from 6:30 a.m. until sunset.

> **i** The beautifully painted Key West mural on the side of the wall at the Cuban Coffee Queen Margaret Street location is reminiscent of a vintage postcard, making it the perfect place to get a great Key West vacation photo.

★**DION'S QUICK MART,** 1127 Truman Ave., Key West, FL 33040; (305) 294-7572; dionsbest.com; Southern; $. Locals turn to Dion's Quick Mart for everything from gas for their car to bread, milk, magazines, and the best fried chicken you have ever tasted. Don't be turned off by the fact that you are buying fried chicken in a gas station. Do what the locals do and grab a box of fried chicken to take out on the boat or for a beachside picnic at Fort Zach. Call ahead for large orders. Two additional locations in Key West are at 3228 Flagler Ave. (305-294-4574) and 5350 US 1 on Stock Island (305-296-9901).

**EL MESON DE PEPE,** 410 Wall St., Key West, FL 33040; (305) 295-2620; elmesondepepe.com; Cuban; $$. Situated just off Mallory Square, El Meson de Pepe draws a large post-sunset crowd. A salsa band plays nightly as the sun sinks into the Gulf of Mexico, which adds to the festive and welcoming atmosphere. Look for Cuban-Conch classics on the menu: Mollete a la Pancho; Cuban bread stuffed with picadillo, a spicy combination of ground beef, capers, raisins, olives, and seasonings; and *ropa vieja* (shredded beef). Quench your thirst with Pepe's Lemonade, a refreshing cocktail made with Bacardi Limon, cranberry, and orange juice. El Meson de Pepe is open for breakfast, lunch, and dinner daily. Large groups are welcome, and reservations are appreciated.

★**EL SIBONEY,** 900 Catherine St., Key West, FL 33040; (305) 296-4184 or (305) 743-9090; elsiboneyrestaurant.com; Cuban; $$. A cascade of bilingual chatter washes over the enthusiastic diners at El Siboney, an informal restaurant specializing in Cuban cuisine. Portions are enormous here. You'll find myriad Cuban twists with beef, including the popular *ropa vieja* and *boliche* (Cuban pot roast). Crab, shrimp, and chicken all get the wonderful Cuban garlic treatment, and you can order paella for two. You can also choose from an array of sandwiches or sides of tamales, yucca, black beans, platanos, and tostones. For a cocktail with a kick, try the homemade sangria, and for dessert (if you have room), try the rice pudding, flan, or natilla. El Siboney is open daily for lunch and dinner.

★**5 BROTHERS,** 930 Southard St., Key West, FL 33040; (305) 296-5205; 5brothersgrocery.tripod.com; $. If you're headed downtown along Southard Street any weekday morning between 6 and 8 a.m., expect to encounter a traffic jam at the corner of Grinnell Street. It's just the locals pulling over to pick up their "fix" at 5 Brothers, which has been serving this island for more than 30 years. This is where Key West goes for bucci, that tiny cup of industrial-strength Cuban coffee that satisfies your caffeine habit with a single swig. This little corner grocery also makes a mean Cuban mix—a combination ham, pork, salami, Swiss, lettuce, and pickle sandwich served on Cuban bread. 5 Brothers is cash only.

**GOLDMAN'S BAGEL, SALAD AND SANDWICH DELI, OVERSEAS MARKET,** 2796 N. Roosevelt Blvd., Key West, FL 33040; (305) 294-3354; goldmansdeli.com; $. At this wildly popular full-service restaurant-deli in the Overseas Market, the hot corned beef and pastrami sandwiches are sliced thin and piled high in traditional deli style, the bagels are baked fresh daily, and the potato salad is tops. You can carry out such delicacies as chopped liver, potato knishes, smoked whitefish, and kosher franks, along with the bagels and an array of flavored cream cheeses sold by the pound. Breakfast and lunch are served daily at tables and at the counter. Deli platters and catering are also available.

**THE GRAND CAFE,** 314 Duval St., Key West, FL 33040; (305) 292-4740; grandcafekeywest.com; Contemporary American; $$. Sit on the patio overlooking Duval Street or inside in the air-conditioning among vibrant artwork by local artists. Start with the carpaccio of beef tenderloin, served with shaved Parmesan cheese, red onions, capers, arugula, and white truffle oil, or the bruschetta, crostini piled high with chopped Roma tomatoes and basil pesto. The lunch menu offers crunchy paninis, hot pressed sandwiches served with a small salad of mixed greens with the amazing house vinaigrette dressing. The Grand Cafe prides itself on excellent wine selections and simply grand martinis, and is open for lunch and dinner daily. Reservations are recommended.

**HALF SHELL RAW BAR,** 231 Margaret St., Key West, FL 33040; (305) 294-7496; halfshellrawbar.com; Seafood; $–$$. The Half Shell Raw Bar is inches from the water and beyond casual. Located at the Key West Historic Seaport, the restaurant is known for local seafood. Expect oysters, clams, shrimp, and stone crabs that are simply prepared, reasonably priced, and served with plastic utensils on paper plates at picnic tables. The full bar offers beer, wine, and frozen drinks. Patrons may opt for outdoor dining on the patio. Reservations are accepted for parties of more than six. Half Shell Raw Bar is open daily for lunch and dinner. Off-street parking is abundant.

**HARBOURVIEW CAFÉ,** Pier House Resort; 1 Duval St., Key West, FL 33040; (305) 296-4600; pierhouse.com; Seafood; $$. Located in the Pier House Resort (see the Accommodations chapter), the menu is full-blown "Floribbean" with all the trimmings. The restaurant lives up to its name with the stunning views of Key West Harbor. Dine inside or out on the harbor and get your taste buds in gear with the white conch chowder—it will make you melt right into your entree of sautéed herb-crusted yellowtail snapper with a shrimp garnish served over Parmesan risotto with lemon caper sauce or the New York strip, served with port wine demi, garlic mashed potato, and seasonal vegetables. The HarbourView serves breakfast, lunch, and dinner daily.

If you like to choose a restaurant by its bill of fare, grab a copy of *The Menu*. This quarterly restaurant guide, published by the *Key West Citizen*, features menus from more than 45 Key West eateries. You'll find free copies at hotels, attractions, grocery stores, and newsstands all around Key West. You can also visit their website: keywestmenu.com.

★HARPOON HARRY'S, 832 Caroline St., Key West, FL 33040; (305) 294-8744; harpoonharryskeywest.com; Classic American; $. Located across from Key West Historic Seaport, Harpoon Harry's ecletic decor combines Tiffany light fixtures with sleds, carousel horses, and antique toy cars. The restaurant's movie-star wall boasts Elvis, Sophia, and Lucy and Desi. The luncheon menu at Harpoon Harry's is much less eccentric than the decor: Daily blue plate specials consist of baked meat loaf or chicken potpie made from scratch. Breakfast is highlighted by Harry's Special: two extra large eggs, two pieces of sausage and bacon, ham, toast, and jelly served with home fries or grits. Two counters, booths, and tables are available daily for breakfast, lunch, and dinner. Cash only. Reservations are not accepted.

★HELP YOURSELF, 829 Fleming St., Key West, FL 33040; (305) 296-7766; helpyourselffoods.com; $. Eating healthy is the way to go, and folks come here for the best in natural and organic eats. No dairy, refined sugars, or bad fats allowed, and the line outside the door proves one thing: People are helping themselves. Help Yourself is a combined shop, cafe, and juice bar that also offers juice and raw-food detox programs. Organic fruit smoothies like the Happy Monkey, made with banana, peanut butter, coconut milk, and coconut palm sugar, and organic juices like the Green Immunity with cucumber, celery, kale, green apple, broccoli, and garlic are both hugely popular. A wide selection of wraps and salads are also available. Open daily for breakfast and lunch.

HOGFISH BAR AND GRILL, 6810 Front St., Stock Island, FL 33040; (305) 293-4041; hogfishbar.com; Seafood; $$. One of the last frontiers of true Keys hangouts, Hogfish Bar and Grill is where the locals go and the fishing boat captains congregate—if you can find it. To get there, take US 1 North out of Key West and across the Cow Key Channel Bridge. At the third stoplight, bear to the right and onto MacDonald Avenue. Follow this for approximately 1 mile and make a right on Fourth Avenue. Take your next left on Front Street and drive almost to the end—you'll see the Hogfish Bar and Grill on the right. Once you are there, belly up to a picnic table and order the signature Hogfish

"Killer" sandwich, which is a fish sandwich smothered with onions and mushrooms on freshly baked Cuban bread. Open daily for lunch and dinner.

**HOG'S BREATH SALOON, 400 Front St., Key West, FL 33040; (305) 296-4222; hogsbreath.com/keywest/; Classic American; $.** Here, nautical charts of Caribbean waters are lacquered onto wooden tables, and patrons dine indoors or outside on a brick patio from which large trees sprout. In addition to the favorite fish sandwich served blackened or grilled with lemon, Hog's Breath's smoked-fish dolphin dip is extremely popular. The restaurant's full-service bar features the medium-bodied Hog's Breath beer, brewed in the Midwest. The name of the joint comes from an old saying of the owner's grandmother, that "hog's breath is better than no breath at all." Hog's Breath is open for lunch and dinner, and live bands play throughout the day and evening. Reservations are not accepted.

**HOT TIN ROOF, Ocean Key Resort, Zero Duval St., Key West, FL 33040; (305) 296-7701 or (800) 328-9815; oceankey.com; Contemporary American; $$–$$$.** The Hot Tin Roof name comes from Tennessee Williams's (a past resident of Key West) most famous play, *Cat on a Hot Tin Roof.* The dining room and outdoor deck enjoy panoramic views of Key West Harbor and its famed sunset. The chef has combined elements of South American, Asian, and French cuisine in an interpretation of flavors and attitudes of Key West he calls "Conch-fusion." Prime examples include the scallop piccata with pappardelle pasta and tomatoes or the caramelized grouper served with coconut, corn, poblano, and carrots. Hot Tin Roof is open for breakfast, lunch, and dinner daily.

**HURRICANE HOLE WATERFRONT BAR AND SEAFOOD GRILL, MM 4.5 Oceanside, 5130 Overseas Hwy., Stock Island, FL 33040; (305) 294-0200; hurricaneholekeywest.com; Classic American; $.** Situated upon pilings overlooking Cow Key Channel, the location may look informal because it is inside the Hurricane Hole Marina compound, but what awaits the diner is one great meal. The atmosphere and dress code are Keys-comfortable. The menu is varied enough that it will please everyone's palate. The appetizers range from peel-and-eat shrimp to chicken tenders to bruschetta. The fish of the day is served numerous different ways, but the most popular entrees include the fish-and-chips. Hurricane Hole is open for lunch and dinner daily, with happy hour specials.

**JIMMY BUFFETT'S MARGARITAVILLE CAFÉ, 500 Duval St., Key West, FL 33040; (305) 292-1435, margaritavillekeywest.com; Classic American; $$.** Lunch really could last forever at Jimmy Buffett's Margaritaville Cafe, and patrons who frequent this place quite often remain throughout much of the day. Margaritas are de rigueur and made fresh per order with Margaritaville tequila. "Parrothead" and other island music plays in the background, and decorations include oversize props from stage settings of Buffett tours. The burger fixin's—lettuce and tomato, Heinz 57, and french-fried potatoes—are not forgotten. Margaritaville is open for lunch and dinner daily. Live music is offered nightly, beginning at 10:30 p.m. Reservations are not accepted, but those on the waiting list may shop for souvenirs in Buffett's adjacent store.

**KELLY'S CARIBBEAN BAR, GRILL & BREWERY, 301 Whitehead St., Key West, FL 33040; (305) 293-8484; kellyskeywest.com; Classic American; $.** Named after actress Kelly McGillis, this Caribbean restaurant is on the site of the original Pan American World Airways offices. Outdoor dining is available on a stone patio with gardens. Among the house specialties here are the whole yellowtail snapper, flash-fried and served with a citrus-chili drizzle, and braised beef short ribs, served with roasted root vegetables in a Young's Chocolate Stout gravy. Kelly's Caribbean also is home to the Southernmost Brewery, which whips up an all-natural selection including Key West Golden Ale, Havana Red Ale, and Southern Clipper Wheat Beer. The restaurant is open for lunch and dinner 7 days a week.

★**KOJIN NOODLE BAR, 502 Southard St., Key West, FL 33040; (305) 296-2077; $$.** Kojin is definitely on the locals' top-ten list of favorite places to dine. This tiny noodle bar offers traditional noodle bowls that are large in flavor and portion size. Insider tip: Half portions of most noodle dishes are not on the menu, but are available if you ask your server. Start with the house-made steamed buns, available with pork belly or tofu, and served with pickled cucumber, scallion, and hoisin sauce. Then make sure to check out the special board, as off-menu dishes like the red curry shrimp and the Saigon salad are both local favorites. A selection of sake, beer, and wine is also on offer. Kojin is open daily for lunch and dinner.

**LA TE DA, 1125 Duval St., Key West, FL 33040; (305) 296-6706; lateda .com; $$.** La Te Da is a combination hotel, cabaret, restaurant, and bar that has been an icon of the Key West party scene since 1978. The main building has been a landmark in Key West since Cuban revolutionary José Martí made it his residence in America. They not only offer a bar that faces lively Duval Street, but also live entertainment in their Cabaret Lounge. There is also a Terrace Bar overlooking the beautiful tropical pool. With the great island drinks and delicious food being served here, you may find it difficult to leave. La Te Da serves breakfast, lunch, and dinner daily.

★**LATITUDES, Sunset Key, boat docked at 245 Front St., Key West, FL 33040; (305) 294-4000; sunsetkeycottages.com/latitudes-key-west; Contemporary American; $$$$.** When you think of dining seaside somewhere on a secluded island, this is the kind of place that comes to mind. Just 5 minutes across the water from the hustle and bustle of Mallory Square, Latitudes might just as well be half a world away. It is that peaceful, that serene. Launches for Sunset Key leave regularly throughout the day from the pier at the Westin Key West Resort and Marina at 245 Front Street. If you are not living or staying on the island, you must make a reservation for your meal at Latitudes with the Westin concierge to secure a boarding pass. Latitudes is open daily for breakfast, lunch, and dinner.

**LA TRATTORIA, 524 Duval St. and 3593 S. Roosevelt Blvd., Key West, FL 33040; (305) 296-1075; (305) 296-2345; latrattoria.us; Italian; $$$.** A romantic taste of old Italy favored by locals, visitors, and Keys residents from as far away as Key Largo, La Trattoria redefines the traditional pasta, veal, chicken, lamb, and seafood dishes of the mother country. Try Agnello alla Griglia (lamb with fresh rosemary) or Cheese Tortellina alla Romana, with smoked ham and peas in a parmigiana cream sauce. Penne Arrabbiata, quill-shaped pasta, delivers a bit of a bite, and the traditional Linguine e Vongole does not disappoint. La Trattoria serves dinner nightly at both locations, and reservations are suggested. After dinner at the Duval Street location, retire to Virgilio's, the charming little cocktail lounge with live music just around the corner.

★**LOUIE'S BACKYARD, 700 Waddell Ave., Key West, FL 33040; (305) 294-1061; louiesbackyard.com; Contemporary American; $$$.** Louie's Backyard combines island manor-house ambience with cutting-edge cuisine. A sweeping veranda for outdoor dining overlooks Louie's "backyard," which is actually a prime piece of Atlantic oceanfront property. In the 1970s this spot was a favorite with next-door neighbor Jimmy Buffett, who often played for his supper. For lunch, try the Not Just Any Fish Sandwich served with potato chips they make every morning. A dinner favorite is the sautéed Key West shrimp with bacon, mushrooms, and stone-ground grits. Louie's Backyard serves lunch and dinner daily. Reservations are recommended. The Afterdeck outdoor oceanside bar is the locals' favorite place for a sundowner and is open all day and into the wee hours.

> **i** Hunter S. Thompson, an American journalist and author famous for his flamboyant writing style known as "gonzo journalism," lived in the Keys for part of his life. One of his favorite haunts was Louie's Backyard restaurant.

**MANGIA MANGIA, 900 Southard St., Key West, FL 33040; (305) 294-2469; mangia-mangia.com; Italian; $$.** Meaning "eat, eat" in Italian, Mangia

Mangia offers a plethora of homemade fresh pasta (made daily on the premises with semolina and fresh eggs) and finely seasoned sauces. You can always order the basic sauces—marinara, Alfredo, pesto, meat, and red or white seafood—but for something out of the ordinary, try Bollito Misto di Mare: pappardelle with fresh scallops, shrimp, conch, salmon, mussels, and mahimahi in a garlic white-wine clam sauce. Outdoor seating is delightful where the patio area is enclosed with palm trees and flowers. Mangia Mangia serves dinner daily and offers beer and wine.

**MARTIN'S, 917 Duval St., Key West, FL 33040; (305) 296-0111; martins keywest.com; German; $$.** Martin's has taken its expansive German menu with its island flair and shines bright on upper Duval Street. You'll find classic German dishes such as sauerbraten with spaetzle and red cabbage, and Wiener schnitzel, but Martin's also prepares island seafood creations *à la deutsch*. Yellowtail snapper is encrusted with almonds, flambéed with cognac, and served with a medley of vegetables and wild rice. Choose from a large selection of fine German wines and beers or one of the signature cocktails, like the espresso martini. Martin's serves lunch and dinner, and offers Sunday brunch with dining indoors or out in their tropical garden. Reservations are suggested.

**MICHAEL'S, 532 Margaret St., Key West, FL 33040; (305) 295-1300; michaelskeywest.com; Contemporary American; $$$$.** Located in Old Town, several blocks off Duval, is this casual yet elegant local favorite. Owners Melanie and Michael Wilson have been serving up some of the best food on the island for more than 15 years. Michael, the former corporate chef for Morton's Steakhouses, knows how to cook a piece of beef. His prime beef, rubbed with roasted garlic and Roquefort, is not to be missed. The menu also includes seafood and pasta specialties, and a good selection of fondues is available in the Garden Bar. There is a full bar with a martini menu. Michael's is open nightly for dinner. Reservations are recommended for both indoor and outdoor seating.

★**MR. Z'S, 501 Southard St., or 2798 North Roosevelt Blvd., Key West, FL 33040; (305) 296-4445; mrzskeywest.com; Italian; $.** Mr. Z's serves up Philly-style Italian-American food fast. This is Mr. Z's claim to fame in Key West: If you have an urge for a cheesesteak at 3 a.m. or pizza at midnight, one call will curb your craving, as Mr. Z's is open nightly until 4 a.m. Locals don't consider an order complete if it doesn't contain cheese fries. Dieters beware! At the Old Town location, eat on one of the few bar stools, or take it to go. There is also free delivery in Old Town, and the more expansive New Town location delivers to Key West, Stock Island, and Key Haven as well. Open daily for lunch and dinner. Cash only.

**NINE ONE FIVE,** 915 Duval St., Key West, FL 33040; (305) 296-0669; 915duval.com; Contemporary American; $$$. Nine one five is housed in a stately Victorian home right on Duval Street. Choose a table on the wraparound porch and people-watch while you dine. Try the tuna dome made with Dungeness crab with a lemon miso dressing, wrapped with sushi-grade ahi tuna, and don't miss the Devils on Horseback—bacon-wrapped dates stuffed with sweet garlic and served with a ginger-soy dipping sauce. And for dessert, how about an artisan cheese plate replete with fresh Florida honeycomb? Postdinner, head upstairs to Point 5 and relax in the hip atmosphere with a full bar and light bites on the menu. Open nightly for dinner. Reservations suggested.

**OLD TOWN MEXICAN CAFE,** 609 Duval St., Key West, FL 33040; (305) 296-7500; oldtownmexicancafe.com; Mexican; $$. Have a seat in the open-air dining room right on Duval Street or inside, tucked back away from the crowds. No matter where you sit, you are in for a fiesta of flavor. It all starts with the salsa. The freshly made salsa is so good here that when heading back to the mainland, locals first stop by Fausto's—the local grocery store that carries Old Town Mexican Cafe salsa by the pint—for the perfect hostess gift. But the salsa isn't the only reason to stop in. Authentic dishes like the tortilla soup and the enchiladas verdes keep locals coming back, along with the inventive veggie plates. Old Town Mexican Cafe is open for lunch and dinner daily.

**ORIGAMI JAPANESE RESTAURANT,** 1075 Duval St., Key West, FL 33040; (305) 294-0092; Japanese; $$. Like the Japanese art of folding paper into decorative or representational forms—origami—this restaurant fashions fresh, local seafood into exquisite sushi and sashimi. The dragon roll must not be missed. Origami also offers traditional Japanese cuisine, such as teriyaki, chicken katsu, steak yakiniku, and tempura. Sit at the cafe-style tables or at the sushi bar and watch the masters at work. Beer, wine, and sake are served. Origami is situated in Duval Square. Free parking is available in the adjoining lot off Simonton Street. Origami is open for dinner daily, and reservations are suggested.

**PEPE'S CAFÉ & STEAK HOUSE,** 806 Caroline St., Key West, FL 33040; (305) 294-7192; pepeskeywest.com; Classic American; $$. Billed as the "Eldest Eating House in the Florida Keys, established 1909," Pepe's is beloved by locals. Options include oysters served raw or baked, New York strip steaks, filet mignon, pork chops, even barbecue. And Pepe's burgers sound as intriguing as they taste: White Collar Burger, Blue Collar Burger, Slit Ray Burger, and Patty Melt. Be sure to try a margarita here (the lime juice is squeezed fresh) and, for dessert, the brownie pie, served warm with ice cream—ask for Cuban coffee flavor instead of vanilla. The restaurant is open every day for breakfast, lunch, and dinner. Reservations are not accepted.

**PISCES,** 1007 Simonton St., Key West, FL 33040; (305) 294-7100; pisces keywest.com; Seafood; $$$. At this enduring tropical French establishment, creativity culminates in such delicacies as the Lobster Tango Mango—lobster flambéed in cognac with shrimp in saffron butter, mango, and basil—and roast half duckling served with raspberry sauce. Other favorite menu items include the yellowtail snapper Atocha, sautéed in lemon brown butter with shrimp and scallops, and the pan-roasted halibut, served with chive clam butter, jumbo lump crab, poached oysters, and applewood-smoked slab bacon. The extensive wine list features some of the best of the vineyards of France and California. Pisces is open daily for dinner only, and reservations are recommended.

**PRIME STEAKHOUSE,** 951 Caroline St., Key West, FL 33040; (305) 296-4000; primekeywest.com; Steak House; $$$. The ambience of Prime Steakhouse includes tables covered with crisp white linen cloths and tall drinking vessels. The staff is dressed all in black, and the hushed atmosphere takes everyone down about two notches. Even though Prime has a limited menu, each and every selection is superb. They offer a local seafood special prepared Keys style, and their steak selections are outstanding. One of the favorite house specialties is home-fried potatoes that are mashed and then fried. Desserts are homemade key lime pie with a graham cracker piecrust and a chocolate cake that is worth the calories. Prime Steakhouse is open daily for dinner, and reservations are recommended.

**ROOF TOP CAFE,** 308 Front St., Key West, FL 33040; (305) 294-2042; rooftopcafekeywest.com; Contemporary American; $$$. High amid the treetops, the Roof Top Cafe bustles with dining activity, but the atmosphere remains unhurried and removed from the fray. Diners may sit on a second-floor balcony, which extends on two sides of the building, under the canopy of ancient leafy trees. Inside, ceiling fans mounted on the white vaulted ceiling gently move the air about the open-air, pavilion-style dining room. Dinner creations have included grilled ancho-rubbed mahimahi served with yucca frites and a coconut curry aioli, as well as grilled duck breast with a port-fig demi-glace, served with gorgonzola mashed potato. Rooftop Cafe is open daily for breakfast, lunch, and dinner. Reservations are recommended.

**THE RUSTY ANCHOR SEAFOOD RESTAURANT,** MM 5 Oceanside, 5510 Third Ave., Stock Island, FL 33040; rustyanchor.com; (305) 294-5369; Seafood; $$. The seafood here is fresh, for in the back of the Rusty Anchor is a commercial seafood market that supplies many of Key West's restaurants. The restaurant holds rope-edged tables, wooden buoys, nautical art prints, and photographs of the fishing fleets of old Key West. Pan-fried yellowtail is their specialty, but make sure to try the teriyaki-grilled tuna sandwich on Cuban bread if it is offered as a special. If seafood is not your favorite, Rusty Anchor also serves burgers, steaks, and ribs. Open Mon through Sat for lunch and dinner, the Rusty Anchor does not require reservations. It's a great place to bring the kids.

**SALUTE! ON THE BEACH,** 1000 Atlantic Blvd., Key West, FL 33040; (305) 292-1117; saluteonthebeach.com; Italian; $$. To "see" Salute is to "see" the "sea," as it is located right smack dab on Higgs Beach with the Atlantic Ocean as your front yard. Salute serves yummy seafood and great Italian choices, like the antipasti platter and the calamari sautéed in marinara. The linguini with mussels, white wine, and butter is also a favorite menu item, as are the mussels steamed in white wine, lemon, and garlic. And don't miss the homemade ice-cream cookie sandwich! But perhaps the best part of this place is the free show that goes on at the beach in front of you. Salute is open daily for lunch and dinner.

★**SANDY'S CAFÉ,** 1026 White St., Key West, FL 33040; (305) 295-0159; kwsandyscafe.com; Cuban; $. Lodged in the same building as the popular M & M Laundry, this hole-in-the-wall Cuban walk-up joint is one of the best places in the Keys for authentic Cuban "fast food." The lines outside the order windows (with a few bar stools available for seating) indicate how loyal Sandy's customers are. The café con leche, cheese tostada, and Cuban mix sandwiches will have you clamoring for more. Sandy's is open 24 hours a day and delivery is available until midnight in Old Town. No credit cards . . . this is cash and carry only. *Bueno! Bueno!*

**SANTIAGO'S BODEGA,** 207 Petronia St., Key West, FL 33040; (305) 296-7691; santiagosbodega.com; Tapas; $$$. Tucked away on a small street with a neighborhood setting is Santiago's Bodega. Wooden floors, warm colors, and wide-open windows looking out onto a porch for dining under gossamer lanterns capture the setting for this unique tapas experience. The food is fresh and simple with more than 30 selections on the menu, including soups and salads. Smoked salmon carpaccio, fresh yellowfin ceviche, and the local-favorite beef tenderloin topped with blue cheese are on offer. There are also loads of vegetarian dishes. Wine, beer, lovely sherry, and ports are also served. Open daily for lunch and dinner, and reservations are recommended.

**SARABETH'S,** 530 Simonton St., Key West, FL 33040; (305) 293-8181; sarabethskeywest.com; Contemporary American; $$$. There is a real Sarabeth, and she is an award-winning jam maker, pastry chef, and restaurateur. Not only does her "empire" include locations in New York City and Key West, but her legendary spreadable fruits and pastries can be purchased on her website as well as in her establishments. The menus include from-scratch pancakes, salads, sandwiches, meat loaf, grilled meats, and fish. Seating, indoors or out, in this historic 19th-century clapboard building is a wonderful way to make a Keys memory. Sarabeth's is open for breakfast and lunch Wed through Fri, brunch Sat and Sun, and dinner Wed through Sun. Reservations are suggested.

★**SEVEN FISH,** 632 Olivia St., Key West, FL 33040; (305) 296-2777; 7fish.com; Seafood; $$. Although the seafood here is excellent, this restaurant, located at the corner of Olivia and Elizabeth Streets, has much more to recommend it. In addition to fresh fish, the menu also includes grilled banana chicken, meat loaf with mashed potatoes, and a New York strip steak cooked the way you like it. Salads—Three Cheese Caesar, mixed greens with balsamic vinegar, or roasted red pepper and goat cheese—are available in two sizes. Seven Fish is small—go early or you may have to wait—and the tables are quite close together. The restaurant is open for dinner every night of the week except for Tues. Reservations are recommended.

**SQUARE ONE,** 1075 Duval St., Key West, FL 33040; (305) 296-4300; squareonekeywest.com; Gastropub; $$$. Square One's New American cuisine includes ethnic twists on old standbys, incorporating influences from Latin America, the Mediterranean, and Asia by using seasonal produce, exotic spices, and homemade condiments. Standouts include the Shanghai-style fried calamari with chili-honey-garlic sauce, and the pork potsticker with pineapple-hoisin sauce. Wine, craft beer, and cocktails are all on offer, and many menu choices are gluten-free. Square One serves brunch Wed through Sun, is open Mon through Sat for happy hour and dinner, and has free parking in the Duval Square parking lot, the entrance to which is on Simonton Street.

**THAI CUISINE,** 513 Greene St., Key West, FL 33040; (305) 294-9424; keywestthaicuisine.com; Thai; $. Thai curry is actually a cooking method, not an ingredient. Together with spices, herbs, and aromatic vegetables, hot chile peppers are ground into a dry paste. At the same time, coconut milk, fish sauce, sugar, and kaffir lime leaves—ubiquitous to every variation of Thai red and green curry—confuse the palate with a riot of sweet-and-sour sensory stimuli. For a traditional delight, try the pad thai, spicy rice noodles sautéed with shrimp, chicken, and egg. Enjoy a selection of Thai and Japanese beers, house wines, plum wine, and sake. Thai Cuisine serves lunch Mon through Fri, is open for dinner nightly, and offers free delivery in Key West.

★**THAI ISLAND,** Garrison Bight Marina, 711 Palm Ave., Key West, FL 33040; (305) 296-9198; thaiislandrestaurant.com; Thai; $. Located at the foot of the bridge in the historic Garrison Bight, Thai Island has become a favorite of locals. Dine on their rooftop patio overlooking the bight as the boats come in with their catches of the day. Start with the tasty Tom Kha Gai or Tom Kha Tofu soup, sour coconut milk blended with chicken or tofu, mushrooms, lemongrass, scallions, and galanga root. Then opt for one of four different kinds of curry with your choice of seafood, beef, chicken, pork, or tofu that promises to be as spicy as you dare. Thai Island is open daily for lunch and dinner, with free parking at Garrison Bight Marina.

**TURTLE KRAALS RESTAURANT AND BAR,** 231 Margaret St., Key West, FL 33040; (305) 294-2640; turtlekraals.com; Classic American & Southern; $$. Turtle Kraals occupies the site of a former turtle cannery, hence the name—which essentially means "turtle pen." Make sure to try the ceviche, served five ways, or the housemade chorizo and goat cheese empanadas with a golden raisin chipotle sauce. Then move on to the locally caught yellowtail snapper served with sautéed Cuban-style black beans, grilled pineapple, and pineapple mojo. Dine inside in the dockside air-conditioned restaurant or upstairs at the Tower Bar while watching the sun as it sets over the Key West Seaport. Turtle Kraals has a full bar and is open daily for lunch and dinner and Sat and Sun for breakfast.

★ **2¢,** 416 Appelrouth Ln., Key West, FL 33040; (305) 414-8626; 2centskw .com; Gastropub; $. James Beard–honored chef Chris Otten (who also created the local favorite, Bad Boy Burrito) has partnered with Chris Shultz, the mastermind behind the local bar hangout, the Porch. Together, the two Chrises have created 2¢, Key West's first gastropub and beer garden, and it is a major hit with the locals. The lights are usually low, emanating from metallic chandeliers that are more sculptural than traditional, and the place is typically humming with locals and travelers alike. Grab a table indoors or out in the garden area and order the tacos of the day, or shishito peppers along with a Bell's Two Hearted IPA or other craft beer or glass of wine.

## BARS

Sometimes, you just need a drink. If an establishment offers food as well as cocktails, you can find it in our restaurant section, and if it offers live music, you can find it in our Entertainment section. See below for those just focusing on serving up a cold beverage (or four). We encourage you to have fun and enjoy our casual Keys pubs and restaurants, but keep in mind that the DUI limit here is 0.08 percent, less than some other states. Remember, too, that driving-under-the-influence laws apply to all vehicles—scooters, boats, and bikes included. So if you drink, don't drive. Or pedal. Take a cab, or take along a designated driver. In Key West, you can request a cab with a bike rack at no extra charge. If you are on foot, pedicabs are a good alternative to transporting yourself, and you can usually flag one down in Key West without any hassle.

RESTAURANTS

★**CHART ROOM BAR**, Pier House Resort, 1 Duval St., Key West, FL 33040; (305) 296-4600 or (800) 327-8340; pierhouse.com. You want to experience a slice of Key West history? Step into this tiny bar located in the Pier House Resort and you will be stepping back in time. Tom Corcoran, author of the popular Alex Rutledge Key West mystery series, used to tend bar here while Jimmy Buffett played for tips. The bar has changed little since then, and the bartender can usually regale you with many a story about the duo.

**DONS' PLACE**, 1000 Truman Ave., Key West, FL 33040; donsplacekeywest .com. Opened in 1998 by two friends named Don, Dons' Place is made up of an inside air-conditioned bar, an outside tiki bar, and a liquor store, replete with a drive-up window. In addition Dons' has 19 TVs for game-watching, a pool table, dartboard, and outdoor games like corn hole, Ping-Pong, and foosball.

**FAT TUESDAY**, 305 Duval St., Key West, FL 33040; (305) 296-9373; fat tuesdaykeywest.com. Stop in at Fat Tuesday and choose from one of 26 flavors of frozen drinks, including margaritas, piña coladas, and 190-octane rum runners. Our favorite is the Pain in the Ass, a combination piña colada and rum runner. The motto here is "One daiquiri, two daiquiri, three daiquiri, floor," and you can even buy a T-shirt that says just that.

★**THE OTHER SIDE**, 429 Caroline St., Key West, FL 33040; (305) 517-6358; theothersidekw.com. Located behind door number 1 in the historic Porter Mansion, The Other Side is serious about cocktails. Head straight to their marble-topped bar for an Old Fashioned made the old-fashioned way: by muddling an Italian sour black cherry and a Florida orange with sugar and Angostura bitters before adding double-aged Jim Beam Black whiskey and serving it over one giant ice cube. As you wait for your cocktail, make sure to admire the amazing black-and-white photography by famed local photographer Michael Marrero.

★**POINT 5**, 915 Duval St., Key West, FL 33040; (305) 296-0669; 915duval .com. In its lofty aerie above the chic nine one five restaurant, the decor at Point 5 only enhances the drinks. The walls, ceilings, and floors are covered in fabulous Dade County pine, and the second-floor porch beckons you with its cool breezes: Submit to a cheese plate from the bar menu while relaxing at your table on the open-air porch overlooking Duval Street.

★**THE PORCH**, 429 Caroline St., Key West, FL 33040; (305) 517-6358; theporchkw.com. Locals head to The Porch, located behind door number 2 in the beautiful Porter Mansion on Caroline and Duval, for craft beers on tap and wine by the glass or bottle. Seasonal selections and popular events like regular wine tastings, costume parties, and DJ nights are also part of the fun. Beers on tap rotate, but typically include Chimay Blonde Trappist Ale, Magic Hat #9, and Shipyard Export Ale, among others.

> **i** If you can't wait until "it's five o'clock somewhere" for alcohol, in Key West there are two bars that open with the sunrise. Schooner Wharf Bar has a "Breakfast Club" where regulars show up at 8 a.m. for a beer buzz rather than coffee. Over at Dons' Place, at 7 a.m. you can have an espresso martini made with vodka, Kahlua, Tia Maria, and, oh, I almost forgot, coffee.

**SCHOONER WHARF BAR,** 202 William St., Key West, FL 33040; schooner wharf.com. Locals head to this open-air bar and restaurant for great live music and to attend one of the numerous special events throughout the year, like the Lighted Boat Parade, the Chili Cook-off, and the Battle of the Bars, a competition to benefit Key West charities during which members of the service industry race through bar-themed obstacle courses.

**VIRGILIO'S,** 524 Duval St., Key West, FL 33040; (305) 296-8118; virgilios keywest.com. This fun little New York–style bar is not really on Duval; it's actually situated on Appelrouth Lane, just around the corner from La Trattoria, one of Key West's best Italian eateries (see the Restaurants chapter). Martinis and their cousins—Gibsons, Manhattans, and Cosmopolitans—are the specialty here, and on "Martini Mondays" you can pay just $5 for one. Grab a seat at the bar or in one of the overstuffed easy chairs while you sip your cocktail and listen to live music from some of Key West's finest musical talent.

# Specialty Foods, Cafes & Markets

Here in the Florida Keys, we think our fish is pretty special. It's certainly the freshest—sometimes only minutes from line to linen. Its pedigree is elite; most species are not marketed outside South Florida. And the abounding variety of innovative culinary presentations is astounding. When you stop at one of our many seafood markets, you will undoubtedly meet the three royal families of our tropical waters: snapper, hogfish, and dolphin, also known as mahimahi. The famed yellowtail or the equally desirous mangrove or mutton snapper most often represents the moist, sweet snapper dynasty. The firm, mild-flavored hogfish clan competes in popularity with the large-flaked and sweetly moist dolphin fish (not to be confused with the porpoise dolphin, which is a mammal).

You won't want to miss our Florida lobster, a delicacy any way you look at it (see the "Diving for Lobster" Close-up in the Diving & Snorkeling chapter). And if you have never tasted a stone crab claw, you are in for a treat (see the Close-up in this chapter). To round out your palate, we have provided you with a rundown of shops selling specialty foods.

## UPPER KEYS

**BOB'S BUNZ ISLAMORADA RESTAURANT AND BAKERY, MM 81.6 Bayside, 81620 Overseas Hwy., Islamorada, FL 33036; (305) 664-8363; bobsbunz.com.** The banner out front proclaims "best buns in town," and these oversize cinnamon rolls live up to the hype. Topped with cream-cheese icing, the buns are undoubtedly one of the local favorites. Also available are "gooey" or sticky buns, bagels, muffins, scones, croissants, key lime pie, cakes, and cookies, which can be ordered online as well. Bob's Bunz features more than 100 items on their menu, so you won't leave hungry. As you might imagine, this restaurant and bakery is a wildly popular Islamorada breakfast and lunch spot.

**KEY LARGO FISHERIES, MM 99.5 Oceanside, 1313 Ocean Bay Dr., Key Largo, FL 33037; (305) 451-3782 or (800) 432-4358; keylargofisheries .com.** The family-run Key Largo Fisheries ships wholesale to hundreds of clients throughout the country and also offers retail sales at their Key Largo store and via overnight delivery. At Key Largo Fisheries, customers will find choice seafood, including snapper, mahimahi, shrimp, and, in season, Florida lobster

# Close-up

## Florida Stone Crab Claws

Now, Yankees can brag about your blue crabs, and West Coasters may boast of Dungeness. But here in the Florida Keys we crow about crab claws like none other—those of the Florida stone crabs.

The stone crabs, large nonswimming crabs found in deep holes and under rocks in the waters surrounding the Keys, have the unusual ability to release their legs or pincers if caught or when experiencing extreme changes in temperature. The separation always occurs at one of the joints to protect the crab from further injury. What is unique about this situation is that the stone crab regenerates the severed appendage, a feat it can accomplish three or four times during its lifetime. This makes it a renewable resource.

The stone crab's two claws serve distinct purposes: The larger claw, or crusher, is used to hold food and fight predators. The smaller claw, known as the ripper, acts as scissors for cutting food.

The crabs are harvested commercially in the Florida Keys with baited traps. It is illegal in the state of Florida to harvest whole stone crabs. They are one of our most precious resources.

A stone crab claw has a hard, heavy, porcelainlike shell with a black-tipped pincer. Seafood markets sell stone crab claws fully cooked. When cooked, the meat inside the shell is sweet and firm-textured. A mild, sweet odor indicates freshness.

The shells must be cracked before serving. If you plan to eat your stone crab claws within an hour of purchase, have the seafood market crack them for you. It is not recommended that you crack the claws until you are ready to eat them.

Stone crab claws are in season from Oct 15 to May 15. They do not freeze particularly well, but most seafood markets listed in this chapter will ship iced, fresh stone crab claws anywhere in the United States.

and stone crab claws. The conch here is imported from the Bahamas and the West Indies, and the scallops are from Boston.

**THE TRADING POST, MM 81.5 Bayside, 81868 Overseas Hwy., Isla-morada, FL 33036; (305) 664-2571; tradingpostfloridakeys.com.** Family-owned and -operated since 1966, the Trading Post is definitely Islamorada's "super" market. Here you'll discover super grocery selections, supergood deli items, a super meat market with a butcher on hand to help you, super wine offerings, and super hours. The Trading Post is open 24 hours a day, 7 days a week! The store also offers customized catering.

## MIDDLE KEYS

**FISH TALES MARKET & EATERY,** MM 53 Oceanside, 11711 Overseas Hwy., Marathon, FL 33050; (305) 743-9196; floridalobster.com; $$. This tiny eatery offers fish and seafood baskets and sandwiches, along with a few heartier specials daily. Fish Tales will cook, smoke, or ship your catch if you've had a productive day on the water. The well-stocked seafood market offers Key West shrimp, stone crabs, tuna, swordfish, the Keys trio (snapper, grouper, and dolphin), and more. Fish Tales Market will ship seafood anywhere in the US. A choice-grade meat counter offers aged steaks, pork tenderloin, and rack of lamb as well. Fish Tales is closed on Sun.

## LOWER KEYS

★**BABY'S COFFEE,** MM 15 Oceanside, 3180 Overseas Hwy., Saddlebunch Key, FL 33040; (800) 744-9866; babyscoffee.com. Late last century (ca. 1991), Gary and O. T. left New York City looking for a home for their new coffee-roasting company. They set up shop in a small building on Key West's famed Duval Street named "Baby's Place," formerly "Baby" Rodriguez's cantina, where, legend has it, Ernest Hemingway occasionally indulged in shooting craps with the locals. Baby's Coffee grew so large that they had to relocate up the Keys at MM 15, and locals still bike up for some fresh brew. They ship their coffee fresh within 48 hours; it is not vacuum-packed or freeze-dried. You'll find all their Key West roasts, Hawaiian roasts, specialty roasts, flavored coffees, and decaf roasts on their website, and you can buy it by the pound at Fausto's in Key West.

**FANCI SEAFOOD,** MM 22.5 Oceanside, 22290 Overseas Hwy., Cudjoe Key, FL 33042; (305) 745-3887; fanciseafood.com. Shelves and shelves of marinades and seafood sauces will inspire you to try your culinary skills in a new creation when you stop in at Fanci Seafood. The very complete fish and seafood selection brought in by local fishermen lets you choose among the usual Keys finfish (grouper, snapper, and dolphin) and golden crab, stone crab claws, lobster, blue crabs, oysters, and mussels. Fanci Seafood is closed on Sun.

**GOOD FOOD CONSPIRACY,** MM 30.2 Oceanside, 30150 Overseas Hwy., Big Pine Key, FL 33043; (305) 872-3945. A full assortment of health foods, homeopathic remedies, vitamins, organic poultry, and organically grown produce is offered at the Good Food Conspiracy. If you browse the shelves, you'll find interesting specialty foods as well. Part of the Conspiracy is a juice and sandwich bar, which features an "outgoing menu" of healthful selections. In addition to the products and produce, Good Food Conspiracy also houses a holistic health center and even a reverend who performs commitment ceremonies and weddings. Talk about one-stop shopping! Open daily.

**KICKIN' BACK FOOD MART, MM 21.4 Oceanside, 21362 Overseas Hwy., Summerland Key, FL 33042; (305) 745-2528.** Life here in the Keys is really laid-back, so why not our grocery stores? This local oasis is easy on and off US 1, offering beer, wine, lottery tickets, an ATM machine, and limited groceries. You won't have to worry about finding a parking spot at Kickin'—it's a gravel parking pad. Pretty simple. That's the way folks around here like it!

★**MURRAY'S FOOD MARKET, MM 24.5 Oceanside, 24550 Overseas Hwy., Summerland Key, FL 33042; (305) 745-3534.** This familiar landmark is Summerland Key's lifeline for provisions. Murray's sells most all your food and household needs. Murray's—with its wonderful fresh deli selection, meat counter, daily baked breads, and beer and wine—saves all the locals in the area from driving south into Key West or north to Big Pine just for a gallon of milk.

**SUGARLOAF FOOD COMPANY, MM 24 Bayside, 24171 Overseas Hwy., Summerland Key, FL 33042; (305) 744-0631; sugarloaffood.com.** This tiny treasure encased in a sunny yellow building is bright and upbeat with goodness galore. Grab a corned beef and Swiss sandwich: house-cured brisket, which is sliced, then steamed, served with Swiss cheese, deli mustard, and Mama Nellie's Famous Slaw on hand-sliced rye bread. Then choose a sweet treat from their extensive in-house bakery before you hit the road.

## KEY WEST

**COFFEE PLANTATION, 713 Caroline St., Key West, FL 33040; (305) 295-9808; coffeeplantationkeywest.com.** This is a great place to enjoy delicious coffee, smoothies, or frappes with light bites like bagels and pastries. They also offer computers with Internet access. Rates and services are reasonable, and the staff is most helpful. The cozy ambience with local art hanging on the walls makes this an inviting stop.

★**COLE'S PEACE ARTISAN BAKERY, 1111 Eaton St., Key West, FL 33040; (305) 292-0703; colespeace.com.** Long a favorite with locals, Cole's Peace Artisan Bakery will become your favorite too. Everything here is authentic, from their famous Cuban bread and honey-walnut cream cheese to their original Ciabatta-Lotta sandwich. For a quick (but fabulous) breakfast, load up on the addictive café con leche and try any one (or four) of the assorted scones, muffins, and sticky buns on offer.

**CORK & STOGIE, 1218 Duval St., Key West, FL 33040; (305) 517-6419; corkandstogie.com.** Just as the name implies, head here to the "closest cigar shop to Cuba," which sells original Key West Cigar Factory cigars and bottles of fine wine. Throughout the year Cork & Stogie hosts wine tastings, book signings, and live music Fri and Sat night. Sit inside or outside on the porch and enjoy your purchases.

**FAUSTO'S FOOD PALACE, 522 Fleming St. and 1105 White St., Key West, FL 33040; (305) 296-5663; faustos.com.** This gourmet food emporium has been serving Key West since 1926. The Fleming Street site is its largest and oldest. Here, in addition to the usual bread, milk, produce, canned goods, and kitchen staples, you will also find fresh local seafood, premium meats and poultry, and numerous varieties of wine, as well as pâtés, rare cheeses, and desserts. The deli counter is especially busy at noontime, when the folks who work downtown line up for sushi and fresh-made sandwiches. The White Street location (305-294-5221) is more like a neighborhood grocery, with a smaller deli counter and a limited selection of produce, bread, frozen foods, and canned goods.

**FLAMINGO CROSSING, 1105 Duval St., Key West, FL 33040; (305) 296-6124.** Since 1987, this has been a favorite with locals and visitors alike. Flamingo Crossing is the place to pause for refreshment as you make your way up and down Duval Street. Homemade ice cream is the business here. You can choose from such flavors as Cuban coffee, raspberry cappuccino, coconut piña colada, key lime, passion fruit, and green tea, among others. Flamingo Crossing also makes its own sorbet and yogurt.

★**GRAND VIN, 1107 Duval St., Key West, FL 33040; (305) 296-1020.** Buy a bottle of wine or champagne to take back to your hotel room or enjoy a glass (or four) on the porch as you watch the crowds navigate Duval Street. People-watching is a favorite pastime here in Key West, and the porch at Grand Vin offers great views. Friendly, knowledgeable bartenders and wines of every grape variety imaginable make Grand Vin truly toast-worthy.

> **i** Harvesting conch (pronounced konk) in Florida waters is illegal. Therefore, most seafood markets import conch from the Turks and Caicos Islands. Firmer in texture than that from most other waters, conch from Turks and Caicos waters is some of the best in the world.

**KERMIT'S KEY WEST KEY LIME SHOPPE,** 200 Elizabeth St. and 802 Duval St., Key West, FL 33040; (305) 296-0806 or (800) 376-0806; keylime shop.com. You can't miss the Elizabeth Street location because Kermit, the key lime chef (as seen on the Food Network and *The Today Show*), is usually outside waving you into this key lime heaven. Everything inside is made with key lime juice, including oils, cookies, candy kisses, salad dressings, juice concentrate, pie filling, and sweets of all sorts. You'll also find key lime soaps and lotions here.

**PEPPERS OF KEY WEST,** 602 Greene St., Key West, FL 33040; (305) 295-9333 or (800) 597-2823; peppersofkeywest.com. Peppers, where chile peppers are the name of the game, bills itself as "the hottest spot on the island." More than 300 varieties of hot sauces already grace the shelves, and more arrive from all over every day. Peppers always has a basket of chips and a few open bottles at the front counter so you can have a taste. Al Roker and Matt Lauer of *The Today Show* barely survived their pepper encounter, so sample if you dare. Peppers bottles its own brands of "hot"—#1, #2, and Goin' Bananas.

★**SUGAR APPLE NATURAL FOODS,** 917 Simonton St., Key West, FL 33040; (305) 292-0043; sugarapplekeywest.com. A longtime favorite of health-conscious Key Westers, Sugar Apple stocks organic and hard-to-find groceries, vitamins, beauty aids, homeopathic remedies, books, and herbs. A juice bar and deli serve up sandwiches, smoothies, specials, and teas.

# Campgrounds

Just as the whooping crane, the Florida panther, and the green sea turtle are on the endangered species list . . . so are campgrounds in the Florida Keys. The locations of most mobile-home parks are on prime real estate. A vast majority of these parks are situated on waterfront/view parcels and are being gobbled up by developers building condos, hotels, or private condotels (condotels are condos privately owned, then placed in a pool of properties to be rented by a management company). Whether you enjoy pitching a tent or traveling with a self-contained motor home, the campgrounds of the Keys offer a reasonably priced alternative to motels and resort accommodations, even though camping rates in the Florida Keys are generally much higher than in other areas of the US. All of our recommended campgrounds do have water access, however, and many are perched at the edge of the Atlantic or the Gulf of Mexico.

A wide range of amenities distinguishes each campground, but one thing is certain: If you wish to camp in the Keys during Jan, Feb, or Mar—those winter months when the folks up north are dusting off their snow boots—you must reserve your site a year in advance. The Keys have a second high season in the summer months, when Floridians locked into triple-digit temperatures head south to our cooling trade winds and warm, placid waters. During sport lobster season, the last consecutive Wed and Thurs of July, it is standing room only in the Keys.

## OVERVIEW

We have listed our recommended Keys campgrounds and RV parks by alphabetical order beginning in Key Largo and ending at Stock Island. Key West devotes its land use to megahotels and quaint guesthouses, presenting a dearth of recommendable campgrounds.

If you think you might fancy a really unusual camping experience, be sure to see the Camping in the Beyond section in this chapter for information on camping in Dry Tortugas National Park or Everglades National Park.

You may assume that all our inclusions maintain good paved interior roads, clean restrooms and showers, laundry facilities, and 20- and 30-amp electrical service. Most campgrounds accept pets if they are kept on a leash at all times and walked only in designated areas and never on the beach. Exceptions will be noted.

Rates vary by the type of site you secure.

## Price Code

Rate ranges are based on a per-diem stay during high season without the 12.5 percent state tax. High season is considered Dec 15 through May 31. Some campgrounds also consider the summer months as high season. Weekly and monthly rates are usually available at a reduced cost; be sure to inquire when you make your reservation.

$     $20 to $40
$$     $40 to $60
$$$     $60 to $80
$$$$     More than $80

## UPPER KEYS

**CALUSA CAMPGROUND RESORT AND MARINA, MM 101.5 Bayside, 325 Calusa St., Key Largo, FL 33037; (305) 451-0232; calusacampground.com. $$–$$$$.** Escape to this family-friendly camp resort on the Gulf of Mexico with all the relaxation you can handle. Paved interior roads lead to gravel pads with full hookups and pull-through sites. Laundry facilities, a clubhouse, LP gas, a swimming pool, playground, boat ramp, and dockage are featured. There is access to the bay and the ocean via Marvin Adams Cut or Tavernier Creek. Pets are welcome as long as they are on a leash.

**JOHN PENNEKAMP CORAL REEF STATE PARK, MM 102.5 Oceanside, 102.5 Overseas Hwy., Key Largo, FL 33037; (305) 451-1202 or (800) 326-3521; pennekamppark.com. $.** Aesthetically, the gravel sites at John Pennekamp Coral Reef State Park don't begin to compare to their waterfront siblings at the Keys' other two state parks, Bahia Honda and Long Key, but a canopy of mature buttonwoods shades most of the sites. Also, the wide range of fabulous recreational opportunities within Pennekamp and its proximity to the nightlife in Key Largo more than make up for any lack of romantic oceanfront ambience (see Beaches & Public Parks in the Recreation chapter).

**KEY LARGO KAMPGROUND AND MARINA, MM 101.5 Oceanside, 101551 Overseas Hwy., Key Largo, FL 33037; (305) 451-1431 or (800) KAMP-OUT; keylargokampground.com. $–$$$$.** Settle down and enjoy this village-like campground laden with palm trees. About one-third of the condo campsites, with full hookups and free cable TV, are available for overnighters. Some sites front the canal and have boat slips. Two beaches look out on Newport Bay, and a heated swimming pool and kiddie pool and volleyball courts add to the fun. John Pennekamp Coral Reef State Park is only a mile north of this 40-acre campground. Rates are based on 4 people (2 adults and 2 children younger than age 6) and 1 camping unit per site. A maximum of 6 people are allowed per rental unit at any time.

CAMPGROUNDS

## MIDDLE KEYS

**LONG KEY STATE PARK, MM** 67.5 Oceanside, 67400 Overseas Hwy., Long Key, FL 33001; (305) 664-4815; floridastateparks.org/park/long-key; $. Every site is oceanfront when you camp at Long Key State Park. You can't get closer to the ocean than this campground in the Florida Keys. Half of the 60 sites offer water and electric, and all have picnic tables fronting the shallow saltwater flats. Each deep site runs from the park road to the ocean. Like John Pennekamp Coral Reef State Park and Bahia Honda State Park, Long Key State Park follows a strictly regimented reservation policy. The park opens at 8 a.m. and closes at sunset.

## LOWER KEYS

**BAHIA HONDA STATE PARK, MM** 37 Oceanside, 36850 Overseas Hwy., Big Pine Key, FL 33043; (305) 872-2353; floridastateparks.org/park/bahia -honda; $–$$. Claiming the Florida Keys' best natural beach (2.5 miles long), the 524-acre Bahia Honda State Park offers roomy sites at Buttonwood that can accommodate large motor homes—Sandspur is limited to tents, vans, and pop-ups. Because these sites sit deep in a tropical hardwood hammock, the park is very selective as to which rigs are allowed to camp here. All these sites have water, and more than half offer electricity. Large cabins literally perch on the water near the bayside campsites. The park has a boat ramp, so you may bring your own craft and try your luck at catching a tarpon.

**BIG PINE KEY FISHING LODGE, MM** 33 Oceanside, 33000 Overseas Hwy., Big Pine Key, FL 33043; (305) 872-2351; bpkfl.com. $$. The sites here range from rustic grass or dirt for tents without water or electricity to dockside locations with full hookups. The boat basin, a part of the Big Pine Fishing Lodge since the late 1950s, accommodates small fishing boats for a daily charge. Ample fish-cleaning stations are provided, so you can ready the spoils of the day for the frying pan. The lodge has an oval swimming pool overlooking a peppering of statuesque coconut palms, all grown from seed. Air-conditioning, phone outlets, and cable hookups are included in the camping fee.

**BLUEWATER KEY RV RESORT, MM** 14.5 Oceanside, 2950 Overseas Hwy., Stock Island, Key West, FL 33040; (305) 745-2494 or (800) 237-2266; bluewaterkey.com. $$–$$$$. Bluewater Key RV Resort's individually owned and landscaped sites feature metered utility hookups, including telephone and cable TV. The friendly management team will make sure you find the site that is perfect for you. Fishing and sunbathing on the private docks is offered to those staying on the premises. Visitors will also be privy to incredible views of the sun and moon rising over the Keys. If some action is needed after your days of quiet solitude, the center of Key West is just a short drive away. We suggest you book at least a year in advance if you'd like a waterfront spot.

**BOYD'S KEY WEST CAMPGROUND, MM 5 Oceanside, 6401 Maloney Ave., Stock Island, Key West, FL 33040; (305) 294-1465; boydscampground .com; $$–$$$$.** Although its brochures state a Key West address, Boyd's is actually on Stock Island, just outside the Key West city limits. Most of the level, shaded sites have cement patios. Bordering the ocean, Boyd's offers a boat ramp, a small marina, extensive dock space, a heated swimming pool, and 4 bathhouses. You can catch the city bus into Key West for unlimited diversions, hang out at Boyd's game room, or watch the large-screen TV, which is tucked in a tiki hut near the pool. A modern hookup is available, along with 30–50 amp service. Please note: They have strict rules about pets—check their website for details.

**GEIGER KEY MARINA AND CAMPGROUND, MM 10.5 Oceanside, 5 Geiger Rd., Geiger Key, Key West, FL 33040; (305) 296-3553; geigerkey marina.com; $$$$.** In the mangroves "on the backside of Paradise" you'll discover Geiger Key Marina and Campground. The setting on the Atlantic Ocean is what makes this quiet location a hidden gem. Geiger Key Marina and Campground is only 10 miles from Key West, yet it seems a million miles away with its laid-back 1950s aura. The property offers campers RV hookups, laundry facilities, ocean-view private tent sites, transient boat slips, kayak rentals, and fishing-charter boats. Their popular restaurant and tiki bar cooks up fantastic BBQ on Sun, often accompanied by live, local music for your enjoyment.

**LAZY LAKES CAMPGROUND AND RV RESORT, MM 19.5 Oceanside, 311 Johnson Rd., Sugarloaf Key, FL 33042; (305) 745-1079 or (866) 965-2537; lazylakesrvresort.com; $$–$$$$.** Off the beaten path, this 28-acre property with a 7-acre saltwater lake is a real Insiders destination for your full-size RV (99 spots available), Big Rigs, tent sites, or mobile homes you can rent. Hike the paths leading around the lake or jump into one of the free kayaks and paddle around for a water view. Lazy Lakes offers 30–50 amp service, laundry facilities, restrooms, a heated pool, general store, and umbrella tables with lounge chairs. During the year they have activities for their guests that include bingo, horseshoes, darts, concerts, and even holiday celebrations. You may never want to leave!

**LEO'S CAMPGROUND AND RV PARK, MM 4.5 Oceanside, 5236 Suncrest Rd., Stock Island, Key West, FL 33040; (305) 296-5260; leoscamp ground.com; $$–$$$.** Minutes from downtown Key West, you can ride a bike or take the bus from this campground park. Rent a tent and settle in—Leo's is ideal for a relaxing spot while in the Lower Keys. Full RV setup with water, sewer, electric (some up to 50 amp), cable TV, barbecues, and picnic tables. Laundry facilities and a bathhouse are also on-site. Pets are permitted, but only if traveling in RVs.

**SUGARLOAF KEY RESORT KOA KAMPGROUND, MM 20 Oceanside, 251 State Road 939, Sugarloaf Key, FL 33042; (305) 745-3549 or (800) 562-7731; koa.com/campgrounds/sugarloaf-key; $$$-$$$$.** Pelicans perched in mangroves near thatched tiki huts on a palm-speckled beach create an island ambience in this comprehensive KOA on Sugarloaf Key. Nearly 200 gravel, grass, or dirt sites offer a choice of hookups. Optional cable hookup is available at an additional charge. The facility offers what you have come to expect from a KOA Kampground—all the necessities, plus the amenities of a resort. A full marina covers the gamut of boating and fishing needs. A large heated pool, hot tub, mini golf, horseshoes, and bicycle rentals offer landlubbers relaxing diversions while volleyball, a game room, and a playground amuse the children.

**SUNSHINE KEY RV RESORT AND MARINA, MM 39 Bayside, 38801 Overseas Hwy., Big Pine Key, FL 33040; (305) 872-2217 or (877) 362-6736; rvonthego.com; $$-$$$$.** Sunshine Key RV Resort and Marina occupies an entire key, officially named Ohio Key. This bustling place, with nearly 400 sites, is more like a small Midwestern town than a tropical camping resort. The 75-acre spot, with its winding signposted streets and myriad amenities, is friendly and family-oriented. The oceanside portion of Sunshine Key remains a tangle of mangroves, buttonwoods, and palm trees that shield a feathered montage of wildlife popular with bird-watchers. Tennis courts, a heated swimming pool, volleyball, horseshoes, and a full schedule of adult activities in the clubhouse keep things hopping. A game room, playground, and water sports occupy the children.

## CAMPING IN THE BEYOND

If there is a little part of you that longs to forge through uncharted territory and live off the land (or the sea), you can fulfill your fantasies here. Everglades National Park and Dry Tortugas National Park, both day-trip excursions from the Florida Keys, offer unique camping experiences for the adventuresome spirits among you.

> **i** Camping and campfires are not permitted in national wildlife refuges.

### Everglades National Park
Canoe or commandeer a small motor craft into the backcountry wilderness of Everglades National Park. This 99-mile route, which is recommended for

experienced canoeists only, connects Flamingo and Everglades City. (Allow at least 9 days to complete the trip.) The charted routing through such colorfully named spots as Darwin's Place, Camp Lonesome, Lostman's Five, and Graveyard Creek encompasses 47 primitive campsites of 3 basic types.

You will need a permit (small fee in season) to camp in one of the backcountry sites. Apply in person at the Gulf Coast or Flamingo Visitor Center up to 24 hours before your trip begins. Everglades National Park also offers camping in 2 in-park campgrounds. Seasonal reservations (Nov through Apr) can be made for these campsites by calling (800) 365-2267 or at the online reservations center, accessed by link from the park's website at nps.gov/ever. Guided tours are offered through Everglades Adventures. Visit evergladesadventures .com for more information.

**Chickees:** These elevated, 10-by-12-foot wooden platforms with roofs are placed along interior rivers and bays where no dry land exists. A design originally used by the Miccosukee Indians, these open-air structures allow the wind to blow through, keeping the insects away. A narrow walkway leads to a self-contained toilet. You will need to have a freestanding tent, because stakes and nails are not allowed.

**Beach Sites:** These are set on coastal beaches that have been built up through time from a conglomeration of fragmented shells. Campers are warned that gulf waters can become extremely rough. Loggerhead sea turtles nest on Highland Beach and Cape Sable in the spring and summer. If you see evidence of their nesting, refrain from lighting a campfire nearby. (Campfires are allowed at beach sites only.)

**Primitive Ground Sites:** These consist of mounds of earth just a few feet higher than the surrounding mangroves. Willy Willy, Camp Lonesome, and Canepatch are old Indian mound sites. Coastal aborigines, who lived here before the Seminole Indians, constructed mounds of shells or soil as dry dwelling sites amid the mangroves. The ground sites, along interior bays and rivers, have a heavier preponderance of insects than either the beach sites or the chickees. Always be prepared for mosquitoes and tiny biting insects called no-see-ums, especially at sunrise and sunset. Mosquito season corresponds with the rainy season, Apr through Oct. We do not recommend you try to camp in the Everglades during these months.

For more information on park or backcountry camping, visit the aforementioned Everglades National Park website, or contact the main park number at (305) 242-7700.

## Dry Tortugas National Park

Roughing it takes on gargantuan proportions when you consider camping at Dry Tortugas National Park, but it's worth the effort, because this remote bit of Paradise has been preserved in a virginal state. You'll find the 11 palm-shaded tent sites—available on a first-come, first-served basis—in a sandy area on Garden Key in front of Fort Jefferson. You must pack in all your supplies, including freshwater; only saltwater toilets, grills, and picnic tables are provided. There is no food, freshwater, electricity, or medical assistance of any kind on the island.

You must take your chances on securing a campsite, because reservations are not taken for the individual sites. A small fee per person, per night must be paid upon arrival at Fort Jefferson. (The park service says securing a site usually is not a problem.) Campsites accommodate up to 8 people. You can reserve a group site for as many as 15 people, however, by contacting the park service, (305) 242-7700. If the group site is available when you submit your completed application, a permit reserving the site will be issued. You may stay up to 14 days at either individual or group sites, but keep in mind you must bring complete provisioning for the duration of your stay and pack out your trash.

You may have left the civilized world behind you in Key West, but the arena of natural splendor surrounding you in the Dry Tortugas is endless. Tour Fort Jefferson (self-guided), America's largest 19th-century coastal fort. The walls of the fort are 50 feet high and 8 feet thick.

A white coral beach—nature-made, not man-made—provides a tropical backdrop for doing nothing at all. But you can snorkel just 60 yards off the beach or dive the seemingly bottomless blue waters, which, preserved as a sanctuary, are filled with fearless battalions of finfish and squadrons of crawfish that are oblivious to your presence.

Bird-watching is superb. Sooty and noddy terns by the thousands gather in the Dry Tortugas from the Caribbean, nesting on nearby Bush Key. Single eggs are laid in depressions in the sand, and parent birds take turns shading them from the hot sun. The entire colony leaves when the babies are strong enough.

Getting to the Dry Tortugas presents a bit of a challenge—and expense. Seaplane is the fastest means of transportation to the Dry Tortugas, but it's also the most expensive. You can also reach the Dry Tortugas by sea. (See the Recreation chapter for information on the *Yankee Freedom III* ferry service to Fort Jefferson.) The National Park Service provides a list of sanctioned transportation services to the Dry Tortugas, which means they are insured and bonded and they maintain good safety records. The park service advises that the criteria are stringent and the list is constantly monitored. Contact the park service, (305) 242-7700, to get the current recommendations. The Dry Tortugas National Park website is nps.gov/drto.

# Boating

The voice of the sea speaks to the soul, no more so than in the Florida Keys. Surrounded by the shimmering aquatic prisms of the Gulf of Mexico and the Atlantic Ocean, the Keys volunteer unlimited vistas for watery exploration. Our depths offer famed fishing grounds (see the Fishing chapter) and unparalleled dive sites (see the Diving & Snorkeling chapter). Cruisers from around the world seek out our remote, pristine anchoring-out spots as well as our resort marinas (see the Cruising chapter). And peppering the Keys, from Key Largo to Key West, a proliferation of water-sports facilities afford anyone visiting our shores the opportunity to get out on the water via canoe, sea kayak, water skis, personal watercraft, sailboard, even paddleboard and paddleboat (see the Recreation chapter). The waters surrounding the Florida Keys are protected as part of a marine sanctuary, so regulations concerning the use of personal watercraft are more stringent here than in other parts of Florida. (See the Florida Keys National Marine Sanctuary Regulations section of this chapter.) For more information, contact the sanctuary office at (305) 743-2437 or log on to florida keys.noaa.gov.

In this chapter we will introduce you to our waters, alert you to the rules of our hydrous highways and byways, and share some safety and navigational tips. We'll provide you with a primer of available public boat ramps, marine supply stores, and boat sales and service businesses, as well as motor and sailboat rentals, boat charters, and other sources to enhance your time on the water.

## BODIES OF WATER

The waters of the Florida Keys conceal multiple habitats that sustain an impressive array of sea life not encountered anywhere else in the US. Depths range from scant inches (which often disappear altogether at low tide) in the nearshore waters, the flats, and the backcountry of Florida Bay to the fathoms of the offshore waters of the deep blue Atlantic. And buried at sea 4 to 5 miles from our shores runs the most extensive living coral reef track in North America. (See the Welcome to the Florida Keys, Cruising, Fishing, and Diving & Snorkeling chapters for more information on these waters and the creatures dwelling within.)

### Flats, Backcountry & Shallow Nearshore Waters

Perhaps the most complex of our waters are the shallows of the nearshore waters, those directly off both our coasts, which vary from a few inches to several feet in depth and sometimes stretch for a mile or more from shore. These "flats" of the Atlantic and backcountry waters of the Gulf of Mexico and Florida Bay (that portion of the gulf bordered by the Upper Keys and Everglades National Park) prove a challenge to navigate. Popular with anglers searching for bone-fish, permit, tarpon, redfish, snook, and sea trout and inhabited by an array of barracuda, sharks, and lobsters, the shallow waters cover meadows of sea grass punctuated with patches of sand, which also function as the nursery waters for many offshore species.

As a boater in the Florida Keys, you should familiarize yourself with the necessary nautical charts before venturing off the dock. Learn to "read" the water (see the Aids to Navigation section in this chapter) because waters are littered with unmarked shoals. Nearshore waters are best traversed in a shallow-draft flats boat or skiff, or by dinghy, canoe, or sea kayak. Operators of personal watercraft should steer clear of the flats to avoid disturbing the aquatic life dwelling below.

If you do happen to run aground here, turn off your motor immediately; the rotating propeller will kill the sea grass. Usually all you need to do is get out of the boat to lighten the load and push the craft to deeper water. Then trim up your motor and proceed. If this doesn't work, wait until the tide rises a bit and try to push off the flat again.

## Intracoastal Waterway

The primary navigable waterway in Florida Bay and the Gulf of Mexico is the Intracoastal Waterway. In the Keys it leads from Biscayne Bay at the mainland, under Jewfish Creek, and then parallels the Keys, accommodating boats with drafts of up to 4 to 6 feet. The Intracoastal runs about 2 to 3 miles off the gulf side of our islands, between shallow nearshore waters and the scattered man-grove islands that lie varying distances from the coast.

The Intracoastal is well marked to about Big Pine Key, where it meets the Big Spanish Channel and heads north into the Gulf of Mexico. (Red day markers should be kept to the starboard, or right, side of the vessel when travel-ing down the Keys in the Intracoastal Waterway.) From the Spanish Channel to Key West, boaters must pay close attention to nautical charts to navigate safe passage. Boaters will enter Key West through the well-marked Northwest Channel.

## Patch Reefs, Hawk Channel & the Barrier Reef

Between the nearshore waters of the Atlantic and the barrier reef some 4 to 5 miles offshore lies a smattering of patch reefs submerged at depths as shallow as 3 feet, with some even exposed at low tide. Surrounding waters vary in depth, but generally are much deeper than the flats and nearshore waters.

Hawk Channel—a safely navigable superhighway frequented by recre-ational boaters and cruisers—runs the length of the Florida Keys, bordering the reef at depths between 11 and 16 feet. Square red and triangular green day markers guide boaters through these waters; red markers should be kept to the starboard, or right, side of the vessel when traveling down the Keys in Hawk Channel.

Outside this marked area, the waters are scattered with dive sites designated with anchor buoys and red-and-white flags, as well as marked and unmarked rocks and shoals. If red-and-white diver-down flags are displayed, boaters should steer clear. These flags indicate that a diver is beneath the water.

Lighthouses now mark shallow reef areas, which, at one time, claimed ships that encountered bad weather or navigated carelessly close to the coral mountains. Waters covering the coral reef can run as deep as 20 to 40 feet, but as history attests, depths can vary considerably. Always consult your nautical chart and "read" the water.

### The Florida Straits

Outside the reef in the Florida Straits, the water depth of the Atlantic increases dramatically to as much as 80 feet, deepening farther with distance from shore. Although on some days these waters are relatively calm, all offshore boaters should check wind and weather advisories before venturing out.

### Creeks & Channels

The channels, or "cuts," between our islands often have extremely strong currents that make traveling between bridge pilings a bit dicey. Current continuously flows from the Gulf of Mexico into the Atlantic because sea level in the gulf is slightly higher than that of the ocean. Exercise caution when boating in these waters.

### Key West Harbor

The southernmost city's ports have traditionally been gracious, welcoming tall ships, steamships, ferries, barges, powerboats, and seaplanes. Pirates, wreckers, spongers, shippers, naval officers, and Cuban émigrés all have found shelter here in the midst of their work, play, and quest for worldly wealth and freedom.

Key West's port, the deepest in all the Florida Keys, has a main channel depth of anywhere from 13 to 34 feet; it is even deeper on the Atlantic side. Passenger cruise ships now include this island among their ports of call. Key West is ranked among the busiest cruise-ship ports of call in the world. Also in that ranking are the Virgin Islands, Puerto Rico, and the Caymans. Recreational cruisers often head for Key West's bustling harbor to prepare themselves and their boats for a Caribbean journey.

Like the rest of the Florida Keys, Key West is protective of its coral reefs and sea-grass beds, and despite the fact that harbors run deep, waters in the backcountry are shallow everywhere. First-time and novice boaters often run aground here and by Fleming Key and Sand Key west of the harbor.

## AIDS TO NAVIGATION

### Nautical Charts

Always use nautical charts and a magnetic compass for navigation when boating in the waters of the Florida Keys. Use electronic means of navigation (GPS) only for confirmation of position. Be sure your vessel is equipped with a VHF marine radio.

The US Coast Guard recommends you follow charts issued by the National Oceanic and Atmospheric Administration (NOAA). To secure nautical charts for the entire Florida Keys, you'll need to purchase a chart kit that includes charts for each section. You can also purchase NOAA charts individually. For instance, to navigate the waters surrounding Key West, the US Coast Guard recommends you use navigational chart No. 11441 for the approaches to Key West Harbor and chart No. 11447 for the harbor itself.

Readily available in many marine supply stores throughout the Florida Keys and Key West (see store listings in this chapter), these charts are accurate based on the date marked on them. Store personnel will be able to help you secure the proper up-to-date chart for the area you will be exploring. Be sure you know how to read the nautical charts before you set off. To view them online before your trip, visit nauticalcharts.noaa.gov.

### Channel Markers

In most waters, boaters follow the adage "red, right, return," meaning that the triangular red channel markers should be kept to the right, or starboard, side of the vessel when heading toward the port of origin. This jingle is confusing at best, for in the Florida Keys it does not appear to apply. Red markers should be kept to the starboard side of the vessel when heading down the Keys, from Key Largo to Key West, through Hawk Channel on the oceanside or the Intracoastal Waterway in the gulf. Conversely, when traveling up the Keys, in either Hawk Channel or the Intracoastal Waterway, square green markers should be kept to your starboard side; keep red markers on your vessel's port, or left, side.

When traversing creeks and cuts from oceanside to the gulf, red markers should be kept on your starboard side, and when coming from the gulf, the opposite holds true. In any event, always consult your nautical chart to determine the channel of safe passage and the corresponding positioning of the navigational markers.

### Tide Charts

It's important to determine mean low tides within the waters you plan to travel so that you do not run aground. In the Florida Keys tides typically rise and fall about 1 to 2 feet. During spring, autumn, and a full moon, tides tend to rise to the higher and lower ends of this scale. Boaters should, therefore, rely on a tide conversion chart. Most marinas, bait and tackle shops, and other businesses that cater to boaters can provide tide information for specific areas in conjunction with a current tide chart available from the US Coast Guard.

## "Reading" the Water

In the Florida Keys visual navigation often means "reading" the water—that is, recognizing its potential depth by knowing which colors indicate safe passage and which connote danger. As water depth decreases, its underlying sea bottom is indicated by distinctive coloration. Be aware that readings may be difficult in narrow channels and in strong currents where the waters often are murky and restrict visibility. Wear polarized sunglasses to better distinguish one color from another.

The easiest way to remember what each water color signifies is to follow some poetic, but fundamental, guidance:

- *Brown, brown, run aground.* Reef formations and shallow sea-grass beds close to the surface cause this color.

- *White, white, you might.* Sandbars and rubble bottoms may be in waters much shallower than you think.

- *Green, green, nice and clean.* The water is generally safe above reefs or sea-grass beds, but larger boats with deeper drafts may hit bottom. If you are renting a boat, find out what the draft is.

- *Blue, blue, cruise on through.* Water is deepest, but changing tides may cause coral reefs to surface. Allow time to steer around them.

## WHEN YOU NEED HELP

Although the US Coast Guard and the Florida Marine Patrol work closely together and will make sure you contact the proper party in any event, they do handle different aspects of our waters in the Florida Keys.

### Florida Marine Patrol

The Florida Fish and Wildlife Conservation Commission's law enforcement arm is the Florida Marine Patrol. They deal with violations such as environmental crime, fish and crawfish bag limits, and illegal dumping. They also enforce boating safety laws, responding to reports of unsafe boating and wake violations, as well as any perceived illegal activity on the water. You can reach the Florida Marine Patrol on a cell phone by dialing FMP (367), which is a free phone call when you are on your vessel and in need of the Florida Marine

Patrol, or on a regular telephone line at (800) DIAL-FMP (342-5367). The Marine Patrol vessels also monitor VHF channel 16.

### US Coast Guard

The US Coast Guard maintains three bases in the Florida Keys and Key West. Their mission is to ensure maritime safety and handle life-threatening emergencies at sea, such as vessel collisions, drownings, onboard fires, or other accidents at sea. The Coast Guard monitors VHF channel 16 at all times. In an emergency, call (305) 743-6388. By cell phone, call *CG (*24). If for some reason you do not have a radio or cell phone on board, flag a passing boat and ask someone on it to radio for assistance.

### Sea Tow

Run aground? Out of fuel? Motor problems? Instead of calling the Coast Guard, call Sea Tow, a nationally recognized boater assistance service that maintains facilities the length of the Keys. Convey the details of your problem and what you think you need. Don't just ask for a tow if you have run out of gas or need only a minor repair. Describe your problem; the difference in cost between having gas delivered to your stranded boat and a multihour tow back to land could be a lot of money. Sea Tow also will provide free advice, such as projected weather changes or directions in unfamiliar territory. Call the Sea Tow offices at (800) 473-2869 or visit seatow.com for more information.

## VESSEL REGULATIONS & EQUIPMENT

Vessels must be equipped with Coast Guard–approved equipment, which varies according to the boat's size, location, and use. All vessels must either be documented or registered, and the appropriate paperwork must be carried on board.

Federal, state, and local law enforcement officials may hail your boat so that they can come aboard and inspect it. Among their reasons for imposing civil penalties: improper use of a marine radio and misuse of calling the distress channel VHF channel 16; boating under the influence (a blood alcohol level of 0.08 percent or higher); and negligence. Negligence includes boating in a swimming area, speeding in the vicinity of other boats or in dangerous waters, bow riding, and gunwaling. Boaters without the required Coast Guard–approved equipment on board or with problematic boats that are considered hazardous may be directed back to port.

### Vessel Registration

Whether or not you are a resident of the Florida Keys, your vessel must be registered in the state of Florida within 30 days of your arrival if one of our islands is its primary location. Registration renewals require your old registration form and a valid Florida driver's license, if you have one; for registering new boats, bring your manufacturer's statement of origin, dealer's sales tax statement, and bill of sale. If you are registering a used boat you have just purchased, you will need a title signed over to you and a bill of sale, one of which must be notarized, and the previous owner's registration if available.

Boats must be registered annually; only cash is accepted as payment. Excluded from registration requirements are rowboats and dinghies with less than 10-hp motors that are used exclusively as dinghies. All other boats may be registered any weekday between 8 a.m. and 4:45 p.m. at one of the Monroe County Tax Collector's Offices. For a list of locations, call (305) 295-5010 or visit flhsmv.gov/offices/monroe.html.

## Required Equipment

The US Coast Guard requires that vessels using gasoline for any reason be equipped with a ventilation system in proper working condition. With the exception of outboard motors, gasoline engines must also be equipped with a means of backfire flame control. In addition, Coast Guard–approved fire extinguishers are required for boats with inboard engines, closed or under-seat compartments with portable fuel tanks, and other characteristics. There are additional requirements for vessels of more than 39 feet and boats used for races, parades, and other specific purposes. Personal flotation devices, night distress signals, and navigation lights are also required. Visit uscgboating.org or contact the US Coast Guard at (305) 743-6778 or (305) 664-8078 for specific requirements for your size and style of boat.

## Recommended Equipment

Regardless of your boat's size, location, and use, the US Coast Guard recommends that you have the following equipment on board: VHF radio, visual distress signals, anchor and spare anchor, heaving line, fenders, first-aid kit, flashlight, mirror, searchlight, sunscreen and sunburn lotions, tool kit, ring buoy, whistle or horn, fuel tanks and spare fuel, chart and compass, boat hook, spare propeller, mooring line, food and water, binoculars, spare batteries, sunglasses (polarized to see water-color variations better), marine hardware, sound-producing device, extra clothing, spare parts, paddles, and a pump or bailer.

## FLORIDA KEYS NATIONAL MARINE SANCTUARY REGULATIONS

The Florida Keys fall within the boundaries of the Florida Keys National Marine Sanctuary, created by the federal government in 1990 to protect the resources of our marine ecosystem. And while, for the most part, visitors can freely swim, dive, snorkel, boat, fish, or recreate on our waters, there are some regulations to guide these activities. For a complete copy of the regulations and marine coordinates of the areas, contact the sanctuary office at (305) 809-4700, or visit floridakeys.noaa.gov.

### Sanctuary-wide Regulations

These mandates focus on habitat protection, striving to reduce threats to water quality and minimize human impact on delicate resources. Visit floridakeys .noaa.gov for a complete list. The following are prohibited in our waters:

- Moving, removing, taking, injuring, touching, breaking, cutting, or possessing coral or live rock

- Discharging or depositing treated or untreated sewage from marine sanitation devices, trash, and other materials

- Dredging, drilling, prop dredging, or otherwise altering the seabed, or placing or abandoning any structure on the seabed

- Operating a vessel in such a manner as to strike or otherwise injure coral, sea grass, or other immobile organisms attached to the seabed, or cause prop scarring

- Having a vessel anchored on living coral in water less than 40 feet deep when the bottom can be seen (*Note:* Anchoring on hardbottom is allowed.)

- Except in officially marked channels, operating a vessel at more than 4 knots / no wake within 100 yards of residential shorelines, stationary vessels, or navigational aids marking reefs

- Operating a vessel at more than 4 knots / no wake within 100 yards of a diver-down flag

BOATING

- Diving or snorkeling without a dive flag

- Operating a vessel in such a manner that endangers life, limb, marine resources, or property

- Releasing exotic species

- Damaging or removing markers, mooring buoys, scientific equipment, boundary buoys, and trap buoys

- Moving, removing, injuring, or possessing historical resources

- Taking or possessing protected wildlife

- Using or possessing explosives or electrical charges

- Harvesting, possessing, or landing any marine life species except as allowed by the Florida Fish and Wildlife Conservation Commission Rule (68B-42 FAC)

## Marine Zoning Regulations

The sanctuary's marine zoning regulations focus protection on portions of sensitive habitats, while allowing public access in others. Only about 2 percent of the sanctuary's waters fall into the five zoning categories. All sanctuary-wide regulations apply in the special zones, along with a number of additional rules and restrictions. The marine zones are under review until 2016, so make sure to check the full list at floridakeys.noaa.gov.

With certain exceptions, the following activities are prohibited in the Ecological Reserves (ERs), Sanctuary Preservation Areas (SPAs), and Special-Use Research Only Areas:

- Discharging any matter except cooling water or engine exhaust

- Fishing by any means

- Removing, harvesting, or possessing any marine life

- Touching or standing on living or dead coral

- Anchoring on living or dead coral, or any attached organism

- Anchoring when a mooring buoy is available

- Catch-and-release fishing by trolling is allowed in Conch Reef, Alligator Reef, Sombrero Reef, and Sand Key SPAs only.

- Bait fishing is allowed in SPAs by Florida Keys National Marine Sanctuary permit.

### Additional Regulations for Tortugas South ER

- Vessels may enter only if they remain in continuous transit with fishing gear stowed.

- Diving and snorkeling are prohibited.

### Additional Regulations for Tortugas North ER

- An access permit is required to stop or use a mooring buoy.

- Anchoring is prohibited.

- Mooring vessels more than 100 feet in total or combined length overall is prohibited.

- No access permit is necessary if vessel remains in continuous transit with fishing gear stowed.

### Activities Prohibited in Special-Use Research Only Areas

The sanctuary's four Special-Use Research Only Areas are located at Conch Reef, Tennessee Reef, Looe Key (patch reef), and Eastern Sambo. Sanctuary Preservation Areas, Special-Use Areas, and the Western Sambo Ecological Reserve are marked by 30-inch round yellow buoys. Tortugas Ecological Reserve is not marked.

The following activities are prohibited:

- Entry or activity without a Florida Keys National Marine Sanctuary permit

- Discharging any matter except cooling water or engine exhaust

- Fishing by any means; removing, harvesting, or possessing any marine life

- Touching or standing on living or dead coral

- Anchoring on living or dead coral, or any attached organism

### Wildlife Management Area Restrictions
Wildlife Management Areas (WMAs) are marked by white-and-orange information/regulatory cylindrical spar buoys and signs. Public access restrictions in these areas include idle speed only/no wake, no access buffer, no motor, and limited closures, and are marked as such.

### Activities Prohibited in the Key Largo and Looe Key Existing Management Areas
Removing, taking, spearing, or otherwise damaging any coral, marine invertebrate, plant, soil, rock, or other material is prohibited. However, commercial taking of spiny lobster and stone crab by trap and recreational taking of spiny lobster by hand or hand gear consistent with applicable state and federal fishery regulations are allowed.

Spearfishing and possession of spearfishing equipment is prohibited, except while passing through without interruption.

## PUBLIC BOAT RAMPS

If you trailer your boat to the Florida Keys, you can launch it at any number of public ramps. Here is a list of boat-launching sites maintained year-round for your use. Parking is limited except at park sites. Please note that at some sites, you must pay a launch fee.

### Upper Keys
**Sunset Point Park,** MM 95.2 Bayside, 20 Sunset Rd., Key Largo, FL 33037
**John Pennekamp Coral Reef State Park,** MM 102.5 Oceanside, 102601 Overseas Hwy., Key Largo, FL 33037
**Caribbean Club Ramp,** MM 104 Bayside, 104080 Overseas Hwy., Key Largo, FL 33037
**Pontunes Boat Rentals and Marina,** MM 107.6 Bayside, 107690 Overseas Hwy., Key Largo, FL 33037
**Gilbert's Resort Marina,** MM 107.9 Bayside, 107900 Overseas Hwy., Key Largo, FL 33037
**Crocodile Lake,** Card Sound Rd. at Steamboat Creek, Tubby's Creek, and Mosquito Creek, 10750 County Road 905, Key Largo, FL 33037
**Card Sound Bridge,** East and West Sides, 1500 Card Sound Rd., Key Largo, FL 33037
**Mangrove Marina,** MM 92 Bayside, 200 Florida Ave., Tavernier, FL 33070

**Florida Keys Dive Center,** MM 90.5 Oceanside, 90451 Old Hwy., Tavernier, FL 33070

**Founder's Park,** MM 87 Bayside, 87000 Overseas Hwy., Islamorada, FL 33070

**East Ridge Road Public Boat Ramp,** Oceanside end of East Ridge Rd., Islamorada, 33070

**Harbor Lights at Holiday Isle,** MM 84 Oceanside, 84001 Overseas Hwy., Islamorada, FL 33070

### Middle Keys

**Hawk's Cay Resort and Marina,** MM 61 Oceanside, 61 Hawks Cay Blvd., Duck Key, FL 33050; (305) 743-7000 or (888) 395-5539

**Sombrero Resort & Marina,** MM 50 Oceanside, 19 Sombrero Blvd., Marathon, FL 33050; (305) 289-7662 or (800) 433-8660

**Marathon Yacht Club,** MM 49 Bayside, 825 33rd St., Marathon, FL 33050; (305) 743-6739

### Lower Keys

**Bahia Honda State Park,** MM 37 Oceanside, 36850 Overseas Hwy., Big Pine Key, FL 33043; (305) 872-2353

**Spanish Harbor Wayside Park,** MM 33 Bayside, Spanish Harbor Key, FL 33042

**Dolphin Marina,** MM 28.5 Oceanside, 28530 Overseas Hwy., Little Torch Key, FL 33042

**Little Torch Key,** MM 27.5 Bayside on State Road 4A between County Rd. and Linda St., Little Torch Key, FL 33042; (305) 292-4560

**Cudjoe Key Boat Ramp,** MM 21.2 Bayside, at the north end of Blimp Rd., Cudjoe Key, FL 33040

**Shark Key Boat Ramp,** MM 11, Oceanside, Shark Key, FL 33040

**Barcelona Boat Ramp,** MM 9.3, Bayside, Big Coppitt Key, FL 33040

### Key West

**Key Haven,** MM 6 Oceanside, Stock Island, FL 33040

**Garrison Bight Marina,** Palm Ave. and Eisenhower Dr., Key West, FL 33040; (305) 294-3093

**Simonton Beach Boat Ramp,** Bayside at 0 Simonton St., Key West, FL 33040

**11th Street Boat Ramp,** 11th St. and Riviera Dr., Key West, FL 33040

**KEY WEST HARBOR SERVICES/BOAT US TOWING SERVICES,** 7281 Shrimp Rd., Key West, FL 33040; (305) 454-3121 (operations), (305) 454-3121 (emergency), or (800) 888-4869 (national contact); kwharborservices .com. Being stranded in a vessel on the water is not fun! This local branch of Boat US Towing Services has been expanding its fleet in order to meet the growing demands of the maritime community. Never pay a towing charge again when you join this marine towing and salvage service with 24-hour assistance. Call their 800 number for membership and protect yourself with marine assistance.

## MARINE SUPPLY STORES

Marine supplies and NOAA charts recommended by the US Coast Guard may be purchased at the following facilities.

### Upper Keys

**WEST MARINE**, 103400 Overseas Hwy., Key Largo, FL 103400; (305) 453-9050 or (800) 262-8464; westmarine.com. West Marine is an expansive store that carries a variety of supplies for sailboats and powerboats. Hardware and electric, safety, plumbing, and maintenance needs can all be met at West Marine. There are 3 additional locations, at 2109 Overseas Hwy., Marathon (305-289-1009); 5790 Second St. on Stock Island (305-294-2025); and 951 Caroline St. in Key West (305-295-0953).

### Middle Keys

See the West Marine listing in the Upper Keys section for their Marathon location.

### Lower Keys

**SEA CENTER**, 29740 Overseas Hwy., Big Pine Key, FL 33043; (305) 872-2243; sea-center.com. Sea Center is family-owned and professionally operated, offering boat sales services and supplies, including hardware, electric, and maintenance needs.

### Key West

See West Marine in the Upper Keys section for their Stock Island and Key West locations.

**KEY WEST MARINE HARDWARE INC.**, 818 Caroline St., Key West, FL 33040; (305) 294-3519 or (305) 294-3425. This is the place to go for every cleat, bolt, snap, or thingamajig your powerboat or sailboat requires—Key West Marine Hardware has it all. You'll find the complete set of official NOAA nautical charts to the Keys and Caribbean waters, along with cruising, fishing, and sailing publications of every description. The stock of fishing tackle is limited, but you can really dress your boat in style with all the add-on amenities offered here. You can also dress yourself: Key West Marine carries a large selection of stylish boating togs.

## BOAT SALES, REPAIRS, FUEL & STORAGE

Facilities throughout the Florida Keys carry a wide variety of new and used boats. For boat owners, most of these sales centers provide all the necessary services, including local hauling, repairs, bottom painting, and fuel.

### Upper Keys

**CARIBEE BOAT SALES,** 81500 Overseas Hwy., Islamorada, FL 33036; (305) 664-3431; caribeeboats.com. This offshore anglers shop has been in business for over 60 years. Family-owned, Caribee Boat Sales deals with new and pre-owned boats alike. Yamaha and Mercury engines are sold here. Indoor and outdoor storage is available, and certified mechanics are on duty Mon through Sat, 8 a.m. to 5 p.m. Bottom painting and boat hauling are provided. Caribee also carries fuel and sells live bait, frozen bait, and ice. Let their friendly staff help you find what you need.

**PLANTATION BOAT MART & MARINA, INC.,** 90400 Overseas Hwy., Tavernier, FL 33070; (800) 539-2628; plantationboat.com. Their selection is always changing, but currently features beautiful Glacier Bay, Palmetto Custom, Jupiter, Sea Pro, and Hydrasport brand boats. You may also buy Yamaha, Johnson, and Evinrude engines here. Plantation Boat Mart maintains a full-service repair department that continues to grow and is now one of the most complete parts departments in South Florida. Stroll through over 40,000 square feet of under-roof service and a large parts inventory.

**SMUGGLERS COVE RESORT AND MARINA,** MM 85.5, Bayside, 85500 Overseas Hwy., Islamorada, FL 33036; (305) 664-5564; smugscove .com. The folks at Smugglers Cove Resort and Marina have developed a nice package over the years in the Upper Keys. Their building at the marina is located in a lovely nautical setting and has 33 slips that berth boats of various sizes. Leave your vessel in good hands while you check out the ship's store that carries live bait and tackle or sample some seafood at the nearby restaurant. You can rent boats here or hang out with one of the captains and go on a charter for backcountry or offshore fishing.

**UNIQUE MARINE,** MM 93 Bayside, 93160 Overseas Hwy., Tavernier Key, FL 33070 (305) 853-5370; uniquemarine.com. For more than 10 years, Unique Marine has been the established dealer for Hurricane, World Kat, Belzona, Glacier Bay Catamarans, and Sea Fox. This dealership takes pride in educating the public about Catamaran fishing boats. They are there for you long after the sale, as they value long-term relationships with their loyal customers. Stop in and see why Unique Marine continuously receives prestigious customer service awards from various boat manufacturers year after year.

**Middle Keys**

**THE BOAT HOUSE MARINA,** MM 53.5 Oceanside, 33050 Overseas Hwy., Marathon FL 33050; (305) 481-0653; theboathousemarina.com. State-of-the-art dockage exists in Marathon. Owned by the Singh Company (see the Tranquility Bay Beachfront Hotel & Resort and Parrot Key Resort listings in the Accommodations chapter), this complex is like no other in the Keys. It was constructed to withstand 155-mph winds and has high-tech security, online web cams, and auto fire suppression. The boathouse currently offers unlimited in-and-out concierge services to ensure that you get the best out of your stay.

**KEYS BOAT WORKS INC.,** MM 49 Bayside, 700 39th St. Gulf, Marathon, FL 33050; (305) 743-5583; keysboatworks.com. Keys Boat Works provides a comprehensive range of services for boats up to 67 feet in length and maintains 15-ton and 50-ton travel lifts. This full-service yard offers fiberglass work, carpentry, and Awlgrip topside painting. A variety of on-premises businesses contribute to the one-stop shopping for boat service, including diesel mechanics, an electronics specialist, a yacht refinisher, sign painter, and fiberglasser. Keys Boat Works can store vessels up to 60 feet, either in or out of the water. The facility has a capacity for 150 boats.

**MARATHON BOAT YARD MARINE CENTER,** 2059 Overseas Hwy., Marathon, FL 33050; (305) 743-6341 or (888) 726-9004; marathonboat yard.com. Marathon Boat Yard has become the first in the Florida Keys to be designated as a "Clean Boatyard." This ensures that the normally messy job of working on boats doesn't harm the environment. Marathon Boat Yard is a full-service marine yard, and on their 2-acre site, they handle new boats, yacht brokerage, sportfishing boats, center consoles, cocktail cruisers, and more.

**Lower Keys**

**SEA CENTER,** MM 29.5 Oceanside, 29740 Overseas Hwy., Big Pine Key, FL 33043; (305) 872-2243; sea-center.com. Sea Center offers full-service inside and outside rack storage. They are repower specialists with the latest products from Mercury, Evinrude, and Suzuki Marine. They maintain a complete marine store with parts, fuel, and accessories.

> **i** If you see a red-and-white diver-down flag displayed while you are boating, stay at least 100 feet away. Divers or snorkelers are in these waters. Motoring between 100 feet and 300 feet from a diver-down flag must be at idle speed.

## Key West

**FISH AND RACE, 5555 College Rd., Key West, FL 33040; (305) 292-2291; fishandrace.com.** Dedicated and admittedly aggressively passionate, the expert mechanics at Fish and Race are not fooling around. Decades of combined experience help them keep your fishing or racing boat in top shape. An extensive inventory of repair parts and a vast selection of new Mercury and Honda outboard engines offer top-of-the-line tune-ups to powerhead and gear-case rebuilding on engines that range in size from 2.5 to 300 horsepower.

> **i** Tycoon Henry Flagler was not only famous for his overseas railroad from Miami to Key West but also operated three cargo ships that sailed from Key West to Havana, Cuba. Measuring up to 350 feet in length, each one held a capacity of 30 refrigerated railroad cars on board.

**GARRISON BIGHT MARINA, Palm Ave. and Eisenhower Dr., Key West, FL 33040; (305) 294-3093; garrisonbightmarina.net.** This full-service marina offers both long- and short-term dry or in-water storage for those who always want their boats available to go back out on a quick adventure. Their fuel dock is equipped with two pumps available for fast fueling, and Yamalube and OMC oil are also available. Garrison Bight Marina is the only authorized Yamaha dealer in Key West.

**OCEANSIDE MARINA KEY WEST, 5950 Peninsula Ave., Stock Island, FL 33040; (305) 294-4676.** Formerly Kings Point Marina, this marina facility has wet slips available up to 80 feet, and the T-Head accommodates yachts up to 120 feet. Amenities include a large bathhouse with laundry, fuel, ice, and bait.

**PROP DOCTOR OF KEY WEST, MM 5 Oceanside, Peninsular Ave. #4, Stock Island, FL 33040; (305) 292-0012.** The owners go by the creed "Boats need to be on the water, not out of the water." A lot of boat owners know that if you shear a prop or damage it by striking something, you could be landlocked for weeks. Now at Prop Doctor, you can be back on the high seas in just a few days. They do all the work themselves on Stock Island and do not send the repairs to the mainland. You can call them and they will send a driver out to the marina to pick up the damaged prop and bring it back to you, sometimes in only a matter of hours. Prop Doctor can also handle shafts, struts, and rudders. Their goal is to keep you fishing!

## KAYAKING

The first kayaks were created by Arctic Indians, the Inuit. Constructed of wooden frames covered in sealskin, the kayaks varied by design from region to region. Today, kayaks are equally creative and beautiful in design. Using one of these ancient forms of water transportation in the eco-sensitive Florida Keys is a great way to reduce our carbon footprint and further protect this fragile spot on Earth. A wonderfully impressive book on kayaking is *Florida Keys Paddling Atlas*, written by Mary and Bill Burnham (burnhamguides.com). It is a great companion on the beaches of the Keys.

### Upper Keys

**BACKCOUNTRY COWBOY OUTFITTERS, MM 82.2 Bayside, 82240 Overseas Hwy., Islamorada, FL 33036; (305) 517-4177; backcountrycowboy .com.** Living large in the Florida Keys but not wrestling herds of cattle, Backcountry Cowboy Outfitters deals with a huge range of kayaks and welcomes customers to paddle and explore the beautiful waters here. Noted for their 2-hour guided kayak tours, plus camping and kayaking equipment, these folks fulfill your every request and are open 7 days a week. Ask about their sunset tour as well as their historical Indian Key excursion.

**FLORIDA BAY OUTFITTERS, MM 104 Bayside, 104050 Overseas Hwy., Key Largo, FL 33037; (305) 451-3018; paddlefloridakeys.com.** Florida Bay Outfitters is one of South Florida's largest kayak, paddleboard, and canoe dealers, with loads of accessories in stock. This place will have you sport-paddling in no time! The knowledgeable and dedicated staff know their business well. They offer sales and rentals with 3-hour and full-day trips, plus water trips during a full moon.

**THE KAYAK SHACK, MM 77 Oceanside, at Robbie's Marina, 77522 Overseas Hwy., Islamorada, FL 33036; (305) 664-4878; kayakthefloridakeys .com.** Explore the backcountry waters by renting a kayak or paddleboard from the Kayak Shack. You can paddle into the unknown by yourself, or take one of several guided tours through their mangrove canopy system or to Lignumvitae or Indian Key State Parks (see the Attractions chapter).

### Middle Keys

**MARATHON KAYAK, Marathon, FL 33050; (305) 395-0355; marathon kayak.com.** Well-known for kayaking tours throughout the Keys, Marathon Kayak is a top-notch group to outfit and guide you in your journey. After customers purchase their gear, they are encouraged to get the feel for their equipment and product line to ensure satisfaction. Marathon Kayak offers multiple locations for outings, including adventures through the Everglades, mangrove canals, and sunset tours. Run by avid outdoor enthusiasts, Marathon Kayak is dedicated to providing visitors with a fun and memorable kayaking experience.

## Lower Keys

**REELAX CHARTERS,** MM 17 Oceanside, Sugarloaf Key; (305) 744-0263 or (305) 304-1392; keyskayaking.com. Enjoy backcountry trips on the water in the mangroves and across the untouched sand flats of the tranquil Lower Keys with Reelax Charters' own Captain Andrea. Take the opportunity to have fun with the family (Reelax is pet-friendly!), or take a romantic trip for two out on the water.

**REFLECTIONS NATURE TOURS,** Big Pine Key, FL 33043; (305) 872-4668 or (305) 872-7474; floridakeyskayaktours.com. Reflections is a mobile nature tour company that trailers their kayaks to a number of tour locations in the Lower Keys to take advantage of the tides and the prevailing winds. With more than 20 key kayaking and paddleboarding spots, Captain Bill Keogh can always find a favorable paddling site in any wind condition. Marine life, birds, plant life, and indigenous Keys animals can be viewed up close and personal to restore your sense of wonder and relaxation.

## Key West

**BLUE PLANET KAYAK ECO-TOURS,** Key West, 33040; (305) 809-9110 or (855) 249-1159 or (305) 294-8087 (rentals); blue-planet-kayak.com. Join in the fun with Blue Planet Kayak and take one of their informative and lively kayak tours. Offering everything from eco-tours to sunset, starlight, birding, and custom tours, these folks know their stuff. They also rent kayaks on an hourly basis or until sunset for some on-your-own paddling adventures. Pick up and drop off at your hotel is provided!

**LAZY DOG KAYAKING,** 5114 Overseas Hwy., Key West, FL 33040; (305) 295-9898; lazydog.com. Stop by the Lazy Dog shack and sign up for a 2- or 4-hour kayak tour around Key West. You can rent a single or double kayak, or try your hand (and balance) at paddleboarding, too!

## POWERBOAT RENTALS

The following rental facilities offer US Coast Guard–approved, safety-equipped vessels. Rental boats vary in size and number of configurations. Call the establishments to inquire about specific boats offered, their features, and prices. (Prices are usually quoted without tax or gasoline.) Purchase the nautical chart you need (see the Aids to Navigation section in this chapter) and bring it with you to the boat-rental facility of your choice. Most facilities will provide you with an operational briefing before you set off. Some require that you remain within a specific locale at all times, sometimes based on weather conditions.

## Upper Keys

**ROBBIE'S BOAT RENTALS & CHARTERS,** MM 77.5 Bayside, 77522 Overseas Hwy., Islamorada, FL 33036; (305) 664-8070 or (877) 664-8498; robbies.com. One of the Florida Keys' more interesting boat-rental facilities, Robbie's is behind the Hungry Tarpon Restaurant. Visitors come to Robbie's just to feed the many tarpon that lurk close to shore (see the Kidstuff chapter). Boat rentals are popular as well—especially since Robbie's is only half a mile from historic Indian Key (see the Attractions chapter). Robbie's rents boats from 18 to 21 feet in length, accommodating 8 people comfortably.

## Key West

**BOAT RENTALS OF KEY WEST,** The Galleon Resort and Marina, 617 Front St., Key West, 33040; (305) 791-1909; boatrentalsofkeywest.com. Park for free in one of the several spots available and then rent a Boston Whaler, or a Center Console, or how about a Deck boat—all ranging from 16 to 24 feet. Walk up and hop on a Jet Ski rental as well. Boat Rentals of Key West guarantees the lowest prices. Guided Boat and Jet Ski tours are also offered. Set out and snorkel, dolphin-watch, fish inland, or watch the sunset as you cruise.

**GARRISON BIGHT MARINA,** Palm Ave. and Eisenhower Dr., Key West, FL 33040; (305) 294-3093; garrisonbightmarina.net. Open 7 days a week, Garrison Bight Marina offers a modern fleet of boats to rent ranging from 15 to 29 feet. They rent by the hour, half day, or full day. Find all the bait, ice, and refreshments you need for an afternoon of very happy boating!

> **i** The 26 segments of the Florida Circumnavigational Saltwater Paddling Trail allow kayakers to explore every Florida coastal habitat type, from barrier island dune systems to salt marsh to mangroves. The trail traces the state of Florida shoreline, and segment 15 encompasses the Florida Keys. For maps of the trail and information on primitive campsites specifically for paddlers, visit dep.state.fl.us/gwt/paddling/saltwater.htm.

## SAILING

The Florida Keys are often described by sailors as the "American Caribbean." Our offshore barrier reef provides protection from swells, allowing many skippers with low-draft boats to trim up their sails and guide their craft through the Intracoastal Waterway. It is important to note that monohulls with 6-foot drafts have difficulty getting out of bayside marinas, but most marinas and harbors run deep enough to accommodate virtually any type of sailboat (see the Cruising chapter). Local Keys sailing clubs organize their own informal races. Sailing in the Florida Keys can include cruising, limited bareboat (no crew or provisions provided) charters, and a combination of snorkeling, fishing, or diving.

### Sailing Courses

Several facilities throughout our islands offer sailing courses for beginner through advanced levels, along with bareboat certification and brush-up sessions. Prices vary greatly depending upon the duration and complexity of the courses and the number of people participating. Be sure to ask about all your options when you call to book your instruction.

### Bareboat Charters

If you already know how to sail or you prefer to explore our waters on your own, the Florida Keys also offers captained and bareboat charters for anywhere from 2 hours to several weeks. Prices vary depending upon the size of the vessel and the length of the bareboat excursion.

**TREASURE HARBOR CHARTERS,** 200 Treasure Harbor Dr., Islamorada, FL 33036; (305) 852-2458 or (800) FLA-BOAT; treasureharbor.com. Treasure Harbor maintains a fleet of yachts ranging in size from 23.5 to 41 feet, including Watkins, Hunter, and Morgan varieties. Skilled sailors can charter any one of these boats on their own, and written and verbal "exams" will test your sailing experience. Professional captains will provide nautical charts, overviews of Florida Keys waters, and suggestions of places to visit. Skippers are available. A security deposit is required.

### Sailing Clubs & Regattas

Avid sailors throughout our islands have formed sailing clubs, which sponsor casual regattas. These are not your upscale yacht clubs, but membership does have its privileges, such as discounted race-entry fees and dinners, and the opportunity to meet individuals who share your interests.

**KEY WEST COMMUNITY SAILING CENTER,** 705 Palm Ave., Garrison Bight Causeway, Key West, FL 33040; (305) 292-5993; keywestsailingcenter .com. The Key West Community Sailing Center (formerly the Key West Sailing Club) is a nonprofit organization open to anyone who wants to learn about the great sport of sailing. This is an active club of avid world travelers, competitive racers, and casual day sailors dedicated to their tight-knit nautical community. Offering educational programs for sailors of all ages and skill levels, they cover the basics of sailing and racing on a variety of boats they own, including Opti Prams, Hobie Waves, Sunfish, Lasers, and 420s. Age group determines which boat will be used for teaching. Dates and times of courses change seasonally; call for details.

> **i** High-profile fleets, intense competition, and superb sailing conditions draw the boat-racing crowds to Quantum Key West, a major international sailing regatta held annually during the third week of January. Typically more than 150 boats in 13 classes compete in this exciting race.

**UPPER KEYS SAILING CLUB, MM 100 Bayside, 100 Ocean Bay Dr., Key Largo, FL 33037; (305) 451-9972; upperkeyssailingclub.com.** Established in 1973, the Upper Keys Sailing Club is based in a club-owned house on the bay and comprises Upper Keys residents of all ages. Races on Buttonwood Sound and social events are held on a regular basis; non-member spectators watch from clubhouse grounds for a small charge. Two offshore races take place over a 2-week period. As a community service, members provide free 2-day sailing seminars 4 times a year. Seminars combine 2 hours of classroom instruction with extensive time on the water aboard the club's 19-foot Flying Scot. Members contend that they have the best view of the sunset from their clubhouse.

## HOUSEBOAT RENTALS

Florida Keys houseboats provide all the comforts of home combined with a camplike experience. Whether you seek a weekend excursion or a gently rocking place to spend your vacation, a houseboat rental may very well float your boat. (And, yes, the pun was intended.)

**KEYS HOUSEBOAT RENTALS, 107900 Overseas Hwy., Key Largo, FL 33037; (877) 744-9442; keyshouseboatrentals.com.** Here is a perfect chance to try something new and relax while you do it. Renting a houseboat is a unique, fun, and affordable alternative to staying in a landlocked hotel. All houseboat rentals are located within Gilbert's Resort and do not leave the dock. Most of them have been newly remodeled and fashioned for the utmost in comfort and convenience. Your vacation rental provides you with full resort privileges, including pool access, a tiki bar, use of a small (but pleasant) beach, outdoor dining, and a boat ramp. Powerboat, stand-up paddleboard, kayak, and personal watercraft rentals are available for anyone staying here as well.

# Cruising

Regarded as America's out-islands by seasoned cruisers of motor and sailing yachts, the Florida Keys can justifiably boast about the sheltered harbors and easily navigated waters enveloping the serpentine stretch. Our waters are well marked; our charts, up-to-date; and the US Coast Guard keeps channels dredged to the proper depth. The Atlantic's Hawk Channel runs along the ocean side of the Keys, protected by the only coral reef in the continental US. The Intracoastal Waterway—called the Big Ditch in the North's inland waters—cuts through the causeway from the mainland at Jewfish Creek and then parallels the Keys through Florida Bay and the Gulf of Mexico. To help you plan your Keys cruising adventure, we guide you on a tour of our preeminent marinas and little-known anchoring-out destinations (in descending order from the Upper to Lower Keys). Be sure to read our Key West and Beyond section, where the junket continues.

## THE FLORIDA KEYS

### Marinas

All marinas listed in this chapter take transient boaters, but we suggest you make reservations at least a month in advance from Dec through Mar. Most marinas have stores or are within walking distance of a convenience market. The marinas keep an active list of expert marine mechanics who are generally on call. We highlight fuel dock facilities and availability of laundry, showers, and restrooms. We also point out restaurants and the hot spots for partying while ashore. Dockmasters monitor VHF channel 16, but they will ask you to switch channels once you have established contact. They will give you detailed directions to the marinas.

> **i** "Wet-foot, dry-foot" is the name of the 1995 revision to the Cuban Adjustment Act of 1996. The revision designates that any Cuban caught on the waters between two nations ("wet feet") would be sent back to his country. Make it ashore ("dry feet"), and he would get a chance to remain in the US.

**THE MARINA CLUB AT BACKWATER SOUND, MM 104 Bayside, 103950 Overseas Hwy., Key Largo, FL 33037; (305) 453-0081; marinaclub keylargo.com.** The future of boat storage is deeded rackominiums, and the Marina Club at Backwater Sound has plenty of options for those seeking these state-of-the-art dry racks. This club is in an ideal location and offers several amenities, including showers, a lounge, fuel, boat care, restaurant, Wi-Fi access, concierge, diving, and spa services.

**MARINA DEL MAR MARINA, MM 100 Oceanside, 527 Caribbean Dr., Key Largo, FL 33037; (305) 453-7171 or (305) 451-4107; marinadelmarkey largo.com.** Plan ahead if you want to stay at one of the 77 slips at the Marina Del Mar Marina, which lies within the underwater boundaries of John Pennekamp Coral Reef State Park and the Key Largo National Marine Sanctuary. Located on the largest deep sea marina in Key Largo, all but a select few are usually booked far in advance from Jan through Mar. Guests have access to 4 pools, 3 Jacuzzis, fitness center, tennis courts, shower and laundry facilities, on-site boat ramp, and continental breakfast for anyone staying on your boat. If you're still hungry, grab a bite at Bogie's Cafe or the Poolside Tiki Bar.

**THE PILOT HOUSE MARINA, MM 99.5 Oceanside, 13 Seagate Blvd., Key Largo, FL 33037; (305) 747-4359 or (305) 393-3638 (after hours); pilothousemarina.com.** Sitting alongside the Pilot House Restaurant (see the Restaurants chapter), this marina offers an array of services to boaters. Deep dockage with slips that can accommodate up to 85-foot-long boats, repairs for your boat, 30-, 50-, and 100-amp, restrooms, showers, laundry facilities, cable TV, Wi-Fi, bait for fishing, diesel, and gasoline are available. Enjoy the glass-bottomed tiki bar at the restaurant next door.

**PLANTATION YACHT HARBOR MARINA, MM 87 Bayside, 87000 Overseas Hwy., Islamorada, FL 33036; (305) 852-2381; marinalife.com.** Grab a slip close to the Keys' fabled backcountry at the bayside Plantation Yacht Harbor, a municipal marina located in the famed sportfishing capital of the world! This 85-slip marina offers easy access to the Florida Bay and Atlantic Ocean. The newly renovated facilities offer on-site laundry, showers, and restroom facilities, wireless Internet, kayak rentals, cable TV, and a fuel dock with gas and diesel. Sit back with some of the finest fishing captains in the area as you enjoy a day onshore with a swimming pool, tennis courts, a sandy beach, and playground. Call ahead for availability.

**ISLAMORADA MARINA, MM 80.5 Bayside, 80461 Overseas Hwy., Islamorada FL 33036; (305) 664-8884; islamoradamarina.com.** Facing Florida Bay, the location of Islamorada Marina provides clear passage into the flats and bay of the Florida Keys, Everglades National Park, and the Atlantic Ocean.

This sprawling marina has storage racks to accommodate up to 200 boats ranging from 15 to 35 feet in length. Committed to constantly improving, the owners have undergone several construction projects to ensure that customers have the most satisfying experience possible. Boat maintenance and repair services are available, as well as competitively priced gas and diesel. If you are looking to fish, kayak, or just sit back and slow down for a bit, this marina is for you.

> **i** Due to the city of Key West's bay-bottom lease, cruise ships may only dock at Mallory Square Pier 12 times a year during sunset. The ships must either moor elsewhere the rest of the year or leave at least one hour before sunset so as not to block the view!

**HAWK'S CAY RESORT AND MARINA, MM 61 Oceanside, 61 Hawks Cay Blvd., Duck Key, FL 33050; (305) 743-7000 or (888) 395-5539; hawkscay.com.** Probably the best all-around marina in the Keys, Hawk's Cay offers a totally protected boat basin and all the amenities of its fine resort hotel (see our Accommodations and Restaurants chapters). Dock your boat at one of the 85 full-service marina slips with fuel, freshwater, cable TV, and phone. Hawk's Cay maintains an extensive list of qualified marine mechanics on call. Rest easy as you leave your boat behind in their care and enjoy the laid-back ease of Hawk's Cay. This marina is accessed via Hawk Channel at marker no. 44 when traveling down the Keys, or at marker no. 45 when approaching from Key West.

**DOLPHIN MARINA AND COTTAGES, MM 28.5 Oceanside, 28530 Overseas Hwy., Little Torch Key, FL 33042; (305) 872-2685 (800) 553-0308; dolphinmarina.net.** Dolphin Marina offers not only boat rentals and dockage but also quaint, nearby lodging. The lodging quarters consist of small cottages overlooking Newfound Harbor and cozy apartments with 1 or 2 bedrooms. Just minutes from luxurious Little Palm Island (see the Accommodations chapter), this down-to-earth marina offers all you need for a day afloat on the open waters of the Atlantic. Dolphin Marina has a fleet of boats that visitors can rent. The marina's ship's store can stock you with all the supplies you may have forgotten. Located at 24.39.95 north latitude and 81.23.28 west longitude.

**LITTLE PALM ISLAND RESORT & SPA, MM 28.5 Oceanside, 28500 Overseas Hwy., Little Torch Key, FL 33042; (305) 872-2524 or (800) 343-8567; littlepalmisland.com.** This exquisite jewel is more reminiscent of the

South Seas than South Florida. Even though it is the most expensive marina in the Florida Keys, staying at this marina is a good deal. As marina guests, you are invited to use all of the recreational facilities: fishing gear, canoes, snorkeling gear, the beach, swimming pool, showers, laundry, and sauna. Children younger than 16 are not permitted at Little Palm Island, and pets must be kept on a leash and in designated areas. Little Palm Island is accessed via the Atlantic at the entrance to Newfound Harbor, red marker no. 2.

**SUGARLOAF MARINA, MM 17 Bayside, 17015 Overseas Hwy., Sugarloaf Shores, FL 33042; (305) 745-3135; sugarloafkeymarina.com.** Housed next to the Sugarloaf Lodge, this marina has ramp access, fuel, beer, soda, bait, tackle, and ice. It may be a little rough around the edges, but locals give it a thumbs-up. Air tours are also offered, allowing those who try it to experience what ultralight sport seaplane flying is all about (plus actually getting some hands-on experience if you like!). Discover the pristine beauty and marine life of the Florida Keys from just inches off the water to hundreds of feet in the air. Make sure to call ahead to reserve a chance to experience this for yourself!

## Anchoring Out

*Barefoot elegance, breathtakingly beautiful,* and *peaceful* all describe anchoring out in the pristine waters lacing the Florida Keys. From the northernmost keys of Biscayne Bay to Loggerhead Key at the end of the line, remote havens remain unspoiled, many reachable only by boat. Ibis, white pelicans, and bald eagles winter among select out-islands, and whole condominiums of cormorants take over the scrub of tiny mangrove islets. Gulf waters simmer with snapper, redfish, lobster, and stone crabs. The Atlantic Ocean sparkles with the glory of the living coral reef beneath. So pack up and push off for an Insiders' bareboat cruise of the Florida Keys, from top to toe.

### *Elliott Key*

On the eastern side of Biscayne Bay, the island of Elliott Key, which has the ranger station for Biscayne National Park, guards a complex ecosystem from the ocean's battering winds. A strong current rushes through the shallow channel between Sands Key and Elliott Key, and small-boat traffic is heavy on weekends. Although the fishing and diving here are first-rate, take care. At the southern tip of Elliott Key, Caesar Creek—named for notorious pirate Black Caesar, who dipped in to stay out of sight in the 1600s—offers dicey passage to Hawk Channel for boats carefully clearing a 4-foot draft at high tide. The more forgiving Angelfish Creek, farther south at the north end of Key Largo, is the favored route from Biscayne Bay to the ocean in this wild and deserted area. Angelfish Creek is the Intracoastal Waterway's last outlet to the ocean until after Snake Creek Drawbridge, for large boats, or those heading for Hawk Channel.

### Pumpkin Key

Safe anchorage surrounds Pumpkin Key, making this island an ideal choice for winds coming from any direction. Be sure to test your anchorage, because Pumpkin Key's waters cover a grassy sea bottom. Nearby Angelfish Creek—filled with grouper, snapper, and angelfish—almost guarantees dinner. Scoot out the creek to take advantage of the diving at John Pennekamp Coral Reef State Park. Approachable from Hawk Channel or the Intracoastal, this area remains virginal even though it rests in the shadow of Key Largo.

### Blackwater Sound

As you anchor in the placid ebony waters of Blackwater Sound, the twinkling lights of Key Largo remind you that civilization is but a dinghy ride away. Anchor along the southeast shoreline of Blackwater Sound for a protected anchorage in east to southeast winds. The Cross Key Canal, which connects Blackwater Sound to Largo Sound, passes under a fixed bridge at the Overseas Highway in Key Largo. If your boat clears 14 feet safely, traverse the canal to dive or snorkel in John Pennekamp Coral Reef State Park.

### Tarpon Basin

Enter Tarpon Basin through Dusenbury Creek or Grouper Creek. Both passages teem with snapper and grouper.

### Largo Sound (John Pennekamp Coral Reef State Park)

John Pennekamp Coral Reef State Park and the adjacent Key Largo National Marine Sanctuary encompass the ocean floor under Hawk Channel from Broad Creek to Molasses Reef. Exit the Intracoastal Waterway at Angelfish Creek and enter Hawk Channel to proceed to Largo Sound. Enter Largo Sound through South Sound Creek. Park staff supervise this anchorage, which is completely sheltered in any weather. Call on VHF channel 16 to reserve a mandatory mooring buoy in the southwest portion of the sound; anchoring is prohibited. A nominal fee for the moorings entitles boaters to full use of park facilities and its pump-out station. The reefs of John Pennekamp Coral Reef State Park shine brighter than others in the Keys. More sun filters through the shallow water, causing the coral to flourish. Much of this reef breaks the surface of the water during low tide.

### Butternut Key & Bottle Key

Don't worry. Those baby sharks you see in the waters surrounding Butternut Key won't hurt you. The skittish infants leave this nursery area when they reach 2 to 3 feet in length. Prevailing winds will determine anchorage sites near these islands, which offer good holding ground. On the Florida Bay side of Tavernier, Butternut Key and Bottle Key showcase voluminous birdlife. Roseate spoonbills breed on Bottle Key, feeding upon the tiny killifish of the flats. A pond on the island attracts mallard ducks in the winter.

### Cotton Key

Approach Cotton Key from the Intracoastal Waterway. This anchorage, protected from north to southeast winds, offers the best nightlife in the Keys north of Key West. Take your dinghy around the entire island of Upper Matecumbe and the community of Islamorada. Catch the action at the Lorelei or Atlantic's Edge at Cheeca Lodge (see the Restaurants chapter). Check out the fishing charters at Bud n' Mary's Marina (see the Fishing chapter). Stop in at the Islamorada Fish Company and take ready-to-eat stone crabs back to your boat for a private sunset celebration (see the Specialty Foods, Cafes & Markets chapter). Dinghy through Whale Harbor Channel to the Islamorada Sandbar, which at low tide becomes an island beach. And, if you'd just like to commune with nature, the forested northeast section of Upper Matecumbe Key hosts a rookery for good bird-watching. *Note:* There is a no-motor zone on the tidal flat.

### Lignumvitae Key

Government-owned Lignumvitae Key stands among the tallest of the Keys, at 17 to 18 feet above sea level. A virgin hammock sprinkled with lignum vitae trees re-creates the feeling of the Keys of yesteryear, before mahogany forests were cut and sold to Bahamian shipbuilders. From 1919 to 1953 the Matheson family, of chemical company notoriety, owned the island, where they built a large home and extensive gardens of rare plantings. Hug the northwest side of the island for good anchorage in east to southeast winds. Dinghy to the Lignumvitae Key dock for guided tours conducted by the state parks service. Nearby Shell Key almost disappears at high tide, so exercise caution. Pods of playful dolphins romp in Lignumvitae Basin, and a sighting of lumbering sea turtles is not unusual. But be sure to bait a hook—fishing is prolific.

### Matecumbe Bight

If winds are not good for anchoring near Lignumvitae, Matecumbe Bight provides good holding ground, except in a north wind. Two miles south, Channel Five—east of Long Key—offers a good crossover between Florida Bay and

Hawk Channel for large sailboats. Strong currents run in the channel beneath the bridge, which is a fixed span with a 65-foot overhead clearance.

### Long Key Bight
Anchor in Long Key Bight, which is accessed via Hawk Channel oceanside or through Channel Five from the Intracoastal Waterway. Bordering Long Key State Park—a 300-acre wilderness area with a good campground, tables, and grills—the bight is protected yet open. Legendary author Zane Grey angled at the former Long Key Fishing Club during the days of Flagler's railroad. Beachcomb for washed-up treasure on the southeast shores of Long Key.

### Boot Key Harbor
Boot Key Harbor in Marathon serves as a good, safe port in a bad blow, but, crowded with liveaboards, it is a bit like anchoring out in Times Square. Enter this fully protected harbor from Sister's Creek or at the western entrance near the beginning of the Seven Mile Bridge. Moser Channel goes under the hump of the Seven Mile Bridge, creating a 65-foot clearance. The draw span of the old bridge has been removed, but the rest remains. A portion on the Marathon end now functions as the driveway to Pigeon Key (see the Attractions chapter). A stretch on the Bahia Honda end is maintained for bridge fishing and is referred to locally as the "longest fishing pier in the world." The Moser Channel and the Bahia Honda Channel (with 20-foot clearance) are the last crossover spots in the Keys. You must decide at Marathon if you will travel the Atlantic route or via the gulf to Key West. If you need fuel, note that the marina at Sunshine Key is the last bayside marina until Key West.

### Big Spanish Channel Area
Leave all traces of civilization behind and head out the Big Spanish Channel toward the out-islands. Proceed with care, for this remote sprinkling of tiny keys is part of the Great White Heron National Wildlife Refuge. Obey no-entry, no-motor, and idle-speed zones. Get your Florida bird guide out of the cabin and count the species.

### Little Spanish Key
The western side of Little Spanish Key provides the best protection from northeast to southeast winds. Explore the surrounding clear waters by dinghy, where the endangered green turtles, which weigh between 150 and 450 pounds, have been spotted feeding on sea grass. Catch your limit of snapper, and share your bounty with the friendly pelicans.

### Newfound Harbor
Newfound Harbor—formed by the Newfound Harbor Keys and the southern extension of Big Pine Key—stars as the premier oceanside harbor between

Marathon and Key West. Dinghy to exquisite Little Palm Island, the setting for the film *PT-109*, the story of John F. Kennedy's Pacific experience during World War II. Newfound Harbor lies within easy reach of Looe Key National Marine Sanctuary, a spur-and-groove coral reef ecosystem popular with divers and snorkelers.

## KEY WEST & BEYOND

Welcome to the ultimate cruising destination: Key West. Full of history and histrionics, this vibrant, intoxicating port pumps the adrenaline, pushes the envelope, and provides a rowdy good time for all. And when you signal a turn back into the slow lane again, dust off your charts and head out to the wild beyond of the Dry Tortugas, the end of the line.

### Marinas

All of our suggested marinas take transient boaters, but with the frequent special events in this area, we suggest you reserve a slip as far in advance as possible. You may assume, unless otherwise stated, that all of our recommended marinas supply hookups for both 30-amp and 50-amp service, as well as freshwater. Key West offers extensive self-provisioning facilities ranging from supermarkets to gourmet take-out shops (see the Specialty Foods, Cafes & Markets chapter). The marina dockmasters will represent you should the need for help arise. Contact the dockmaster on VHF channel 16 for directions, and read your charts closely.

**A&B MARINA,** 700 Front St., Key West, FL, 33040; (305) 294-2535 or (800) 223-8352; aandbmarina.com. A&B Marina is situated in the heart of Old Town, right in the middle of all the action. A&B offers dockage for vessels up to 190 feet in length. The marina maintains a diesel fuel dock and has a convenience store, air-conditioned shower facilities, and a laundry room. A&B Lobster House, upstairs, welcomes one and all. People-watching is great from their dockside bar. Approach A&B Marina by finding the red day marker no. 4, at the entrance of Key West Bight near the end of the rock jetty. Hail them when you reach the Bight and they will welcome you with possible slip assignments.

**THE GALLEON RESORT AND MARINA,** 617 Front St., Key West, FL 33040; (305) 296-7711 or (800) 544-3030; galleonresort.com. The excitement of Duval Street pulsates only a few blocks away, but the ambience at the Galleon remains unhurried (except when hosting championship boat-racing events!) The 91 dockage slips will accommodate vessels up to 140 feet and 9-foot drafts. Fuel is available in Key West Bight or at Conch Harbor Marina. The Galleon indulges you with all the usual amenities, as well as moped or bicycle rentals that aid you in your exploration of Key West. Follow Mainship channel, NOAA Chart No. 11445 to marker no. 24, then steer to marker no. 4 at the east end of the breakwater to enter.

**KEY WEST BIGHT MARINA, Key West Historic Seaport, 201 William St., Key West, FL 33040; (305) 809-3983; keywestcity.com.** Situated in the heart of the Key West Historic Seaport, Key West Bight Marina has 33 deepwater transient slips that will accommodate vessels up to 140 feet in length with a maximum draft of 12 feet. Tourists and locals alike utilize this marina, close to the current action offered by nearby restaurants and shops, while also connecting patrons to the many historical landmarks of Old Town. At reasonable rates, dockage includes 30-, 50-, and 100-amp power, water hookups, 24-hour security, a pump-out station, ice, and laundry facilities. Arrive at Key West Bight Marina from the Gulf of Mexico or Atlantic waters.

**THE WESTIN KEY WEST RESORT AND MARINA, 245 Front St., Key West, FL 33040; (305) 294-4000 ext. 7575 or (866) 837-4250 (reservations); westinkeywestresort.com.** The Westin Key West Resort and Marina offers transients all the perks of its lavish property. Make reservations up to 6 months in advance to dock at the Westin Key West Resort and Marina. Only 1 block off famed Duval Street, its location can't be beat and it fills up quickly. The adjoining resort owns the private offshore Sunset Key, where guests may take a day trip and enjoy its pristine beach, away from the fray.

## Anchoring Out

The highway may stop in Key West, but the path to adventure continues into the sunset. The Dry Tortugas, the brightest gems in the necklace, mark the real end of the line in the Florida Keys. Once you leave Key West Harbor, you join the ranks of the swashbucklers who have abandoned the safety of civilization to explore the vast unknown. Be sure you know the range and capabilities of your craft, because only self-sufficient cruising vessels can make the 140-nautical-mile trek to the Dry Tortugas and back. There is no fuel, freshwater, provisioning, or facilities of any kind once you leave Key West. Unpredictable foul weather could keep you trapped at sea for days, so make sure you are fueled for 200 miles, and stock the larder for extenuating circumstances.

### Key West

If you want to anchor out in busy Key West Harbor, look for a spot west of Fleming Key in about 10 to 15 feet of water. You'll find less current, good holding ground, and less fishing-vessel traffic than around Wisteria Island. The municipal dinghy dock at the foot of Simonton Street is the only official place to land your dinghy, but you might want to arrange secured short-term dockage for your dinghy from one of the marina dockmasters.

# Lighthouses of the Florida Keys

Nostalgic memories are aroused when you think of lighthouses. Rugged, isolated, beautiful in their strength, and haunting in their history, these beacons of light hold the imagination of anyone interested in sea navigation.

General George Gordon Meade's first career may have been a commander of Union forces, but his interest and real love was in pharology. His genius in marine engineering led him to Delaware Bay and the building of lighthouses along that body of water. Known for his screw-pile design in lighthouses, most of his structures remain standing today. Meade came to the Florida Keys, where he designed and built Carysfort, Sombrero, Rebecca, and Sand Key Lighthouses. To end his dignified career, he went on to design the beautiful Fairmount Park in Philadelphia.

**Carysfort Reef Lighthouse:** Placed on the National Register of Historic Places in 1984, this red lighthouse was built in 1825 and first lit in 1852. Carysfort is the oldest iron screw-pile lighthouse still functioning in the US, and the first of this type in the Florida Keys. Named for the HMS *Carysfort*, which ran into the reef in 1770, and automated in 1960, it stands at 112 feet and is shaped in a skeletal octagonal pyramid.

**Alligator Reef Lighthouse:** This still-functioning lighthouse was built in 1873 and sits 4 miles east of Indian Key off Islamorada. Automated in 1963, this old beauty is an iron pile with a platform and painted white and black. The height is 136 feet, and it is skeletal in its shape.

**Sombrero Key Lighthouse:** Built in 1858 in the skeletal octagonal pyramidal design, brown in color, and automated in 1960, Sombrero still

## Boca Grande Key

A string of shoals and keys snakes west from Key West, offering unparalleled diving and fishing opportunities. Beyond Man and Woman Keys—popular snorkeling spots—Boca Grande Key offers a good day anchorage on the northwestern side with a beautiful white-sand beach. The current is too swift to anchor overnight. Be alert to the constantly shifting shoals around the entrance channel. Note also that this island is a turtle nesting ground—all or parts of it are off-limits during specific times of the year, and fines are possible.

helps boats navigate the waters off Marathon. Not open to the public, this 160-foot lighthouse is operated by the US Coast Guard.

**American Shoal Lighthouse:** Built in 1880, this lighthouse sits in the Atlantic off Sugarloaf Key. The brown-and-white sentinel was automated in 1963. It reaches a height of 103 feet and was constructed in the skeletal octagonal pyramidal shape.

**Key West Lighthouse:** Located at 938 Whitehead Street in historic Old Town, this 86-foot black-and-white structure is a real gem. Built in 1847 for the purpose of helping ships navigate the perilous reefs off the Lower Keys, it was listed on the National Register of Historic Places in 1998. It was automated in 1915, then deactivated in 1969. Built in the West Indian vernacular style, it now is open as a museum and operated by the Monroe County and City of Key West Historical Society.

**Loggerhead Key Lighthouse:** Used as an active aid for navigating Dry Tortugas National Park off Key West, this black-and-white structure was built in 1858 and was automated in 1988. Standing 157 feet, the lighthouse is operated by the National Park Service and is open to the public.

**Tortugas Harbor Lighthouse** (also known as the Garden Key Lighthouse): This hexagonal-shaped black beauty stands proudly in Garden Key, off Key West. It is operated by the National Park Service and open to the public. Built in 1876, activated in 1912, and deactivated in 1921, the lighthouse sits in Dry Tortugas National Park and is accessible only by boat or seaplane.

**Sand Key Lighthouse:** Seven miles southwest off Key West, this lighthouse with its red and black colors stands 120 feet out of the water. Built in 1826, automated in 1938, and deactivated from 1989 to 1998, it's not open to the public. Built in the square skeletal with center column design, it is listed on the National Register of Historic Places.

## Marquesas Keys

About 24 miles from Key West, a broken collar of low-lying, beach-belted islands forms the Marquesas Keys. If you pass Mooney Harbor Key on your way into the inner sanctum, watch for coral heads about 1,100 yards offshore. Prevailing winds will determine at which side to anchor, but you should be able to achieve a protected anchorage. Many a ship has crashed on the coral heads in this area, leaving interesting wrecks, but check with the Coast Guard before you dive, because the US Navy has been known to use the area west of the Marquesas as a bombing and strafing range. Explore the big rookery of frigate birds or take aim with a little spearfishing. This pit stop on the way to the

Dry Tortugas rates as an end point in itself. *Note:* A 300-foot no-motor zone is established around the three smallest islands; a 300-foot no-access buffer zone is established around one mangrove island; and an idle-speed-only / no-wake zone is established in the southwest tidal creek.

### Dry Tortugas

Open water stretches like a hallucination from the Marquesas to our southernmost national park, the Dry Tortugas. Ponce de León named these islands the Tortugas—Spanish for "turtles"—in 1513, presumably because the waters teemed with sea turtles, which he consumed as fresh meat. Lack of freshwater rendered the islands dry.

The first sight of the massive brick fortress of Fort Jefferson, the colorful history of which began in 1846, is breathtaking (see the Attractions chapter). Unparalleled diving exists in these unsullied waters. Colors appear more brilliant because the waters are clearer than those bordering the inhabited Keys. The entire area is a no-take zone, so don't be alarmed if you spot a prehistoric-size lobster or jewfish. Be sure to snorkel the underwater nature trail. From your dinghy, watch for the nesting sooty and noddy terns in their Bush Key sanctuary (landing is forbidden).

Fishing and anchoring to anything except mooring buoys is strictly prohibited in the 46-square-mile Research Natural Area (RNA) in Dry Tortugas National Park. Overnight anchoring can only occur on sand bottoms within 1 nautical mile of the Harbor Light at Fort Jefferson. Combined with the Tortugas Ecological Reserve and now the RNA, this is the largest no-take marine reserve in the continental US. The popular fishing area in the Dry Tortugas— the anchorage around Fort Jefferson and Garden Key—remains open for recreational fishing.

### Loggerhead Key

Just beyond Garden Key dozes Loggerhead Key, called the prettiest beach in the Keys by those in the know. A good day anchorage with a legion of interesting coral, this is literally the end of the line for the Florida Keys. Nothing but 900 miles of water lies between this point and the Mexican coast. Hope you remembered to fuel up in Key West!

# Fishing

Anglers fish here with an intensity rarely seen anywhere else in the US . . . the world, even. Eavesdrop on a conversation anywhere in the Keys, and someone will be talking about fishing. As you drive down the Overseas Highway and look out at our acres of shimmering waters, you will feel an overwhelming urge to join in the battle of power and wits—fish against angler—that makes the Keys so special.

The Florida Keys have more than 1,000 species of fish; most are edible, all are interesting. To pursue our bonefish, permit, tarpon, snook, or any other species, you will need a saltwater fishing license (see the Fishing Licenses section in this chapter). You must obey catch and season restrictions and size limits. These regulations change often. Ask for an up-to-date listing when you purchase your fishing license.

The Florida Keys fall within the boundaries of the Florida Keys National Marine Sanctuary, created by the federal government in 1990 to protect the resources of our marine ecosystem. And while, for the most part, visitors freely swim, dive, snorkel, boat, fish, or recreate on our waters, some regulations took effect in July 1997 to guide these activities. Refer to the Boating chapter for information on these regulations before you venture into our waters. For a complete copy of the regulations and marine coordinates of the areas, contact the Sanctuary office, (305) 292-0311, or check their website, floridakeys.noaa.gov.

## CATCH-AND-RELEASE ETHICS

Preserve our natural resources. "A fish is too valuable to be caught only once," the US Department of Commerce, the National Oceanic and Atmospheric Administration, and the National Marine Fisheries Service maintain. We agree. The spirit behind the catch-and-release policy is to enjoy the hunt and the score, but take a photograph of the fish home with you, not the quarry itself. Taxidermists do not need the actual fish to prepare a mount for you; they only need the approximate measurements. Take home only those food fish you plan to eat.

To properly release a fish, keep the fish in the water and handle it very little whenever possible. Dislodge the hook quickly with a hook-removal tool, backing the hook out the opposite way it went in. If the hook can't be removed quickly, cut the leader close to the mouth. Hold the fish by the bottom jaw or lip—not the gills—with a wet hand or glove so that you don't damage its mucus or scales. Have your photo taken with the fish, then cradle the tired fish, rocking it back and forth in the water until it is able to swim away under its own power. This increases the oxygen flow through its gills, reviving the fish and thereby augmenting its chances for survival against a barracuda or shark.

## WHERE TO FISH

To introduce you to our complex watery ecosystem and the species of fish dwelling therein, we have divided fishing destinations into four distinct sections: the flats, the backcountry, blue water, and the bridges.

### The Flats

The continental shelf is nature's gift to the Florida Keys. Stretching from the shoreline like a layer of rippled fudge on a marble slab, it lingers for many shallow miles before plunging to the depths of the blue water. In the Keys we rather reverently call this area the flats. Waters ranging from mere inches to several feet in depth cover most of the flats, but some areas completely surface during low tide, exposing themselves to the air and intense sunlight. Changing winds, tides, temperatures, and barometric pressure ensure that conditions in the flats fluctuate constantly.

An unenlightened observer might think the flats uninteresting, for most of this watery acreage is covered with dense turtle grass, shell-less sand, or muddy muck. But far from being a wasteland, the flats are the feeding grounds and nursery for a city of marine families whose members inspire dramatic tales of daring and conquest from every person who has ever baited a hook here.

The 4,000 square miles of flats, from Key Biscayne to Key West and beyond, yield a trio of prize game fish—bonefish, permit, and tarpon—which, when caught in one day, we refer to as the Grand Slam. And keeping company in the same habitat are the bonus fish—barracuda and shark—that regularly accommodate anglers with exciting runs and fights. Fishing the flats is really a combination of angling and hunting, for you must first see and stalk the fish before you ever cast the waters. The hunt for bonefish, permit, and tarpon requires patience and unique angling skills, but most essentially, you must be at the right place at the right time.

We cannot even begin to teach you how to fish for these formidable fighters of the flats in this chapter. You should hire a professional guide, for which there is no substitute—at least while you are a novice. Guides know the local waters well and keep detailed records of where to find fish under every condition, saving you precious hours and money in the pursuit of your mission (see the Guides & Charters section of this chapter). But we will introduce you to the exciting species you will encounter on our flats, relate their personalities, tattle about their habits, and point you in the right direction so you can learn all you wish to know and share in the angling experience of a lifetime: fishing the flats in the Florida Keys.

First in the see-stalk-cast sequence so important in fishing the skinny waters of the flats is the visible interpretation of the watery hallucination under the surface. To see the fish of the flats, you must have polarized sunglasses to cut the sun's glare so that you can concentrate on looking through your reflection on the top of the water to the shallow bottom. Under the water, fish often look like bluish shadows, or they may appear as indistinct shadings that simply look different from the waters surrounding them.

Most waters of the flats in the Keys are fished from a shallow-draft skiff, or flats boat, although you can wade out from shore in many areas if you prefer. Never motor onto a flat; the fish can hear the engine noise and spook easily. Use an electric trolling motor or, better yet, pole in, using a push pole. A push pole is a fiberglass or graphite dowel, 16 to 20 feet long, with a V-crotch on one end for traversing the soft bottom of the flats and a straight end on the other for staking out. Using it requires body power and coordination and more than a little practice. A flats boat has a raised poling platform that gives the poler or guide a height advantage to more readily distinguish the fish from its shadowy surroundings, in preparation for an accurate cast.

> **i** Former president George H. W. Bush once landed a monster 130-pound tarpon in Lignumvitae Channel off Islamorada. After a 45-minute fight with this trophy catch, he tagged the fish and released it back into the wild.

At the turn of the tide, the fish begin to move into the flats, grazing like sheep in a pasture. Guides know where the fish congregate during an incoming (flood) tide and an outgoing (ebb) tide. While it may prove dangerous for the fish to come up on the flats—they expose themselves to predators—the concentration of food is too enticing for them to resist. The fish prefer feeding during the low, incoming tide; the food is still easy to find, but they won't risk becoming stranded on the flats.

### Bonefish: Phantom of the Flats

A sighting of the glistening forked tail of the Gray Ghost—alias of the famed bonefish (*Albula vulpes*) haunting our flats—has been known to elevate the blood pressure of even the most seasoned Keys angler to celestial heights. This much-respected, skittish silver bullet is considered the worthiest of all opponents, a wily, suspicious street fighter, here one moment, gone the next. The bonefish's superior eyesight, acute hearing, keen sense of smell, and boundless speed routinely befuddle anglers, some of whom dedicate their lives to thwarting the fish's Houdini-like escape attempts.

You can spot a bonefish three ways: tailing, mudding, or cruising. When the slender, silvery bonefish feeds, its head goes to the bottom and the fork of the tail will break the surface of the water—a tailing fish. The bonefish feeds into the current because its food source is delivered in the drift. As the fish puts its mouth down into the sand and silt, rooting around on the bottom of the flats, looking for shrimps, crabs, and other crustaceans, the water clouds up. This is called "making a mud." As the mudding bonefish continues feeding, the current takes the cloudy water away so it can see its prey once again. Bonefish require water temperatures of 70 degrees and higher for feeding on the flats.

Spotting a cruising fish takes some practice. Look for "nervous water." The bonefish pushes a head wake as it swims, which sometimes shows as an inconsistency on the surface of the water. On other occasions, a mere movement by the fish underwater will cause the surface water to appear altered. Most of the time that the bonefish is cruising, however, it is swimming in deeper water; you will have to spot it. The back and sides of the bonefish are so silvery, they act as a mirror. The fish swims right on the bottom of the flats in 8 or more inches of water, and the sun shining through the water causes the bottom to reflect off the sides of the fish. So if you think you have seen a ripple of weeds, the image may actually be a bonefish.

The best bait for bonefishing is live shrimp. A guide with an experienced eye will put you on the fish by calling out directions like the hands of a clock. The bow of the boat will always be 12 o'clock. You will be instructed by the guide to look in a direction—for instance, 2 o'clock—and, at a specified distance, to spot the bonefish in preparation for a cast. The cast is the most crucial part of successfully hooking a bonefish. You should be able to cast 30 feet quickly and accurately. A cast that places the bait too close to the fish will spook it and cause the bonefish to dart away at breakneck speed. If the bait is cast too far away, the fish won't find it at all. The bait should land 2 to 3 feet in front of the fish and be allowed to drift to the ocean floor.

Many times the bonefish will smell the bait prior to seeing it because the fish is downcurrent of the bait and swimming into the current. The bonefish begins to dart back and forth and goes in circles, looking for the scented prey. Once the fish locates the source of the scent, it tends to suck in the bait. You, the angler, must make sure there is no slack in the line and that your rod tip is low to the water. Then firmly but gently lift up to set the hook. Hold on tight and raise your rod straight up in the air, holding your arms as high above your head as possible. Once the fish realizes something is wrong—that it's hooked—it will peel away in an electrifying run, taking out 100 to 150 yards of line in a heartbeat. This whole process—from sighting to hooking—explodes in adrenaline-pumping nanoseconds. Ten to 30 minutes later, after the bonefish makes several pulse-pounding sprints, you can reel in the tired fish to the side of the skiff, where the guide will photograph both victor and spoils. Then quickly release the bonefish so that it may rest up and thrill another angler on yet another day (see the previous section in this chapter on catch-and-release ethics).

Bonefish usually range in size from 5 to 10 pounds, but the size of this fish belies its strength. A 5-pound bonefish fights like a 20-pound wannabe. The Keys are the only place in the continental US where an angler can fish for bonefish. Locals boast that the Keys have the biggest and best-educated bonefish this side of the Gulf Stream. Expect bonefish to grace our flats during Apr, May, June, Sept, Oct, and occasionally into Nov. Cool weather and cold fronts push them into deeper waters from Dec through Mar. The hot weather of July and Aug drives them to cooler, deeper waters as well, although some will stay all year.

### Permit: Ultimate Flats Challenge

Though sharing the same waters as the bonefish and stalked in the same manner, the permit (*Trachinotus falcatus*) proves to be a more elusive catch. Spooky, skittish, and stubborn, this finicky eater, which can take out line like a long-distance runner, is so difficult to catch that most anglers never even see one. Three or four times the size of a bonefish—averaging 20 to 30 pounds—the silvery, platter-shaped permit forages in the safety of slightly deeper waters, not risking exposure of its iridescent blue-green back. Its sickle-shaped, black-tipped tail pokes out of the water as it feeds on bottom-dwelling crabs and shrimps, often tipping off its location. The permit's shell-crushing jaws, rubbery and strong, can exert 3,000 pounds of pressure per square inch, enabling it to masticate small clams and crustaceans and dash many an angler's expectations.

The best days to find permit are those glorious, cloudless sunny smiles from Mother Nature, cooled by a slight ocean breeze. Schools of permit will graze the top of the flats and near rocky shorelines in higher tides and poke around in basins and channels during low tides, searching for a meal of small crabs and crustaceans. They often hover above submerged objects such as lobster pots. If

FISHING

you pass above an area littered with sea urchins, be on the lookout for permit searching for gourmet fixings.

Not easily duped, a tailing permit will make you forget all about a bonefish because, if you manage to hook one, you've got a street brawl on your hands that could last an hour or more. When hooked, the permit instinctively heads for deeper water. In the transition zone between the flats and the blue water, the permit will try to cut the line by weaving through coral heads, sea fans, and sponges. The fish will pause in its run to bang its head on the bottom or rub its mouth in the sand to try to dislodge the hook. If you manage to follow the permit through this obstacle course, you may actually catch it a quarter-mile from where you hooked it.

### Tarpon: The Silver King

It is little wonder that the tarpon (*Megalops atlanticus*) is dubbed the "silver king," for it wins 9 out of every 10 encounters with an angler. The tarpon's lung-like gas bladder allows it to take a gulp of atmospheric air from time to time, enabling the fish to thrive in oxygen-depleted water. This magnificent super-hero of the sea, ranging in size from 50 to 200 pounds, will break the surface and "roll" with a silvery splash as it steals an oxygen jolt and powers on for an intensified fight. The tarpon frequents the deeper flats of 4 to 8 feet or hangs out in the rapidly moving waters of channels, or under one of the many bridges in the Keys. Live mullet, pinfish, and crabs will entice this hungry but lazy despot, which faces into the current, effortlessly waiting for baitfish to be dragged into its mouth. The tarpon's toothless lower jaw protrudes from its head like an overdeveloped underbite, filled with bony plate that crushes its intended dinner.

The successful angler will use heavy tackle and a needle-sharp hook. Hold the rod with the tip at 12 o'clock and wait. When the fish strikes and eats the bait, let the rod tip drop with the pressure, giving minimal resistance. When the rod is parallel to the water and the line is tight, set the hook through the bony structure with a series of short, very strong jabs. Once hooked, the stunned fish runs and leaps repeatedly, with reckless abandon, entering the water headfirst, tail-first, sideways, belly-flopped, or upside down—an Olympian confounding its rod-clutching judge. It is important to have a quick-release anchor when fishing for tarpon because, once the action starts, you must be on your way, chasing the cavorting fish. Be prepared to duke it out, for it is often a standoff as to who tires first, the angler or the tarpon.

Exciting to catch on light tackle is the schooling baby tarpon, which, at up to 50 pounds, sprints and practices its aerobatics like its older siblings. Look for baby tarpon in channels and in harbors.

Tarpon season generally begins in Apr and continues until mid-July. Because the tarpon is primarily a nocturnal feeder, the best fishing is at daybreak and dusk or during the night. This magnificent creature grows very slowly, not reaching maturity until it is at least 13 years old. Since the tarpon is not an edible fish, some people consider killing it akin to murder. If you want a simulated mount of your catch, estimate the length and girth for the taxidermist. Take a photograph with your prize, and release the fish quickly and carefully.

### Barracuda: Tiger of the Flats

Look for the barracuda (*Sphyraena barracuda*), which packs a wallop of a fight, anywhere the water is about 2 feet deep, especially grassy-bottom areas. This toothy, intelligent predator has keen eyesight and moves swiftly. The barracuda's inquisitive nature causes it to make investigative passes by your boat, where it is oft tempted to sample your baited offerings intended for other species. Pilchards make good bait for catching barracuda. Cut off part of the tail fin of a pilchard before baiting the hook. This injury causes the bait to swim erratically, attracting the insatiable 'cuda. When casting to a barracuda, your bait should land at least 10 feet beyond the fish and be retrieved across its line of sight. A cast that lands the bait too close—5 feet or less—will frighten the 'cuda into deep water. If you are using artificial baits such as a tube lure, be sure to retrieve the bait briskly to pique the barracuda's interest.

Humans eat barracuda in some tropical areas, but not in the Keys. The flesh is sometimes toxic, and it is not worth the risk. You are better off quickly releasing the fish so that it might fight another round.

### Sharks

Several shark species (order *Selachii*) roam our flats looking for a free meal. Sand sharks and nurse sharks are relatively docile, but bonnetheads and black-tip sharks will readily take a shrimp or crab intended for a bonefish or permit, putting up a determined fight. If you happen to catch a shark, release the fish while it is in the water when possible, using a de-hooking device to remove hooks safely. If you use non-stainless steel hooks, you can simply cut the leader and leave the hook in the shark as the hook can dissolve if it remains in a fish. For more information on catch-and-release regulations, visit catchandrelease.org/sharks.

### The Backcountry

When Mother Nature bestowed the prolific oceanside saltwater flats on the Florida Keys, she didn't stop at our rocky isles. As the Gulf of Mexico meets mainland Florida, a lively ecosystem flourishes in a body of water known as Florida Bay. Hundreds of tiny uninhabited keys dot the watery landscape, referred to locally as "the backcountry." Loosely bordered by the Keys—from Key Largo to Long Key—and Everglades National Park, backcountry waters offer a diverse habitat of sea grass or mudflats, mangrove islets, and sandy basins. The southernmost outpost of Everglades National Park is at Flamingo, which maintains a marina, boat rentals, houseboats, and guide services.

You'll usually be able to find snappers, sheepshead, ladyfish, and the occasional shark along the grass-bed shorelines, the open bays, and in the small creeks flowing out of the Everglades. The silver king, the mighty tarpon, frequents backcountry creeks and channels, flats, and basins, and is rumored to be particularly partial to the Sandy Key Basin in the summer months. But beckoning anglers to these waters is another sporting trio—redfish, snook, and spotted sea trout—which when caught in one day is boasted far and wide as the Backcountry Grand Slam.

### Redfish, aka Red Drum

The coppery redfish, or red drum (*Sciaenops ocellatus*), all but disappeared in the 1980s from overfishing, but conservation measures by the state of Florida and the federal government caused a rebirth. This fast-growing fish migrates offshore to spawn when it reaches about 30 inches (4 years). It is a protected species in federal waters. Regulations open a scant 9-inch window for anglers to keep 1 captured redfish per day, which must measure between 18 and 27 inches. All redfish measuring less than 18 inches or more than 27 inches must be released, always. Because it grows so rapidly, the redfish is exposed to harvest for only one year of its life. It is highly coveted for eating, put on the culinary map by New Orleans's Chef Prudhomme and his famed Cajun blackening process.

As with fishing for bonefish or permit, you will look for redfish on an incoming tide, when they will be rooting for crabs on the shoals and flats. As the water gets higher, the fish work their way up on the flats. You will want to use a shallow-draft boat with a push pole or electric trolling motor, and be prepared with polarized sunglasses for enhanced vision in spotting a tailing fish. You'll hear experienced anglers say, "A tailing red is a feeding red." The reddish, squared-off profile of the redfish's tail can be spotted from several hundred feet. When the fish is really hungry, you may see its entire tail exposed, even the shady eyelike spot at the base. Cruising redfish will push a head wake similar to that of a bonefish.

Although a redfish isn't nearly as easily spooked as a bonefish, you should still stay as far away from the fish as possible while still casting a right-on winner. Live shrimps or crabs will entice the fish, which, with poor eyesight, hits almost any bait coming its way. The hooked redfish often sticks around and puts up a hard fight. Attracted to its discomfort, other redfish swim to the scene of the accident. You can often catch another redfish if you can get another baited hook into the water fast enough.

The backcountry of the Florida Keys is one of the few places in the world where you can fish for redfish year-round, although they prefer cooler waters. It is illegal, however, to buy or sell our native redfish, and they must be kept whole until you reach shore. You are forbidden to gig, spear, or snatch the red drum.

### Snook

The second member of the Backcountry Grand Slam, the snook (*Centropomus undecimalis*) likes to tuck against the shady mangrove shorelines to feed on baitfish that congregate in the maze of gnarled roots. A falling tide will force the baitfish out of their rooted cages and into deeper holes, where the snook can get at them. But the baitfish aren't the only ones getting snookered. This cagey, sought-after game fish, once hooked, has buffaloed many an angler, vanishing back into the mangroves and snapping its tenuous connection to the rod-wielder like a brittle string. If you win the battle of the bushes or find the snook pushing water in the open or at the mouth of a creek, you still haven't won the war. Once hooked, the snook thrashes about violently, trying to dislodge the barbed intruder. Its hard, abrasive mouth and knife-sharp gill covers can dispense with your line in a flash.

This silvery, long-bodied fish—thickened around the middle—faces its foes with a depressed snout and a protruding lower jaw. A distinctive lateral, black racing stripe extends the length of its body, all the way to its divided dorsal fin. The snook is unable to tolerate waters colder than 60 degrees. And while some anglers feel snook is the best-tasting fish in the Keys, Florida law mandates that in Monroe County you may not fish for snook from Dec 15 through Jan 31, nor in the months of May, June, July, and Aug. The fish must measure between 26 and 34 inches. The limit is 1 snook per person per day. Snook may not be bought or sold, and you must purchase a $2 snook stamp for your saltwater fishing license in order to fish for them.

### Spotted Sea Trout, aka Spotted Weakfish

Even though this backcountry prize is called a weakfish, it can be a challenging catch. The weakfish moniker derives from its clan's easily torn mouth membranes. The spotted sea trout (*Cynoscion nebulosus*)—actually a member of the fine-flavored drum family—nevertheless resembles a trout, with shimmering iridescent tones of silver, green, blue, and bronze.

The sea trout's lower jaw, unlike a true trout's, projects upward, and a pair of good-size canine teeth protrude from the upper jaw. These predatory, opportunistic feeders enjoy a smorgasbord of offerings but are particularly fond of live shrimp. The sea trout makes a distinctive splash and popping sound when it feeds on a drift of shrimp. These weakfish are easily spotted in the shallow backcountry waters, popular with light-tackle enthusiasts who enjoy the stalk-and-cast challenge.

Sea trout prefer temperatures between 60 and 70 degrees. Each must measure at least 12 inches to be fished, and the catch is limited to 4 fish per person per day. They are highly ranked as a table food because they are so delicately flavored, but the flesh spoils rapidly. Ice it quickly, and fillet the fish immediately upon returning to shore.

FISHING

## The Blue Water

The Gulf Stream, or Florida Current, moves through the Florida Straits south of Key West and flows northward, along the entire coast of Florida, at about 4 knots. This tropical river, 25 to 40 miles wide, maintains warm temperatures, hosting a piscatorial bounty from the prolific Caribbean that constantly restocks the waters of the Keys. The blue water encompasses deep water from the reef to the edge of the Gulf Stream and is particularly prolific at the humps, which are underwater hills rising from the seafloor. The Islamorada Hump is 13 miles offshore from Islamorada. The West Hump lies 23 miles offshore from Marathon and rises from a depth of 1,100 feet to 480 feet below the surface.

Blue-water fishing is synonymous with offshore fishing here in the Keys. To an angler, it means big game: billfish, tuna, dolphin, cobia, wahoo, and kingfish. Also offshore, at the edge of the coral reef and the nearshore patch reefs, you will find a palette of bottom fish, snappers, and groupers coveted more for their table value than their fighting prowess, and a grab bag of bonus fish—some good to eat, all fun to catch.

Until you are experienced in our waters, you will need a guide. To troll for big game fish in the blue water, you should book a private charter, which will put you on the fish and supply everything you need, including the professional expertise of the captain and mate, who know when to hold 'em . . . and when to fold 'em. These charters usually accommodate 6 anglers and, though pricey, provide the most instruction and individual attention. You can divide the cost with 5 other anglers or join with another party and split the tab (see the Guides & Charters section of this chapter).

Alternately, sign on to a party boat, or head boat, which usually accommodates 50 or more anglers. These boats usually take anglers to the reef for bottom fishing, where you can drop a line and try your luck for snapper, grouper, and even kingfish and some of their sidekicks. Mates on deck untangle lines, answer questions, and even bait your hook. And although it is a little bit like taking the bus during rush hour instead of a limousine, at $50 per day—rods, tackle, and bait included—a party boat remains the most economical means of fishing offshore. In Key West, try the *Greyhound,* located at Garrison Bight. Call (305) 296-5139 for more information.

### Billfish: Marlin & Sailfish

Before you head out to the blue water to hunt for sailfish and marlin, you might want to have a cardiac workup and check your blood pressure because, if your trolled bait takes a hit, it will prove a battle of endurance.

The cobalt-blue marlin (*Makaira nigricans*), largest of the Atlantic marlins, migrates away from the equator in warmer months, enigmatically gracing the Keys waters on its way northward. Females of the species often reach trophy proportions—1,000 pounds or more—but males rarely exceed 300 pounds. Tuna and bonito provide the mainstay of the blue marlin's diet, but some blue marlin have been found with young swordfish in their stomachs. Anglers trolling ballyhoo or mullet have the chance of latching on to a blue marlin, especially in tuna-infested waters. A fighting blue marlin creates a specter of primitive beauty: A creature the size of a baby elephant plunges to the depths, then soars in gravity-defying splendor, only to hammer the water once again and shoot off in a torpedo-like run.

Less often caught in our waters is the white marlin (*Tetrapturus albidus*), which is much smaller than the blue, averaging 50 to 60 pounds and rarely exceeding 150 pounds. Both marlin use their swordlike bills to stun fast-moving fish, which they then consume. Unlike other members of its family, the white marlin's dorsal and anal fins are rounded, not sharply pointed. The upper portion of its body is a brilliant green-blue, abruptly changing to silvery white on the sides and underslung with a white belly. White marlin will strike trolled live bait, feathers, and lures, hitting hard and running fast with repetitive jumps. The white marlin begins its southward migration as the waters of the North Atlantic cool in the autumn.

A shimmering dorsal fin, fanned much higher than the depth of its streamlined steel-blue body, distinguishes the sailfish (*Istiophorus platypterus*) from its billed brethren. Fronted with a long, slender bill, this graceful creature—averaging 7 feet long and 40 pounds in Florida waters—is meant to be captured and released, but stuffed no more. Probably the most popular mount of all time—the flaunted mark of the been-there, done-that crowd—the sailfish, at least in the Florida Keys, is generally allowed to entertain, take a bow, and go back to the dressing room until the next show. Taxidermists now stock fiberglass blanks, so you need only phone in the prized measurements to receive your representative mount.

The migration of the sailfish coincides with that of the snowbirds, those Northerners who spend the frigid months in the balmy Florida Keys. In late autumn and early winter, the sailfish leave the Caribbean and gulf waters and head up the Gulf Stream to the Keys. A fast-growing fish—4 to 5 feet in a year—it seldom lives more than 5 years. Feeding on the surface or at mid-depths on small fish and squid, the sailfish also is amenable to trolled appetizers of outrigger-mounted live mullet or ballyhoo that will wiggle, dive, and skip behind the boat like rats after the Pied Piper. The sailfish, swimming at up to 50 knots, will give you a run for your money, alternating dramatic runs and explosions from the depths with catapults through the air. It delights novice and expert alike. The inexperienced angler can glory in the pursuit with heavy tackle, while the seasoned veteran can lighten up, creating a new challenge. Both will savor the conquest.

Florida law allows you to keep 1 billfish per day and mandates size limitations. Sailfish must be at least 63 inches; blue marlin, 99 inches; and white marlin, 66 inches. We recommend, however, that you follow the ethical considerations of catch-and-release, recording your conquest on film instead.

FISHING

### Blackfin Tuna

Highly sought by anglers and blue marlin alike, the blackfin tuna (*Thunnus atlanticus*) is set apart from the other six tunas of North America by its totally black finlets. Rarely exceeding 50 pounds, this member of the mackerel family is not as prized as the giant bluefin of North Atlantic waters, but Keys anglers still relish a substantial battle and the bonus of great eating.

Primarily a surface feeder, the blackfin terrorizes baitfish from below, causing them to streak to the surface and skitter out of the water like skipping stones, a move that attracts seabirds. A sighting of diving gulls will tip off the presence of tuna at the feed bag. Blackfin tuna are partial to a chumming of live pilchards but will also attack feathers and lures trolled at high speeds. Tuna fishing on the humps is usually good in the spring months.

### Dolphin: Schoolies, Slammers & Bulls

Anyone who has ever seen a rainbow of schooling dolphin (*Coryphaena hippurus*), aka mahimahi, knows the fish's identity crisis is unfounded. Nothing about this prismatic fish suggests the mammal sharing its name. The dolphinfish resembles a Technicolor cartoon. Its bright green, blue, and yellow wedge-like body looks like the fish just crashed into a paint cabinet, and its high, blunt, pugnacious forehead and Mohawk-style dorsal fin evoke a rowdy, in-your-face persona not wholly undeserved. Once out of the water, however, the brilliant hues ebb like a fading photograph, tingeing sweet victory with fleeting regret.

Second only to billfish and tuna, dolphin are prized by blue-water anglers. Frantic fights follow lightning strikes, and the dolphin often throws in some aerobatics besides. This unruly fighter rates as a delicacy at the table as well, celebrated as moist white-fleshed dolphin fillets in the Keys and South Florida, but marketed as mahimahi elsewhere. Dolphinfish are surface feeders, attracted to the small fish and other tasty morsels associated with floating debris or patches of drifting sargassum weed. Flying fish, plentiful in the Gulf Stream waters, form a large portion of their preferred diet. A school of dolphin will actually attack a trolled bait of small, whole mullet or ballyhoo, streaking from a distance in a me-first effort like schoolboys to the lunch gong. It is not unusual for 3 or 4 rods to be hit at one time, an all-hands-on-deck effort that approaches a marathon. And as long as you keep one hooked dolphin in the water, alongside the boat, its buddies will hang around and wait their turn for a freshly baited hook.

Dolphins are rapidly growing fish, living up to 5 years. The young are called schoolies, generally in the 5- to 15-pound range. Slammers make an angler salivate, as they each weigh 25 pounds and more, and an attacking school can get your heart pumping. Doing battle with the heavyweight, the bull dolphin, quite often happens by accident while you are trolling for some other species. But the bull can hold his own in any arena. Dolphin season is generally considered to be from Mar until Aug, but the fish tend to stay around most of the year. Limit is 10 per person per day.

### Cobia: The Crab Eater

The cobia (*Rachycentron canadum*), the orphan of the piscatory world, enjoys no close relatives and is in a family by itself. Excellent on the table or on the troll, the adult cobia is a favorite bonus fish, often caught during a day in the blue water looking for sailfish. Particularly partial to crabs, the cobia also feeds on shrimp, squid, and small fish. The young cobia is often found in the flats of nearshore bays and inlets around the mangroves and buoys, pilings, and wrecks.

### Wahoo

A fine-eating bonus fish, generally caught by fortunate accident while trolling for sailfish or kingfish, the wahoo (*Acanthocybium solandri*) is far from an also-ran. One of the fastest fish in the ocean, the wahoo is a bona fide member of the mackerel family, similar in many ways to the Spanish mackerel. Its long, beaklike snout and slender silver-and-blue-striped body contribute to its prowess as a speed swimmer, for when hooked, the wahoo runs swiftly, cutting and weaving like a tailback heading for a touchdown. This loner rarely travels in schools. Wahoo season is in May, but the fish are here year-round.

### Kingfish, aka King Mackerel

Here in the Florida Keys, we call the king mackerel—which goes by assorted aliases in other parts of the country—the kingfish. At the turn of the 20th century, kingfish was the most popular catch off the Keys. Sailfish, then unrevered, were considered pests because they crashed the kingfish bait. The streamlined kingfish (*Scomberomorus cavalla*) travels in large schools, migrating up and down the coast in search of warm waters. Kingfish commonly frequent the waters of the Keys during the winter months, heading north in the spring.

Kings can be caught by drift fishing, where anglers cut the boat's engines and drift, fishing over the schools. Alternately, you can troll for kingfish with whole mullet or ballyhoo. Some captains prefer to anchor and chum, lacing the slick from time to time with live pilchards. Any method you use, a wire leader is essential when angling for kingfish because the fish displays razor-sharp teeth that it is not reluctant to use. Kingfish caught in our waters commonly weigh in at about 20 pounds, although the fish have been recorded reaching upward of 40 pounds. The kingfish is a good sport fish and also makes a fine meal. Limit is 2 per person per day.

### Amberjack

When all else fails in the blue water, you can always find a deep hole and battle an amberjack (*Seriola dumerili*). This powerful, bottom-plunging fish—nicknamed AJ—guarantees a good brawl. Bringing in an amberjack is like pulling up a Volkswagen Beetle with light tackle. Limit is 1 per person per day.

### The Reef Elite: Snapper & the Mackerels

Inhabiting the edge of the barrier reef that extends the length of the Florida Keys and in the smaller patch reefs closer in to shore, several finned species noteworthy for their food value coexist with the brightly painted tropicals and other coral-dwelling creatures. Like a well-branched family tree, these fish encompass many clans, all entertaining to catch and most delectable to eat. Startled anglers have even brought in permit while fishing the wrecks along the reef line. The brooding presence of the barracuda is always a strong possibility on the reef because the 'cuda is partial to raw snapper "stew" or grouper "tartare" when given the opportunity. It thinks nothing of stealing half the hooked fish in one mighty chomp, leaving the angler nothing but a lifeless head.

You will need a boat at least 20 feet long to head out to the reef, some 4 to 5 miles offshore. But with a compass, your NOAA charts, GPS, tackle, chunked bait, and some information gathered locally at the nearest bait and tackle shop, you should be able to find a hot spot on your own. Then all you need to do is fillet the captives, find a recipe, and fry up the spoils.

The snapper family is a popular bunch in the Florida Keys. The prolific cousins—all pleasurable to eat, delightful to catch, and kaleidoscopic to see— confuse Northerners with their dissimilarity. Snappers travel in schools and like to feed at night. Most common on the Keys table is probably the sweet, delicate yellowtail snapper (*Ocyurus chrysurus*), which usually ranges from 12 to 16 inches in length. Big yellowtails, called flags, approach 5 to 6 pounds and 20 inches in length and are prevalent from late summer through Oct. The yellowtail's back and upper sides shade from olive to bluish with yellow spots. A prominent yellow stripe begins at the yellowtail's mouth and runs midlaterally to its deeply forked tail, which, as you would expect, is a deep, brilliant yellow. The yellowtail is skittish, line-shy, and tends to stay way behind the boat. The fish's small mouth won't accommodate the hooks most commonly used in the pursuit of the other snappers. Successful anglers use light line, no leaders, and small hooks buried in the bait.

The mangrove snapper, or gray snapper (*Lutjanus griseus*), though often haunting the coral reef, also can be found inshore in mangrove habitats. Grayish in color with a red tinge along the sides, the mangrove snapper displays two conspicuous canine teeth at the front of the upper jaw. The mangrove is easier to catch than the yellowtail or the mutton snapper. Live shrimp and cut bait, added to a small hook, will induce these good fighters to strike. Anglers enjoy taking mangrove snappers on light tackle.

The brightly colored mutton snapper (*Lutjanus analis*) shades from olive green to red, with a bright blue line extending from under its eye to its tail and a black spot below the dorsal fin marking its side. Mutton snappers are most often caught in blue holes, so called because the water color of these deep coral potholes appears bluer than the surrounding waters. You will also find muttons in channels and creeks and occasionally even on a bonefish flat. The fish range in weight from 5 to 20 pounds. Mutton snappers are rumored to be shy and easily spooked by a bait that is cast too closely, but they love live pilchards. Usually caught in cloudy, churned-up water, the muttons provide a fierce confrontation. The limit for snappers is 10 per person per day.

Ergonomically designed for speed, the torpedo-shaped Spanish mackerel (*Scomberomorus maculatus*) distinguishes itself from the king and the cero with a series of irregular, buttercup-yellow spots on its stripeless sides, which look like the freckles on the Little Rascals. Cherished by light-tackle enthusiasts, the Spanish mackerel averages less than 2 pounds and 20 inches in length. Its razorlike teeth dictate that you carefully consider your choice in terminal tackle, for slashing your line rates right up at the top of the Spanish mackerel's getaway tactics. Spanish mackerel migrate into Florida Bay in Feb. Limit is 15 per person per day.

Larger than its Spanish cousin, the cero mackerel (*Scomberomorus regalis*) displays yellow spots above and below a bronze stripe that runs down its silvery sides, from the pectoral fin to the base of its tail. The cero is the local in our visiting mackerel lineup, not straying far from the waters of South Florida and the Keys, where it feeds on small fish and squid. The cero makes excellent table fare when consumed fresh, but fillets do not freeze well.

You may encounter the tripletail (*Lobotes surinamensis*) if you fish around wrecks, buoys, or sunken debris. Nicknamed the "buoy fish," the tripletail has been known to reach 40 pounds and a length of 3 feet. The fish's dorsal and anal fins are so long that they resemble two more tails, hence the name tripletail. The tripletail is a mottled palette of black, brown, and yellow, looking like an autumn leaf. Young tripletails, which like to stay close to shore in bays and estuaries, often are spotted floating on their sides at the surface, mimicking a leaf on the water. The tripletail will put up a valiant fight, and, though not seen on restaurant menus, it will make a tasty dinner. You must catch tripletail with a hook and line only, no snatch hooks.

## The Bridges

The bridges of the Florida Keys attract fighting game fish and flavorful food fish like magnets draw paper clips. The state of Florida replaced many of the original bridges of the Overseas Highway with wider, heavier spans in the late 1970s and 1980s, subsequently fitting many of the old bridges, no longer used for automobile traffic, for use as fishing piers. These bridges are marked with brown-and-white signage depicting a fish, line, and hook. (Many of the old bridge structures have been closed because lack of maintenance has left them unsafe. Be sure to fish only from those bearing the county signage.) The fishing bridges offer the general public free fishing access to many of the same species that frequent more far-flung areas of our waters. Parking is provided at the fishing-pier bridges. The Seven Mile Bridge, the Long Key Bridge, and the Bahia Honda Bridge have been designated historical monuments.

The waters beneath the bridges host a lively population of tarpon, mangrove snappers, snook, baby groupers, and yellowtails (see the Flats, Backcountry, and Blue Water sections of this chapter for information on these fish). Grunts (*Haemulon plumieri*) also are commonly caught at the bridges. Though little respected in other Keys waters, this small, bluish-gray fish is, nevertheless, fun to catch and makes a tasty meal. The grunt's name is derived from the sounds escaping the fish's bright orange mouth when it is captured. This grunting sound is actually the grinding of the pharyngeal teeth, which produces an audible noise amplified by the air bladder.

Night fishing is popular from the bridge piers, too. An outgoing tide with a moderate flow inspires the fish to continue feeding after dark. Baitfish and crustaceans, a temptation too great for many of the finned predators to pass up, are funneled through the pilings and out to sea.

Stop in at one of the local bait and tackle shops to get rigged out for bridge fishing. The local fishing experts working in these shops are encyclopedias of knowledge and will be able to guide you as to times, tides, and tackle. Locals recommend you use stout tackle when fishing from one of our bridges. You not only have to retrieve your catch while battling a heavy current, but you also must lift it a great distance to the top of the bridge.

Live shrimp, cut bait, or live pinfish will attract attention from at least one of the species lurking below. You will need to keep your shrimp alive while fishing from the bridge. Put the shrimp on ice in a 5-gallon bucket with an aerator or in a large Styrofoam cooler with an aerator. You can also lower a chum bag (filled with a block of chum, available at all bait shops) into the water. Tie a couple of dive weights to a long rope, lower the chum bag down the surface of a piling on the downcurrent side of the bridge, and tie it off to the railing. Then fish the slick. The chum will drift with the current, attracting sharks and any finfish in the neighborhood.

You will need sinkers on your line in order for your baited hook to drop to the bottom because a swift current pulses under the bridges. Don't launch your cast away from the bridge. Drop your bait straight down, near a piling or downcurrent, at the shore side of the bridge. Rubble from past construction sometimes piled here creates a current break, allowing the fish a place to rest, feed, or hide in the swirls or eddies. Don't forget to buy a fishing license.

## FISHING LICENSES

Florida law states you must possess a saltwater fishing license if you attempt to take or possess marine fish for noncommercial purposes. This includes finfish and such invertebrate species as snails, whelks, clams, scallops, shrimps, crabs, lobsters, sea stars, sea urchins, and sea cucumbers.

Exempt from this law are individuals younger than age 16 and Florida residents age 65 and older. You are also exempt if you are a Florida resident and a member of the US armed forces not stationed in Florida and home on leave for 30 or fewer days, with valid orders in your possession.

Florida residents who are fishing in salt water or for a saltwater species in freshwater, from land, or from a structure fixed to land need not purchase a license. Land is defined as "the area of ground located within the geographic boundaries of the state of Florida that extends to a water depth of 4 feet." This includes any structure permanently fixed to land such as a pier, bridge, dock or floating dock, or jetty. If you use a vessel to reach ground, however, you must have a license. And if you are wading in more than 4 feet of water or have broken the surface of the water wearing a face mask, you also must have one.

You are not required to have a license when you fish with one of our licensed captains on a charter holding a valid vessel saltwater fishing license or if you are fishing from a pier that has been issued a pier saltwater fishing license. Other, more obscure exemptions also apply. Check floridafisheries.com for more information.

A Florida saltwater fishing license is available from most bait and tackle shops and from any Monroe County tax collector's office. You can also obtain a license by calling (888) 347-4356 or online at myfwc.com. Residents and nonresidents pay differing amounts for this license. The state defines a resident as anyone who has lived in Florida continuously for at least 6 months; anyone who has established a domicile in Florida and can provide evidence of such by law; any member of the US armed forces who is stationed in Florida; any student enrolled in a college or university in Florida; or an alien who can prove residency status.

There is a penalty for fishing without the required license or stamps.

## TOURNAMENTS

If you're an angler who would like to compete against your peers instead of just yourself, the Florida Keys offers a plethora of exciting tournaments—more than 50 a year—encompassing most of the finned species enriching our waters. These tournaments, scheduled year-round from Key Largo to Key West, award prizes, cash, or trophies in a variety of categories ranging from heaviest or longest to most caught and released in a specified time period.

Generally, the tournaments fit into one of three categories, although some tournaments have multiple divisions. The billfish tournaments—white marlin, blue marlin, and sailfish—are the most prestigious and the most expensive. Billfish tournaments are catch-and-release events. Proof of the catch usually requires a photograph and a sample of the leader, which will be tested for chafing. Scoring follows an intricate point system. A catch of a white marlin, a blue marlin, and a sailfish in one day—not your average day, even in the Keys—constitutes a slam.

Dolphin tournaments are more family-type competitions. Anglers use their own boats without guides, and if the dolphin exceeds prespecified poundage, it may be brought in and weighed. Anglers can keep the fish, which are excellent eating.

Flats tournaments—tarpon, bonefish, and permit—are always catch-and-release, usually scored by a point system. A catch on a fly rod scores more points than one retrieved on light tackle. The fish must be measured, a photo must be taken, and the process must be witnessed. We recommend you book one year in advance for tarpon tournaments.

Some of our tournaments are restricted to a specific category of angler—women only or juniors only, for instance—or to a particular type of tackle, such as light tackle or fly rods. Others award a mixed bag of catches ranging from game fish to groupers to grunts. Many of the tournaments donate at least a portion of their proceeds to a charitable organization.

In the following section we introduce you to a sampling of the most important fishing tournaments held annually in the Keys. For a complete listing, visit fla-keys.com.

**BAYBONE CELEBRITY TOURNAMENT, Key Largo; (305) 664-2002; redbone.org.** Event no. 2 in the Redbone Celebrity Tournament Series, the prestigious catch-and-release Baybone tournament is typically in early to mid Oct. The Redbone Trilogy Series, which includes the S.L.A.M. (Southernmost Light-tackle Anglers Masters), donates proceeds to the Cystic Fibrosis Foundation for research. The stalked catch for the Baybone is bonefish and permit, which are photographed against a measuring device and released. Points are awarded for catches on fly, spin/plug, or general bait. An intricate point system determines the winners, who receive original paintings and sculptures as prizes.

**CHEECA LODGE & SPA PRESIDENTIAL SAILFISH TOURNAMENT, MM 82 Oceanside, Islamorada; (305) 664-4651 or (800) 327-2888; cheeca .com.** Perhaps the most prestigious of all tournaments in the Florida Keys is this tournament, held in mid-Jan. The former president, George H. W. Bush himself, typically competed in this event. Preceded by a kickoff meeting, 2 days of intense fishing are followed by an awards banquet at Cheeca Lodge. Fifty boats participate, 2 anglers per boat. Other than those included in the most-catches category, bonefish must weigh at least 8 pounds to qualify. All must be released. Trophies are awarded to winners, and proceeds benefit a variety of Keys environmental groups.

**ISLAMORADA SAILFISH TOURNAMENT, Islamorada; (305) 852-2102; islamoradasailfishtournament.com.** This annual sailfish tournament takes place in Dec. Scoring is as follows: 100 points for each released sailfish. Completed tagging cards must be submitted to the Committee Boat in order to qualify for the most-tagged trophy. Only 12-pound-test lines or less may be used, and live or dead bait as well as artificials are acceptable. Hooks may not be altered.

> **i** The most famous blue-water angler in Key West's collective consciousness remains Ernest Hemingway, who augmented his famous writing with a passion for fishing these waters. Photographs of Hemingway with his prized monster-size tarpon and sailfish cause many a covetous angler to turn green with envy.

**KEY WEST FISHING TOURNAMENT, Key West; (305) 295-6601; keywestfishingtournament.com.** This unusual tournament must have been designed for the angler who just can't fish enough. It lasts from Mar to Nov and encompasses a potpourri of divisions and species. Both charters and individuals can register for the tournament and also participate in a 2-day kickoff tournament-within-a-tournament, which in itself awards cash prizes. Anglers weigh their food-fish catches or record their releases at participating marinas and are awarded citations for their efforts. At the grand finale of the tournament, the tabulated results are announced and all prizes are presented.

**LEON SHELL MEMORIAL SAILFISH TOURNAMENT, Key Colony Beach; (305) 289-1310.** This is 2 days of fishing, with the proceeds benefiting the Keys Hospice and Visiting Nurses Association of the Florida Keys. The tournament is named after Leon Shell, best known as the inventor of the Leon Lure, an artificial lure regarded as one of the top bubble-creating lures ever invented. With more than $150,000 donated since its inception, this tournament draws a huge crowd. In the yearly tourney, cash prizes are awarded and the prize for the boat releasing the most sailfish is given out at an awards dinner. Weight fish divisions are given for dolphin, tuna, wahoo, and kingfish. Also, there is a junior division for youngsters ages 9 to 15½ years old.

FISHING

**S.L.A.M. TOURNAMENT, Key West; (305) 664-2002; redbone.org.** First in the Redbone Tournament Series each year is the S.L.A.M. (Southernmost Light-tackle Anglers Masters) event in early Sept, for the benefit of cystic fibrosis research (also see the Baybone Tournament event). Participants in this 2-day fishing event angle to score a Grand Slam: the catch and release of a bonefish, permit, and tarpon in 2 days. Points are awarded for each release in categories of fly, spin/plug, and general bait. Each release is photographed against a measuring device. Like the other tournaments in this series, the S.L.A.M. awards original artwork to its winners.

## GUIDES & CHARTERS

There are many captains and guides in the Florida Keys offering their services on the flats, blue water, or backcountry. Our guides are the most knowledgeable in the world—licensed captains who maintain safe, government-regulated watercraft. Hiring a guide allows the first-time visitor or the novice angler an opportunity to learn how to fish the waters of the Florida Keys and catch its bounty without having to spend too much time learning about the fish's habits. And guides will be your best teachers, for they usually have a lifetime of experience. Once you fish our waters, however, you will be the "hooked" species, for this unforgettable angling experience is addictive.

Book a guide as soon as you know when you are coming to the Keys, because the guides here book up quickly, especially during certain times of the year. If you hope to fish our waters with a guide during tarpon season, especially the months of May and June, plan a year ahead. Holidays such as Christmas and New Year's book up quickly also. Traditionally, the months of Aug through Nov are a bit slower. You may be able to wing it during those months, but we wouldn't advise it. Even if you don't take a charter trip, stop at a fishing marina around 4 p.m. and check out the catch of the day.

Blue-water or offshore fishing charters can accommodate 6 anglers. The captain guides the vessel to his or her favorite hot spots, which are anywhere from 6 to 26 miles offshore and usually closely guarded secrets. Often the captain will stop on his or her blue-water trek so the mate can throw a cast net for live bait. The mate will rig the baits, ready the outriggers, and cast the baited hooks for you. Big game fish are usually stalked by trolling, as are dolphin. You need do nothing but relax, soak in the sea air, and wait for the call, "Fish on!" Then the action is up to you.

Blue-water charter boats range in size from 35 to 50 feet. Each generally has an enclosed cabin and a head (toilet) on board. Everything you need for

FISHING

a day's fishing is provided except your refreshments, lunch, and any personal items you may need. It is customary to tip the mate 10 to 15 percent in cash if you have had a good day.

Guides for flats fishing or backcountry angling usually take a maximum of 2 anglers per boat. The guide will pole the skiff or flats boat through the skinny water, attentively looking for fish from atop the poling platform. This sight fishing dictates both guide and anglers stand alert, all senses engaged. The angler, whether fly-fishing or spin-casting, casts to the desired location directed by the guide.

Flats boats measure 16 to 18 feet. They are not outfitted with any shading devices, nor do they have a head. Be aware, you may have to use rather primitive facilities. Many of the guides will dip into shore for a pit stop, but others will not, so inquire before you leave the dock. All fly or spin rods, reels, tackle, and bait are provided. Some guides even tie their own flies, providing special furry or feathery creations proven to entice the fish. It is customary to tip the guide 10 to 15 percent in cash if you were happy with the excursion.

When booking a charter, inquire about penalties for canceling your reservation. No-shows frequently will be charged the full price.

Always bring sunscreen, polarized sunglasses, a cap with a long bill lined with dark fabric to cut the glare, and motion-sickness pills (even if you've never needed them before). Anglers are responsible for providing their own lunches and refreshments. Keys tradition is to bring lunch for the captain and mate on a blue-water charter or for the guide on a flats trip.

Many guides are known only on a word-of-mouth basis, but we have compiled a source list of fishing marinas and outfitters you may call to secure an offshore charter or flats or backcountry guide. The chambers of commerce in Key Largo, Islamorada, Marathon, the Lower Keys, and Key West also act as referral sources (see subsequent listings).

Perhaps even more than the rest of the Keys, you'll need a guide to find the fish in the waters surrounding Key West. A busy harbor for centuries, Key West's marinas and bights are a bustling maze to the uninitiated. Many of the more than 60 charter boats in the Key West fleet dock at the City Marina at Garrison Bight, which is accessed on Palm Avenue, just off N. Roosevelt Boulevard. This marina is locally referred to as Charter Boat Row. From 7 to 7:30 a.m. and 3:30 to 5 p.m., the captains are available at their vessels to take direct bookings. You can meet them and their crews, see the offshore vessels, and save money to boot. Booking a charter directly with the captain instead of a charter agency nets you a sizable discount. Other charter boats dock at Key West Bight, in the Key West Historic Seaport.

Some guides are willing to captain your private vessel at a much-reduced charter rate. If this interests you, inquire when you call one of these booking sources. Often hotels maintain a source list of guides or charter captains they will recommend. Inquire when you reserve your accommodations.

## Offshore & Backcountry Guide Booking Sources

Establishments acting as booking services will determine your needs and book your flats/backcountry guide or blue-water/offshore charter directly. Cancellation policies vary and change from year to year, so be sure to inquire about procedures and penalties before you book your charter. The top guides in the Florida Keys book out of the establishments listed below. Be sure to log on to their websites to find out more information on the guides they represent.

### Upper Keys

**Bay and Reef Company,** MM 81.5 Bayside, La Siesta Marina, Islamorada, FL 33036; (305) 393-1779 or (305) 393-0994; bayandreef.com.

**Bud n' Mary's Marina,** MM 79.8 Oceanside, 79851 Overseas Hwy., Islamorada, FL 33036; (305) 664-2461 or (800) 742-7945; budnmarys.com.

**Florida Keys Outfitters,** MM 81.2 Oceanside, 81219 Overseas Hwy., Islamorada, FL 33036; (305) 664-5423; floridakeysoutfitters.com.

**Over Under Sportfishing,** MM 82 Oceanside, at the Islander Resort, 82100 Overseas Hwy., Islamorada, FL 33036; (866) 682-8862; overundercharters.com.

**Whale Harbor Marina,** MM 81.9 Oceanside, 83413 Overseas Hwy., Islamorada, FL 33036; (305) 664-4511; whaleharborcharters.com.

**World Wide Sportsman Inc.,** MM 81.5 Bayside, 81576 Overseas Hwy., Islamorada, FL 33036; (305) 664-4615; basspro.com/islamorada.

### Middle Keys

**Captain Hook's Marina & Dive Center,** MM 53 Oceanside, 11833 Overseas Hwy., Marathon, FL 33050; (305) 743-2444 or (800) 278-4665; captainhooks.com.

### Lower Keys

**Strike Zone Charters,** MM 29.5 Bayside, 29675 Overseas Hwy., Big Pine Key, FL 33043; (305) 872-9863; strikezonecharter.com.

### Key West

In addition to the limited number of fishing marinas and outfitters booking guides or charters, Key West's fishing excursions are put together by charter agencies operating out of booths peppering Mallory Square, Duval, and other major streets of Key West. You can book party boats at these booths as well.

FISHING

**Capt. Tony Murphy's Saltwater Angler,** 243 Front St., at the Westin Key West Resort and Marina, Key West, FL 33040; (305) 296-0700; saltwater angler.com.

## Chambers of Commerce

These chamber of commerce offices throughout the Florida Keys will provide you with a list of guides for any style of fishing excursion via their phone numbers or websites.

**Key Largo Chamber of Commerce & Florida Keys Visitor Center,** MM 106 Bayside, 106000 Overseas Hwy., Key Largo, FL 33037; (305) 451-1414 or (800) 822-1088; keylargochamber.org.

**Islamorada Chamber of Commerce,** MM 87 Bayside, 87100 Overseas Hwy., Islamorada, FL 33036; (305) 664-4503 or (800) FAB-KEYS; isla moradachamber.com.

**Greater Marathon Chamber of Commerce,** MM 53.5 Bayside, 12222 Overseas Hwy., Marathon, FL 33050; (305) 743-5417 or (800) 262-7284; floridakeysmarathon.com.

**Lower Keys Chamber of Commerce,** MM 31 Oceanside, 31020 Overseas Hwy., Big Pine Key, FL 33943; (305) 872-2411 or (800) 872-3722; lowerkeyschamber.com.

**Key West Chamber of Commerce,** 510 Greene St., 1st Floor, Key West, FL 33040; (305) 294-2587 or (800) 527-8539; keywestchamber.org.

## Party Boats

Party boats, sometimes called "head boats," offer a relatively inexpensive way to fish the waters of the Keys. The party boats, US Coast Guard–inspected and certified vessels, generally hold 50 passengers or more, but most average no more than 25 to 30 anglers. Party boats take anglers out to the reef, where they anchor or drift and bottom-fish for more than 40 species of fish. Spring and summer seasons sport a plethora of snappers, dolphinfish, and yellowtails, while kingfish and cobia are more apt to make an appearance in the winter months. Porgies, grunts, and some species of snappers show up all year. Occasionally even a sailfish or a big shark has been caught from a party boat here.

Party boats offer rod and reel rentals at a nominal fee per trip. This

> **i** More than 10 percent of the International Game Fish Association (IGFA) saltwater line-class and fly-fishing world records have been set in the Florida Keys.

FISHING

includes your terminal tackle—hook, line, and sinker—and all bait. If you bring your own fishing gear, bait is included in the excursion fee. You do not need a fishing license on a party boat. While most party-boat information mentions your license is included in the excursion fee, this actually is only a temporary license, good for the duration of your fishing trip only. Two or more mates will be working the boat, helping you bait hooks, confiding fishing tips, and untangling the inevitable crossed lines.

Most of the party boats have seats around the periphery of the lower deck and a shaded sundeck up top. You are advised to wear shorts rather than swimsuits and durable sneakers or deck shoes, not flip-flops or sandals. Remember, there will be a lot of anglers and many flying hooks on the boat. Put some sturdy cloth between your skin and that accidental snag. Most captains recommend bringing a lightweight long-sleeved shirt for protection against the sun and a jacket to ward off cool breezes. Bring sunglasses, sunscreen, a hat, and motion-sickness pills (many people who never suffered from seasickness before find drifting in the swells causes them *mal de mer*). Also bring a fishing rag or towel to wipe your hands with throughout the day.

After you land a fish, a mate will help you take it off the hook and will check the species to make sure it is not one of those protected by law, such as Nassau grouper. The mate then will measure the fish to ensure it meets the required size limit, tag it with your name, and place it on ice. At the end of the fishing trip, you may reclaim your catch. The mate will clean your fish, usually for tips. Party boats with a set cleaning-fee policy will be noted in the descriptions. Mates work for tips aboard party boats, the standard tip being 10 to 15 percent if you had a good day and if the mate was helpful.

The following party boats may be booked for day or evening charters. It is always a good idea to arrive at the docks 30 minutes before departure to stow your gear on the boat and secure a good position on deck. All boats have restrooms on board. Most have an enclosed cabin and offer a limited snack bar, beer, and soda. Exceptions will be noted.

In all cases, you are allowed to bring your own cooler filled with lunch and refreshments. All party boats recommended in this section take credit cards unless otherwise stated. Children's rates for youngsters age 12 and younger are often available.

> **i** Before green turtles were placed on the endangered and protected list and no longer allowed to be caught, they were a source of food throughout Florida's history. The pens that held the turtles were called "kraals."

## Upper Keys

*CAPTAIN MICHAEL,* **ROBBIE'S OF ISLAMORADA,** MM 77.5 Bayside, 77522 Overseas Hwy., Islamorada, FL 33036; (305) 417-6520 or (888) 316-7754; robbies.com. Get the thrill of sportfishing without a care in the world (and at a reasonable price!). The 65-foot *Captain Michael,* with spacious decks and an air-conditioned cabin, is available for private charters, sunset cruises, and wedding receptions. Both day and night party-boat excursions are available.

*MISS ISLAMORADA,* Bud N' Mary's Marina, MM 79.8 Oceanside, 79851 Overseas Hwy., Islamorada, FL 33036; (305) 664-2461 or (800) 742-7945; budnmarys.com. *Miss Islamorada* is a 65-foot party/fishing boat that entertains up to 49 people. All tackle, bait, and licenses are provided along with an experienced crew and clean restrooms. There is a deli on-site before you leave, should you need last-minute provisions, as none are available on board without prior arrangement. So be sure to bring your own snacks along with you for your fishing trip, sunset cruise, or corporate meeting. The daily excursion for this boat is from 9:30 a.m. to 4 p.m. Individuals may also hold a poignant memorial service or unforgettable wedding aboard the boat.

*SAILOR'S CHOICE,* **HOLIDAY INN RESORT AND MARINA,** MM 100 Oceanside, 66701 Overseas Hwy., Key Largo, FL 33037; (305) 451-1802 or (800) 979-3370 (reservations); sailorschoicefishingboat.com. *Sailor's Choice,* a 65-foot, aluminum, custom-built craft with lounge, offers plenty of shade and seating for anglers on its daily fishing excursions. Children are welcome on both day and evening trips. During the afternoon they can easily see the big fish in the water along with seabirds, porpoises, and sea turtles. The 2 daily excursions are from 9 a.m. to 1 p.m. and 1:30 to 5:30 p.m., while the evening excursion is from 7:30 p.m. to midnight.

## Middle Keys

*MARATHON LADY,* MM 53 Oceanside, 11711 Overseas Hwy., Marathon, FL 33050; (305) 743-5580; fishfloridakeys.com/marathonlady. Children fish for significantly reduced rates aboard the 73-foot *Marathon Lady.* Inquire when you make your reservations. If you rent a rod and reel for the 4-hour excursion, your tackle is included, but if you prefer to bring your own gear, terminal tackle is available for a nominal fee. The mates will clean your catch for a small fee as well.

## Lower Keys

**SEA BOOTS CHARTERS,** MM 24.5 Oceanside, Summerland Key; FL 33042; (305) 745-1530 or (800) 238-1746; seaboots.com. With a Coast Guard Masters License under his belt, Captain Jim Sharp has been on the water most of his life. His vast experience (more than 50 years!) fishing the cool blue waters of the Florida Keys and the Bahamas makes an outing with him a thrilling experience. On his 6-passenger boat, *Sea Boots,* you are provided fishing license, tackle, bait, and ice for the trip.

### Key West

Key West party boats are docked at Charter Boat Row on Palm Avenue off North Roosevelt. You can call the numbers listed to make reservations, book a space at one of the booths on Duval Street and in the Mallory Square area, or simply come down to the docks and make arrangements directly with the captain. Vessels usually operate at far less than maximum capacity during most seasons, so finding a spot should not present a problem.

**GREYHOUND V, Charter Boat Row, City Marina, Garrison Bight, Amberjack Pier #5, 1801 North Roosevelt Blvd., Key West, FL 33040; (305) 296-5139 or (305) 296-5923; greyhoundv.com.** Daily trips are from 11 a.m. to 4 p.m. On any given outing, you are likely to encounter serious local fishermen and -women on this boat. Mates charge a nominal fee to clean your fish. Make sure to arrive 15 to 20 minutes early so you can be properly assisted when boarding.

**GULFSTREAM IV, Charter Boat Row, City Marina, Garrison Bight, 1801 North Roosevelt Blvd., Key West, FL 33040; (305) 296-8494; gulfstream keywest.com.** The 58-foot *Gulfstream IV* provides a full-service lunch counter offering snacks, beer, and soda. They have his/her restrooms on the boat and an inside cabin and an outdoor bench, both with plenty of seating. The mates will clean your catch for a small fee. Children under 5 ride for free.

### This Isn't Kansas

The months of June through Nov make up hurricane season in South Florida. Here in the Florida Keys, summer alerts us to keep a watchful eye peeled on the skies over open water for yet another weather concern: water spouts. Water spouts are tornadoes or vortexes that form over open water, and here in the Keys there are as many as 400 to 500 each year. We hold the title as the most frequent spot on Earth for water spouts to form. The reason for this is our islands and shallow water heat the air; then add to the mix our high humidity. With that heat, the air rises and the water in the humidity forms water droplets that make up clouds. As the water vapor condenses, more heat is released, thus causing the air to rise faster. Then throw in the east-to-northeast "trade winds" and boom—the perfect water spout. Ranging in height from 18,000 to 20,000 feet, they are dramatic to witness. Rarely do they come ashore, but nevertheless, it's a good idea to keep a watchful eye on them, especially if you are in or on the water.

## OUTFITTERS

### Upper Keys

**FLORIDA KEYS OUTFITTERS, MM 81.2 Oceanside, 81219 Overseas Hwy., Islamorada, FL 33036; (305) 664-5423; floridakeysoutfitters.com.** The focus here is on fly fishing, and this outfitter's personnel rank as some of the most experienced in the sport. You'll find such brands as Hardy, Sage, and G. Loomis fly rods and Tiber and Nautilus fly reels, plus a wide selection of flies and fly-tying materials. In addition to Simms, Patagonia, and Columbia clothing, Florida Keys Outfitters sells Simms and Patagonia shoes and booties.

**WEST MARINE, MM 103.4 Bayside, 103400 Overseas Hwy., Key Largo, FL 33037; (305) 453-9050; westmarine.com.** West Marine is your one-stop shop for all of your boating and fishing needs. Great inventory, large selection, and helpful sales folks are available to assist with questions. Check out their website for other locations in the Upper Keys.

**WORLD WIDE SPORTSMAN INC., MM 81.5 Bayside, 81576 Overseas Hwy., Islamorada, FL 33036; (305) 664-4615 or (800) 227-7776; basspro .com/islamorada.** This two-story superstore is owned by Bass Pro Shops and is stocked to the rafters with a wide assortment of fishing tackle by manufacturers such as Penn, Sage, Daiwa, Shimano, Orvis, and more. You'll find fly-tying materials and a huge assortment of flies here. A rod and reel repair center is on the premises. North Face, Natural Reflections, and Columbia fishing clothes for both men and women are just a few of the many brands offered. Several area guides launch from these facilities. The marina also offers a fuel dock as well as frozen, live, and fresh bait.

### Middle Keys

**THE TACKLE BOX, MM 48 Oceanside, 1901 Overseas Hwy., Marathon, FL 33050; (305) 289-0540; thetacklebox.com.** The Tackle Box sells anything and everything you'll need for saltwater fishing, as they stock plenty of brand names of rods, reels, and fishing gear. They offer advice, equipment, bait, tackle, or charters for any type of fishing you wish to do. They even sell bowfishing equipment and can clean, recondition, or repair any Penn, Shimano, Daiwa, or other reels quickly and for a reasonable price with one or more of their 20,000 parts in stock.

### Lower Keys

**LOWER KEYS TACKLE, MM 29.7 Oceanside, 29770 Overseas Hwy., Big Pine Key, FL 33043; (305) 872-7679; reeflighttackle.com.** Stop in and swap fish stories about the one that did not get away because you came here for

FISHING

your outfitting! They have it all, including a live-bait room. The crew call their inventory "fish candy." They have special fishing seminars every week in season, as well as inside tips on their website. In-store, they offer Penn rod and reel repair as well as a host of rods, reels, tackle, beer, and even unique pieces for sale by local artists. Also in stock are shirts, hats, and polarized eyewear.

## Gentle Giants

Two fishermen anchored in the reef off Marathon recently spotted a 19-foot juvenile whale shark. These are the largest sharks in the ocean, with adults measuring 33 feet long and weighing up to 60 tons. Their identifying marks are spotted backs, and they have broad, flat faces. They scoot along feeding on whatever they can filter through their giant mouths. Whale sharks are gentle, and the only danger is getting slapped with their fins or tail. You just never know what you will see in the sea in the scenic Florida Keys!

### Key West

**CAPT. TONY MURPHY'S SALTWATER ANGLER,** 243 Front St., at the Westin Key West Resort and Marina, Key West, FL 33040; (305) 296-0700; saltwaterangler.com. The Saltwater Angler specializes in fly tackle. Look for Sage, G. Loomis, Orvis, Tibor, Abel, and Shimano rods and reels. The store also stocks a full assortment of flies and fly-tying materials. You can also select from a complete line of top-brand fishing apparel by Orvis, Patagonia, and Columbia. Books and artwork with an angling theme round out their offerings.

# Diving & Snorkeling

Ranking as the third-largest reef system and one of the most popular dive destinations in the world, the Florida Keys' reef runs 192 miles from Virginia Key in Biscayne Bay all the way to the Dry Tortugas in the Gulf of Mexico. A fragile symbiotic city of sea creatures crowds our reef—fish, sponges, jellyfish, anemones, worms, snails, crabs, lobsters, rays, turtles, and, of course, both soft and stony corals—sometimes mixing it up with sunken bounty of a different kind: shipwrecks of yesteryear. Although our coral reef appears sturdy, this toothsome barrier is actually made up of colonies of tiny living animals. These coral polyps develop so slowly that it can take years for some species to grow just 1 inch. The careless toss of an anchor or slightest touch can destroy decades of coral growth in just seconds. When polyps are damaged or killed, the entire colony becomes exposed to the spread of algae or disease, and the reef is at risk.

To protect and preserve our marine ecosystem, Congress established the Florida Keys National Marine Sanctuary in 1990. Extending on both sides of the Florida Keys, the 2,800-square-nautical-mile sanctuary is the second-largest marine sanctuary in the US (see the Welcome to the Florida Keys chapter). The sanctuary encompasses two of the very best diving areas in the reef chain of the Keys: the Key Largo National Marine Sanctuary, which in turn envelops John Pennekamp Coral Reef State Park, and the Looe Key National Marine Sanctuary.

The state of Florida adjusted its offshore boundaries from 7 miles to 3 miles. This means many of the underwater dive and snorkel sites that used to be referred to as John Pennekamp Coral Reef State Park are now actually part of the Key Largo National Marine Sanctuary. To clear up the confusion, remember: Key Largo National Marine Sanctuary encompasses the waters of John Pennekamp Coral Reef State Park, but Pennekamp is not synonymous with the sanctuary.

## OVERVIEW

In this chapter we provide you with a rundown of great reef and wreck dives and snorkel adventures from Key Largo to the Dry Tortugas. Our reefs are not within swimming distance of the shore, so you will need to make your way by boat. If you plan to venture out on your own craft or in a rental boat, be sure to stop at a dive center or marine supply store and purchase a nautical map that denotes the exact coordinates for dive and snorkel sites (see the listings in this chapter). Motor to the reef only if you know the waters, are an experienced boat handler, and can read the nautical charts well. You are financially liable for damage to the reef, so always anchor only at mooring buoys when provided or on sandy areas of the sea bottom. Florida law dictates you fly the diver-down flag, which is red with a diagonal white stripe, to warn other boaters that divers are underwater within 100 feet of your craft.

Probably the most popular and hassle-free way to dive or snorkel in the Florida Keys is to go out with a dive charter. Most reputable dive centers in the Keys belong to the Keys Association of Dive Operators, which sets standards of safety and professionalism. Crews are trained in CPR, first aid, and handling dive emergencies. Emergency oxygen supplies are kept on board. The dive captains, who must be licensed by the US Coast Guard, judge weather conditions and water visibility each day and select the best sites suited to your experience level. Often their coveted knowledge of little-visited patch reefs and wrecks affords you an experience you could not duplicate on your own. We offer you a guide to dive centers, noting the comprehensive services ranging from instruction and underwater excursions to equipment rentals and sales.

In the Florida Keys, usually neither the crew nor the dive master accompanies divers in the water. Divers spread out across a shallow reef, two by two, swimming in a buddy system. The dive master stays on board and watches everyone from the boat. You must prove your experience level by showing current dive certification and your dive log before you may go out on a dive charter. If you have not made a comparable dive within the past six months, you should hire an instructor or dive master to accompany you in the water. Be sure you are comfortable with the sea conditions and that they are consistent with your level of expertise.

Whether you dive on your own or go out to the reef with a charter, you should be aware of the strong current of the outgoing tidal flow and in the Gulf Stream. It is easy to overlook the current in the fascination of your dive until, low on both energy and air, you must swim against it to get back to the boat. Begin your dive by swimming into the current. To determine the direction of the current, watch the flow of your bubbles or lie back into a float position and see which way the current carries you.

Be careful around bridges. The tremendous energy of the tides passing through the pilings of our bridges creates coral outcroppings that would not normally be so close to shore. Divers and snorkelers without boat transportation to the patch reefs or the gulf waters like to take advantage of this underwater terrain to look for lobsters. Be forewarned: It is very dangerous to dive or snorkel under and around our bridges. The currents are swift and the tidal pull is strong. Boat traffic is often heavy. If you do decide to dive or snorkel here, be sure to carry a diver-down flag with you on a float, and follow the buddy system. The best and safest time to tackle these turbulent waters is just before slack tide, during slack tide, and immediately following slack tide. The time of this cycle varies with wind, the height of the tide, and the phase of the moon.

i Funded by Sanctuary Friends Foundation of the Florida Keys, Ken Nedimyer and a group of volunteers have successfully propagated and transplanted native staghorn corals in the wild. Some of the corals Ken "babysat" for more than 12 years, and by using polyps that settled on his "livestock," the staghorn thickets have been successfully established. Contact the foundation at (305) 289-2288 or visit sanctuaryfriends .org for more information.

Whether you'd like to spend a few hours, days, weeks, or a lifetime exploring our coral reefs and wrecks, you'll find in this chapter all you need to know to "get wet," as divers like to say, in the Florida Keys.

## In Emergencies

Before you dive, you should check out the Divers Alert Network (DAN), a nonprofit, dive-safety organization. DAN's mission is to help divers in need of medical emergency assistance and to promote dive safety through research, education, products, and services.

The DAN Emergency Hotline, (919) 684-9111, is available 24 hours a day, 7 days a week, to assist with medical emergencies and to facilitate medical evacuation services. DAN also provides a Medical Information Line, (919) 684-2948, during normal business hours for nonemergency questions. For more information, visit diversalertnetwork.org.

Divers in the Florida Keys are in good hands in the face of a recompression emergency. The Florida Keys Hyperbaric Center (305-853-1603) is located at Mariners Hospital in the Upper Keys. Dive-shop personnel, instructors, dive masters, and boat captains have joined with members of the local EMS, US Coast Guard, Marine Patrol, NOAA, Monroe County Sheriff's Office, and the Florida State Highway Patrol to develop a coordinated evacuation program to get injured divers off the water and to the hyperbaric chamber quickly. In case of a decompression injury, call 911 and get the victim to the nearest emergency room as rapidly as possible.

## THE KEYS TO THE REEF

Most diving and snorkeling takes place on the barrier reefs of the Florida Keys. These linear or semicircular reefs, larger than the inner patch reefs, have claimed a graveyard of sailing vessels, many laden with gold and silver and other precious cargo. Salvaged by wreckers for centuries, the remains of these wrecks entice experienced divers, some of whom still hope to discover a treasure

## Great Annual Fish Count

The Reef Environmental Education Foundation (REEF), headquartered in Key Largo, invites divers to participate in the Great Annual Fish Count each July. More than 120,000 volunteer surveys have been submitted. The information is then used for fish population studies of marine protected areas and artificial reefs, and to see if a particular species is being overfished. No wildlife is harmed in this effort. Visit fishcount.org or reef.org to learn more.

trove. Lighthouses were erected on the shallower, more treacherous sections of the barrier reef during the 19th century as an aid to navigation. They now also mark popular dive and snorkel destinations.

The coral reef system of the Florida Keys is distinctively known as a spur-and-groove system. Long ridges of coral, called spurs, are divided by sand channels, or grooves, that merge with the adjoining reef flat, a coral rubble ridge on the inshore edge of the reef. The ridges of elkhorn coral thrive in heavy surf, often growing several inches a year. The spurs extend 100 yards or more, with shallower extremities sometimes awash at low tide while the seaward ends stand submerged in 30 to 40 feet of water. Small caves and tunnels wind through to the interior of the reef, home to myriad species of marine plants and animals. The white grooves separating the spurs are covered with coarse limestone sand, a composite of coral and mollusk shell fragments and plates from green calcareous algae. The wave action passing between the spurs of coral creates furrows in the sand floor of the grooves.

Generally, the shallower the reef, the brighter the colors of the corals, because strong sunlight is a prerequisite for reef growth. Legions of fish sway back and forth, keeping time with the rhythm of the waves. While deep dives yield fascinating discoveries—such as long-lost torpedoed ships—for those with advanced skills, sport divers will not be disappointed with the plethora of sea life within 60 feet of the surface. Night dives reveal the swing shift of the aquatic community. While the parrotfish may find a cave, secrete a mucous balloon around itself, and sleep the night through, sparkling corals blossom once the sun sets, and other species come out of hiding to forage for food.

Supplementing our coral barrier and the broken bodies of reef-wrecked ships, artificial reefs have been sunk to create underwater habitats for sea creatures large and small. The Florida Keys Artificial Reef Association, a nonprofit corporation of Keys residents, banded together in 1980 to capitalize on putting to use the many large pieces of concrete that became available during the removal of some of the old Keys bridges. More than 35,000 tons of rubble were deep-sixed throughout the Keys' waters between 1981 and 1987, creating acres of artificial reefs. In recent years, steel-hull vessels up to 350 feet long have been scuttled in stable sandy-bottom areas, amassing new communities of fish and invertebrates and easing the stress and strain on the coral reef by creating new fishing and diving sites. You'll find a comprehensive list of the artificial reef locations at the Florida Fish and Wildlife Conservation Commission website: myfwc.com.

Always use a mooring buoy if one is available. The large blue-and-white plastic floats are drilled directly into the sea bottom and installed with heavy chains or concrete bases, and are available on a first-come, first-served basis. If you are in a small craft, however, it is courteous to tie off with other similar boats, allowing larger vessels use of the mooring buoys. Approach the buoy from downwind against the current. Secure your boat to the pickup lines using a length of your own rope. Snap shackles provide quick and easy pickup and release. Large boats are advised to give out extra line to ensure a horizontal pull on the buoy. If no mooring buoys have been provided, anchor only in a sandy area downwind of a patch reef so that your boat's anchor and chain do not drag or grate on nearby corals.

## DIVE SITES

In the Upper, Middle, and Lower Keys parts of this section, we highlight some of the better-known and most enchanting dive and snorkel sites, listed in descending order from the top of the Keys in the Key Largo National Marine Sanctuary to the Looe Key National Marine Sanctuary in the Lower Keys.

In Key West our coral reef system heads west into the sunset as it swings by Cayo Hueso into the untamed and isolated but charted waters leading to the Marquesas and the Dry Tortugas. (The half-day dive excursions based in Key West do not venture as far as these outer, uninhabited Keys. You will have to charter private overnight dive excursions or travel the distance in your own motor or sailing yacht if you wish to explore these waters; see the Cruising chapter.) In the Key West and the And Beyond parts of this section, we highlight 20 of the most interesting dive and snorkel sites from Key West to the Dry Tortugas National Park.

### Underwater History

In August 2008 underwater archaeology students from across the country took part in a deep mystery 25 feet below the surface off Key Largo. Their discovery of weathered metal bands of a paddle wheel, parts of a smokestack, and boiler plates helped them to solve the puzzle of the shipwrecked *Menemon Sanford*. This 237-foot side-paddle steamship sank in 1862 while on a secret Civil War mission. The vessel was built in 1854 and named after Captain Sanford, founder of the Sanford Independent Line that later became the Royal Caribbean Cruise Line.

## Upper Keys

### Carysfort Reef

Situated at the extreme end of Key Largo National Marine Sanctuary, Carysfort Reef appeals to both novice and intermediate divers. British vessel HMS *Carysfort* ran aground here in 1770. The reef, now marked by the 100-foot steel Carysfort Lighthouse, undulates between 35 and 70 feet. Lush staghorn corals, which look like bumpy deer antlers, and masses of plate coral, which overlap each other like roofing tiles, cascade down the 30-foot drop to the sandy bottom. Schools of algae-grazing blue tang and pin-striped grunts circulate among the coral heads of a secondary reef. The HMS *Winchester,* a British man-of-war built in 1693, hit the reef in 1695 after most of her crew died of the plague while en route from Jamaica to England. The wreck, discovered in 1938, was cleaned out by salvagers in the 1950s. It rests southeast of Carysfort Light in 28 feet of water. Location: North Carysfort: Lat. 25° 13.80, Long. 80° 12.74; South Carysfort: Lat. 25° 13.00, Long. 80° 13.06.

### The Elbow

Aptly named, the Elbow looks like a flexed arm as it makes a dogleg turn to the right. Prismatic damselfish and angelfish, so tame they will swim up and look you in the eye, belie this graveyard of sunken cargo ships, the bones of which litter the ocean floor. The 191-foot *Tonawanda*, built in 1863 in Philadelphia, ended its short career as a tug and transport vessel in 1866 when it stranded on the reef. The ca. 1877 passenger/cargo steamer *City of Washington*, cut down and sold as a barge, piled up on the Elbow Reef in 1917 as it was towed by the USS *Edward Luckenbach*. Dynamited so it would not impede navigation, the barge's scattered remains rest near the *Tonawanda* in about 20 feet of water covered with purple sea fans and mustard-hued fire coral trees. The unidentified Civil War wreck, now nothing more than wooden beams held together by iron pins, sits in 25 feet of water. A search of the area may yield a sighting of an old Spanish cannon, probably thrown overboard to lighten the load when one of the ships ran aground. The Elbow, marked by a 36-foot light tower, provides good diving for the novice. Depths at this spur-and-groove reef range between 12 and 35 feet, and currents vary. Location: Lat. 25° 08.82, Long. 80° 15.19.

### Christ of the Deep Statue

Perhaps one of the most famous underwater photographs of all time is of the Christ of the Deep statue, which stands silhouetted against the sapphire-blue ocean waters bordering Key Largo Dry Rocks. This 9-foot figure of Christ, arms upraised and looking toward the heavens, was donated to the Underwater Society of America by Egidio Cressi, an Italian industrialist and diving equipment manufacturer. Designed by Italian sculptor Guido Galletti and cast in Italy, the statue is a bronze duplicate of the Christ of the Abysses, which stands underwater off Genoa. Surrounded by a flotilla of nonchalant skates and rays, the statue's left hand appears to be pointing to the massive brain corals peppering the adjoining ocean floor. With depths ranging from shallow to 25 feet, snorkeling is outstanding. Schools of electric-blue neon gobies congregate in cleaning stations, waiting to service other fish that wish to be rid of skin parasites. A slow offer of an outstretched arm may net you a goby-cleaned hand. Location: Lat. 25° 07.45, Long. 80° 17.80.

## Grecian Rocks

This crescent-shaped patch reef, which ranges in depth from shallow to 35 feet, ranks as a favorite among snorkelers and novice divers. Colonies of branched elkhorn corals, resembling the racks of bull moose or elk, provide a dramatic backdrop for the curious cruising barracuda, which often unnerve divers by following them about the reef but rarely cause a problem. Colossal star corals dot the area, which is populated by a rainbow palette of Spanish hogfish and a scattering of protected queen conch. An old Spanish cannon reportedly is concealed in one of the more luminous of the star coral, placed there some time ago by rangers of John Pennekamp Coral Reef State Park. Look for a small patch of reef near Grecian Rocks where old cannon and fused cannonballs litter the landscape. At low tide this reef rises out of the water. Location: Lat. 25° 06.70, Long. 80° 18.55.

## San Pedro *Underwater Archaeological Preserve*

This shipwreck park named after the Spanish ship *San Pedro* lies in 18 feet of water approximately 1.25 nautical miles south of Indian Key. The ship went down in 1773, and the remains can be found on the white-sand bottom. The park is located approximately 1.25 nautical miles south from Indian Key at GPS coordinates N24 51.802'/W80 40.795'. To prevent anchor damage, make sure to tie up to mooring buoys located at the site. Visit floridastateparks .org for more information.

## *USS* Spiegel Grove

The USS *Spiegel Grove*, a decommissioned Thomaston-class dock landing ship (LSD 32), was scuttled as an artificial reef in May 2002 in the waters off Key Largo. The largest vessel ever sunk as an artificial reef in the US, the *Spiegel Grove* did not go down without a fight. The ship unexpectedly began to sink ahead of schedule, turtling and sinking upside down and at an angle that kept it from completely submerging. The ship's bow stuck up out of the water for three weeks before a Resolve Marine Group salvage crew rolled it onto its starboard side, allowing it to sink completely on June 10, 2002. The *Spiegel Grove* rests at a depth of 130 feet, midway between the *Benwood* wreck and the Elbow reef.

## Benwood

The English-built freighter *Benwood*, en route from Tampa to Halifax and Liverpool in 1942 with a cargo of phosphate rock, attempted to elude German

U-boats early in World War II by running without lights. Unfortunately, the American freighter *Robert C. Tuttle* also took a darkened route. In their ultimate collision, the American ship ripped the *Benwood*'s starboard side open like a can opener. As it limped along, a fire broke out on deck and attracted a German U-boat, which finished her off with two torpedo hits. A memorable first wreck for novice divers, the bow of the ship remains in about 50 feet of water, while the stern rests in but 25 feet. It lies in line with the offshore reef about 1.5 miles north of French Reef. Location: Lat. 25° 03.16, Long. 80° 20.02.

### French Reef
Even novice divers can negotiate the caves at French Reef. Swim through the 3- to 4-foot limestone ledge openings or just peer in for a glance at the vermilion-painted blackbar soldierfish, which often swim upside down, mistakenly orienting themselves to the cave ceilings. Limestone ledges, adorned with tub sponges, extend from the shallows to depths in excess of 35 feet. Follow the mooring buoys for the best route. A mountainous star coral marks Christmas Tree Cave where, if you swim through the two-entrance passage, trapped air bubbles incandescently flicker in the cave's low light. Hourglass Cave sports a shapely column of limestone that divides the space in half, and White Sand Bottom Cave, a large swim-through cavern, shelters a potpourri of groupers, dog snappers, moray eels, and copper-colored glassy sweepers. Location: Lat. 25° 02.06, Long. 80° 21.00.

### White Bank Dry Rocks
A garden of soft corals welcomes snorkelers and novice divers to these patch-reef twins. With calm waters and depths ranging from shallow to 25 feet, White Bank Dry Rocks extends north and south along Hawk Channel at the southern end of Key Largo National Marine Sanctuary. You will feel as if you are swimming in a giant aquarium, for the lacy sea fans, feathery sea plumes, and branching sea whips create surreal staging for the fluttering schools of sophisticated black-and-yellow French angelfish. Location: 1.25 miles inshore of French Reef.

### Molasses Reef
Shallow coral ridges of this well-developed spur-and-groove reef radiate from the 45-foot light tower that marks Molasses Reef. Mooring buoys bob in deeper water, about 35 feet. Just off the eastern edge of the tower lies a single windlass, all that remains of the so-called Winch Wreck, or Windlass Wreck. Look for Christmas tree worms among the masses of star coral. The conical whorls, resembling maroon and orange pine trees, are actually worms that reside in living coral. If you slowly move a finger toward these faux flowers, they will sense your presence within half an inch and disappear like Houdini into their coral-encased tube homes. Location: Lat. 25° 01.00, Long. 80° 22.53.

## USCG Bibb *and* USCG Duane

Advanced divers will relish the exploration of the two US Coast Guard cutters sunk as artificial reefs 100 yards apart near Molasses Reef. These vessels, ca. mid-1930s, saw action in World War II and the Vietnam War. Both did search and rescue in their later peacetime years and were decommissioned in 1985. A consortium of dive shops and the Monroe County Tourist Development Council bought the cutters, which were subsequently stripped of armament, hatches, and masts, then cleaned. In 1987 the US Army Corps of Engineers sank the 327-foot vessels on consecutive days. The *Bibb* rests on her side in 130 feet of water, with her upper portions accessible at 90 feet. The upright *Duane* sits in more than 100 feet of water, but you can see the wheelhouse at 80 feet and the crow's nest in 60 feet of water. Location: Bibb: Lat. 24° 59.71, Long. 80° 22.77; Duane: Lat. 24° 59.38, Long. 80° 22.92.

## Pickles Reef

Pickles Reef got its name from the coral-encrusted barrels strewn about the ocean floor near the remnants of a cargo ship, called the Pickles Wreck, that carried them to their demise. The kegs are said to resemble pickle barrels, hence the name of the reef, but more likely were filled with building mortar bound for burgeoning construction in Key West. Look for the distinctively marked flamingo tongue snails, which attach themselves to swaying purple sea fans, grazing for algae. Flamboyantly extended around the outside of the flamingo tongue's glossy cream-colored shell is a bright orange mantle with black-ringed, leopard-like spots. Don't be tempted to collect these unusual creatures, for the colorful mantle is withdrawn upon death. With depths between 10 and 25 feet and a moderate current, Pickles Reef is a good dive for novice to intermediate skill levels. Location: Lat. 24° 59.23, Long. 80° 24.88.

## Conch Reef

Dive charters usually anchor in about 60 feet of water at Conch Reef, but the area actually offers something for everyone. With depths ranging from shallow to 100 feet and currents varying from moderate to strong, beginners as well as intermediate and advanced divers will be entranced here. The shallow section, festive with swirling schools of small tropicals, extends for a mile along the outer reef line. Conch Wall steeply drops from 60 to 100 feet, where sea rods, whips, fans, and plumes of the gorgonian family's deepwater branch congregate with an agglomeration of vaselike convoluted barrel sponges. The coral of Conch Reef was nearly decimated by heavy harvesting in bygone eras; dead stumps of pillar corals can still be seen. Location: Lat. 24° 57.11, Long. 80° 27.57.

## Hens and Chickens

A brood of large star coral heads surrounds a 35-foot US Navy light tower within 7 feet of the water's surface on this inshore patch reef, bringing to mind a mother hen and her chicks. Less than 3 miles from shore, this easily accessed 20-foot-deep reef remains popular with novice divers. Plumes, fans, and candelabra soft corals intermingle with skeletons of the coral graveyard (almost 80 percent of the reef died in 1970 after an unusually cold winter). Jailhouse-striped sheeps-head mingle with shy notch-tailed grunts and the more curious stout-bodied groupers, but don't be tempted; spearfishing is not allowed here. Remains of the Brick Barge, a modern casualty, and an old steel barge torpedoed during World War II lie among the coral heads. Location: Lat. 24° 55.9, Long. 80° 32.90.

### *The* Eagle

In 1985 an electrical fire disabled the 287-foot *Aaron K*, a freighter that carried scrap paper between Miami and South America. Declared a total loss, she was sold to the Monroe County Tourist Council and a group of local dive shops and then scuttled for use as an artificial reef. The vessel was renamed the *Eagle* after the Eagle Tire Company, which provided much of the funding for the project. A must-do for advanced divers, the *Eagle* landed on her starboard side in 120-foot waters, though her upper portions lurk within 65 feet of the surface. Densely packed polarized schools of silversides flow and drift within her interior. The tiny fork-tailed fish will detour around divers swimming through the school. Location: Lat. 24° 52.18, Long. 80° 34.21.

## Middle Keys

### *Alligator Reef*

Launched in 1820 in Boston, the USS *Alligator* hunted pirates in Florida as part of the West Indies Squadron. A 136-foot light tower now marks her namesake, Alligator Reef, which claimed the copper-and-bronze-fitted warship in 1825. The navy stripped the ship's valuables and blew her up. The *Alligator* rests offshore from the 8- to 40-foot-deep reef, now a bordello of brilliant tropicals, corals, and shells. Location: Lat. 24° 51.07, Long. 80° 37.21.

### *American, Maryland & Pelican Shoals*

American, Maryland, and Pelican shoals lie just offshore of the Saddlebunch Keys. They are east of Summerland and Cudjoe Keys where dive boats depart. Teeming with fish, these reefs are less visited than others in the Florida Keys.

### *Coffins Patch*

Gargantuan grooved brain corals join staghorns and toxic fire corals at Coffins Patch, a 1.5-mile reef popular with Middle Keys divers. A drift of yellow-finned French grunts and festive angelfish join an escort of mutton snappers, each distinctively branded with a black spot below the rear dorsal fin, as they guard the remains of the Spanish galleon *Ignacio*, which spewed a cargo of coins across the ocean floor in 1733. Location: Lat. 24° 40.60, Long. 80° 58.50.

### *The* Thunderbolt

In 1986 the artificial reef committee bought the *Thunderbolt*, a 188-foot cable-laying workboat, from a Miami River boatyard. The vessel was cleaned and her hatches removed. She then was towed south of Coffins Patch, where she was sunk as an artificial reef. Sitting majestically upright in 115 feet of water, the *Thunderbolt*'s bronze propellers, cable-laying spool, and wheelhouse are still recognizable. A stainless-steel cable leads from the wreck to a permanent underwater buoy. Current is strong at this wreck. Clip a line to the eye on the buoy and walk down the line. This dive is suitable for those with advanced certification. Location: Lat. 24° 39.48, Long. 80° 57.90.

### *Delta Shoals*

This shallow 10- to 20-foot shoal claimed many an unsuspecting ship through the centuries. Perhaps the most colorful history is that of an old vessel that ran aground in the 1850s. The ship yielded no treasure, but recovery of unique relics and elephant tusks led to the name Ivory Wreck. Among the wreckage were leg irons and brass bowls, leading historians to believe this was a slave ship from Africa. Location: Lat. 24° 37.78, Long. 81° 05.49.

### *Sombrero Reef*

A 142-foot lighthouse tower marks this living marine museum. Coral chasms, ridges, and portals support a proliferation of fuzzy, feathery, or hairy gorgonians as well as a salad bowl of leafy lettuce coral. A battalion of toothy barracuda swims reconnaissance, but don't be alarmed. You are too big to be considered tasty. Location: Lat 24° 37.50, Long. 81° 06.50.

## Lower Keys

### *Looe Key National Marine Sanctuary*

In 1744 Captain Ashby Utting ran the 124-foot British frigate HMS *Looe* hard aground on the 5-square-mile Y-shaped reef now bearing her name. Remains of the ship are interred between two fingers of living coral about 200 yards from the marker in 25 feet of water. The ballast and the anchor remain camouflaged with centuries of vigorous coral growth. Preserved as a national marine sanctuary since 1981, the 5- to 35-foot-deep waters surrounding Looe Key protect the diverse marine communities from fishing, lobstering, and artifact collecting, all forbidden.

The sanctuary, like Key Largo National Marine Sanctuary in the Upper Keys, offers interesting dives for novice, intermediate, and advanced divers alike. The spur-and-groove formations of Looe Key National Marine Sanctuary are the best developed in the Keys, and you can observe a complete coral reef ecosystem within the sanctuary's boundaries (see the Welcome to the Florida Keys chapter).

Take a laminated reef-creature guide sheet (readily available in dive shops) on your dive to identify the senses-boggling array of sea life at Looe Key. Look for some of these interesting species: The yellowhead jawfish excavates a hole in the sand with its mouth and retreats, tail-first, at the first sign of danger. The wary cottonwick sports a bold black stripe from snout to tail. The prehistoric-looking red lizardfish rests camouflaged on rocks and coral. The occasional blue-spotted peacock flounder changes color, chameleonlike, to match its surroundings.

Commercial dive charters provide excursions to Looe Key from Big Pine Key, Little Torch Key, and Ramrod Key. Location: Lat. 24° 32.70, Long. 81° 24.50.

## Astronauts under the Sea

NASA's National Oceanic and Atmospheric Administration's Aquarius underwater laboratory is the site for "splash down." This is tech talk for astronaut training underwater. The lab at Aquarius is a 45-foot-long complex that rests 62 feet beneath the surface, 3 miles off Key Largo in the Florida Keys National Marine Sanctuary. This setting provides a habitat for astronauts training for possible missions in space. During the NASA Extreme Mission Operations, astronauts imitate moonwalks, testing for mobility using specially designed space suits and weights to simulate lunar gravity. Aquarius is also the world's only undersea science facility.

### *The* Adolphus Busch

Scuttled in 1998 between Looe Key and American Shoal, this 210-foot freighter is named for one of the founders of the brewing industry. The *Adolphus Busch* sits upright in 100 feet of water. A tower comes within 40 feet of the surface and can be penetrated. *Adolphus Busch* is rapidly becoming a thriving tenement of fish and marine organisms. Location: Lat. 24° 31.81, Long. 81° 27.64.

### Key West

### *Eastern Sambo*

An underwater ridge at 60 feet dropping off sharply to the sand line at 87 feet goes by the name of Eastern Drop-off in this immensely popular reef area southeast of Key West. Reddish-brown honeycomb plate corals encrust the sloping reef face, while boulder corals pepper the base at the outer margin of the reef. The Hook, a long spur-and-groove canyon, extends south from the Eastern Sambo reef marker. Look for cruising tarpon during the summer months. West of Eastern Sambo is a site commonly referred to as marker no.

28, where sea turtles and nurse sharks make their rounds of the elkhorn coral. Location: Lat. 24° 29.50, Long. 81° 39.80.

### Middle Sambo

Coral heads and soft corals cover the sand beneath the 30- to 40-foot depths of Middle Sambo. You won't be alone as you observe the prolific lobsters haunting this area, especially in the summer months. Look for squadrons of tarpon and snook. Location: Lat. 24° 29.71, Long. 81° 41.79.

### Western Sambo

Mooring buoys mark this popular reef area with a variety of dives to 40 feet. Fields of branch coral stretch into the blue infinity, while mountains of sheet, boulder, star, and pillar corals cover the dramatic drop from 28 to 40 feet. Small yellow stingrays, which are actually covered with dark spots and can pale and darken protectively when the environment dictates, lie on the bottom with their stout, venomous tails buried in the sand. In the protected midreef area of the Cut, goggle-eyed blennies mill about with a colony of yellowhead jawfish, which retreat tail-first into their sand holes when frightened.

Half a mile south of Western Sambo, the remains of the *Aquanaut*, a 50-foot wooden tugboat owned by Chet Alexander, were scuttled in 75 feet of water as an artificial reef. Scattered about amid drifts of mahogany snappers and nocturnal glasseyes, the wreck is alive with spiderlike yellow arrow crabs. Location: Lat. 24° 29.38, Long. 81° 42.68.

### *The* Cayman Salvager

The 187-foot-long, steel-hulled buoy tender *Cayman Salvager*, built in 1936, originally sank at the Key West docks in the 1970s. Refloated and innards removed, she went back down in 1985 for use as an artificial reef, coming to rest on her side. Hurricane-force waves later righted her, and she now sits in 90 feet of water on a sandy bottom. Look for the fabled 200-pound jewfish and 6-foot moray eel residing in her open hold. Location: 6 miles south of Key West, 1 mile southwest of Nine Foot Stake, which is 1 mile west of marker no. 1.

### Joe's Tug

Sitting upright in 60 feet of water, *Joe's Tug*, a 75-foot steel-hulled tugboat, was scuttled as an artificial reef in 1989. The boat rests inshore from the *Cayman Salvager* on a bed of coral. This is one of the most popular wreck dives in the Key West circuit. Look for Elvis, the resident jewfish, who hangs out at the tug with yet another large moray eel. Location: 6 miles south of Key West.

### Eastern Dry Rocks

Shells, conchs, ballast stones, cannonballs, and rigging of disintegrating wrecks litter the rubble zone, coral fingers, and sand canyons of Eastern Dry Rocks.

With depths between 5 and 35 feet and only light current, this dive is suited to novices. Location: Lat. 24° 27.50, Long. 81° 50.44.

## Rock Key

Twenty-foot cracks barely as wide as a single diver distinguish Rock Key from nearby cousins at Eastern Dry Rocks. A 19th-century ship carrying building tiles from Barcelona went aground on Rock Key, scattering her bounty about the ocean floor. Tiles carrying the Barcelona imprint are reportedly still occasionally recovered. Location: Lat. 24° 27.21, Long. 81° 51.60.

## Stargazer

Billed as the "world's largest underwater sculptured reef," Stargazer stands 22 feet below the surface, 5 miles off Key West between Rock Key and Sand Key. The creation of artist Ann Lorraine Labriola, Stargazer mimics a primitive navigational instrument, its giant steel sections—ranging between 2,000 and 8,000 pounds—emblazoned with constellation symbols and emblems. A "mystery chart" sends divers on an underwater treasure hunt with a series of puzzles that require a certain amount of celestial knowledge to solve. Location: Lat. 24° 27.49, Long. 81° 52.09.

## Sand Key

Originally called Cays Arena by early Spanish settlers, Sand Key, 6 miles south of Key West, is partially awash at low tide. Topped by a distinctive 110-foot red iron lighthouse, Sand Key's shape, composed of shells and ground coral, changes with each hurricane and tropical storm. Sand Key shines as a good all-weather dive and, with depths ranging to 65 feet, appeals to all skill levels. The shallows of the leeward side provide good snorkeling. In spring and summer the Gulf Stream movement over the shallows provides great visibility and vibrant colors. You can easily reach Sand Key on your own in a 17- to 18-foot boat on a calm day. Location: Lat. 24° 27.19, Long. 81° 52.58.

## Ten-Fathom Bar

Advanced divers peruse a gallery of deep dives on the western end of the outer reef system, which is nearly 4 miles long. The southern edge, Fennel Ridge, begins at about 60 feet deep, giving the site its name, then plunges to the sand line, undulating between 90 and 120 feet. Encrusted telegraph cables at 45 to 55 feet, apparently snaking a line to Havana, cut across the eastern end of the Ten-Fathom Bar, competing with man-size sponges and dramatic black coral.

Near the cable, Eye of the Needle sports a plateau of coral spurs. Deep, undercut ledges shelter the spotted, white-bellied porcupinefish. Divers can swim under a ledge and up through a broad "eye" to the top of the plateau. Depths max out at 120 feet, but you'll see much more between 40 and 80 feet.

Be prepared for a sea squadron of fin-driven tropicals to shadow your every move. Location: 0.5 mile due south of Sand Key.

### Toppino's Reef (#1 Marker Reef)
Four and a half miles south of Boca Chica Channel and 5 miles south of Key West is one of the most beautiful shallow dive spots in the Keys. Famous for 8- to 10-foot-high coral fingers rising from the bottom, marine life congregate to eat off the hard and soft coral. This is a very popular nighttime dive spot in 25 feet of water. The USS *Vandenberg* was sunk near this spot in 2009 (see below, this section).

### Western Dry Rocks
Experts will love the unusual marine life at Western Dry Rocks. Novices and snorkelers will, too, because this site ranges in depth from 5 to 120 feet, averaging 30 feet with lots of light. Coral fingers with defined gullies and coral formations laced with cracks and caves showcase species normally found more in the Bahamas than in the Keys. The deep-dwelling candy basslets hide themselves away at 90 feet, while their more gregarious cousins, the orangeback bass, hang out in the open. The dusky longsnout butterflyfish prefer dark recesses, though they will sometimes curiously peer out to see what's happening. Sharks have been witnessed regularly enough to prompt advice against spearfishing. Location: 3 miles west of Sand Key.

### Alexander's Wreck
Commercial salvor Chet Alexander bought a 328-foot destroyer escort from the US Navy at the bargain price of $2,000 and sank her (still sporting her deck guns) in about 40 feet of water west of Cottrell Key as an artificial reef in 1972. Though the current fluctuates from moderate to strong, the relatively shallow depths here allow conscientious novices a chance to swim among fascinating sea creatures: The bodies of the prison-bar-striped spadefish resemble the spade figures in a deck of playing cards. Zebra-striped sheepshead are so curious that if you remain stationary, they may come over to investigate. The flashy metallic gold-and-silver-striped porkfish is apparently the victim of a cruel creator—two bold, black, diagonal bands slash across its glittery head. Location: Lat. 24° 36.97, Long. 81° 58.91.

### Cottrell Key
A snorkeler's paradise at 3 to 15 feet, Cottrell Key, on the gulf side, saves the day for divers when the weather is foul on the Atlantic. The grassy banks of the adjoining lakes protect the reef in east-southeast to southwest winds. Ledges and solution holes run for several miles amid intermittent coral heads and swaying gorgonians. The pits, crevices, and coral caves hold great treasures: encrusting orange sponges, which look like spilled cake batter; lustrously mottled cowries,

camouflaged by their extended mantles; Florida horse conchs, which will venture out of their long conical spire if you wait patiently; and spindle-shaped freckled tulip snails. Location: Gulf side, 9 miles out of N.W. Channel.

### ★ *USS* Vandenberg

Key West has its newest artificial reef: a 13,000-ton, 520-foot-long, 100-foot-tall decommissioned vessel, the *General Hoyt S. Vandenberg*. Located near marker no. 32 in 140 feet of water, 6 miles off the coast of Key West in the Florida Keys National Marine Sanctuary, and costing nearly $6 million, the *Vandenberg* is one of the premier dive sites in the world. Experts boast you can dive there for days and not see it all. Suitably trained and equipped deep divers can penetrate the superstructure using the multiple horizontal and vertical swim-through flooding and venting holes that are cut into the ship. The *Vandenberg*, a US Air Force missile-tracking ship, was decommissioned in 1983. The ship also tracked US space missions in the early 1960s. Local videographers from Digital Island Media won an Emmy for their work on filming the sinking of the *Vandenberg*.

> **i** Local honorary Conch and ocean explorer Sylvia Earle convinced Google executives to launch Google Ocean. Using existing maps and databases to reveal parts of the ocean world, Google's downloadable programs allow views under the Florida Keys of marine protected areas, dive sites, and shipwrecks. All this without getting your hair wet! Visit earth.google.com/ocean.

### And Beyond

*The Shipwrecks of Smith Shoals*

Between June and Aug 1942, four large ships met their demise near Smith Shoals, apparent unwary victims of American military mines. The USS *Sturtevant*, a 314-foot-long four-stack destroyer, was only two hours out of port escorting a convoy when two consecutive explosions ripped her apart. She rests in 65 feet of water. The 3,000-ton American freighter USS *Edward Luckenbach*, en route from Jamaica to New Orleans with a cargo of tin, zinc, and tungsten, joined the *Sturtevant* after hitting the same minefield. The *Bosiljka* also made a navigational misstep, succumbing to an American mine as she carried her pharmaceutical cargo from New Orleans to Key West. Groupers, jewfish, snappers, and cobia populate the sunken 277-foot Norwegian ship *Gunvor*, taken by a mine on her way to Trinidad from Mobile, Alabama. The wreckage is scattered in 60 feet of water. Location: Lat. 24° 45.30, Long. 81° 01.18.

## Marquesas Keys

This group of 10 mangrove islands surrounded by shallow waters has alternately been called the remains of a prehistoric meteor crater and an atoll. The ring of keys was named for the Marquis de Cadierata, commander of the 1622 Spanish fleet that included the wrecks *Nuestra Señora de Atocha* and *Santa Margarita*. The wrecks were partially salvaged until 1630 by the Spanish, who enticed slave divers to search the remains, promising freedom to the first diver to recover a bar of silver from the site. Mel Fisher rediscovered the ships in 1985. Fisher, the famous 20th-century salvor, found a mother lode of treasure in the holds.

The Marquesas Keys evidence little human influence, for they remain uninhabited. Clusters of coral heads shrouded in groupers and snappers mark the southern edge of the islands. Twenty-five miles from Key West, the Marquesas appeal to divers cruising in their motor yachts or on an overnight charter, and to hale and hearty day-trippers. West of the Marquesas several wrecks dot the suboceanic landscape. Exercise caution before diving, however, because the US Navy has been known to use them as bombing and strafing targets from time to time. Before you strap on your tanks, check your radio for a Coast Guard bulletin regarding this area. Location: 25 miles west of Key West.

## *The* Northwind

The *Northwind*, a large metal tugboat belonging to Mel Fisher's Treasure Salvors Inc., tragically sank in 1975 while working on the *Atocha* project. Said to have a malfunctioning fuel valve and a leaky bulkhead, the *Northwind* capsized while at anchor, taking Fisher's son and daughter-in-law to a watery grave. The vessel lies on her side in 40 feet of water 3.5 miles southwest of the Marquesas.

## Cosgrove Shoal

A 50-foot skeletal lighthouse marks the northern edge of the Gulf Stream, 6 miles south of the western Marquesas. This rocky bank runs for miles, a prehistoric dead reef where caves and ledges support gardens and forests and social clubs of marine fin and flora. A contingent of giant barracuda patrols the shallows, and black coral grows up from the depths, which extend beyond recreational diving capacities. Be sure to take the strong outgoing tide into consideration before you dive here. Location: 6 miles south of the western edge of the Marquesas.

## Marquesas Rock

Moderate to strong currents and depths to 120 feet dictate that this dive is suited only to advanced skill levels. A can-buoy marks the rocky plateau of Marquesas Rock, the cracks and crevices of which reveal a potpourri of sea life. A school of jacks, apparently attracted by your bubbles, may make a swing past. Saucer-eyed reddish squirrelfish, with elongated rear dorsal fins resembling squirrel tails, mind their own business in the shaded bottom crevices.

Occasional sightings of sailfish, sperm whales, and white sharks have been reported. Keep in mind that when diving at Marquesas Rock you are 30 miles from the nearest assistance.

## Florida Keys Menace

The lionfish, a small fish with spines that are venomous, is prolific and voracious and has been spotted in Florida Keys waters. The lionfish is native to the Pacific Ocean and has been known to upset local ecosystems off the coast of North Carolina as well as in the Bahamas. REEF (Reef Environmental Education Foundation) and the Florida Keys National Marine Sanctuary sponsor derbies throughout the year with cash prizes to help rid our waters of this invasive species.

### *Dry Tortugas National Park*

The end of the line in the Florida Keys, the Dry Tortugas lie some 60 miles beyond Key West. Small boats are discouraged from making the trip because strong tidal currents flowing against prevailing winds between Rebecca Shoals and the reef of the Tortugas can be treacherous. There is no fuel, freshwater, or facilities offering provisions, nor will you find any emergency assistance. Nonetheless, if your vessel is self-sufficient, if you are with a charter out of Key West, or if you have traveled to the Dry Tortugas by seaplane or ferry to camp on Garden Key (see the Recreation and Campgrounds chapters), you are in for the treat of a lifetime.

The eight-island chain is guarded as our southernmost national park. All living creatures below are protected from collection or capture, so a virtual mega-aquarium exists beneath the sea. The constant Gulf Stream current cleanses the waters, allowing visibility of 80 to 100 feet over the 100-square-mile living coral reef. Just off the beach on the west side of Loggerhead Key slumbers a snorkeler's paradise. About a mile offshore lies the remains of a 300-foot, steel-hulled French wreck. Divers report that a monster-size jewfish estimated to be 150 years old resides under the wreck. Other wrecks are littered about the ocean floor, claimed by the reef during centuries past.

## DIVE CENTERS

As you drive down the Overseas Highway from Key Largo to Key West, you will notice banner-size, red-and-white diver-down flags heralding one dive shop after another. More than 100 such establishments are listed in the phone book alone. To help you navigate this minefield of choices, we supply you with the best ammunition: information.

Many of the dive operations offer the same basic services and will take you to similar, if not the same, spots. But each also differs in many ways. Snorkelers and divers often are taken to the reef in the same excursion, for the varied depths of our spur-and-groove reefs can be experienced with multiple levels of expertise. Snorkel-only trips also are an option. The size of dive excursions varies greatly, ranging from 20 individuals or more to a small-boat group.

Dive rates are based on a two-tank, two-site daylight dive. If you don't have your own equipment, full-gear packages—generally including two tanks, buoyancy compensator, weight belt, regulator, octopus breathing device, gauges, and occasionally mask, snorkel, and fins—are available. A wet suit is advisable in winter. Always ask exactly what is included if you need a full-gear package. All our recommended dive centers make a one-tank, night-dive excursion on request unless otherwise specified.

Virtually all of our listed dive centers offer optional dive packages, either for multiple days of diving or for hotel-dive combinations. If you plan to dive on several days of your holiday, you will save money with a package, but you will be limited to diving with one exclusive dive center.

You may assume, unless otherwise noted, all featured dive centers rent full equipment and maintain a retail dive shop where you can purchase equipment, accessories, and underwater camera housings if needed. You may also count on the fact that all recommended dive centers offer a one-day "let's give it a try" resort course. These courses are based on participation of two or more people. Private courses also are available at a considerably higher fee. Many of our recommended dive centers offer a wide selection of Professional Association of Diving Instructors (PADI), National Association of Underwater Instructors (NAUI), and other advanced classes.

You will be required to show your certification card and logbook, and you must wear a buoyancy compensator and a submersible pressure gauge. Snorkels are required equipment for all divers. To dive deeper than 60 feet, considered a deep dive, you must hold advanced certification or a logbook entry showing dives to equivalent depths within the last six months. If you cannot meet these specifications, you will be required to be accompanied by an instructor or guide, which often entails an additional fee. You must wear an octopus (an emergency breathing device to share air with your dive buddy) or carry spare air for a deep dive, and you must be equipped with a depth gauge or a timing device. You do not need advanced certification to participate in a night dive, but you must own or rent a dive light and carry a Cyalume stick as a backup lighting system.

All dive centers request you check in at least 30 minutes prior to the excursion's departure. Allow even more time if you are renting a full-gear package. We list the dive centers in alphabetical order from Key Largo through Key West.

# Close-up

## Diving for Lobster

You may envision the mighty Maine, but when we say lobster in the Florida Keys, a totally different creature comes to mind. Equally delectable, the Florida lobster, or spiny lobster, is a crustacean akin to crabs, shrimp, and crawfish. Unlike its Downeast cousin, the Florida lobster is clawless. Ten spiderlike legs support its spiny head and hard-shell body, and radarlike antennae make up for weak eyesight. But its best defense, most coveted by hungry humans, remains its powerful tail muscle, which propels the lobster backward at breakneck speed.

Diving for lobster is a popular sport in the waters of the Florida Keys. Nocturnal feeders, spiny lobsters hide underwater in crevices, between rocks, in caves, under artificial reefs, near dock pilings, or in dead coral outcroppings during the day. They are not easy to spot. They occasionally peek out from their protective holes, but most often only a single antenna will be visible. The good news is that a whole gang may be hiding out together.

So how do you catch these potentially tasty morsels locals call bugs? Here are a few basic tools—and tricks—to help swing the scales in your favor:

- You will need a pair of heavy-duty dive gloves, for the two large horns on the lobster's head and the sharp spines of its whipping tail can draw blood.

- To store your captive prizes, get an easy-to-open mesh game bag with a fastener that you can hook to your weight belt. Be sure this bag does not drag over the reef, which would damage coral and other marine life.

- Instead of poking your arm into a crevice or hole to coax out a lobster, it's much safer and smarter to use a probe or "tickle stick," a long metal or fiberglass rod with a short, 90-degree bend on one end. That hole could just as easily house a dangerous moray eel as a lobster.

- And a lobster net is a must for capturing the tickled lobster.

To harvest lobsters in the Florida Keys recreationally, you need a valid Florida saltwater fishing license with a current crawfish stamp (see the Fishing chapter). Florida law mandates lobster hunters carry a device to measure the lobster's carapace, that portion of the shell beginning between the eyes and extending to the hard end segment just before the tail. The carapace should measure at least 3 inches or the lobster—deemed a "short"—must be returned to the sea. The measuring device can be secured to your game bag. Measure the lobster before you put it in your bag; do not bring it to the boat to be measured.

Look for lobsters in the patch reefs on the ocean side by using NOAA navigational charts. Look for relatively shallow areas (15 to 20 feet) surrounded by deeper water (25 to 30 feet). If your boat has a chart recorder, use it to detect bottom contours and the presence of fish. Look for irregular bottom areas, which often mean coral outcroppings and sponges. When you find the suspected patch reefs, check them out with a quick dive to the bottom before anchoring your boat. You will need to scuba-dive for lobsters in the patch reefs.

Alternately, look for lobster "holes" in the shallow gulfside waters and, wearing mask, snorkel, and fins, free-dive for the crustaceans. Watch for patches of brightness in the turtle-grass floor from your skiff. Sandy sea bottom looks bright also, so slow to idle speed and look for coral. Throw a buoy marker here (connect a dive weight to a Styrofoam buoy with line), because coral outcroppings are rare. Send a dive scout over the side to bird-dog the outcropping for antennae and, with a little luck, the hunt will begin.

When frightened, the wily lobster will contract its powerful tail and propel itself like a bullet backward into its shelter or the sea grass. Slowly slide your tickle stick behind the lobster and tap its tail. Bothered from behind, the lobster is persuaded to slowly leave its shelter to investigate. Once the lobster is out of the hole, place the net behind (yes, behind!) the lobster with the rim firmly resting on the sandy bottom if possible. Tap the lobster's head with the tickle stick. This time, irritated, the lobster will propel backward into your net. Quickly slam your net down on the seafloor so the lobster cannot escape. Then secure the net closed with your other hand. The lobster may thrash and become tangled in the net.

Holding the netted lobster firmly with one hand, measure the carapace. Carefully remove the lobster from the net. If short, release it. If legal size, place it securely in your game bag, tail-first. One thrust of the vigorous tail could negate all your efforts. Also, be careful not to release any other bugs you have already bagged. If you see a dark spot or reddish orange nodules under the tail, this lobster is an egg-bearing female. By Florida law you must release her.

Place your captured lobsters in the saltwater-filled bait well of your boat or store them on ice in a cooler with a lid. It is against Florida law to separate the tail from the body while on Florida waters. On dry land pull the tails, which must measure more than 5½ inches. There is little meat in the body, so it may be discarded or boiled to make lobster stock. After wringing the tail, break an antenna from the severed body. Insert the antenna, larger end first, into the underside base of the tail and then pull it out. The spiny thorns of the antenna will snag the intestinal tract, which will be removed with the antenna. To freeze the tails, place them in small plastic ziplock bags, filled with freshwater, and freeze for up to six months.

## Upper Keys

**AMY SLATE'S AMORAY DIVE RESORT,** MM 104.2 Bayside, 10425 Overseas Hwy., Key Largo, FL 33037; (305) 451-3595 or (800) 426-6729; **amoray.com.** From this resort, you can hop out of bed, onto the deck, and take off for a scuba excursion. The Amoray Dive Resort's villa lodging amenities, complete with hot tub and pool, cater to your every diving whim (see the Accommodations chapter). Amoray's catamaran will whisk you to the reefs of the Key Largo National Marine Sanctuary for a two-tank dive. Night dives are available.

**CAPTAIN SLATE'S SCUBA ADVENTURES,** MM 90.7 Oceanside, 90791 Overseas Hwy., Unit 1, Tavernier, FL 33037; (305) 451-3020 or (800) 331-3483; **captainslate.com.** After 36 years in business, Captain Slate's has opened at a brand-new location with renewed energy. Snorkelers can make a snorkel-only excursion to one destination or they can accompany divers as "bubble watchers" to specially selected reef locations if they'd rather stay dry. A special feature of Captain Slate's is the custom underwater wedding package. Divers are married in front of the Christ of the Deep statue at Key Largo Dry Rocks. Vows are made via underwater slates as guest-divers watch the ceremony from the ocean floor and guest-snorkelers view the proceedings from overhead. Videos and still-photography of the blessed event are also available.

**CORAL REEF PARK COMPANY,** MM 102.5 Oceanside, John Pennekamp Coral Reef State Park, 102601 Overseas Hwy., Key Largo, FL 33037; (305) 451-6300 or (305) 451-6322 (reservations); **pennekamppark.com.** John Pennekamp Coral Reef State Park offers varied options for adventure seekers. Snorkeling trips begin at 9:30 a.m. or 1 p.m. Destinations include Molasses Reef, North Dry Rocks, Grecian Rocks, Benwood, Elbow, or Carysfort. Another option, above the surface, is a 2.5-hour ride to the surrounding reefs on the *Spirit of Pennekamp*, the resort's flagship glass-bottomed boat. If you want to stay closer to shore, you can rent a mask, snorkel, and fins and paddle around in the water off Cannon Beach, where, yes, there really are a couple of sunken cannons and ancient anchors.

**DIVERS DIRECT,** MM 99.6 Oceanside, 99621 Overseas Hwy., Key Largo, FL 33037; (305) 451-0118 or (800) DIVE-USA; **diversdirect.com.** Divers Direct, a water lover's emporium with 6 locations in the state of Florida (see the website for details), offers one of the largest selections of men's, women's, and children's clothing along with snorkeling and scuba gear, kids' equipment, videos, books, and a repair service. In business since 1984, the owners are divers as well. They have trained their staff to know their products well and make sure their customers have the right gear and advice for the perfect dive.

**FLORIDA KEYS DIVE CENTER, MM 90.5 Oceanside, 90451 Overseas Hwy., Tavernier, FL 33070; (305) 852-4599 or (800) 433-8946; floridakeys divectr.com.** The Florida Keys Dive Center is one of the few that offers technical diving. This refers to diving beyond the limits that apply to recreational diving. Their staff is highly trained and eager to teach beginners how to get started and experienced divers new skills. The Florida Keys Dive Center is also one of only two PADI 5-Star Career Development Centers in the Keys. If you get there early, take some time and enjoy the relaxing atmosphere of their tiki hut before taking the plunge.

**HORIZON DIVERS, MM 100 Oceanside, 100 Ocean Dr., Bldg. #1, Key Largo, FL 33037; (305) 453-3535 or (800) 984-DIVE; horizondivers.com.** Horizon Divers runs clean and fast, ensuring divers the maximum amount of bottom time to study large varieties of fish species found in more than 100 locations off the coast of Key Largo. Videotape or photograph the sea life in these waters while you perfect your diving technique and deepen your connection with nature. Whether you're novice or advanced, Horizon Divers has instructors to help you hone your skills. Saturday-night dives are also an option for those who want to see the world of sea life that comes alive after dark. Be sure to call ahead to make reservations; at least six divers are required to make this a go.

**JOHN PENNEKAMP CORAL REEF STATE PARK BOAT RENTALS & DIVE CENTER, MM 102.5 Oceanside, 102601 Overseas Hwy., Key Largo, FL 33037; (305) 451-1202 or (305) 451-6300 (reservations); pennekamp park.com.** The Pennekamp State Park Dive Center prides itself on being the only dive center actually situated inside Pennekamp's grounds. This company's scuba shuttles regularly to visit such novice sport dives as Molasses Reef, the wreck of the *Benwood*, and the Christ of the Deep statue. Average dives range from 30 to 45 feet deep, and certification requirements are stringent. For more serious divers, they have a PADI 5-Star Dive Shop where inquiring minds can receive instruction on becoming a fully certified diver. No one has to be left out; *Encounter* is a wheelchair-accessible snorkeling vessel that allows even more individuals the chance to take part in the fun.

**OCEAN DIVERS, MM 100 Oceanside, 522 Caribbean Dr., Key Largo, FL 33037; (305) 451-1113 or (800) 451-1113; oceandiversdc.com.** Adjacent to Marina Del Mar Resort, Ocean Divers has had over 500,000 customers come through their center. Ocean Divers, operating for over 33 years now, maintains a rotating schedule of trips frequenting several set dive sites if conditions allow. Visiting the popular sites within the Key Largo National Marine Sanctuary, Ocean Divers slips into Eagle Ray Alley and Fire Coral Cave, and between the stands of the rare day-feeding pillar coral. Divers who enjoy wreck dives can visit the *Bibb*, the *Duane*, and the *Spiegel Grove*. Night dives to Molasses Reef are offered regularly and upon request.

**RAINBOW REEF, MM 100.8, 100800 Overseas Hwy., Key Largo, FL 33037 or Courtyard by Marriott and Holiday Inn, MM 100, 99725 Overseas Hwy., Key Largo, FL 33037; (305) 451-7171 or (800) 457-4354; rainbowreef .us.** Rainbow Reef, with 2 locations, offers extensive dives to coral and artificial reefs, ledges, walls, and centuries-old wrecks. Oh, and don't forget the fish! Depths go up to 90 feet, with each dive site offering its own unique qualities. The charters hit all the spectacular spots from Elbow Reef down to Conch Reef and Wall. Rainbow Reef's engaging staff make your dive personal and pleasurable. (Their Facebook page is full of happy posts and solid reviews!) Plus, they are a full-service PADI 5-Star Gold Palm Instructor Center. See you beneath the sea!

**SILENT WORLD DIVE CENTER, 47 Garden Cove Dr., Key Largo, FL 33037; (305) 451-3252; silentworld.com.** Now under new management and in a new location, Silent World is dedicated to bringing the best of recreational and technical diving to the Keys. Their custom dive boat makes regular visits to the Elbow, Key Largo Dry Rocks, the *Benwood*, French Reef, Carysfort Reef, and other popular sites within Key Largo National Marine Sanctuary. And no crowds, no rush! There is a maximum of 12 divers at a time and at least an hour spent at each site.

## Middle Keys

**ABYSS DIVE CENTER, MM 53.5 Oceanside, 12565 Overseas Hwy., Marathon, FL 33050; (305) 743-2126; abyssdive.com.** The Abyss Dive Center in Marathon sticks to the less-is-more approach of diving, which guarantees lots of personal attention. The company takes a maximum of 6 divers or snorkelers at a time to over 50 sites spread over the reefs, including Sombrero Gardens, Shrimp Boat Reef, and the Gap. Abyss will take you to the *Thunderbolt* if your certs are current or your dive experience warrants, or you can hire an instructor and explore the wreck with a guide. Since it is such an experience, they suggest making reservations well in advance.

**HALL'S DIVING CENTER, MM 48.5 Bayside, 5050 Overseas Hwy., Marathon, FL 33050; (305) 743-5929 or (800) 331-HALL; hallsdiving.com/ halls.** If you are an advanced certified diver or have an 80-foot dive under your weight belt, head out to the *Thunderbolt* with Hall's. Divers of other skill levels will enjoy plunging down 25 to 90 feet, to sites like Coffins Patch near Sombrero Reef. In addition to standard equipment, a deluxe full-gear package, featuring top-of-the-line Nitrox clean gear, is available. Hall's also provides certification in the use of a rebreather and specialty dives with diver propulsion vehicles. Or you can rent mask, snorkel, and fins and explore the shallow gulf waters or the Atlantic Ocean off Sombrero Beach with a buddy.

**TILDEN'S SCUBA CENTER, MM 49.5 Bayside, at the Blackfin Resort and Marina, 4650 Overseas Hwy., Marathon, FL 33050; (305) 743-7255 or (888) SCUBA-FL; tildensscubacenter.com.** Long known as a top-notch dive center in the Florida Keys, Tilden's heads to such thriving reef locations as Cannon Reef, Porkfish Reef, and Shark Harbor, and takes advanced divers on guided excursions to shipwrecks such as the famed *Thunderbolt* site. Tilden Scuba Center operates one of the largest dive vessels in the Middle Keys—it's licensed to carry 40 passengers—but limits its excursions from 12 to 20 divers and snorkelers. Want to try something new? SNUBA! This combination of *scuba* and *snorkel* is perfect for non-divers, this special system allows anyone 8 and older to explore to a maximum of 20 feet!

### Lower Keys

**LOOE KEY REEF RESORT & DIVE CENTER, MM 27.5 Oceanside, 27340 Overseas Hwy., Ramrod Key, FL 33042; (305) 872-2215 or (877) 816-3483; diveflakeys.com.** Twice a day the friendly crew at Looe Key Reef Resort whisks you off to the Looe Key National Marine Sanctuary, one of the healthiest reefs in the United States. You will visit 2 sites with at least an hour of bottom time at each location. On Wed and every other Sun, trips are made to the *Adolphus Busch* wreck. Call to confirm times. Snorkelers may accompany divers. Looe Key Reef Resort & Dive Center offers dive/lodging packages at its adjoining motel. The dive boat leaves from its mooring directly behind the motel, so schlepping your gear is not a burden here.

**STRIKE ZONE CHARTERS, MM 29.6 Bayside, 29675 Overseas Hwy., Big Pine Key, FL 33043; (305) 872-9863; strikezonecharter.com.** Docked out back, Strike Zone Charters' glass-bottomed catamarans are ready to transport you to the Looe Key National Marine Sanctuary for a spectacular two-tank dive. The depth of this reef (ranging from 6 to 30 feet) makes it perfect for divers and snorkelers alike!

i **Soldiers Undertaking Disabled Scuba (SUDS) is a nonprofit organization designed to help improve the lives of injured soldiers returning from Iraq and Afghanistan. As part of soldiers' physical rehab, SUDS often takes them to Key Largo to finalize their scuba certification. For more information, visit sudsdiving.org.**

**UNDERSEAS INC., MM 30.5 Oceanside, 30678 Overseas Hwy., Big Pine Key, FL 33043; (305) 872-2700 or (800) 466-LOOE; underseasinc.com.** In the Lower Keys when you've said, "Looe Key National Marine Sanctuary," you've said it all. Underseas will take you to the depths of this pristine sanctuary and satisfy all levels, from snorkelers and novice divers to those with advanced skills. Looe Key is endlessly fascinating, and the good people of Underseas Inc. have been revealing its best-kept secrets to divers since 1969! Call for times of departure and get ready for adventure.

## Key West

**CAPTAIN'S CORNER DIVE CENTER, 125 Anne St., Key West, FL 33040; (305) 296-8865 or (305) 296-8918; captainscorner.com.** Captain's Corner Dive Center's scuba and snorkel excursions feature wreck and reef dives, and double wreck dives are available by special arrangement. Dive a wreck, then watch the sunset from the deck of the boat. Private trips may be booked to the wreck of the *Nuestra Señora de Atocha*, 30 miles west of Key West. Captain's Corner always has instructors in the water with you, so you can sign on even if you are a novice diver. The boat departs from 631 Greene Street, corner of Greene and Elizabeth Streets, at the Conch Republic Seafood Restaurant.

**DIVE KEY WEST INC., 3128 North Roosevelt Blvd., Key West, FL 33040; (305) 296-3823 or (800) 426-0707; divekeywest.com.** Dive Key West offers "reef du jour," customizing the schedule based on diver demand and weather conditions. It concentrates on the 30-foot reef lines where the light is better and the colors are more brilliant, allowing you more bottom time to enjoy the heightened beauty. The inner reefs have large stands of coral and a high concentration of tropical fish, while at the outer reefs you will see less coral, more big sea fans and sponges, and larger finfish. Dive Key West visits the wrecks of the *Cayman Salvager, Joe's Tug,* and the *Vandenberg,* all ranging from 60 to 100 feet, respectively, offering a skill level for everyone.

**LOST REEF ADVENTURES, 261 Margaret St., on Key West Bight, Key West, FL 33040; (305) 296-9737 or (800) 952-2749; lostreefadventures .com.** Lost Reef Adventures customizes its dive trips a day before departure based upon the skill levels and dive-site desires of interested divers. Excursions visit the celebrated *Joe's Tug, Cayman Salvager,* and *Vandenberg* wreck sites. With their dedication to detail and individual attention, you will be sure to feel taken care of when you explore the deep with Lost Reef Adventures.

# Recreation

If you want to scuba-dive or snorkel, fish, sail, or motor in our abundant waters, see the related chapters in this book. For a plethora of other stimulating diversions, read on. We show you where the action is—from skydiving, parasailing, and water sports to sunset cruises, eco-tours, and bicycling. You'll find out about our beaches and public parks in this chapter. And if the weather isn't fine—which is rare—or you would just like to stay indoors, we tell you where to see a first-run movie or even a local play.

## OVERVIEW

Expect to pay a fee for your recreational choices. We will indicate which diversions are free. Recreation facilities are organized by category from Key Largo to Key West.

## AIR·TOURS & SKYDIVING

**KEY WEST BIPLANES, Key West International Airport, 3469 S. Roosevelt Blvd., Key West, FL 33040; (305) 851-8359; keywestbiplanes.com.** For a bird's-eye view of Key West and beyond, take a ride in a vintage open-cockpit biplane. Key West Biplanes' sightseeing plane rides take you over the coral reef to view shipwrecks in Fleming Key Channel, along the south shore of Key West, to Boca Grande Key, across the backcountry waters, and up the Keys as far as Little Palm Island (see the Accommodations chapter). Tours range from 6 minutes to more than an hour. Prices are based on 2 people riding in the front seat. They also offer aerobatic rides.

**SKYDIVE KEY WEST, MM 17 Bayside, Lower Sugarloaf Airport, Sugarloaf Key, FL 33042; (305) 745-4386; skydivekeywest.com.** Try tandem skydiving from 10,000 feet over the Lower Keys and Key West with Skydive Key West. First-timers are welcome. Allow 1 hour per person for this venture, including training and the jump. Soft landings are provided on Lower Sugarloaf Key. Skydive expeditions aboard a Cessna 182 depart Sugarloaf Airport between 10 a.m. and sunset 7 days a week. Skydivers are advised not to scuba-dive for 24 hours before their jump. Videos and photographs are available for purchase as souvenirs. Jumps are by reservation only, and you must be at least 18 years of age to take the plunge.

## BEACHES & PUBLIC PARKS

Life's a beach, the T-shirts say, but first-time visitors to the Keys who expect to find soft, white, endless sand along the ocean are bound to be disappointed. The coral reef protects the Keys from the pounding surf that grinds other shorelines into sand, and so most of ours must be carted in by the truckload. Nevertheless, if stretching out in the sand tops your recreational must-do list, humans and nature have teamed up here to bring you a stretch or two. Some of our parks and beaches charge admission fees, and most have specific hours of accessibility.

Keys beaches do not maintain lifeguard stations. Riptides are rare here, but jellyfish are not. Swim at your own risk, and never venture out alone or after dark.

> **i** For your safety, Florida has warning flags posted on our public beaches statewide. Double red lines: no swimming at all. Yellow: medium hazard, moderate surf and/or currents. Green: low hazard, calm conditions, but exercise caution. Purple: dangerous marine life.

### Upper Keys

**ANNE'S BEACH, MM 73.5 Oceanside, Islamorada, FL 33036.** At low tide, tiny Anne's Beach holds enough sand to accommodate several blankets, but it attracts sun worshippers by the dozens. Swimming waters are shallow. A wooden boardwalk meanders for about 0.3 mile along the water, through the mangroves, and 5 picnic pavilions jut out from the boardwalk. Parking is limited. To find Anne's Beach, slow down along the Overseas Highway southwest of Caloosa Cove Resort and look toward the ocean for 2 small parking lots. The boardwalk connects the lots. Blink and you'll miss it. There is no charge.

**BEACH BEHIND THE LIBRARY, MM 81.5 Bayside, Islamorada, FL 33036.** This stretch of beach has no more official name than its general location, but it does offer a playground, restrooms, and showers. There is no admission charge.

**DAGNY JOHNSON KEY LARGO HAMMOCK BOTANICAL STATE PARK, MM 106 Oceanside, County Road 905, Key Largo, FL 33037; (305) 451-1202; floridastateparks.org/park/key-largo-hammock.** Encompassing almost 2,500 acres stretched over nearly 11 miles of north Key Largo, this state park is a jewel. The park is located in a tropical jungle of mangrove swamp, coastal rock barren, and a rockland hammock. Some of the resident species are rare tree snails, the Schaus swallowtail, the silver-banded hairstreak, and mangrove and hammock skippers. There is a guided walk every Thurs and Sun on a beautiful 0.5-mile nature trail. A backcountry permit, obtained at John Pennekamp Coral Reef State Park (see listing in this section), gives you access to an additional 6 miles of tranquil Keys flora and fauna.

**FOUNDERS PARK, MM 87 Bayside, Plantation Key, FL 33036; (305) 853-1685; Islamorada.fl.us/founders_park.** Islamorada, Village of Islands, is proud of its green spaces. One of its gleaming examples is the 40-acre municipal Founders Park on Plantation Key. This multipurpose park offers fun for the entire family—including the family dog! The park features playgrounds, sandy beaches, a dog park, baseball diamonds, picnic areas, an Olympic-size pool with restrooms, bocce, and tennis courts, a vita course with 18 exercise stations, a skate park, and unforgettable views of the Gulf of Mexico. Various community events are held here throughout the year, so check local publications. Some fees may apply to some areas.

**FRIENDSHIP PARK, MM 101.3 Oceanside, 69 Hibiscus Dr., Key Largo, FL 33037.** This park sports a playground, a Little League field, swings, and a basketball court. It's perfect for those lazy afternoons with children in tow, and it's especially inviting for picnics. The park is open from 8 a.m. until dusk or when a Little League game is scheduled. Admission is free.

**HARRY HARRIS PARK, MM 92.5 Oceanside, Tavernier, FL 33070; (305) 852-7161.** Bring the kids along to Harry Harris, where a small beach fronts a tidal pool protected by a stone jetty. You'll find a playground, ball field, volleyball net, in-line skating park, and picnic grounds. Restrooms are also available. To reach the park, follow signs leading toward the coast along the oceanside by MM 92.5 (Burton Drive). Stay on Burton Drive about 2 miles and follow the signs to the left. Admission is free, except on weekends and federal holidays when nonresidents (persons residing outside Monroe County) must pay a per-person admission fee as well as a docking fee to use the boat ramp. The park is open from 8 a.m. to sunset.

**INDIAN KEY BEACH, MM 78 Oceanside, Islamorada, FL 33036.** Although there isn't much of a beach here, a swimming area and boat access are available. Admission is free.

**JOHN PENNEKAMP CORAL REEF STATE PARK, MM 102.5 Oceanside, 102601 Overseas Hwy., Key Largo, FL 33037; (305) 451-6300 or (305) 451-1202 (pavilion rentals); pennekamppark.com.** Well known to divers and snorkelers as the first underwater state park in the US, John Pennekamp also offers a wide range of diversions within its land-based boundaries. You can explore most of the fascinating habitats of the Florida Keys here (see the

Welcome to the Florida Keys chapter), and enjoy campfire programs, guided walks, and canoe trips. The park offers a nature trail, beaches, picnic areas, campsites (see the Campgrounds chapter), restrooms, showers, and water-sports concessions (see listings in this chapter) where you can rent any equipment you might desire, from scuba gear to sailboats. Expect to pay a nominal admission fee per person and per vehicle. The park is open from 8 a.m. to sunset.

**KEY LARGO COMMUNITY PARK,** MM 99.6 Oceanside, 500 St. Croix Place, Key Largo, FL 33037. This huge community park offers playgrounds, ball fields, a skate park, and tennis and volleyball courts. It is co-located with Jacob's Aquatic Center (see listing in the Water Sports section of this chapter).

★**LIGNUMVITAE KEY BOTANICAL STATE PARK,** MM 78.5 Oceanside, Islamorada, FL 33036; (305) 664-9814, floridastateparks.org/park/lignumvitae-key. The only way to get to this park is by boat. The trails here provide real access to an almost untouched tropical spot. Tours are available by calling the number above.

★**LONG KEY STATE PARK,** MM 67.5 Oceanside, 67400 Overseas Hwy., Long Key, FL 33001; (305) 664-4815; floridastateparks.org/park/long-key. A long, narrow sand spit makes up the "beach" at this state park, which is fronted by a shallow-water flat. You can rent a canoe and enjoy the calm, easily accessible waters while you bird-watch and fish in ideal conditions. The picnic area is equipped with charcoal grills. Long Key State Park offers oceanfront campsites (see the Campgrounds chapter), restrooms, and shower facilities. Expect to pay a nominal admission fee per person and per vehicle. Long Key State Park is open from 8 a.m. to sunset.

**SEA OATS BEACH,** MM 74 Oceanside, 74501 Overseas Hwy., Islamorada, FL 33036. This long stretch of beach offers a full mile of open water with grass flats for wade-fishing for bonefish and tarpon. It is not unusual for a flats skiff to go poling by or to see folks just hanging out on the beautiful white sand with the sea oats blowing in the Atlantic breeze.

## Middle Keys

**CURRY HAMMOCK STATE PARK,** MM 56.2 Oceanside, 56200 Overseas Hwy., Marathon, FL 33050; (305) 289-2690; (850) 245-2157 (statewide info line); floridastateparks.org/park/curry-hammock. Curry Hammock is located at Little Crawl Key just north of Marathon Shores. Exuding an untouched charm all its own, the park offers a mix of tropical hammock, mangrove swamp, and a wide expanse of the coral rock sand that passes for a beach in the Keys. Grills and picnic tables abound, many tucked beneath shady buttonwood trees. The kids will enjoy the swings and slides, and anglers will like the shallow, productive bonefish flat that fronts the shoreline. A cut of deeper water on the north side of the park affords the chance for a "real" swim and maybe some snorkeling as well. Changing rooms and restrooms are available. A number of roofed pavilions protect picnic tables and grills from the elements. A nominal fee for entry is charged by honor system. Camping is not allowed here.

**MARATHON COMMUNITY PARK, MM 49 Oceanside, 9805 Overseas Hwy., Marathon, FL 33050.** The city of Marathon can be very proud of their 23-acre public park, which offers 4 tennis courts, a tennis wall, a combination hockey/basketball court (3 courts), 2 Little League fields, and 2 soccer fields. There is also an Xtreme skating park, 2 shuffleboard courts, 2 bocce ball courts, a batting cage, concession stand, amphitheater, picnic areas, and restrooms. This facility is handicapped-accessible. The park hours are 7 a.m. to 10 p.m., and there is no admission charge.

**SOMBRERO BEACH, MM 50 Oceanside, Sombrero Beach Rd., Marathon, FL 33050.** This spacious, popular public beach offers a picnic area, volleyball courts, restrooms, showers, and sweeping views of the Atlantic. Swimming waters run deep off Sombrero Beach. The Marathon Chamber of Commerce and volunteer organizations work to keep this gem of a beach in pristine condition. Sombrero Beach is handicapped-accessible. There is no admission charge, and parking is plentiful.

## Lower Keys

★**BAHIA HONDA STATE PARK, MM 37 Oceanside, 36850 Overseas Hwy., Big Pine Key, FL 33043; (305) 872-2353; floridastateparks.org/park/ bahia-honda.** Bahia Honda State Park sparkles like a diamond and boasts the best natural beach in all of the Florida Keys. Narrow roads wind through the mangrove thickets, many of which have been fitted as campsites (see the Campgrounds chapter). Tarpon fishing beneath the Bahia Honda Bridge attracts seasoned anglers and novices alike, and the park has its own marina with boat ramps and overnight dockage. Bahia Honda offers picnic facilities, restrooms, guided nature walks, and charter boat excursions. Expect to pay a nominal admission fee per person and per vehicle. The park is open 8 a.m. to sunset.

**BIG PINE KEY COMMUNITY PARK, MM 31 Oceanside, 31009 Atlantis Dr., Big Pine Key, FL 33042.** This community park includes a playground, baseball field, basketball and roller-hockey courts, a skate park, and a central building containing a concession stand. Located on the property is an all-purpose field for other sports programs, plus fitness trails circling the park.

**VETERANS MEMORIAL PARK, MM 40 Oceanside, Little Duck Key, FL 33043.** With restrooms and picnic shelters, this beach makes for an ideal lunch spot. The small beach provides a swimming area but no lifeguards. Open from 8 a.m. until dusk, the beach is free to the public. And don't be confused by the name. This beach is on Little Duck Key, not Duck Key. You will find it on the left side of the Overseas Highway, just this side of Bahia Honda, as you are traveling south toward Key West.

## Key West

**BAYVIEW PARK, 1310 Truman Ave., Key West, FL 33040.** You will definitely notice Bayview Park if you are driving into Key West on N. Roosevelt Boulevard, which becomes Truman Avenue. On your left as the road narrows and you head into Old Town, Bayview Park has 5 public tennis courts and a Pro Shop, Pepe Hernandez softball field, basketball courts, playground equipment area, pavilion, 6 restrooms, and an open area for picnics and family gatherings.

★**FORT ZACHARY TAYLOR HISTORIC STATE PARK,** Truman Annex at the end of Southard St., 601 Howard England Way, Key West, FL 33040; (305) 292-6713; floridastateparks.org/park/fort-taylor. Look to the left of the brick fort for a pleasant (although rocky) beach with picnic tables and barbecue grills. The locals call this place "Fort Zach"; this is where they come in droves to sunbathe and snorkel. The water is clear and deep, and you're likely to see many colorful fish congregating around the limestone-boulder breakwater islands constructed just offshore. When it gets too hot on the beach, head for the shade—there's plenty of it available under the lofty pine trees in the picnic area. The beach area is open 8 a.m. to sunset. An admission fee to the park is charged.

**CLARENCE HIGGS BEACH PARK, 1001 Atlantic Blvd., Key West, FL 33040.** Located on the Atlantic Ocean adjacent to the Waldorf Astoria's Casa Marina Resort and composed of approximately 16.5 acres of oceanfront vista, this popular spot is known to the locals as "Higgs Beach." Right across the street near the Casa Marina is an extensive playground called Astro City, a favorite with the kids. (See the Kidstuff chapter for more kid-friendly activities.) Within the park, there is the West Martello Tower, a Civil War–era fort that is listed on the National Register of Historic Places, an African Refugee Burial Ground, the White Street Pier, as well as one of the largest AIDS memorials in the country.

**SMATHERS BEACH, S. Roosevelt Blvd., Key West, FL 33040.** Across from Key West International Airport, Smathers is a long strip of sand that bustles with food vendors, water-sports concessions, and beautiful bods in itsy-bitsy, teeny-weeny suits. Admission here is free, but there are streetside parking meters. If you don't mind carting your beach gear a few extra yards, free parking is available on the far side of S. Roosevelt. The beach is open sunrise to 11 p.m.

## BICYCLING

See the Keys the way locals do—by bicycle! Over the past several years, the state of Florida has spent around $13 million improving the Overseas Heritage Trail. The Heritage Trail parallels the Overseas Highway, a designated National Scenic Highway, and includes 23 of the historic Flagler Railroad bridges. But you don't have to bring your bike with you to the Keys to enjoy the Heritage Trail. Rentals are offered by the day, 24 hours, multiple days, week, or month. Most of these establishments sell parts and new bicycles, do repairs, and rent helmets and other gear.

### Upper Keys

**KEY LARGO BIKE AND ADVENTURE TOURS, MM 91.4 Oceanside, 91946 Overseas Hwy., Tavernier, FL 33070; (305) 395-1551 for tours; (305) 393-2453 for rentals and the shop; keylargobike.com.** There are more than 80 miles of bike paths in the Florida Keys, and the folks at Key Largo Bike use them on a regular basis. They have even created a 54-page document detailing the best places to ride, which can be e-mailed to you for a nominal fee. Rentals and tours are offered daily, including a 2-day bike tour from Key Largo down to Key West.

### Middle Keys

**OVERSEAS OUTFITTERS SPORT & BICYCLE, MM 48 Bayside, 1700 Overseas Hwy., Marathon, FL 33050; (305) 289-1670; overseasoutfitters .com.** Overseas Outfitters is the place to go in the Middle Keys to fully outfit your active lifestyle. They carry everything from snorkeling equipment and sunglasses to bicycle helmets and custom riding jerseys, along with bike sales, service, and rentals.

### Lower Keys

**BIG PINE BICYCLE CENTER, MM 31 Bayside, 31 County Rd., Big Pine Key, FL 33043; (305) 872-0130; bigpinebikes.com.** This is the best source for bicycle rentals and sales in the upper portion of the Lower Keys. They also carry parts and accessories, and they do bicycle repairs as well.

### Key West

Most bike rental places on the island will deliver the bike right to you and pick it up when you are finished, free of charge.

**A & M RENTALS, 523 Truman Ave. or 513 South St., Key West, FL 33040; (305) 896-1921; amscooterskeywest.com.** Here you can rent bikes by the day or week, scooters by the hour or the week, and electric cars for 2- or 4- hour rides.

RECREATION

★**THE BIKE SHOP,** 1110 Truman Ave., Key West, FL 33040; (305) 294-1073; thebikeshopkeywest.com. Since 1981, the Bike Shop has offered bicycle products and services to locals and travelers alike. They rent one-speed cruisers and carry a full line of components and accessories (piggy bike horn, anyone?), along with Trek, Gary Fisher, Giant, and Haro bikes.

**EATON BIKES,** 830 Eaton St., Key West, FL 33040; (305) 294-8188; eatonbikes.com. Have you ever fallen in love with a bicycle? If not, this may be a first! The guys at Eaton Bikes will dazzle you with their artistic, intricate designs on bicycles, choppers, lowriders, and electrical bikes. Their cycles are as beautiful to look at as they are to ride. They also offer rentals and repairs.

**ISLAND BICYCLES,** 929 Truman Ave., Key West, FL 33040; (305) 292-9707; islandbicycle.com. Island Bicycles offers a full selection of bicycles for sale and rent. Repairs and accessories are also available here.

**MOPED HOSPITAL,** 601 Truman Ave., Key West, FL 33040; (305) 296-3344; mopedhospital.com. Moped Hospital rents single-speed bicycles with coaster brakes, baskets, high-rise handlebars, soft seats, balloon tires, and locks by the hour, day, or week.

★**WE-CYCLE BICYCLES,** MM 4.5 Oceanside, 5160 Overseas Hwy., Stock Island, FL 33040; (305) 292-3336; wecyclekw.com. The screaming green building gets your attention even if you don't need a bike. Inside the folks offer a full-service bicycle shop and free pickup and delivery on bike repairs. This is a popular local spot, as it serves as the starting point for the annual Zombie Bike Parade each fall.

## BOAT EXCURSIONS, ECO-TOURS & SUNSET CRUISES

Our crowning glory rests in our encompassing waters. Explore the backcountry and the waters of Everglades National Park on group eco-tour expeditions, take a glass-bottomed boat trip to the reef to view the fascinating creatures residing there, or relax aboard a sunset cocktail cruise.

### Upper Keys

*AFRICAN QUEEN,* MM 100 Oceanside, Marina Del Mar, 527 Caribbean Drive, Key Largo, FL 33037; (305) 451-8080; africanqueenflkeys.com. Board the legendary *African Queen*—featured in the Humphrey Bogart and Katharine Hepburn movie of the same name, and recently restored—in Key Largo for daily canal or dinner cruises and sunset or charter excursions.

**CAPT. STERLING'S EVERGLADES ECO-TOURS,** Tours depart from Sundowner's, MM 104 Bayside, 103900 Overseas Hwy., Key Largo, FL 33037; (305) 853-5161 or (888) 224-6044. pennekamp.com/sterling. Venture 17 miles into the waters of Everglades National Park, in and around mangrove and bird rookery islands, aboard a 23-foot pontoon boat. Tours are limited to 6 passengers and depart at 9 a.m., 11 a.m., 1 p.m., and 3 p.m. daily. The Key Largo *Flamingo Express* charter takes you through Crocodile Dragover, the Dump Keys, and 38 miles to Flamingo in Everglades National Park.

**CARIBBEAN WATERSPORTS ENVIRO TOURS,** MM 97 Bayside, at the Hilton Key Largo Beach Resort, 97000 Overseas Hwy., Key Largo, FL 33037; (305) 852-5553; caribbeanwatersports.com. Glide through the Everglades with Caribbean Watersports' 2-hour guided tour and explore uninhabited mangrove islands all along Florida Bay in a 17-foot rigid inflatable Zodiac that has a fiberglass hull, stabilizing inflatable side pontoons, and a quiet electric trolling motor. Tours are limited to 6 people; you must call ahead to reserve a spot.

**JOHN PENNEKAMP CORAL REEF STATE PARK,** MM 102.5 Oceanside, 102601 Overseas Hwy., Key Largo, FL 33037; (305) 451-6300; penne kamppark.com. Pennekamp State Park's glass-bottomed catamaran, the *Spirit of Pennekamp*, carries as many as 130 people on 2.5-hour tours of the reef. Tours are offered 3 times daily. Snorkeling and scuba tours are also offered, and personal or group in-water guides are also available.

***KEY LARGO PRINCESS* GLASS BOTTOM BOAT,** MM 100 Oceanside, Holiday Inn Docks, Key Largo, FL 33037; (305) 451-4655 or (800) 307-1147; keylargoprincess.com. This princess carries passengers on narrated 2-hour tours that drift above the reef. A full bar is available on board, and guests can buy hot dogs and snacks. *Key Largo Princess* tours are offered 3 times daily. Family rates and private charters are available. The boat is wheelchair-accessible.

***REEF ROAMER* AND *QUICKSILVER* CATAMARANS,** MM 100 Oceanside, Holiday Inn Docks, Key Largo, FL 33037; (305) 451-0105; quicksilver snorkel.com. Daily sails through the sanctuary waters of John Pennekamp Coral Reef State Park vary with the season aboard the 50-foot catamarans *Reef Roamer* and *Quicksilver*. Discounts and family rates are available on snorkeling trips. Private and group charters also can be arranged. Gear rental is extra.

### Middle Keys

**HAWK'S CAY RESORT AND MARINA,** MM 61 Oceanside, 61 Hawks Cay Blvd., Duck Key, FL 33050; (305) 743-7000 or (888) 313-5749; hawks cay.com. Take the Florida Keys Kayak Tour for a guided eco-tour of the out-islands near Duck Key. Many other water-related activities are available at

Hawk's Cay, including chartered fishing excursions to the backcountry or the reef. Other amusements are available, including personal watercraft and small-boat rentals, waterskiing, and parasailing.

**SPIRIT SNORKELING, MM 47.5 Bayside, 1400 Overseas Hwy., Marathon, FL 33050; (305) 289-0614; spiritsnorkeling.net.** A 40-foot catamaran named *Spirit* takes passengers snorkeling to popular Middle Keys, offers private charter cruises and eco-tours as well as a yoga cruise, and sets off for a daily sunset cruise at the end of the day. Call in advance to make reservations.

## Lower Keys

**STRIKE ZONE CHARTERS, MM 29.5 Bayside, 29675 Overseas Hwy., Big Pine Key, FL 33043; (305) 872-9863; strikezonecharter.com.** Strike Zone offers daily snorkel and dive trips to the Looe Key National Marine Sanctuary, as well as fishing excursions and a 5-hour backcountry out-island excursion, which includes a fish cookout on a secluded island. Customizable private charters for anywhere from 6 to 49 people are also available.

## Key West

★**DANGER CHARTERS, 407 Caroline St., Key West, FL 33040; (305) 304-7999; dangercharters.com.** Don't let the moniker fool you: *Danger* is the name of the Chesapeake Bay skipjack sailboat, not any situation you will encounter on this adventurous charter. Excursions include backcountry kayaking and snorkeling on the reef, and usually last about 5 hours. Full-day trips, sunset cruises, and specialized bird-watching trips are also available. Call for details and pricing.

**FURY CATAMARANS, 237 Front St., Key West, FL 33040; (305) 294-8899 or (877) 994-8898; furycat.com.** Climb aboard one of Fury's 65-foot catamarans for a sail by day or night. Fury offers two 3-hour trips to the reef daily for snorkeling—one in the morning, one in the afternoon—plus a 2-hour champagne sunset sail each evening. You can buy separate tickets for day snorkeling or sunset sailing, or purchase a combination snorkeling/sunset sail ticket. In addition, Fury also offers parasailing.

**LAZY DOG, MM 4.2 Oceanside, 5114 Overseas Hwy., Stock Island, FL 33040; (305) 295-9898; lazydog.com.** Locals head to Lazy Dog for their Paddle Fit and Paddle Yoga classes, as well as their 2-hour backcountry kayak tours and 4-hour backcountry kayak/snorkel tours. Children 9 years and older are welcome on all excursions, as are dogs on all trips except the 4-hour kayak/snorkel excursion.

**RESTLESS NATIVE CHARTERS,** 201 William St., Key West, FL 33040; (305) 394-0600; restlessnative.com. Sail away for a 4-hour tour on this luxurious yacht that includes snorkeling, kayaking, and a gourmet lunch with wine, beer, or soda. The *Restless Native* can only carry 6 passengers, with crew, so this is like having your own private vessel to explore the waters off Key West. Sunset and private charters are also available. All charters must be booked 7 days in advance.

**SEBAGO CATAMARANS,** 201 William St., at the Key West Historic Seaport, Key West, FL 33040; (305) 292-4768 or (800) 507-9955; keywest sebago.com. Head out to the reef for a snorkeling/sailing adventure aboard Sebago's 60-foot catamaran, or cruise Key West Harbor at sunset. Complimentary drinks are served on both excursions. Sebago also offers parasailing, as well as a 6-hour eco-trip that includes kayaking, snorkeling, and sailing, plus a luncheon buffet.

**YANKEE FLEET FERRY TO FORT JEFFERSON AND DRY TORTUGAS NATIONAL PARK,** Key West Historic Seaport, 240 Margaret St., Key West, FL 33040; (800) 634-0939; yankeefreedom.com. A voyage to Dry Tortugas National Park, 70 miles west of Key West, requires a full day. You'll be able to take a tour of the massive, historical Fort Jefferson on Garden Key, and enjoy calm seas, pristine natural-sand beaches, and some of the best snorkeling anywhere. The *Yankee Freedom III,* a 250-passenger, high-speed catamaran, whisks passengers from Key West to Fort Jefferson in less than 2.5 hours. Fare includes round-trip transportation; snorkeling gear; en route commentary by a naturalist-historian; a 45-minute guided tour of Fort Jefferson; and breakfast and lunch. Passengers are not permitted to carry alcohol to the Dry Tortugas.

## GOLF & TENNIS

Putters and players drive the Keys links, and racqueteers of all ages love our courts. Read on and be on the ball. Expect to pay for court time by the hour. Greens fees are reasonable at the public course in Key West, and if you belong to a country club back home, be sure to contact Florida Keys Country Club in Marathon, (305) 743-2551, to see about reciprocal privileges.

### Upper Keys

**ISLAMORADA TENNIS CLUB,** MM 76.8 Bayside, 768000 Overseas Hwy., Islamorada, FL 33036; (305) 664-5341; islamoradatennisclub.com. This facility maintains 4 Har-Tru green clay and 2 DecoTurf cushion courts. Private lessons, clinics, round-robins, and tournaments are offered to the general public, and Islamorada Tennis Club will arrange games at all levels. A pro shop is on the premises. Same-day racket stringing is available.

### Middle Keys

**BOONDOCKS GRILLE & DRAFT HOUSE,** MM 27.5 Bayside, 27205 Overseas Hwy., Summerland Key, FL 33042; (305) 872-4094; **boondocks us.com.** Boondocks is a family-fun park that allows kids of all ages to enjoy a round of miniature golf. With its large rock formation shaped like a huge boulder, the state-of-the-art 18-hole course comes complete with waterfalls, tunnels, ponds, tiki hut clubhouse, and towering, giant cavemen.

### Key West

**ISLAND CITY TENNIS,** 1310 Truman Ave., Key West, FL 33040; (305) 294-1346; **islandcitytenniskeywest.com.** These public tennis courts are owned by the city of Key West and keep the lights on till 9 p.m. Island City Tennis is right on Truman Avenue, which leads to Duval Street. It is first-come, first-served, and very popular with visitors as well as locals. There is a pro shop on the premises.

**KEY WEST GOLF CLUB,** MM 5 Bayside, 6450 E. College Rd., Stock Island, FL 33040; (305) 294-5232; **keywestgolf.com.** The only public 18-hole course in the Keys, this par-70 course designed by Rees Jones offers a clubhouse, pro shop, and lessons. Greens fees are hefty in high season but about a third less in the off-season. For late-afternoon golfers, special "twilight" fees are available after 2:30 p.m. Monroe County residents receive discounts, but you must reside here year-round to qualify. Call for details.

## WATER SPORTS

Pick your pleasure and make a splash—parasailing, waterskiing, paddleboarding, kiteboarding, wakeboarding, or kayaking. For a rundown of scuba-diving/ snorkeling trips to the reef, see our Diving & Snorkeling chapter.

### Upper Keys

**CORAL REEF PARK COMPANY,** John Pennekamp Coral Reef State Park, MM 102.5 Oceanside, 102601 Overseas Hwy., Key Largo, FL 33037; (305) 451-6300; **pennekamppark.com;** (305) 451-6300 or (800) 326-3521; **penne kamppark.com.** Coral Reef Park Company rents snorkeling equipment at Pennekamp Park for unguided exploration of the nearshore Pennekamp waters off Cannon Beach, or you can sign on with one of the snorkeling tours to the reef (see the Diving & Snorkeling chapter for details). Rent canoes or kayaks here and paddle the mangrove water trails. Small boats also are available for hire.

**ISLAMORADA WATERSPORTS COMPANY,** MM 84.7 Bayside, Plaza 88, 84771 Overseas Hwy., Islamorada, FL 33036; (305) 853-5483; **sevensports**

.com. Private lessons from Professional Air Sports Association (PASA-certified) instructors for beginners, intermediate, or advanced boarders in the thrilling sport of kiteboarding are on offer. You can also master the art of paddleboarding or try your hand at wakeboarding.

★JACOB'S AQUATIC CENTER, MM 99.6 Oceanside, 320 Laguna Ave., Key Largo, FL 33037; (305) 453-7946; jacobsaquaticcenter.org. Jacob's Aquatic Center is a 3-pool complex with a 25-meter, 8-lane competition pool and contiguous diving pool with 1- and 2-meter diving boards. This facility is suitable for scuba and Red Cross certification, synchronized swimming, youth swim teams, masters' swimming, swim lessons, water aerobics/Pilates, gymnastics, and water polo. They also have an interactive pool/water park featuring a pirate ship, "spray" gym, and "beachfront" entry. Co-located with the Key Largo Community Park (see listing in this chapter).

OTHERSIDE BOARDSPORTS, MM 83 Bayside, 82758 Overseas Hwy., Islamorada, FL 33036; (305) 853-9728; othersideboardsports.com. This shop offers board-sports-minded athletes a chance to skateboard, kiteboard, wakeboard, and paddleboard. With knowledgeable instructors, you will be off and boarding in no time.

### Middle Keys

HAWK'S CAY RESORT AND MARINA, MM 61 Oceanside, 61 Hawks Cay Blvd., Duck Key, FL 33050; (305) 743-7000 or (888) 395-5539; hawks cay.com. The water-sports facility at Hawk's Cay offers parasailing, boat rentals, paddleboard and kayak rentals, water-ski and wakeboard rentals, as well as instruction. A scuba center and sailing school are also on the premises.

### Key West

BAREFOOT BILLY'S, at 3 locations in Key West: Casa Marina, Marriott Beachside, and the Reach Resort; (305) 900-3088; barefootbillys.com. Barefoot Billy's is the one-stop shop in Key West for hourly or daylong rentals of the following: glass-bottomed boats, clear-bottomed kayaks, Jet Skis, paddleboards, snorkeling gear, and Hobie Cats. They even offer flyboarding lessons. James Bond never had it so good.

THE KITE HOUSE, Key West; (305) 879-0549; thekitehouse.com. Kiteboarding is not for the amateur, so the owner of this business urges everyone to take a few lessons with a PASA-certified (Professional Air Sports Association) instructor. Courses for all levels are available. After the lessons the instructor sends you on a few practice runs; then you get into your power zone and you're off! Trips are available from Oct to May.

**SUNSET WATERSPORTS,** located at Smathers Beach, Key West Bight, Parrot Key Resort, and Hurricane Hole Marina; (305) 296-2554; sunset watersportskeywest.com. This outfit offers something for everyone. Parasailing, Hobie Cats, kayaks, and paddleboards are all provided on Smathers Beach. For an all-inclusive day trip, take the "Do It All." From the Key West Seaport, a 44-foot catamaran takes you out about 3 miles to a shallow wreck. From there, take turns exploring with paddleboards, kayaks, and just about anything else you can imagine.

## PHYSICAL FITNESS

### Upper Keys

**FROGGY'S FITNESS,** MM 91.8 Bayside, 91812 Overseas Hwy., Tavernier, FL 33070; (305) 852-8623; froggysfitness.com. Froggy's Fitness is a 6,500-square-foot fitness center that features free weights, treadmills, Stairmasters, elliptical machines, and more. In addition to customized personal training, Froggy's offers yoga, boot camp, Pilates, aerobics, and kickboxing classes, as well as indoor cycling. The center provides individualized diet and nutrition plans and body-fat testing. You can purchase gym wear, aerobics footwear, vitamins, protein supplements, and other health foods here, too.

**KEY LARGO YOGA & HOLISTIC HEALTH COACHING,** MM 99 Bayside, Ste. 9, 99198 Overseas Hwy., Key Largo, FL 33037; (305) 879-0377; keylargoyoga.com. Owner and yoga teacher Kathy Shirley has been practicing yoga for more than 15 years and has even completed the 200-hour training for Vinyasa yoga. Her yoga studio is focused on the yoga method as a means to connect mind, body, and spirit. Classes include all levels of Vinyasa, as well as beginner yoga, guided meditation, and Mommy and Me Yoga. Various workshops are also on offer year-round.

★**PILATES IN PARADISE,** MM 98.8 Bayside, 103400 Overseas Hwy., Ste. 255, Key Largo, FL 33037; (305) 453-0801; pilatesinparadise.net. Owner and instructor Christi Allen is a certified Romana's Pilates instructor with more than 1,500 hours of training in the Pilates method from teachers all over the country. Allen is also a certified nutrition and lifestyle coach, and therefore takes a holistic approach to fitness, which is reflected in her classes. Pilates in Paradise offers classes in mat, tower, reformer, and combo, which is a little bit of everything. Private instruction is also available.

### Middle Keys

**KEYS FITNESS CENTER,** MM 49.5 Oceanside, 5101 Overseas Hwy., Marathon, FL 33050; (305) 289-0788; floridakeysfitness.com. Offering fitness equipment by Paramount, Life Fitness, and Nautilus, Keys Fitness Center also sports a separate free-weights room for the serious workout addict. The facilities offer private showers and a relaxing sauna. Personal trainers are bilingual. Keys Fitness Center is open Mon through Fri from 6 a.m. to 9 p.m., Sat from 8 a.m. to 6 p.m., and Sun from 9 a.m. to 4 p.m.

**YOGA ON THE SEA, on the Spirit Snorkeling boat, docked at MM 47.5 Bayside, 1410 Overseas Hwy., Marathon, FL 33050; (305) 289-0614; yoga onthesea.com.** How many people can say they've done yoga on the ocean? Spirit Snorkeling offers a yoga sunset cruise aboard their 34-foot catamaran taught by an Ananda instructor. No need to worry about the motion of the ocean, as the construction of the watercraft is such that it is almost as wide as it is long, allowing for much more stability than other craft. All levels are welcome. Call for schedules and availability. *Namaste*, mateys!

## Key West

**BIKRAM YOGA STUDIO OF KEY WEST, 927 White St., Key West, FL 33040; (305) 292-1854; kw-yoga.com.** This is the real thing, and not for wimps. Classes are 90 minutes long, and you will need to bring or rent a sticky yoga mat as well as a large towel for $2 each on the premises. At Bikram Yoga the room is kept warm so your muscles will stretch more easily. To that end, it is recommended that ladies wear leotards and men wear bathing suits. Cash or check only.

**BODY ZONE SOUTH, 2740 N. Roosevelt Blvd., Overseas Market, Key West, FL 33040; (305) 292-2930.** A full range of exercise equipment is available here, including Nautilus equipment, treadmills, stationary bikes, stair climbers, and plenty of free weights. Classes include indoor cycling, yoga, and core strength. Personal training and massage are available as well. The juice bar and play care for children are both convenient services. Body Zone South is open daily.

**COFFEE MILL DANCE & YOGA STUDIO, 916 Pohalski St., Key West, FL 33040; (305) 296-9982; coffeemilldance.com.** The Coffee Mill is the place in Key West to get moving! Instructors include members of the Key West Contemporary Dance Company, and classes are taught for beginners and advanced dancers (or wannabe dancers) of all ages. Coffee Mill's extensive class list includes yoga, ballet for beginner adults, aerobics, Pilates, Capoeira, Zumba, jazz, and even belly dancing. Classes are held daily, and visitors are welcome.

**ISLAND GYM, 1119 White St., Key West, FL 33040; (305) 295-8222; key westislandgym.com.** This facility is open 7 days a week for serious athletes. Island Gym hosts a full range of free weights as well as indoor and outdoor workout spaces. Personal training and group fitness sessions are also available, and wireless headsets allow you to watch TV on flat screens while working out on the elliptical or treadmill.

★**KEY WEST YOGA SANCTUARY,** 1130 Duval St., Key West, FL 33040; **keywestyogasanctuary.com.** The Key West Yoga Sanctuary is dedicated to practicing and teaching attention and consciousness on and off the mat. To that end, in addition to yoga, Pilates and meditation classes are offered as well as special workshops. Group and private Pilates classes on both the mat and the reformer are available.

★**LIZ LOVE FITNESS,** (479) 200-4689; info@lizlovefitness.com; lizlove fitness.com. If you are looking to find the best route to run, do a swim workout in the ocean, try your hand at TRX, a Pilates mat session, or even cycle up the Keys, Liz Love is the trainer to call. Liz is a certified personal trainer who is the driving force behind many of Key West's popular races, like the Southernmost Marathon & Half, and the Key West Triathlon (TRIKW) in addition to numerous 5Ks on the island. She is available to train at Stay Fit Studio, or she can come to you to guide you through a custom workout, whether it is for an hour-, day-, week-, or month-long stay.

**PARADISE HEALTH AND FITNESS,** 1706 N. Roosevelt Blvd., Key West, FL 33040; (305) 294-4120; **paradisehealthandfitness.com.** In addition to a full-circuit weight room, Paradise offers a wide range of group classes, including yoga, Pilates, extreme fitness, and lower and upper body challenges for all ages and fitness levels. They also offer ballroom and salsa classes on the weekends for beginners or advanced dancers. Personal trainers are on staff to assist you, and will make home visits if you're so inclined. Short- or long-term memberships as well as daily rates are available.

**STAY FIT STUDIO,** 804 White St., Key West, FL 33040; (305) 294-0693; **stayfitstudiokeywest.com.** Start off another perfect day in paradise with an invigorating workout with Stay Fit Studio. They have classes in spinning, Pilates, boot camp, and yoga, among many others. Stay Fit also offers massages, so you can truly relax post-workout.

# Attractions

Don't wait for a rainy day (you might not have one) to explore our historical sites, out-islands, museums, nature preserves, and marine research centers. You'll find the majority of our most popular land-based diversions bordering the Overseas Highway, for our string of islands is not very wide. So put on your sandals, grab your hat, and don't forget the sunscreen! You are about to set out on an adventure in the Florida Keys.

*Price Code*
Codes are based on adult admission.

| | |
|---|---|
| $ | Less than $5 |
| $$ | $5 to $10 |
| $$$ | $10 to $20 |
| $$$$ | More than $20 |

## HISTORIC HOMES & MUSEUMS

### Upper Keys

**FLORIDA KEYS HISTORY OF DIVING MUSEUM, MM 83 Bayside, 82990 Overseas Hwy., Islamorada, FL 33036; (305) 664-9737; diving museum.org; $$$.** The Florida Keys History of Diving Museum displays historic diving equipment and research documents representing more than 4,000 years of underwater exploration from around the world and the Keys. Self-guided tours begin with "Timeline of Diving" (featuring interactive exhibits that allow visitors to experience the evolution from breath-hold divers to early scuba), the "Treasure Room" (telling the story of Art "Silver Bar" McKee, the father of recreational diving), "Parade of Nations" (a collection of historic hard-hat dive helmets from around the globe), and the gallery, "Deep Diving in the Abyss" (showcasing authentic diving suits, offering endless photo opportunities).

### Middle Keys

**CRANE POINT MUSEUM AND NATURE CENTER, MM 50 Bayside, 5550 Overseas Hwy., Marathon, FL 33050; (305) 743-9100; cranepoint.net; $$$.** The small, interesting Crane Point Museum sits on the skirt of the Crane Point Hammock. Behind the museum's expertly hand-crafted copper doors is a potpourri of Keys icons and exhibits. Choose your path and follow several different nature trails on this sprawling 63-acre property. Read the self-guided tour pamphlet provided by the museum that lists some of the unusual tropical hardwoods you'll see in Hammock Loop and the enchanting varieties of butterflies you'll spot in Butterfly Meadow. Crane Point is open daily. One admission charge allows access to both trails and museums. Children age 4 and younger get in free.

### Key West

**AUDUBON HOUSE & TROPICAL GARDENS,** 205 Whitehead St., Key West, FL 33040; (305) 294-2116 or (877) 294-2470; audubonhouse.com; $$$. In 1832, John James Audubon spent time on the grounds of Captain John H. Geiger's huge garden. During his stay in the Keys, Audubon produced 22 sketches of birds for his "Birds of America" folio; 28 first-edition Audubon works are on display in this special home. The house and environs includes one of the finest tropical gardens in all the Keys. Guests are invited to take their time and linger as long as they like. A free pair of headphones and a tape are provided for guests and help bring the house alive. Audubon House is open daily.

**CURRY MANSION INN,** 511 Caroline St., Key West, FL 33040; (305) 294-5349 or (800) 253-3466; currymansion.com; $. This imposing home evokes images of an opulent old Key West, although now the 3-story Conch house serves as the focal point for a bed-and-breakfast inn and museum. Built in 1905 by Milton Curry, Florida's first homegrown millionaire, the inn's public rooms are furnished with 18th-century antiques. From the attic you can climb the widow's walk for a panoramic view of Key West Harbor. Self-guided tours are available daily between 8:30 a.m. and 5 p.m. See the Accommodations chapter for information on overnight stays in the adjacent buildings.

**ERNEST HEMINGWAY HOME AND MUSEUM,** 907 Whitehead St., Key West, FL 33040; (305) 294-1136; hemingwayhome.com; $$$. The Ernest Hemingway Home and Museum ranks as Key West's most popular attraction. Built in 1851, the home took on historical significance in the 1930s when Ernest and Pauline Hemingway moved in. While Ernest wrote several of his most celebrated works, Pauline spearheaded extensive remodeling and installed the island's very first backyard swimming pool. The exorbitant construction costs once prompted Hemingway to jokingly take a penny from his pocket, press it into the wet cement of the patio, and say, "Here! Take the last penny I've got!" Be sure to check out that very coin as well as the property's infamous six-toed cats!

**FLORIDA KEYS HISTORICAL MILITARY MEMORIAL,** One Mallory Square, Key West, FL 33040; FREE. Flush with military history, Key West honors its best with this handsome memorial dedicated to those who have proudly served their country and the military events directly affecting Key West and the Keys. Beginning in 1822, when the US Navy raised the American flag over Key West, through the era of the Spanish-American War, World Wars I and II, Korea, the Cuban Missile Crisis, Vietnam, Desert Storm, Iraq, and the ongoing war on drugs, this simple, elegant display stands proud as a sentinel, reflecting a community paying homage to these historic events and brave souls.

**FORT EAST MARTELLO, 3501 S. Roosevelt Blvd., Key West, FL 33040; (305) 296-3913; kwahs.com; $$.** This enchanting former fort will bring you up to speed on Key West history. The Civil War–era brick fortress was never completely finished because the circular Martello design became antiquated before it was ever armed. This national landmark is operated by the Key West Art and Historical Society. Its 8-foot-thick walls enclose a small gallery of charming wood carvings of Key West's Mario Sanchez and funky welded sculptures by the late Stanley Papio of Key Largo.

**HARRY S. TRUMAN LITTLE WHITE HOUSE, 111 Front St., Key West, FL 33040; (305) 294-9911; trumanlittlewhitehouse.com; $$$.** President Harry S. Truman came to Key West for the first time in 1946 and went on to spend 11 working vacations in the commandant's quarters, dubbed the Little White House. View Truman's Winter White House as it looked when he spent working vacation days here. Presidents Taft, Eisenhower, Kennedy, Carter, and Clinton all found the Little White House both a restful place to restore body and mind as well as a key location to carry out important government business. Guided tours are conducted daily, offering glimpses into the politics of the Cold War and the naval history of Key West.

i Looking for a quiet, tranquil place to catch your breath? Just a few blocks away from the hustle and bustle of Duval Street is the serene Stations of the Cross Gardens on the grounds of historic St. Mary Star of the Sea Catholic Church. This half-acre garden is open to travelers and islanders alike.

**KEY WEST LIGHTHOUSE AND KEEPER'S QUARTERS MUSEUM, 938 Whitehead St., Key West, FL 33040; (305) 294-0012; kwahs.com; $$.** This 1848 structure, inland just across from the Hemingway Home, affords visitors a bird's-eye view of Key West from atop its 90-foot light tower. The lighthouse was positioned far from the water to avoid the fate of its predecessor on Whitehead Point, which toppled in a hurricane. The lighthouse museum and gift shop are open daily for self-guided tours. Children 6 and under are admitted free. Combination tickets are available for adult admission to this museum, the East Martello Museum, and the Key West Museum of Art and History at the Custom House (see descriptions elsewhere in this chapter).

**THE KEY WEST MUSEUM OF ART AND HISTORY AT THE CUS-TOM HOUSE, 281 Front St., Key West, FL 33040; (305) 295-6616; kwahs .com; $$.** If you like history, do not miss this award-winning museum. The Custom House is on the National Register of Historic Places and remains one of the finest examples of Richardsonian/Romanesque Revival architecture in existence. The house has two floors of exhibitions that weave together two centuries of history, art, people, and events. Exhibits of artwork and historical artifacts change periodically; however, those on the second floor traditionally focus on the history of Key West. In addition to artifacts and art, the Custom House offers beautiful views of the harbor from its many arched windows. The museum is open daily.

**MEL FISHER MARITIME HERITAGE SOCIETY AND MUSEUM, 200 Greene St., Key West, FL 33040; (305) 294-2633; melfisher.org; $$$.** For 16 years, "today's the day" was the hope of treasure salvor Mel Fisher, who literally struck gold in 1985. Finding the *Nuestra Señora de Atocha*, which Fisher estimated to be worth $400 million, ensured his legacy as treasure hunter extraordinaire. Heavy gold chains, jeweled crosses, and bars of silver and gold are among the artifacts on display at the permanent first-floor exhibit. Take a lab tour to see how history is revealed through excavation and conservation of shipwrecks. Exhibits change frequently—call for details. The museum shop offers a variety of pirate and nautical gifts and is open daily.

**RIPLEY'S BELIEVE IT OR NOT MUSEUM, 108 Duval St., Key West, FL 33040; (305) 293-9939; ripleys.com/keywest; $$.** World-famous for fantastically weird artifacts, Ripley's Key West location does not disappoint. Enjoy a self-guided tour of more than 500 exhibits in 13 air-conditioned galleries, featuring items from Ernest Hemingway's home, including his reading glasses, a typewriter, and a shrunken torso. Cruise through the Boutique of Weird Clothing displaying a vest made of human hair and a pair of Madonna's underwear. Study an actual vampire-killing kit and a collection of two-headed animals. Finally, catch a ride on a motorcycle made from 100 percent real bones before you check out a portrait of Vincent van Gogh made entirely of butterfly wings.

**SAN CARLOS INSTITUTE, 516 Duval St., Key West, FL 33040; (305) 294-3887; institutosancarlos.org; FREE.** Founded in 1871 by Cuban exiles, the San Carlos Institute was established to preserve the language and traditions of the Cuban people. Dubbed "La Casa Cuba" by legendary poet and patriot José Martí, the institute united the exiled Cuban community. With the perseverance of the Hispanic Affairs Commission, a state agency headed by Rafael Penalver, restoration of the San Carlos Institute was completed on January 3, 1992, exactly 100 years after José Martí delivered his first address at the museum. Today the San Carlos Institute is a museum, library, school, art gallery, theater, and conference center.

### The Schooner *Western Union* Maritime Museum

The schooner *Western Union* is one of the oldest working wooden schooners in the US. The Schooner *Western Union* Preservation Society is the not-for-profit corporation founded for the purpose of restoring, maintaining, and operating the historic Schooner *Western Union* Maritime Museum in Key West. In addition to the restoration of the schooner, they also operate the boat as a maritime museum with an educational outreach program that includes historical tours, children's activities, and private excursions. This proud 130-foot vessel is built of mahogany timbers and Dade County pine. The beam is 23½ feet, the draft is 8 feet, and the sail area is a whopping 4,800 square feet. Even though the *Western Union* is a sailing vessel, the ship has two engines to steady it at sea. Book her for a sunset sail. You can also reserve the *Western Union* for weddings and special events. Located at 202 William St., Key West; call (305) 292-1766 or visit schoonerwesternunion.org for more information.

**WEST MARTELLO TOWER JOE ALLEN GARDEN CENTER,** 1100 Atlantic Blvd., Key West, FL 33040; (305) 294-3210; keywestgardenclub .com; FREE. Built in 1862, the West Martello Tower, like the other forts on the island, was never involved in an actual war. Today the tower is also the Joe Allen Garden Center, and the Key West Garden Club operates here. Stroll the brick pathways through arched courtyards and lush foliage while you spot local flora, including a key lime tree. Find an inviting spot to relax, perhaps one of the gazebos dotting the area that catch soft sea breezes and provide soothing respite from the tropical sun. West Martello is open seven days a week, except holidays.

## WILDLIFE

### Upper Keys

**DOLPHINS PLUS OCEANSIDE AND BAYSIDE,** MM 100 Oceanside, 31 Corrine Place; MM 101.9 Bayside, 101900 Overseas Hwy., Key Largo,

FL 33037; (866) 860-7946; (877) 365-2683; dolphinsplus.com; $$$$. This marine mammal research and education facility offers you the opportunity to enter the world of the bottlenose dolphin or sea lion for a compatible swim. The natural swim teaches you all about dolphins, how to interact with them, and details about their social pod structure. Experience a structured swim, guided by a trainer, which guarantees participants one-on-one contact with the dolphins as they demonstrate their intelligence through trained behaviors. Can't decide between a natural or structured swim? Try their Dolphin Combo and sample each experience for a discounted combination price. Calling ahead to make a reservation is advised.

**LAURA QUINN WILD BIRD SANCTUARY,** MM 93.6 Bayside, 93600 Overseas Hwy., Tavernier, FL 33070; (305) 852-4486; keepthemflying.org; **FREE.** The Florida Keys Wild Bird Center is dedicated to the rescue, rehabilitation, and release of ill, injured, and orphaned wild birds. Their Laura Quinn Wild Bird Sanctuary (named after the founder of the Florida Keys Wild Bird Center) houses birds that have been rehabilitated but are incapable of living in the wild. Visitors may walk along a boardwalk through the birds' natural habitats, which have been discreetly caged with wire enclosures. The sanctuary is open daily, sunrise to sunset, and is funded by public donations.

**THEATER OF THE SEA,** MM 84.5 Oceanside, 84721 Overseas Hwy., Islamorada, FL 33036; (305) 664-2431; theaterofthesea.com; $$$$. Theater of the Sea offers continuous performances daily. The natural saltwater lagoons are home to popular marine creatures that are featured in the many special programs offered throughout the facility. The Swim with the Stingrays program includes 15 minutes of instruction and 30 minutes in the water snorkeling while you closely observe, feed, and touch these docile and beautiful creatures. Swim with the Dolphins, Sharks, and Sea Lions programs are also offered. Or take the 4-hour Adventure and Snorkel Cruise that covers 13 miles on the Atlantic Ocean and Florida Bay.

### Middle Keys

**THE DOLPHIN CONNECTION,** MM 61 Oceanside, 61 Hawks Cay Blvd., Duck Key, FL 33050; (305) 289-9975 or (888) 251-3674 (for reservations); dolphinconnection.com; $$$$. The Dolphin Connection's Dolphin Discovery provides an interactive, 25-minute, in-water encounter with bottlenose dolphins. You will not actually swim with the Connection's dolphins, but you will get to know them up close and personal. Touch, feed, pet, and play with them from the security of a submerged platform—great for non-swimmers or those with physical limitations. Dockside Dolphins is a 30-minute, behind-the-scenes look at dolphin training sessions that allows participants to take part in the fun without leaving dry land. Plus, their 3-hour

Trainer for a Day program is a dolphin lover's dream come true! Advance reservations are required for all programs.

**DOLPHIN RESEARCH CENTER, MM 59 Bayside, 58901 Overseas Hwy., Grassy Key, FL 33050; (305) 289-1121 or (305) 289-0002 (for reservations); dolphins.org; $$$$.** The Dolphin Research Center's mission is to offer a variety of fascinating dolphin encounters while promoting education, research, and rescue of these precious marine animals. The Dolphin Encounter enables you to see their personality shine through during a series of individual playful yet structured interactions including a dolphin kiss, hand shake, and dorsal pull. Dolphin Explorer allows inquiring minds to discover the excitement of research while having fun with their subjects of study. In Paint with a Dolphin, you can help a dolphin paint a T-shirt just for you. There are many other programs available, so call for more information.

**MARATHON WILD BIRD CENTER, MM 50 Bayside, at Crane Point Hammock, 5550 Overseas Hwy., Marathon, FL 33050; (305) 743-8382; marathonwildbirdcenter.org; FREE.** Safely protected in wooded, 64-acre Crane Point Hammock park, the Marathon Wild Bird Center is a licensed wildlife rehabilitation facility that specializes in migratory birds. Incorporated in 1998, they work with local veterinarians and other caring individuals who are concerned with the rescue, rehabilitation, and return of wild birds back into their natural setting of the Florida Keys. Their website gives step-by-step, detailed instructions on the care of orphaned baby birds. People throughout the Florida Keys know the MWBC as one of the leading wild bird rescue centers for the care and rehabilitation of wild birds in Monroe County.

## Lower Keys

**THE BLUE HOLE, MM 31 Bayside, Key Deer Blvd., Big Pine Key, FL 33043; (305) 872-2411; FREE.** You may wonder why all those cars are parked on the side of Key Deer Boulevard; from the roadside the area looks like an uninhabited stand of slash pines. Trust us—park your vehicle and join the crowd. A few steps into the thatch palm understory you'll see a large, water-filled barrow pit, known as the Blue Hole. Inhabiting this incongruous water hole are a couple of resident alligators, the only known gators in the Keys. If you are lucky, you may catch a glimpse of one of these elusive reptiles, along with turtles and freshwater fish.

**NATIONAL KEY DEER REFUGE AND WATSON NATURE TRAIL, MM 30.5 Bayside, 28950 Watson Blvd., Big Pine Key, FL 33043; (305) 872-2239; fws.gov/nationalkeydeer; FREE.** This refuge protects the habitat frequented by the key deer, a small species—most are around 3 feet high—that is found nowhere else in the world (see the Welcome to the Florida Keys chapter.) Some areas of the refuge are off-limits to visitors and marked accordingly, but designated trails are open for daytime public access. The key deer are protected by law, so even feeding them is a misdemeanor offense. You can sometimes spot key deer beside US 1, but you are more likely to see them along the back roads, especially on No Name Key, where there are fewer human inhabitants.

### Key West

**KEY WEST AQUARIUM,** 1 Whitehead St., Key West, FL 33040; (888) 544-5927; keywestaquarium.com; $$$. Key West's oldest tourist attraction (built in 1934), and still one of the most fascinating our southernmost city has to offer, affords you a diver's-eye view of the marine creatures of our encompassing waters. Stroll at your leisure alongside the backlit tanks re-creating our coral reefs. You will marvel at the frenzy of sharks at feeding time; the stingrays flipping and splashing for their rations; and a wide variety of tropical fish, game fish, and sea turtles recognizing the hands that feed them in the outdoor Atlantic Shores Exhibit, created to look like a mangrove lagoon. The aquarium is open daily.

**THE KEY WEST BUTTERFLY & NATURE CONSERVATORY,** 1316 Duval St., Key West, FL 33040; (305) 296-2988; keywestbutterfly.com; $$$. Celebrate butterflies around the globe at this enchanting attraction. Stop at the Learning Center for a brief introductory film on the wonders of the butterflies' world before proceeding to the main conservatory. The diversity of size, shape, color, and behavior make these delicate winged creatures a delight to see. Make sure to see the owl butterflies—the largest variety on-site. The gardens are a lush, tropical nirvana, inhabited by 50 to 60 species of exotic butterflies and myriad birds from all over the world. Arrive in the morning and see them basking in the sun, warming their muscles to fly.

**KEY WEST WILDLIFE CENTER,** 1801 White St., Key West, FL 33040; (305) 292-1008; keywestwildlifecenter.org; FREE. This wildlife center is dedicated to treating over 1,000 different types of sick, injured, and orphaned animals while educating the public about birds and other wildlife in the Keys. The grounds are full of rare and native species of flora. At any given time approximately 100 animals—ranging from seabirds to raccoons to chickens—are recovering here. You can see them during visiting hours. Key West Wildlife Center will rescue animals anywhere from the Seven Mile Bridge to the Dry Tortugas. The park is open daily and admission is free, but donations are appreciated. Volunteers are always needed.

## OUTDOOR SITES

### Upper Keys

**HURRICANE MONUMENT, MM 81.6 Oceanside, Islamorada, FL 33036; FREE.** This sturdy monument honors the hundreds of residents and railroad workers in Islamorada who lost their lives in the Labor Day hurricane of 1935, a storm that has been classified as one of the strongest to ever hit the United States. This monument depicts the fury of nature's elements, offering images of high seas and wind-battered palm trees. Carved out of local coral limestone and framed by fantastic views on both sides, the Hurricane Monument may be freely viewed just off the Overseas Highway and is worth a quick stop.

**INDIAN KEY STATE HISTORICAL SITE, MM 78.5 Oceanside, Indian Key, Islamorada, FL 33036; (850) 245-2157 or (305) 664-9814 (for rentals); floridastateparks.org/park/indian-key; FREE.** A colorful history surrounds Indian Key, a 10-acre oceanside island about 0.75 mile offshore from Lower Matecumbe Key. Now uninhabited, this tiny key has yielded archaeological evidence of prehistoric Native American cultures. Indian Key is accessible only by boat. The historic site is open from 8 a.m. to sundown. Ranger-led tours are available, and visitors enjoy swimming, sunbathing, hiking, kayaking, and snorkeling among local baby sharks, shells, colorful fish, and coral life. Robbie's Marina, MM 77.5 Bayside (305-664-9814; robbies.com), offers the only regularly scheduled tour transportation to the island. Reservations are preferred.

**LIGNUMVITAE STATE BOTANICAL SITE, MM 78.5 Bayside, Lignumvitae Key, Islamorada, FL 33036; (850) 245-2157 or (305) 664-9814 (for reservations); floridastateparks.org/park/lignumvitae-key; $.** Lignumvitae Key supports one of the best examples of a virgin hardwood hammock in the Florida Keys. Also on the island is the 1919 home of William J. Matheson, a wealthy Miami chemist, who owned the island for many decades. Ranger-guided tours are given twice daily, Fri through Sun. You may not enter the hammock unless accompanied by a ranger. Come equipped with mosquito repellent and sturdy shoes. Like Indian Key, Lignumvitae Key may only be accessed by boat, and limited private dockage for small craft is available (see previous listing for information on Robbie's Marina, which offers transportation to the key).

**PIONEER CEMETERY, MM 82 Oceanside, at Cheeca Lodge, 81801 Overseas Hwy., Islamorada, FL 33036; FREE.** Their gravestones defiled in the hurricane of 1935, the founding fathers and mothers of Islamorada—the Parkers, Pinders, and Russells—still rest in the Pioneer Cemetery, now a part of the extensive grounds of Cheeca Lodge. In 1989, Cheeca Lodge and University of

ATTRACTIONS

Miami historian Josephine Johnson researched the cemetery, leading to the designation of the Pioneer Cemetery as a historical site by the Historical Association of Southern Florida. You will find the tiny Pioneer Cemetery surrounded by a white picket fence near the beach on the Cheeca Lodge grounds. The cemetery is open for free viewing by the general public.

**WINDLEY KEY FOSSIL REEF STATE GEOLOGIC SITE, MM 84.9** Bayside, Windley Key, Islamorada, FL 33036; (850) 245-2157 or (305) 664-2540; floridastateparks.org/park/windley-key; $. Quarried long ago by workers building Henry Flagler's East Coast Railroad Extension in the early 1900s, the ancient fossilized coral reef that forms the bedrock of the Keys (see the Welcome to the Florida Keys chapter) is exposed here for all to see. Borrow the in-house trail guide, which interprets the natural attributes of the land that you will discover on Windley Key's 4 self-guided trails. The visitor center is open Fri through Sun, 9 a.m. to 5 p.m., and features educational exhibits about the history of this site. Feel free to relax at one of the available picnic tables.

## Middle Keys

**PIGEON KEY FOUNDATION & MARINE SCIENCE CENTER, MM 47 Oceanside, Pigeon Key, 1 Knights Key Blvd., Marathon, FL 33050;** (305) 289-0025; (305) 743-5999 (gift shop & ferry); pigeonkey.net; $$$. Though undoubtedly Pigeon Key was known to Native Americans and Bahamian fishermen in the early days of the Keys, it was Henry Flagler's (the "Father of Florida's") East Coast Railroad Extension that put the tiny 5-acre key on the historical map. The volunteer-staffed Pigeon Key Foundation is devoted to preserving the cultural history of the Keys. The island is connected to the mainland by a bridge that was originally built for the railroad. The hurricane of 1935 flooded Pigeon Key and caused so much damage to the railroad that the company decided not to rebuild (see the History chapter).

## Key West

**AFRICAN CEMETERY AT HIGGS BEACH, 1001** Atlantic Blvd., Key West, FL 33040; (305) 294-4633 (Mel Fisher Museum); africanburialground athiggsbeach.org; **FREE.** In 1860, three illegal slave ships were intercepted by the US Navy and diverted to Key West, bringing almost 1,500 Africans to the area. Locals were so appalled by the treatment of those held captive that they rallied and provided food and shelter for the diverted slaves. Despite their efforts, hundreds still died, and the bodies were buried in mass graves in the Higgs Beach area, now known as the African Cemetery. In 2007, a concrete slab was poured over the grave site and the African Cemetery at Higgs Beach sign was erected as a first step in creating a lasting memorial.

**DRY TORTUGAS NATIONAL PARK,** 70 miles west of Key West; (305) 242-7700; nps.gov/drto; $$. Visit Dry Tortugas National Park for a spectacular ride back in history. Accessible only by boat or seaplane, the Dry Tortugas lie almost 70 miles west of Key West. Ponce de León named the seven islands "Las Tortugas" in 1513, presumably for the multitude of sea turtles (tortugas). The "Dry" moniker was added later to indicate the islands' lack of freshwater. The protected waters surrounding the Tortugas sparkle with all the sea creatures of the coral reef as well as a good many shipwreck remains. With natural sand beaches and calm seas, snorkeling and swimming are a must.

**FLORIDA KEYS ECO-DISCOVERY CENTER,** Truman Annex Waterfront, 35 E. Quay Rd., Key West, FL 33040; (305) 809-4750; floridakeys .noaa.gov/eco_discovery.html; FREE. The 6,400-square-foot Eco-Discovery Center is located at historic Truman Waterfront and features more than 6,000 square feet of interactive exhibits that reveal insights into marine life and what research scientists are doing to preserve the vitality of Key West's ocean waters, including a dynamic mock-up of Aquarius, the world's only underwater ocean laboratory. Be sure to check out the Mote Marine Laboratory Living Reef exhibit, a 2,500-gallon reef tank with living corals and tropical fish that you can study on the live Reef Cam. And do not leave without making a quick stop at the gift shop!

**FORT ZACHARY TAYLOR HISTORIC STATE PARK,** 601 Howard England Way, Key West, FL 33040; (305) 292-6713 or (305) 295-0037 (rentals and activities); floridastateparks.org/park/fort-taylor; $. This Key West military bastion served the Union well during the Civil War, when it guarded against Confederate blockade runners. So impressive were its defenses, the fort was never attacked. It saw continuous usage by the military until the federal government deeded the structure to the state of Florida for use as a historic site. The surrounding park offers a beach for fishing, swimming, or snorkeling, as well as picnic areas equipped with tables and grills, outside showers, a snack bar, and restroom facilities. It also boasts one of the best, most unobstructed views of the sunset. Tours of the historic fort are offered at noon daily.

**KEY WEST AIDS MEMORIAL,** Foot of White Street Pier, at White St. and Atlantic Blvd., Key West, FL 33040; keywestaids.org; FREE. The names of many of the victims of the AIDS epidemic are inscribed on this memorial, which consists of flat granite slabs embedded in the walkway approaching White Street Pier. Built with private funds and dedicated on World AIDS Day, December 1, 1997, the memorial has room for 1,500 names. At the unveiling, it contained 730. New names are engraved annually in a ceremony that takes place each December on World AIDS Day. Members of a volunteer group—Friends of the Key West AIDS Memorial—maintain and protect this site that provides a quiet place for loved ones to express grief and feel hope again.

**KEY WEST CITY CEMETERY, 701 Passover Ln., at Margaret and Angela Streets, Key West, FL 33040; (305) 292-8177; FREE.** Built in 1847, after the horrific hurricane the year before washed out the sand sanctuary at the island's southernmost point, the Key West City Cemetery lies right in the center of town. Carved with symbols and prosaic sayings, the gravestones are a living legacy for those lying beneath. The Historic Florida Keys Foundation's self-guided tour pamphlet lists graves of Key West's most prominent or notorious deceased citizens, with brief profiles and the meaning of the carved symbols on the gravestones. Within the fenced-in 19 acres, 80,000 to 100,000 people are buried. This historic cemetery is open every day for viewing.

**KEY WEST HISTORIC SEAPORT AND HARBOR WALK, 201 William St., at Key West Bight, Key West, FL 33040; (305) 294-1100; keywestcity .com; FREE.** Formerly known as Key West Bight, this prime strip of waterfront real estate has undergone a complete metamorphosis. Shops, restaurants, and raw bars now line the wooden boardwalk that stretches from the foot of Front Street to the foot of Margaret Street. Vessels bound for the Dry Tortugas leave from here, as do many of the snorkel and sunset cruises and fishing charters (see our Recreation chapter for details). And if you are on the lookout for the freshest seafood on the island, you have your choice of various waterfront restaurants along the Harbor Walk, with the kind of menus you have been dreaming about.

**KEY WEST HISTORICAL MEMORIAL SCULPTURE GARDEN, Mallory Square, 401 Wall St., Key West, FL 33040; (305) 294-4142; keywest sculpturegarden.org; FREE.** Located on Key West's original shoreline just behind Mallory Square, this humble fenced-in "garden" pays homage to three dozen men and women whose lives and deeds have had tremendous impact on the southernmost city. Here you will find the stories and likenesses of such former influential citizens as wreckers Asa Tift and Captain John Geiger, writer Ernest Hemingway, President Harry S. Truman, railroad magnate Henry Flagler, and Sister Louise Gabriel, whose Grotto to Our Lady of Lourdes is said to have protected Key West from hurricanes for more than 75 years. Open every day, 7:30 a.m. until 9 p.m.

**KEY WEST SHIPWRECK MUSEUM, MALLORY SQUARE, 1 Whitehead St., Key West, FL 33040; (305) 292-8990; keywestshipwreck.com; $$$.** Relive the days of wreckers, lumpers, and divers at the Key West Shipwreck Museum, where actors, video footage, and interactive presentations re-create vestiges of Key West's once-lucrative wrecking industry. During the 1800s, about 100 ships passed by the port of Key West daily, many running aground on the reef. Meet Asa Tift, a 19th-century wrecker and the original owner of what would one day become the Hemingway Home. Listen as he recounts his story of salvaging the goods of the *SS Isaac Allerton*, which was downed by a hurricane in 1856 (see our Kidstuff chapter). Shows run every 30 minutes, daily.

**KEY WEST TROPICAL FOREST & BOTANICAL GARDEN,** 5210 College Rd., Stock Island, FL 33040; (305) 296-1504; keywestbotanicalgarden .org; **$$.** The Key West Botanical Garden Society represents the last undeveloped native hardwood hammock in the environs of Key West. Despite its proximity to US 1 and a busy public golf course, the garden is surprisingly peaceful. It features exotic and native plants that can be viewed from a series of walking trails and is home to numerous birds and butterflies, especially during the spring and fall migration seasons. Enjoy a Hatha Yoga class on-site, and then channel your newly generated calm energy into one of the 8 self-guided information tours of lush courtyards and tropical landscapes. Restrooms and refreshments are available.

**MALLORY SQUARE SUNSET CELEBRATION,** Mallory Square Dock near 0 Duval St., Key West, FL 33040; (305) 292-7700 or (786) 565-7448; sunsetcelebration.org; **FREE.** Every evening, as the sun sinks into the Gulf of Mexico over Sunset Key off Mallory Square, buskers and street players, vaudevillians and carny wannabes alike perform unique acts. Beverage and food vendors hawk refreshments while fire-eaters, furniture jugglers, tightrope walkers, and sword swallowers compete for your attention. Photography, handmade jewelry, T-shirts, wood sculptures, body art, psychics—the bounty is endless! This daily event, a Key West tradition since 1984, is free to all, but pack your pocket with small bills, because the performers play for tips. The fun starts approximately an hour before sunset at Mallory.

**MILE MARKER 0,** Corner of Whitehead and Fleming Streets; **FREE.** The official green-and-white MM 0 signifying the end of US 1 is posted at this corner. Have someone snap a picture of you in front of the sign. It will be a wonderful reminder of the very moment you finally arrived at the end of your road—providing a souvenir hunter has not made off with the sign, which happens with great regularity. In case you might be considering it, tampering with highway signs, including those enticing green mile markers, is against the law. But if you absolutely must own one, replicas of MM 0 are available for purchase in many Key West shops.

**THE SOUTHERNMOST POINT, Corner of Whitehead and South Streets, Key West, FL 33040; FREE.** At the Atlantic end of Whitehead Street you'll see the giant red, white, green, and yellow marker buoy that designates the southernmost point of the continental US. And standing in front of it, in the street, blocking traffic, preens a never-ending stream of tourists, trying to capture the moment they stood a mere 90 miles away from Cuba, closer than anyone else in the country in that moment. The colorful concrete buoy is the backdrop of pictures for virtually every traveler to Key West—about a million people per year.

## GUIDED & SELF-GUIDED TOURS

### Key West

**CITYVIEW TROLLEY, 105 Whitehead St., Key West, FL 33040; (305) 294-0644; cityviewtrolleys.com/keywest; $$$$.** Experience Key West and learn about its rich history from the comfort of this hop-on/hop-off open-air trolley service. The seats are comfortably padded, and the conductors will regale you with tales of Key West's past and present as you cruise around the island aboard the trolley. There are 8 stops on the route, including Mallory Square, Harry Truman's Little White House, the Southernmost Point, and the Hemingway Home. The first tour begins at 9:30 a.m., with the last reboard at 4:30 p.m., and trolleys run at a 30-minute frequency.

**CONCH TOUR TRAIN, 201 Front St., Key West, FL 33040; (888) 916-8687; conchtourtrain.com; $$$$.** The quirky little Conch Tour Train is a great way to garner an overview of Key West in the shaded comfort of a canopied tram. You'll pass by most of the attractions already touched on in this chapter, sometimes twice, because in tiny Key West the train weaves a circuitous route that often changes from one hour to the next depending on road construction, special events, and street closures. Plus, children 12 and younger ride free! They are ranked in the top 20 tour services on Trip Advisor, and offer a 100 percent money-back guarantee for those who still need convincing.

**LLOYD'S TROPICAL BIKE TOUR, 601 Truman Ave., Key West, FL 33040; (305) 304-4700; lloydstropicalbiketour.com; $$$$.** Lloyd, one of Key West's most colorful characters, will expertly lead you on a leisurely 2-hour bike tour of the island, machete in hand. Don't worry—it's okay if you have not been on a bike since before you had your first margarita. The ride is easy and fun. As you stop along the way to hear local stories and sample the local fruits, you may hear Lloyd say, "There is always some kind of fruit in season . . . like a sapodilla or a Surinam cherry. Just sit back, pedal along effortlessly on our flat island, and relax. It all makes so much sense." We could not agree more.

**OLD TOWN TROLLEY TOURS OF KEY WEST**, 201 Front St., Key West, FL 33040; (888) 912-8687; historictours.com/keywest; $$$$. Join the Old Town Trolley Tour for an informative, convenient entry into Key West. Old Town Trolley Tours is one of the longest tours offered on the island, lasting 1.5 hours. They depart every 30 minutes and allow passengers to get off at any of the 12 stops and reboard the same day. All along the way the tour guide will treat you to a Key West history lesson, full of anecdotes and legends. Old Town Trolley Tours run daily and are free for kids 12 and under.

**PELICAN PATH**, 322 Duval St., Key West, FL 33041; (305) 294-9501 or (305) 294-2587; oirf.org; FREE. Visitors who like to wander on their own should be sure to first pick up a copy of the Pelican Path brochure at the chamber of commerce on Greene Street. This map offers a short history of Key West as well as a suggested route that will take you past 50 of our most prominent historic structures, most of which are now private homes. Don't be surprised if you cannot spot the path markers; many of them have disappeared over the years. Even so, the Pelican Path remains relatively easy to follow and is a great way to get acquainted with island history.

**SLOAN'S GHOST HUNT**, (305) 290-3451; keywestghosthunt.com. Love a good ghost story? Sloan's Ghost Hunt offers you the chance to get an in-depth introduction to the most famous ghosts of our island. The tour is a 90-minute stroll through Old Town's "Dead Zone" using ghost-hunting equipment to capture spirits at Key West's most active locations. This is the only tour owned and operated by renowned ghost hunter and originator of ghost tours in the Florida Keys, David L. Sloan. David is also the author of the books *Ghosts of Key West* and *Haunted Key West*, and he is the Haunted History columnist for the *Key West Citizen*. Ghost Hunt winds its way through Key West after dark, seven days a week, rain or shine. Reservations are recommended.

**WILD DOLPHIN ADVENTURES**, William St., Historic Key West Bight; (305) 296-3737; wilddolphinadventures.com; $$$$. Relax and get away from the Key West crowds by taking an adventure on the 21-foot *Coral Reefer* out onto the Gulf of Mexico, interacting with beautifully wild Atlantic bottlenose dolphins. This is an ecology tour that gives you the opportunity to watch a resident pod of dolphins in their natural habitat where they live and play. On your outing you will see local birds, coral reefs, sponges, rays, and more. Snorkeling is also available on these trips, allowing divers to observe shallow-water shipwrecks encrusted with corals, sponges, and curious fish. Seating is limited, and reservations are recommended.

# Kidstuff

There is so much for the little ones to do in the Keys: observe dolphins in their natural habitat, swim with sea creatures in our tropical waters, learn about the area's ecosystem at our museums and parks, and lots more! In this chapter we list highlights of kid-friendly activities by category in each area of the Keys.

## BEACHES, PARKS & PLAYGROUNDS

### Upper Keys

**ANNE'S BEACH, MM 73.5 Oceanside, Islamorada, FL 33036; (305) 664-6400.** This small beach offers a scenic walkway and great views of the shallows surrounding Islamorada. It has restrooms and picnic tables.

**FOUNDERS PARK, MM 87 Bayside, 87000 Overseas Hwy., Plantation Key, Islamorada, FL 33036; (305) 853-1685 or (305) 434-8984 (water sport rentals).** There are many activities at this well-maintained waterfront park, including an impressive Olympic-size pool with diving area, a shallow-water beach, water-sports rentals, ball fields, a fishing jetty, bocce, tennis, and basketball courts, a vita course with 18 exercise stations, a skate park, and a dog park.

**FRIENDSHIP PARK, MM 100 Oceanside, 101.3 Overseas Hwy., Key Largo, FL 33037.** This community park offers a ball field, playground, and tennis courts. Entrance is free for kids 12 and under. Pets are welcome!

**HARRY HARRIS PARK, Turn off US 1 at Burton Dr., MM 92.5 Oceanside, Key Largo, FL 33037; (305) 852-7161.** This gorgeous oceanfront park has been updated with a new toddler playground. You can watch your kids from a convenient covered picnic area. Entry to the park is free Mon through Fri. On weekends it's free for kids under 15, with a small charge for others.

**JOHN PENNEKAMP CORAL REEF STATE PARK, MM 102.5 Oceanside, 102601 Overseas Hwy., Key Largo, FL 33037; (305) 451-6300; pennekamppark.com.** The depths of the sea can be discovered at John Pennekamp Coral Reef State Park, the nation's first underwater preserve. Pennekamp can be explored by glass-bottomed boat or on scuba-diving or snorkeling excursions. (See the Diving & Snorkeling chapter for more information.) When it's time to dry off, feel free to picnic, swim, or set up camp on the premises. Call ahead for rentals.

**KEY LARGO COMMUNITY PARK, turn off US 1 at MM 99.6 Ocean-side, Key Largo, FL 33037.** This huge park has it all: playground, ball fields, tennis courts, volleyball court, and more. Plus, it's a mere 5-minute drive from the Jacob's Aquatic Center pool facility (see the Camps & Outdoor Activities section in this chapter for more information).

**OLD SETTLER'S PARK, MM 92 Oceanside, Key Largo, FL 33037.** This small community park is free and offers swings and slides for children to play on. There is also a trail that leads walkers through butterfly gardens, eventually leading to a large public pavilion near the ocean.

**WINDLEY KEY FOSSIL REEF GEOLOGICAL STATE PARK, turn off US 1 at MM 84.9 Bayside, Islamorada, FL 33036; (305) 664-2540; florida stateparks.org/windleykey.** Examine the fossilized imprints of ancient shells and marine organisms you will find in the coral quarry walls of the Windley Key Fossil Reef Geological State Park. If you bring paper and crayons, you and the kids can make a crayon rubbing of your favorite fossil to take home.

### Middle Keys

**COCO PLUM BEACH, turn off US 1 at Coco Plum Dr., MM 54.5 Ocean-side, Marathon, FL 33050.** Because this site is a destination for turtle nesting, things are kept simple and quiet at Coco Plum Beach. Despite its few ameni-ties, this small, natural beach is a worthwhile stop. It is also dog-friendly, with clean-up baggies provided.

**MARATHON COMMUNITY PARK, 9850 Overseas Hwy., Marathon, FL 33050; (305) 743-6598.** Between 7 a.m. and 10 p.m., Marathon Community Park opens 4 tennis courts, a tennis wall, 3 combination hockey/basketball courts, 2 Little League fields, and 2 soccer fields to the public. There is also an Xtreme skating park, 2 shuffleboard courts, 2 bocce courts, a batting cage, concession stand, amphitheater, picnic areas, and restrooms. This facility is also wheelchair-accessible.

**ROTARY FIELD OF DREAMS, MM 52 Oceanside, Marathon, FL 33050.** This 3-acre landscaped park tends to be a standout for children during their stay in the Keys. It offers a wooden replica of Thomas the Train, plus plenty of tunnels, swings, a playground with two lookout towers, and a sandbox with a toothy, make-believe shark statue. There is plenty for toddlers and older kids as well. (Just note that dogs are not allowed.)

**SOMBRERO BEACH, MM 50 Oceanside, Marathon, FL 33050.** This 12.6-acre beach is one of the most popular stops in Marathon and offers walkways, picnic areas, and a roped-off swimming area. The kids can play in the sand or look for crabs and other crustaceans. There is no admission fee, and it is totally handicapped-accessible. Take care if your kids want to try out the water; it tends to be deeper in this area, and there are typically no lifeguards on duty. Turn off US 1 at Sombrero Beach Boulevard and drive to the end to reach the beach.

## Lower Keys

**BAHIA HONDA STATE PARK,** MM 37 Oceanside, 36850 Overseas Hwy., Big Pine Key, FL 33043; (305) 872-3210 or (305) 872-2353 (reservations); bahiahondapark.com. This state park has 2 beaches. A small one near the concession stand at the south end of the park is calm, sheltered, and roped off for safety. The other, the Sandspur, is much longer. You can wade in the soft sand through waters that vary from several inches to 3 feet deep looking for sea creatures and washed-up treasure (see the Recreation chapter for more on beach options).

**BAY POINT PARK,** MM 15 Oceanside, Key West, FL 33040. This community park offers a soccer field, basketball and tennis courts, and a small playground with swings.

**BLUE HERON PARK,** Wilder Rd. and Lytton Rd., off Key Deer Blvd., Big Pine Key, FL 33043. This is a solid park with all the expected features of well-rounded community space—offering basketball courts, playgrounds, pavilions, a jungle gym, barbecues, and portable toilets.

**VETERANS MEMORIAL PARK AND BEACH,** MM 39 Oceanside, west end of Seven Mile Bridge, Little Duck Key, FL 33043. Enjoy a long walk on this easily accessed beach while you take in the beautiful views it provides of the Atlantic Ocean. There are covered picnic tables for those who need shade, or venture out into the sun to show your children the shallow-water flats habitat of the Keys. Pets are welcome, too.

**WATSON FIELD AND SOUTH STREET PLAYGROUND,** MM 30, Key Deer Blvd. and South St., Big Pine Key, FL 33043. Watson Field and South Street Playground is an all-purpose park with a focus on you and your family's athletic needs. You'll find a baseball diamond here. Behind the field there is a small playground, volleyball court, and the Susann Thisler Tennis Courts.

## Key West

**ASTRO CITY,** 1001 Atlantic Blvd., Key West, FL 33040; (305) 295-4385. This well-equipped playground is conveniently located just across the street from Higgs Beach. It is a popular stop for families on their way to and from the ocean and a lovely compromise between playtime for kids and relaxing beach views for parents.

**BAYVIEW PARK**, 1310 Truman Ave., Key West, FL 33040. This large park offers plenty of room for a fun-filled family ball game. You'll also find a fully equipped playground, basketball court, tennis courts, and restrooms. Lots of community events take place here, so it can get crowded on weekends.

**FORT ZACHARY TAYLOR HISTORIC STATE PARK**, 601 Howard England Way, Key West, FL 33040; (305) 295-0037; floridastateparks.org/park/fort-taylor. Named after the 12th president of the United States, this historic fortress at the southwest end of Key West is a fascinating place to roam. The grounds offer a sandy beach with picnic tables and restrooms. Fishing is allowed on the west side of the park, by the Key West Shipping Channel. Children will enjoy watching the boats sail by out of Key West Harbor after strolling through the wooded natural trails that weave in and out of these protected 54 acres.

## CAMPS & OUTDOOR ACTIVITIES

### Upper Keys

**JACOB'S AQUATIC CENTER**, MM 99 Oceanside, 320 Laguna Ave., Key Largo, FL 33037; (305) 453-SWIM; jacobsaquaticcenter.org. Your children can splash for hours at the water park at Jacob's Aquatic Center. A mock-up of a "spray gym" pirate ship looms in the center of a shallow splash pool that is perfect for toddlers. Older kids will also enjoy swimming in an adjacent pool. Polite and astute lifeguards are on hand, and swim lessons and training are available.

### Middle Keys

**PIGEON KEY MARINE SCIENCE SUMMER CAMP**, MM 47 Oceanside, 1 Knights Key Blvd., Marathon, FL 33050; (305) 509-0345 or (305) 289-0025; pigeonkey.net. This hands-on science expedition into the living history of Pigeon Key and the Florida Keys can be either a day or overnight camp. Students ages 10 to 18 learn about natural animal habitats, marine life, and the fragile ecosystem we live in. Kids are able to spend their downtime in solar-powered cabins on a private island. Classes are usually at the end of July through Aug. Call for details.

### Lower Keys

**BOONDOCKS GRILLE & DRAFT HOUSE**, MM 27.5 Bayside, 27205 Overseas Hwy., Summerland Key, FL 33042; (305) 872-4094; boondocksus

KIDSTUFF

# Close-up

## Things that Go Bump in Plain Sight . . . Robert the Doll

This straw-filled toy doll was a gift, given to Key West resident Robert Eugene Otto as a child by his Jamaican nurse in the early 1800s. The nurse, upset at being dismissed by Robert's mother, handmade the stuffed doll in the likeness of young Master Otto, and some say it was voodoo-cursed. The doll was even given young Mr. Otto's first name of "Robert." With his unblinking eyes, faded sailor suit, and the mysterious stories surrounding him, Robert has become a legend in his own right. Living in their family home on the corner of Eaton and Simonton Streets (see the Artist House listing in the Accommodations chapter), young Eugene became very attached to Robert, and even blamed the doll for mishaps and unusual events, saying "Robert did it!" Eventually, the toy was banished to the attic where, as the story goes, he would taunt schoolchildren from the window, so much so that the kids would take a different route to school. When Mr. Otto died in the 1970s, Robert was given a home in a glass case at the Fort East Martello Museum (see the Attractions chapter), where he resides today. Despite rumors of ruined photographs and unexplained events at the museum from time to time, Robert is the most popular exhibit.

**.com.** Featuring the only public miniature golf course in the Florida Keys, Boondocks is a favorite place for families to play a round . . . or four.

**SEACAMP, MM 29.5 Oceanside, 1300 Big Pine Ave., Big Pine Key, FL 33043; (305) 872-2331 or (877)-SEACAMP; seacamp.org.** This marine science educational program for teenagers is located at the tip of Big Pine Key. Campers visit coral reefs, sandy and grassy areas, mudflats, and natural tide pools, all of them rich in sea plants and animals essential to the study of marine science. Camp facilities include an oceanfront dining and recreation hall, science laboratory, deepwater harbor, arts and crafts building, infirmary, and a man-made holding pool that serves as a temporary habitat for larger specimens campers can study.

## MUSEUMS

### Middle Keys

**CRANE POINT MUSEUM AND NATURE CENTER,** MM 50 Bayside, 5550 Overseas Hwy., Marathon, FL 33050; (305) 743-9100; cranepoint .net. Your children can learn about the rich and exciting history of the Keys at this special little museum, showcasing a collection of artifacts that includes a 600-year-old dugout canoe and recovered pirate treasure from the 1500s. There is a strong focus on the native wildlife at Crane Point, and the many nature trails, sunset boardwalk, and wild bird center all highlight the natural habitat of countless species they are dedicated to safely showcasing.

### Key West

**KEY WEST SHIPWRECK MUSEUM,** 1 Whitehead St., Key West, FL 33040; (305) 292-8990; keywestshipwreck.com. History comes to life here with re-creations of the salvage and wrecking era through live actors, film, and artifacts from the wreck of the *Isaac Allerton,* which sank off the Keys in 1856. The business of salvaging goods from ships wrecked on Florida Keys reefs made Key West the richest US city per capita in the mid-1800s. Wrecking master "Asa Tift" guides guests through the museum, explaining the unique industry, and invites them to climb the facility's 65-foot lookout tower.

## WILDLIFE

### Upper Keys

**DOLPHINS PLUS OCEANSIDE AND BAYSIDE,** MM 100 Oceanside, 31 Corrine Place; MM 101.9 Bayside, 101900 Overseas Hwy., Key Largo, FL 33037; (866) 860-7946; (877) 365-2683; dolphinsplus.com; $$$$. Dolphins Plus offers in-water experiences with bottlenose dolphins and sea lions in addition to myriad other unique activities. Structured and natural dolphin swim encounters are offered, and allow swimmers (ages 7 years and older) to observe the grace, fluidity, and curiosity of these clever mammals firsthand.

**LAURA QUINN WILD BIRD SANCTUARY,** MM 93.6 Bayside, 93600 Overseas Hwy., Tavernier, FL 33070; (305) 852-4486; keepthemflying.org. This Upper Keys landmark is home to more than 100 ill, injured, or orphaned wild birds, all housed in a natural setting on more than 5 acres. The sanctuary boardwalk attracts over 50,000 visitors annually and is kept running through donations.

**ROBBIE'S MARINA, MM 77.5 Bayside, 77522 Overseas Hwy., Islamorada, FL 33036; (305) 664-8070 or (877) 664-8498 (reservations); robbies.com.** Feeding the tarpon at Robbie's Marina is not to be missed. Look for the famous tarpon named "Scarface" as you and your children admire the hungry fish glimmering in the sunshine when they jump up to catch their lunch. You can purchase a cup of baitfish, the tarpon's favorite snack, at the marina. Robbie's also offers small powerboats for rent and a party fishing boat on which you can go reef fishing off Islamorada.

**THEATER OF THE SEA, MM 84.5 Bayside, 84721 Overseas Hwy., Islamorada, FL 33036; (305) 664-2431; theaterofthesea.com.** Islamorada's lush 17-acre tropical oasis features a variety of fish and marine life, native birds, colorful parrots, sea turtles, crocodiles, and exotic plants. General admission includes live performances by dolphins in the main lagoon (created by excavations for Henry Flagler's railroad; see the History chapter), sea lions, and parrots, a guided tour of marine-life exhibits, and a glass-bottomed boat tour of the facility's natural saltwater lagoon. Theater of the Sea also hosts swim programs with dolphins, stingrays, sharks, and sea lions.

## Middle Keys

**CAPTAIN HOOK'S MARINA & DIVE CENTER AQUATIC LEARNING CENTER, MM 53 Oceanside, 11833 Overseas Hwy., Marathon, FL 33050; (305) 743-2444 or (800) 278-4665; captainhooks.com.** Captain Hook's has been around for more than 50 years, so you can bet they know the Florida Keys waters extremely well. A highlight of visiting Captain Hook's is their fishpond and marine life exhibit, including their 48,000-gallon outdoor aquarium. Every day at 4 p.m. you can watch nurse sharks, eels, and other big fish receive their evening meal. It's free fun!

**CRANE POINT HAMMOCK, MM 50 Oceanside, 5550 Overseas Hwy., Marathon, FL 33050; (305) 743-9100; cranepoint.net.** This 63-acre environmental and archaeological preserve includes attractions like the Adderley House, built in 1906 by a Bahamian immigrant; a butterfly meadow; nature trails full of interesting sinkholes and mangroves; and the Marathon Wild Bird Center for injured and orphaned birds.

**DOLPHIN RESEARCH CENTER, MM 59 Bayside, 58901 Overseas Hwy., Grassy Key, FL 33050; (305) 289-1121 or (305) 289-0002 (reservations); dolphins.org.** The Dolphin Research Center is a teaching and research facility with fun-filled interactive programs, including painting with a dolphin and becoming a trainer for a day.

## Lower Keys

**THE BLUE HOLE, MM 31 Bayside, Key Deer Blvd., Big Pine Key, FL 33043; (305) 872-2411 or (800) 872-3722.** This freshwater sinkhole is home to a couple of curious alligators, and they'll swim almost up to the viewing platform. Keep your puppy on a leash, because its barking will ring the alligators' dinner bell. You'll see turtles in the Blue Hole, and key deer come around at dusk. There is no admission charge.

**THE HORSESHOE, MM 35 Bayside, just over the Bahia Honda Bridge, Big Pine Key, FL 33043.** Stop here as you head down the Keys. In the Horseshoe, you will see a natural aquarium of colorful tropical fish, with no danger from sharks or barracuda because they cannot get into this special little body of water.

**NATIONAL KEY DEER REFUGE VISITOR CENTER, MM 30.5 Bayside, Key Deer Blvd., Big Pine Key, FL 33043; (305) 872-2239; fws.gov/ nationalkeydeer.** Just before sunset, simply drive (or ride a bike—cautiously) to the end of Key Deer Boulevard, and you're bound to see key deer strolling out of the woods to feed. The key deer is an endangered species that lives only in the Lower Keys. These shy, appealing creatures are about 3 feet tall and can be found grazing all around Big Pine Key, especially during early morning hours and around dusk. The deer are wild and healthy, so please don't touch or feed them. For more information, stop by the refuge headquarters at the National Key Deer Refuge Visitor Center.

**NO NAME KEY BRIDGE, Big Pine Key, FL 33043.** This scenic bridge that links No Name Key to Big Pine Key is a popular spot to take kids fishing. The evening sightseeing is also excellent for birds and key deer. We suggest you park your car and walk along the pedestrian walkway.

**STRIKE ZONE CHARTERS, MM 29.5 Bayside, 29675 Overseas Hwy., Big Pine Key, FL 33043; (305) 872-9863; strikezonecharter.com.** Hop aboard a glass-bottomed boat for a 5-hour ecological tour of the Lower Keys backcountry with Strike Zone Charters. You will learn the history of the key deer, the tiny out-islands, the hurricanes, the wreckers, and the local Native American tribes. Check out bald eagle nesting sites, great white herons, egrets, and dolphins feeding in the wild. After all that, snorkel and fish a little. And then the perfect finale—a fish cookout picnic on a private island. Bliss.

## Key West

**DOLPHIN WATCH, 201 William St. and Caroline St., Key West, FL 33040; (305) 294-6306 or (800) 979-3370; dolphinwatchusa.com.** Book a trip with Key West's original dolphin charter, Dolphin Watch, and observe the wild dolphins as they frolic in their natural habitat. The boat is a custom-made, 31-foot catamaran and they book only 6 people per trip, so you and your family will have no trouble viewing the magnificent creatures, along with other sea life including turtles, rays, fish, and maybe even a manatee or two.

**THE FLORIDA KEYS ECO-DISCOVERY CENTER, 33 East Quay Rd., Truman Waterfront, Key West, FL 33040; (305) 809-4750 or (305) 809-4700; floridakeys.noaa.gov.** This 6,400-square-foot facility showcases natural wonders both on land and underwater. Highlights include a walk-through version of the Aquarius, a manned underwater research habitat located off Key Largo, and interactive exhibits that spotlight the Keys' diverse ecosystems. A 2,500-gallon living reef tank with corals and tropical fish completes the experience. With its touch screens, stunning photos, and roomy theater, this educational center has become a hit with families. It's a great way to learn about reef and mangrove habitats indoors. The center is operated by the Florida Keys National Marine Sanctuary, and admission is free.

**KEY WEST AQUARIUM, 1 Whitehead St., Key West, FL 33040; (305) 296-2051 or (888) 544-5927; keywestaquarium.com.** Opened in 1935, the Key West Aquarium was one of the first family-friendly attractions offered in the Keys. Today it is home to groupers, moray eels, barracuda, tropical fish, tarpon, sharks, parrotfish, and more. A touch tank features small sea creatures that children can touch and feed. Guided tours of the aquarium include shark feeding and a unique opportunity for guests to bravely "pet" a shark.

**THE KEY WEST BUTTERFLY & NATURE CONSERVATORY, 1316 Duval St., Key West, FL 33040; (305) 296-2988; keywestbutterfly.com.** This is a wonderland housing thousands of tropical plants and hundreds of the delicate creatures known as "flowers of the sky." The solarium and nature exhibit, which is one of only three major butterfly facilities in Florida, features a 5,000-square-foot glass-domed tropical butterfly habitat.

**KEY WEST NATURE PRESERVE, two entrances on Atlantic Blvd. between White and Bertha Streets.** The City of Key West acquired this undeveloped oceanfront property and turned it into an accessible natural area. Wooden walkways and trails take visitors through mangrove forests to a quiet strip of beach. Children will enjoy seeing butterflies, lizards, and birds.

# Annual Events

No one knows how to throw a party better than residents of the Florida Keys! Come join us as we dress in period attire and relive eras from our past. Or join locals and folks from across the world in a challenging road race on a bridge spanning miles of open sea.

We also have boat parades, bikini contests, battle reenactments, and our own unplugged, underwater concert. Or try your angling skills in one of our many fishing tournaments (see the Fishing chapter for an expanded listing). Immerse yourself in Florida Keys arts and culture at our historical observances, music festivals, or arts and crafts fairs.

## OVERVIEW

The following selection of festivals and events is a sampling of what we offer annually in the Florida Keys. Additional events occur sporadically from year to year. Dates and locations often change, and admission prices vary. Call the local chambers of commerce for details: Key Largo, MM 106 Bayside, (305) 451-1414 or (800) 822-1088; Islamorada, MM 82.5 Bayside, (305) 664-4503 or (800) 322-5397; Marathon, MM 53.5 Bayside, (305) 743-5417 or (800) 262-7284; Lower Keys, MM 31 Oceanside, (305) 872-2411 or (800) 872-3722; Key West, 510 Greene St., (305) 294-2587 or (800) 527-8539. You also will find annual event information on the official website of the Monroe County Tourist Development Council: fla-keys.com.

## JANUARY

**ART UNDER THE OAKS, MM 89.5 Bayside, San Pedro Catholic Church, 89500 Overseas Hwy., Tavernier, FL 33070; (305) 360-8556; artunderthe oaks.com.** Begun in 1982, Art Under the Oaks, held in the gardens on the grounds of San Pedro Catholic Church, is always a tremendous community gathering. This 1-day celebration in mid-January is held in a natural setting under a lovely canopy of oak trees. It offers homemade crafts, fine art from local artists, specialty food booths, self-guided nature tours of the gardens, children's arts and crafts, raffle items, and live music. Because of the large turnout, free shuttle bus service runs from the Plantation Key School's parking lot to the event.

★**KEY WEST CRAFT SHOW, Whitehead St., Key West; (305) 294-1241; keywestartcenter.com.** Key West ends the month of January with a weekend-long exhibit of original crafts. Among the one-of-a-kind items offered for sale, you'll find handmade jewelry, leather goods, wood carvings, kitchen accessories, and exquisite hand-thrown pottery from Pottery by Grace, a fifth-generation Conch (potterybygrace.com). Exhibitors come from throughout the Keys and the US. The crafts show takes place in the street—on Whitehead Street between Eaton and Greene. Admission is free.

★**KEY WEST FOOD AND WINE FESTIVAL, Various locations throughout Key West; (800) 474-4319; keywestfoodandwinefestival.com.** The Key West Food and Wine Festival offers 4 fun-filled days of culinary delights and funky events you would expect to experience only in Key West. The festival's signature events are the Kick Off Your Flip-Flops Barefoot Beach Party; the Grand Tasting, with a refined selection of wines; and Duval Uncorked, which leads guests along Duval Street for a mile-long food- and wine-tasting extravaganza. There are also neighborhood strolls, one-of-a-kind fund-raisers like coconut bowling, various informative seminars, and an outdoor wine market.

> **i** If you are "road-tripping" south to the Florida Keys, remember that Florida's Turnpike (built in 1957) is a toll road. If you travel on I-95 or US 1 in Florida, there are no tolls.

**KEY WEST HISTORIC HOUSE AND GARDEN TOURS, Various locations throughout Key West; (305) 294-9501; oirf.org.** Olde Island Restoration, a nonprofit organization that encourages preservation of Key West's many historic structures, sponsors this popular tour—spanning Dec, Jan, Feb, and Mar—to show off some of the city's finest private properties. Typically each event features 5 or 6 privately owned homes. Tours explore shotgun-style cottages, Conch-style mansions, and everything in between. The tours are self-guided, but participants may meet at the Olde Island Restoration offices along Mallory Square and then embark on a Conch Train bound for the tour site. Scheduled dates vary from year to year. There is an admission fee.

★**KEY WEST LITERARY SEMINAR, Various locations throughout Key West; (888) 293-9291 or (888) 293-9291; kwls.org.** Originated in 1983 and dedicated to the celebration of the written word, the Key West Literary Seminar is a very important gathering of notable authors and their admiring public. Key West's San Carlos Institute serves as the home base for these sessions, but events occur at various locations throughout Key West. Writing workshops, tours of legendary local authors' homes, and cocktail parties also are offered to seminar participants. Reserve early. These events are typically sold out up to a year in advance.

FEBRUARY

★**GIGANTIC NAUTICAL FLEA MARKET,** MM 87 Bayside, Islamorada; (305) 664-4503 or (800) 322-5397; giganticnauticalfleamarket.org. The Upper Keys Rotary Club has been producing this giant flea market for more than 15 years. New and used boats, clothing, marine equipment, electronics, dive gear, antiques, fishing gear, and nautical arts and crafts are just some of the items available. Held at the end of Feb in Founders Park on Plantation Key (see the Recreation chapter), the entrance fee is a suggested donation of $5, which goes to the Rotary scholarship fund. There is a free shuttle from Coral Shores High School at MM 89.9 due to limited parking.

**OLD ISLAND DAYS ART FESTIVAL,** Whitehead St., Key West; (305) 294-1241; keywestartcenter.com. If you appreciate art, your heart is bound to beat faster at the sight of several blocks of exhibits by talented local artists. Inspired by the southernmost city, they take this opportunity to showcase their vivid creations. Virtually all artistic media are represented in this juried weekend-long show, usually held at the end of Feb, including oil, watercolor, and acrylic paintings; graphics; wood, metal, and stone sculptures; glasswork; and photography. Judges provide merit awards within each category. Old Island Days Art Festival exhibits line Whitehead Street from Greene Street to Caroline and into Truman Annex. No charge for browsing.

## MARCH

**CONCH SHELL BLOWING CONTEST,** Sunset Pier at Ocean Key House, Duval St., Key West; (305) 294-9501; oirf.org. Come to this fun "Conch Honk." The Conch Shell Blowing Contest offers adults and children the opportunity to sound off. Prizes are awarded to the loudest, the funniest, and the most entertaining conch-shell blowers in several divisions. This 1-day, springtime event takes place on the waterfront and on various dates each year, but usually in Mar or Apr. Participation is free.

**KEY WEST GARDEN CLUB FLOWER SHOW AT WEST MARTELLO TOWER,** Atlantic Blvd. and White St., Key West; (305) 294-3210; keywest gardenclub.com. Established in 1949 by former Key West politician Joe Allen, the Garden Club organizes monthly educational seminars for the public. Held at the West Martello Tower, the flower show features some 800 entries of floral arrangements, potted plants, palms, rare tropical flowers, and hybrids. Judges from garden clubs throughout the state of Florida award ribbons and prizes in several categories. The flower show is typically held during the spring, not necessarily always in Mar. There are admission costs.

## APRIL

**★CONCH REPUBLIC INDEPENDENCE CELEBRATION, Various locations throughout Key West; (305) 296-0213; conchrepublic.com.** This 10-day festival officially commemorates Key West's attempt to secede from the US on April 23, 1982, after the US Border Patrol established roadblocks at the end of the mainland to screen for drugs and illegal aliens. Independent Key Westers rebelled, creating their own flag and attempting to secede. The secession fizzled, of course, but locals here find the brief attempt at independence a reason to party nevertheless. Around this same time every year, officials of the fictitious Conch Republic—secretary general, prime ministers, navy, air force, and all—host events like picnics, balls, Conch cruiser car shows, the Red Ribbon Bed Race down Duval Street, and what has been dubbed "the world's longest parade."

**★COW KEY CHANNEL BRIDGE RUN, Cow Key Channel Bridge, Stock Island; cowkeybridgerun.com.** This is the only 0K race in the Florida Keys that takes place on one of the shortest bridges in the Keys. And there is a bar close to the finish line. Heats include People Competing for Last Place, Costumed Men, Costumed Women, a Family Run, and People Who Forgot to Run. More than 1,000 people turned out for the inaugural run in 2014, and a portion of the proceeds benefit a local nonprofit.

**★SEVEN MILE BRIDGE RUN, Seven Mile Bridge, Marathon; (305) 395-7040; 7mbrun.com.** For more than 30 years, men and women from around the world have flocked to this 7-mile roadway, which spans the open water between Marathon and Bahia Honda. In the wee morning hours, these spirited individuals participate in the most scenic competition of its kind: a run across one of the world's longest bridges. Prizes are awarded in various categories. Usually the run begins on the Marathon end of the Seven Mile Bridge. Expect to pay an entry fee. Spaces are limited, so if you plan to run, reserve your spot early.

## MAY

**HARRY S. TRUMAN LEGACY SYMPOSIUM, 111 Front St., Key West; (305) 294-9911; trumansymposium.com.** From 1945 to 1953 president Harry S. Truman spent 11 working vacations on the Key West Navy Base in what was to be known as the Little White House. The annual Truman Legacy Symposium, held in mid-May, offers a reception and lunch with a VIP tour of the house. Guest speakers, like Florida senator Bob Graham, discuss the various roles Truman played in shaping our nation's history. Topics change each year, as do the speakers. Truman's grandson, Clifton Truman Daniel, usually is in attendance and gives one of the keynote addresses.

★**KEY WEST SONGWRITERS FESTIVAL,** various locations throughout Key West; (305) 292-2032; kwswf.com. You may not recognize the names of the performers at this annual event in early May, but if you're a country music fan, you'll almost certainly know their songs. For more than 15 years, this festival has been bringing over 100 of the country's foremost performing songwriters to the Key West stage. The Songwriters Festival revolves around 5 days and nights of more than 25 free shows staged at the most popular drinking holes and hot spots throughout Key West.

> **i** Heading into "love bug" territory is not an invite for Valentine's Day. In late May and early June, heading north from the Florida Keys, you run smack dab into these pesky critters—literally—which splat all over windshields, hoods, and grilles of cars, not to mention your sunglasses and body parts if you are cycling.

## JUNE

**THE ORIGINAL FKCC SWIM AROUND KEY WEST,** Key West; (305) 809-3562; fkccswimaroundkeywest.com. This is the only sanctioned, insured, and US Coast Guard–permitted race around Key West. The event is a 12.5-mile swim clockwise around the island of Key West. Age groups 18 through 65 and older can register.

## JULY

★**HEMINGWAY DAYS FESTIVAL,** Hemingway Home and Museum, 907 Whitehead St., Key West; (305) 294-2587; hemingwaydays.org. Celebrate the legendary author's birthday with residents of the old man's former hometown by the sea. There's a street fair, a short-story competition, and a Hemingway look-alike contest at what was one of his favorite haunts, Sloppy Joe's. This weeklong event centers on the author's July 21 birthday. Fees for some events are required.

★STAR SPANGLED EVENT AT SOMBRERO BEACH, MM 50 Oceanside, Marathon; (305) 743-5417 or (800) 262-7284. On July 4 follow a parade to the beach, where fireworks decorate the sky, and enjoy all-American hot dogs, hamburgers, and fish sandwiches. Live entertainment is provided, games are available for the kids, and an afternoon volleyball tournament welcomes last-minute sign-ups. Many people see the fireworks display from the decks of their boats, anchoring offshore for the extravaganza. No admission or entry fee is required. Food and games are priced individually.

★UNDERWATER MUSIC FESTIVAL, MM 31 Oceanside, 31020 Overseas Hwy., Big Pine Key; (305) 872-2411 or (800) 872-3722; lowerkeys chamber.com. Whether you dive, snorkel, or merely swim, you can enjoy 6 hours of prerecorded, commercial-free music—from Beethoven to the Beatles to the humpback whale song—in synchronicity with tropical fish swimming across the reefs of the Looe Key National Marine Sanctuary. Dance the day away underwater, and look out for surprises such as mermaids and the Keys' very own Snorkeling Elvises. On land, you'll find a variety of foods, arts and crafts, and family games at the Lower Keys Chamber of Commerce, MM 31 Oceanside. Admission to both the concert and the food festival, usually held the second Sat in July, is free. See the Diving & Snorkeling chapter for a list of dive and snorkel charters that will take you to the reef.

## SEPTEMBER

FLORIDA KEYS POKER RUN, Miami through Key West; (305) 393-4827; petersonsharley.com. Revved up in 1972, bikers have since traveled our roads into Key West for this highly successful and popular motorcycle run. For this event in early Sept, more than 10,000 motorcyclists ride from Miami to Key West, stopping at various points within our islands to pick up playing cards. At the end of the ride, the player with the best poker hand wins, and all enjoy live bands, field events, and runs-within-a-run on Duval Street. Bikers can also get their machines blessed before returning home. Entry is free; each poker hand costs a nominal fee.

ANNUAL EVENTS

**S.L.A.M. CELEBRITY TOURNAMENT,** Key West; (305) 664-2002; red bone.org. First of the annual Celebrity Tournament Series is the Southernmost Light-tackle Anglers Masters (S.L.A.M.). Anglers try to score a Grand Slam by catching and releasing a bonefish, permit, and tarpon in 2 days. Usually held in early Sept; proceeds benefit the Cystic Fibrosis Foundation. (See the Fishing chapter for additional details.)

**WOMENFEST KEY WEST,** Various locations throughout Key West; (305) 294-4603 or (800) 535-7797; womenfest.com. Each week after Labor Day, thousands of women from all over the country and the world gather in Key West for a bit of female bonding, and they have been doing so for more than 30 years. They include women from diverse races, religions, professions, and sexual orientations. This 7-day celebration is produced by the Key West Business Guild and includes women-only water sports, pool and dance parties, cocktail parties, comedy shows, and concerts.

## OCTOBER

**FANTASY FEST,** Various locations throughout Key West; (305) 296-1817; fantasyfest.com. Usually held in late Oct, this is Key West's biggest party of the year—a citywide celebration similar to Mardi Gras in New Orleans, with different themes that dictate the floats and costumes every year (see the Close-up in this chapter).

**GOOMBAY FESTIVAL,** Bahama Village at Petronia St., Key West; (305) 294-2587 or (800) 648-6269. Designed to showcase the cultural customs of the city's Bahamian community through food, music, and crafts, this grassroots affair has grown to include African, Filipino, and Latin traditions, too. Try some festival fare and one of the Bahamian-inspired food booths, dance in the streets to the music of African and steel drummers or calypso bands, then stop by the straw market to see straw hats and fruit baskets being woven. Goombay is held the first weekend of Fantasy Fest (see Close-up).

**SOUTHERNMOST MARATHON & HALF MARATHON,** Key West; (800) 608-1140; somomarathon.com. The Southernmost Marathon & Half Key West offers just that: 26.2, 13.1, or 6.2 miles of ocean and gulf views, as well as iconic Key West landmarks. Their motto is "No hills, no chills." All participants receive an event T-shirt and finisher medal. Special events and an expo take place throughout the weekend.

# Close-up

## Fantasy Fest

Kookier than Carnival and merrier than Mardi Gras, Fantasy Fest is Key West's own decadent and dreamy delight.

Fantasy Fest was originally conceived as a way to boost tourism in an otherwise soft season. It succeeded—and how! Today, more than two decades after its conception, this event more than doubles the island's population for one week in October, culminating with the arrival of some 70,000 revelers on Duval Street for the Saturday-night parade.

Fantasy Fest is a nine-day adult Halloween celebration that commences on a Friday night with the Royal Coronation Ball, where the King and Queen of Fantasy Fest are crowned. The competition is open to all, and campaigning for the titles begins as early as late August. The winners are the ones who "buy" the most votes (translation: They raise the most money for AIDS Help Inc.). The closer it gets to Fantasy Fest, the fiercer the competition becomes, and the more creative the candidates are.

The final tally takes place at the Coronation Ball. The man and woman—or man and man-in-drag—are dubbed "royalty" only after emerging from a field of entrants. The King and Queen receive regal robes, crowns, and scepters and preside over all official Fantasy Fest events. The real winners in all of this, however, are the people served by AIDS Help Inc.

Each year Fantasy Fest features a new theme, which is emblazoned on posters and T-shirts promoting the events—all of which are for sale, of course. During the celebration week you can enjoy a preview of some courageous/outrageous costumes at the Masked Madness and Headdress Ball, and even enter your pet (and yourself) in the Pet Masquerade and Parade. No species is excluded. Visit fantasyfest.com or call (305) 296-1817 for more information.

## NOVEMBER

**AMERICAN POWER BOAT ASSOCIATION WORLD CHAMPIONSHIP RACE, Waters off Key West; (305) 296-6166; superboat.com.** Just as Key West begins to recover from Fantasy Fest, the big boats roar into town to compete in a week's worth of offshore races that culminate in the naming of the world's champ. These are no little putt-putt motorboats; they are high-performance ocean racers costing more than $1 million each and boasting speeds of 125 to 150 mph. There's no charge to watch, and the best viewing spots are along Mallory Square and at the harborside hotels—the Pier House, Ocean Key House, Hyatt, and Westin.

## DECEMBER

**KEY WEST TRIATHLON (TRIKW),** Key West; trikw.com. This annual triathlon consists of a swim in the warm Gulf of Mexico waters on the first leg, biking the Overseas Highway, then running along the Atlantic Ocean to the finish line. There is also an expo with information booths on all things healthy in the Keys. Start training now!

**NEW YEAR'S EVE ON DUVAL STREET,** Key West; (305) 294-2587 or (800) 648-6269; keywestcity.com. Times Square has nothing on us when it comes to ringing in a new year. We close off the street and, in typical Key West style, party outdoors till the bars close at 4 a.m. So come New Year's Eve, grab your hat and horn and head for Duval to watch the conch shell drop from the top of Sloppy Joe's Bar (or the red high heel at Bourbon Street Pub) at the stroke of midnight. Just don't wear your best silks and satins for this celebration, because it will be raining champagne for sure! CNN televises this countdown, so be on your best behavior as you smile at the cameras.

# Entertainment

From live music to live theater, with a few drag shows in between, Key West has your nights (and some of your days, too) covered.

Key West is the cultural center of the Florida Keys. This scintillating port has long attracted free spirits and adventurers—wreckers, sailors, spongers, shrimpers, and pirates—who played an enormous role in Key West's settlement and development. An enigmatic quality inherent in the essence of Key West draws fertile minds and searching souls to its inner sanctum like moths to a flame. From Ernest Hemingway to earnestly trying, Key West has hosted for a time the famous, the infamous, and the obscure.

Enjoy our live music, theater, and dance while you are here, and tour our myriad galleries. Or, if your timing is right, catch an arts festival, literary seminar, or theater gala for a creative night out. Be sure to check the Annual Events chapter for descriptions of special arts festivals and events.

## ARTS ORGANIZATIONS

The Florida Keys Council of the Arts (keysarts.com) is considered the official arts organization of the Florida Keys. They provide services to visual and performing artists in the Keys by offering grants, showcasing art in public places, and sponsoring various festivals and events throughout the year. This and other arts organizations are listed alphabetically.

### Upper Keys

**ART GUILD OF THE PURPLE ISLES,** Key Largo; (305) 451-2396; purple islesartguild.com. Established in 1963, this Upper Keys artists society produces art-related events year-round and has more than 1,000 visitors viewing its annual event, held in the Key Largo Public Library from mid-Feb through the first part of Mar. The mission of the Art Guild of the Purple Isles is to foster camaraderie and support, to encourage visual artists with educational activities and venues for exhibiting their work, and to develop a public awareness and appreciation of the visual arts throughout the community.

### Lower Keys

**LOWER KEYS ARTISTS NETWORK,** MM 30.5 Bayside, 221 Key Deer Blvd., Big Pine Key, FL 33043; (305) 872-1828; artistsinparadise.com. Formed in 1994, the Lower Keys Artists Network has about 30 members, and anyone in the Lower Keys interested in art is welcome to join. Meetings are held in season at Artists in Paradise, a co-op gallery in Big Pine. Members assist in judging student art competitions and work with the public library to provide arts and crafts programs for children. The group raises funds for art scholarships through corporate sponsorships. Lower Keys Artists Network also provides demonstrations and seminars on all forms of art, including watercolor, wood sculpture, food sculpture, stained glass, and etching.

## Key West

**FLORIDA KEYS COUNCIL OF THE ARTS, 1100 Simonton St., Key West, FL 33040; (305) 295-4369; keysarts.com.** The Florida Keys Council of the Arts' mission is "to connect artists and arts organizations with each other, with local audiences, and with the important tourism economy." They maintain an artist registry and website, where you'll find complete, year-round listings of the arts and entertainment events in the Keys. In addition, they get the cultural word out to the public via a weekly calendar in five local newspapers and a quarterly brochure of events. The arts council both writes and provides grants that benefit individual artists, arts organizations, schools, and libraries. It is supported by Monroe County and private donations, and has several hundred members throughout the Florida Keys.

**THE STUDIOS OF KEY WEST, 533 Eaton St., Key West, FL 33040; (305) 296-0458; tskw.org.** The Studios of Key West (TSKW) is a nonprofit cultural organization and Key West's only multidisciplinary arts center. They host artists-in-residence in their studio spaces and hold lectures, classes, concerts, performances, and workshops. Their new location on Eaton Street includes a 200-seat professional theater, a large gallery devoted to contemporary art, 9 studios for practicing artists, and 2 dedicated classrooms, including a digital media lab. Check their online catalog regularly, as they offer everything from classes to concerts throughout the year.

## THEATER

### Upper Keys

**ICE (ISLAMORADA COMMUNITY ENTERTAINMENT), MM 87 Bayside, TIB Bank of the Keys Amphitheater, Founders Park, 87000 Overseas Hwy., Islamorada, FL 33036; MM 89.9 Oceanside, Coral Shores High School, 89901 Overseas Hwy., Tavernier, FL 33070; (305) 395-6344; keysice .com.** "Stars above . . . stars onstage" is the bill for bringing great dance, music, and theater to the Upper Keys. These venues invite friends, neighbors, and visitors to enjoy wonderful performances in the Founders Park amphitheater or in the Coral Shores High School of the Performing Arts. The calendar sparkles with concert series, special events, and plays for every age and artistic taste.

## Middle Keys

**MARATHON COMMUNITY THEATER,** MM 49.5 Oceanside, 5101 Overseas Hwy., Marathon, FL 33050; (305) 743-0408; marathontheater.org. Providing live theatrical entertainment to locals and visitors for decades, the Marathon Community Theater annually stages 4 to 6 productions. Past productions include *The Music Man, 9 to 5: The Musical, Ravenscroft,* and *Applause!* Productions utilize full sets and costuming, and actors hail from throughout the Keys, from Key Largo to Key West. The group also hosts other productions, ranging from art shows and concerts to a summer theater program for children.

## Key West

**FRINGE THEATER OF KEY WEST,** various locations; (786) 598-2221; keywestfringe.org. The Fringe's approach is immersion theater—performing in settings that suit a specific play. Past shows include the Tennessee Williams play *Suddenly Last Summer,* which takes place in a New Orleans garden and was performed at the Peggy Mills garden at The Gardens Hotel; *Boston Marriage* by David Mamet, which called for a Victorian setting and was presented at The Carriage Trade, a Victorian guesthouse; and *Weeds* by Tony Konrath and Vanessa McCaffrey, about the infamous Key West fire chief Bum Farto, which was presented at 1907 Old Firehouse Museum.

★**NUTCRACKER KEY WEST,** Tennessee Williams Theatre, 5901 West College Rd., Stock Island; (305) 304-1726; nutcrackerkeywest.com. The children of Key West, under the direction of founder Joyce Stahl, will leave you breathless with their annual artistic production of *The Nutcracker.* This classic ballet is all done with fabulous professionalism, but with a Keys twist. King Neptune, the queen, and her cavaliers perform their magic along with local kids who dance as baby chicks, toy soldiers, angelfish, reef fish, and tiny shrimp. Worthy of a standing ovation every time, performances are scheduled in the first week of Dec.

**RED BARN THEATRE,** 319 Duval St. (rear), Key West, FL 33040; (305) 296-9911; redbarntheatre.com. The restored carriage house that hosts the Red Barn Theatre has stood in the shadows of one of Key West's oldest houses, now the Key West Women's Club, for more than 50 years. Restored as a professional theater in 1980, the 88-seat structure's size and layout is organized so that there isn't a bad seat in the house. The Red Barn Theatre does 5 or 6 professional shows from Nov through May, including comedies, musicals, and dramas like *Bingo! A Winning Musical, God of Carnage,* and *Forbidden Broadway.* Each July, they host the Key West Summer Stage (keywestsummerstage.com).

**★KEY WEST THEATER,** 512 Eaton Street, Key West, FL 33040; face book.com/keywesttheater. The brand new Key West Theater is the go-to venue for cutting-edge entertainment in the Florida Keys. Housed in a historic Baptist church that was recently renovated, restored, and transformed into a vibrant theatrical venue, the Key West Theater produces the following events annually: world premieres of original plays written by Key West writers; the wildly popular Sunday Ramble, live music featuring Key West's best artists (some of whom have recorded their albums in the theater's music studio); Broadway stars performing cabaret shows; The Bone Island Variety show, during which Key West's favorite acts offer up sketches, comedy, great music, and artist interviews; screenings of original short films and documentaries, and so much more.

**TENNESSEE WILLIAMS FINE ARTS CENTER,** 5901 West College Rd., Stock Island, FL 33040; (305) 296-1520 or (305) 295-7676 (tickets); ten nesseewilliamstheatre.com. The Tennessee Williams Fine Arts Center opened in January 1980 on the campus of Florida Keys Community College with the world premiere of Tennessee Williams's unpublished play, *Will Mr. Merriweather Return from Memphis?* Named for one of Key West's most illustrious writers, this 478-seat, air-conditioned theater produces a full season of dance, theater, chamber music, and shows by nationally known performing artists. Professional touring companies, like *Spamalot* and Alvin Ailey American Dance Theatre, bring a wave of nationally recognized artists to the Florida Keys.

**WATERFRONT PLAYHOUSE,** 310 Wall St., Key West, FL 33040; (305) 294-5015; waterfrontplayhouse.org. Once the site of Porter's warehouse, Waterfront Playhouse's physical structure served as an icehouse in the 1880s, storing blocks of ice cut from New England ponds and brought to Key West as ships' ballast. The Waterfront Playhouse restored the old warehouse into the current theater, infusing the crumbly stone walls with enduring creativity. The Waterfront Playhouse is dedicated to expanding knowledge of dramatic works to the general public

i For listings of current shows in Key West or to purchase tickets, visit keystix .com or call (305) 295-7676.

and presents a variety of musicals, comedies, and dramas, like *The Full Monty*, *August: Osage County*, and *Xanadu: The Musical*.

## CINEMA

### Upper Keys

**B&B THEATRES TAVERNIER CINEMA 5,** MM 92 Bayside, 91298 Overseas Hwy., Tavernier, FL 33040; (305) 853-7003 (movie hotline) or (305) 853-7004 (office); bbtheatres.com. This is a 5-plex theater that features first-run films with Dolby-enhanced sound and the latest technology. Matinees daily, late-night shows on weekends. Located in the Tavernier Towne Center.

### Middle Keys

**MARATHON COMMUNITY CINEMA,** MM 49.5 Oceanside, 5101 Overseas Hwy., Marathon, FL 33050; (305) 743-0288; marathontheater .org. This is no average movie theater. Owned and operated by the Marathon Community Theater, the cinema is small and intimate, although the screen is large. Seating is informally arranged in comfy barrel chairs around cocktail-style tables. A single movie is shown twice nightly. Matinees are offered on Sat and Sun. The theater is tucked behind Marathon Liquors.

### Key West

**REGAL CINEMA KEY WEST 6,** 3338 Roosevelt Blvd., Searstown Shopping Center, Key West, FL 33040; (305) 296-7211; regalcinemas.com. Six movies run concurrently at the Florida Keys' first multiplex cinema. All tickets for shows before 6 p.m. are discounted. Listening devices for the hearing-impaired are available here as well.

★**TROPIC CINEMA,** 416 Eaton St., Key West, FL 33040; (305) 295-9493; keywestfilm.org. The Key West Film Society formed in 1998 to bring the area the best of independent, foreign, and alternative movies. Since then Tropic Cinema has shown hundreds of films and even hosted premieres. Highlights have included the Cuban music documentary *Buena Vista Social Club*; a costumed *Rocky Horror Picture Show*, replete with stage show; and for the avant-garde, *The Celebration*—an ultimate in contrast: no lighting, no music, and shot on video. The purpose of the Key West Film Society and Tropic Cinema is to showcase film in Key West and to be a magnet for this art form.

## CONCERTS

### Upper and Middle Keys

**THE FLORIDA KEYS CONCERT ASSOCIATION, INC.,** Marathon and Islamorada; floridakeysconcerts.com. Islamorada and Marathon venues hold 4 to 6 concerts annually, quite often at San Pablo Catholic Church (MM 53.5

Oceanside). A well-balanced season of offerings includes classical and semiclassical music, encompassing voice, strings, brass, and organ. You may purchase a subscription to all concerts or buy tickets at the door.

## LIVE MUSIC AND SHOWS

### Upper Keys

**CARIBBEAN CLUB, MM 104.5 Bayside, 104080 Overseas Hwy., Key Largo, FL 33037; (305) 451-9970; caribbeanclubkl.com.** Bogie and Bacall are alive and well in this famous Key Largo bar and restaurant. The walls are filled with memorabilia from the 1948 classic movie *Key Largo,* even though most of the movie was filmed on Hollywood soundstages and back lots. Great sunset views and live music Thurs through Sun night draw late-night crowds, making this a popular locals' hangout. The Caribbean Club is cash only.

### Middle Keys

**BRASS MONKEY, MM 50 Oceanside, 234 55th St., Marathon, FL 33050; (305) 743-4028.** This long-established bar and liquor store is a regulars' hangout in Marathon. Billing themselves as "the in place of the out islands," the Brass Monkey serves up not only lunch and dinner but also live music 6 nights a week. The lounge opens early and closes in the wee hours. "That Funky Monkey" is still going strong after more than 30 years!

### Key West

**AQUA NIGHTCLUB, 711 Duval St., Key West, FL 33040; (305) 294-0555; aquakeywest.com.** Live entertainment at the predominantly gay Aqua Nightclub includes nightly drag shows, karaoke, a weekly "Aqua Idol" competition on Tues night, poker games Sat and Sun, and a dance club complete with DJs every weekend. No matter what time you stop in at Aqua, there will be something fabulous going on.

**BOTTLECAP LOUNGE AND LIQUOR, 1128 Simonton St., Key West, FL 33040; (305) 296-2807; bottlecapkeywest.com.** Every Fri during happy hour at the Bottlecap, all the tips go to a Key West nonprofit, and locals turn up in droves to support their favorite charities. The Bottlecap is home to two rooms, a patio bar, a pool table, as well as DJs and live entertainment to keep you occupied all night long.

**BULL & WHISTLE, 224 Duval St., Key West, FL 33040; (305) 296-4545; bullkeywest.com.** This establishment is actually three bars in one. The Bull is downstairs and features live music in an open-air setting. The Whistle is upstairs and offers pool and video games, along with a great view of Duval Street from the balcony. The Garden of Eden, on the very top, has a great view of Key West . . . and more: It's the only clothing-optional roof garden in town.

**CAPTAIN TONY'S SALOON, 428 Greene St., Key West, FL 33040; (305) 294-1838; capttonyssaloon.com.** Just half a block off Duval, this watering hole is the site of Hemingway's original bar stool and Key West's first hanging tree, which grows through the roof of the bar. Captain Tony's is part of Key West's history, as it is the original location of Sloppy Joe's. Once owned by Captain Tony Tarracino, a friend of Jimmy Buffett's and a former Key West mayor, the saloon features walls covered with bras and business cards. Live entertainment is offered nightly.

**801 BOURBON BAR AND CABARET, 801 Duval St., Key West, FL 33040; (305) 294-9354; 801bourbon.com.** With a clientele consisting primarily of gay patrons and tourists, 801 offers two stories of fun. A second floor features live entertainment, with karaoke at 4 p.m. and Drag Queen Bingo at 5 p.m. every Sun, and drag shows nightly, starring the world-famous Sushi. You might have seen her on CNN New Year's Eve counting down the seconds to the new year while being lowered in a giant red high heel. She even managed to make Anderson Cooper blush.

★**THE GREEN PARROT BAR, 601 Whitehead St., Key West, FL 33040; (305) 294-6133; greenparrot.com.** Frequented primarily by locals, and known simply as "The Parrot," this eclectic bar is housed in an 1890s-era building half a block off Duval, down Southard Street. Walls are adorned with unusual oversize portraits and a mural of the Garden of Eden. Weekends feature local and national bands playing everything from ukuleles in harmony to blues and zydeco, and the dance floor is usually crowded.

### Key West Bar Card

Looking for a deal on cocktails in Key West? Most establishments have daily happy hour drink specials between 4 and 6 p.m., but you might have to ask for them, as they aren't always advertised. For a drink special any time of day or night at numerous locations throughout Key West, check out the Key West Bar Card. After purchasing the card, you'll get one 2-for-1 drink in any participating bar per day. You can visit as many bars on the card in one day as you like, but you can only use the card once per bar. The card costs $20 to purchase and is good for one calendar year. Visit keywestbarcard.com for more information.

## Key West's Bettie Page and Burlesque History and Future

Notorious burlesque dancer and actress Sally Rand was featured at the 1933 Chicago World's Fair and in the 1934 film *Bolero*. Sally's claims to fame were her trademark fan dance and bubble dance. Ms. Rand was a Key West winter resident for many years, often visiting the troops at the local Navy Hospital. Her historic gingerbread home on Eisenhower Drive is a far cry from its flamboyant mistress. Also, the world's most famous pin-up model of the 1940s, Bettie Page, met and married a young man in Key West prior to her retirement and leaving the area. Her spirit lives on as numerous burlesque shows are held at various locations around the island throughout the year. Visit keystix.com for individual show information and to purchase tickets.

**RICK'S KEY WEST, 202-208 Duval St., Key West, FL 33040; (305) 296-5513; ricksanddurtyharrys.com.** Rick's Key West offers eight night spots in one complex, including a wine and martini bar, a dance club, a VIP bar, and a daiquiri bar. In addition, Rick's Downstairs Bar offers live entertainment from 4 p.m. until midnight. The Tree Bar allows you to sit and sip a spell, all the while watching the sights of Duval Street pass by. The band at Durty Harry's starts at 8 p.m. and plays live rock 'n' roll until 4 a.m. This bar also has a television wall, which shows all major sporting events. And for a little more risqué entertainment, the Red Garter Saloon is a mirror-and-brass adult club. Pick your pleasure.

**SCHOONER WHARF BAR, 202 William St., Key West, FL 33040; (305) 292-3302; schoonerwharf.com.** Dockside at the Key West Historic Seaport is the open-air, thatched-palm Schooner Wharf, which bills itself as "a last little piece of old Key West." The place offers outdoor thatched-umbrella tables, a covered bar, and grill, and features live jazz, rhythm and blues, and island music nightly.

**SLOPPY JOE'S BAR, 201 Duval St., Key West, FL 33040; (305) 294-5717; sloppyjoes.com.** It's no wonder this was Hemingway's favorite watering hole. The upbeat atmosphere of Sloppy Joe's is contagious. The bar opened in 1933 on the site of what is now Captain Tony's Saloon. In 1937 it moved to its current location. Some say that Hemingway did some writing in the back rooms of the bar and kept a few of his manuscripts locked up here. Photos of the author line the walls. Live entertainment is offered from noon to 2 a.m. daily. A gift shop sells T-shirts, hats, and other Sloppy Joe's souvenirs.

SMOKIN' TUNA, 4 Charles St., Key West, FL 33040; (305) 517-6350; smokintunasaloon.com. The official headquarters of the Key West Songwriters Festival, Smokin' Tuna is the newest venue where you can find popular local musicians playing live nightly. The music starts at 5 p.m. every day of the week. Sit outside in the open-air courtyard under the stars or have some great local seafood at their raw bar.

## ART GALLERIES

Unique galleries dot the Florida Keys, often tucked amid commercial shops in a strip mall or gracing a freestanding building off the beaten track. In Key West, galleries abound along Duval Street, and you'll also find small lofts and garrets secreted off the beaten track down narrow lanes. Come along for a gallery crawl through the high spots of the Florida Keys' art scene, from Key Largo to Key West. Consult keysarts.com for even more information.

### Upper Keys

THE GALLERY AT KONA KAI, Kona Kai Resort, MM 97.8 Bayside, 97802 Overseas Hwy., Key Largo, FL 33037; (305) 852-7200 or (800) 365-7829; konakairesort.com. The Gallery at Kona Kai secrets away a small yet exquisite changing exhibit of fine art treasures. The gallery showcases artists from around the world, as well as prominent South Florida artists such as Clyde Butcher, who is known for his hauntingly surreal black-and-white photography of the Everglades and Big Cypress National Preserve.

> **i** *Seven New Friends,* by renowned sculptor J. Seward Johnson, greets travelers at Key West International Airport. The group stands atop the airport terminal eagerly awaiting your arrival. Johnson's other works are showcased at the Key West Museum of Art and History at the Custom House (see the Attractions chapter).

KEY LARGO ART GALLERY, MM 103 Bayside, 103200 Overseas Hwy., #10 Central Plaza, Key Largo, FL 33037; (305) 451-0052; keylargoartgallery .com. The theme of the Key Largo Art Gallery is to provide a creative haven for artists and to educate the community on various art forms. The camaraderie of the group of artists housed here allows an explosion of creative talent. A few years ago, one of the original "Highwaymen" was featured at the gallery. The Florida African Highwaymen were given that name in the 1950s because they traveled the roads and used their vehicles as showcases for their art, selling alongside highways. The gallery also showcases artists Gloria Avner, Tina Dykes, Liz Queeny, and Michael Mayer, among others.

★**RAIN BARREL VILLAGE OF ARTISTS AND CRAFTSPEOPLE,** MM 86.7 Bayside, 86700 Overseas Hwy., Islamorada, FL 33036; (305) 852-3084; rainbarrelsculpture.com. The infamous *Betsy the Lobster* stands to greet shoppers at the entrance to this artist colony. At 30 feet tall and 40 feet in length, she is a showstopper! The Rain Barrel Village of Artists and Craftspeople is a garden complex of creativity. The 2,000-square-foot mixed-media gallery features an array of paintings, sculptures, woodwork, and decorative glass. You'll find an eclectic assortment of art and craft creations, including ceramics and an expansive wind chime collection.

**REDBONE SALTWATER ART GALLERY,** MM 81 Oceanside, 200 Morada Way, Islamorada, FL 33036; (305) 664-2002; redbone.org. The Redbone Saltwater Art Gallery features a variety of saltwater and marine art and sculptures from local artists and others noted for their works related to sportfishing, such as Don Ray, James Harris, and C. D. Clarke. Redbone is Florida's largest saltwater-fishing art gallery.

**STACIE KRUPA STUDIO GALLERY OF ART,** MM 82.9 Oceanside, 82935 Overseas Hwy., Ste. 1, Islamorada, FL 33036; (305) 942-0614; staciekrupa.com. You can watch Stacie Krupa, artist-in-residence, as she creates her huge, vibrant, mixed-media works on canvas at this contemporary, SoHo-style gallery. A powerful combination of bright colors and massive images, some of which depict Florida Keys birds and fish, Krupa's expressive creations will knock your sandals off.

### Lower Keys

**ARTISTS IN PARADISE,** MM 30.5 Bayside, 221 Key Deer Blvd., Big Pine Key, FL 33043; (305) 872-1828; artistsinparadise.com. Artists in Paradise is a cooperative gallery in Big Pine run by the artists from the Lower Keys Artists Network (see the listing in this chapter), who use the gallery to display their work. More than 30 artists currently show works done in a variety of media: sculpture, oil, watercolor, acrylic, pen and ink, pottery, copper, and stained glass. The gallery is open daily.

### Key West

**ALAN S. MALTZ GALLERY,** 1210 Duval St., Key West, FL 33040; (305) 294-0005; alanmaltz.com. Using the mystical nature of light, Alan S. Maltz, a world-renowned fine-art photographer, is an inspiration with his haunting and magical images. When you enter his gallery and view the art on the walls, you feel as though you are looking at the actual scene he photographed, not just a piece of artwork. His pieces are large and compelling. Alan's framing technique is as unique as his talent, because he has the ability to keep his audience involved in the piece as a whole.

**FLORIDA KEYS COMMUNITY COLLEGE, 5901 West College Rd., Stock Island, FL 33040; (305) 296-9081; fkcc.edu.** Florida Keys Community College stages 4 art shows a year in the Library Gallery. Invitational shows are held in Oct and Feb, and the Florida Artist series is showcased in Jan and Feb. Student work is exhibited during the month of Apr.

**THE GALLERY ON GREENE, 606 Greene St., Key West, FL 33040; (305) 294-1669; galleryongreene.com.** Curated by Nance Frank, the Gallery on Greene is a collection of Key West art with an emphasis on works of authentic, historic importance and local charm, from 1934 to present day. Among the offerings here are works by the late part-time Key West resident Jeff MacNelly (he drew the cartoon strip *Shoe*) and Henry La Cagnina, the last survivor of 12 artists brought to Key West in the 1930s by the WPA.

**GINGERBREAD SQUARE GALLERY, 1207 Duval St., Key West, FL 33040; (305) 296-8900; gingerbreadsquaregallery.com.** Billed as Key West's oldest private art gallery, established in 1974, Gingerbread Square Gallery on upper Duval features sculptures, art glass, one-person shows, and ongoing presentations of the highly acclaimed works of Key West's favorite artists. Sal Salinero, whose oils depict the treasures of the rain forest, is a featured artist.

**GLASS REUNIONS, 825 Duval St., Key West, FL 33040; (305) 294-1720; glassreunions.com.** Glass is the business here, and you can get it in almost any form or color imaginable. Lamps, vases, and mirror wall hangings all showcase the talents of the various artists. For the traditionalist, a wide selection of stained-glass art is available.

**GUILD HALL GALLERY, 614 Duval St., Key West, FL 33040; (305) 296-6076; guildhallgallerykw.com.** More than 20 local artists display their work here, presented in a vast array of media. Most of the pieces focus on island life, with a definite Bahamian and Caribbean influence thrown in. Head upstairs for more unusual, and larger, works of art. This is Key West's original artists' co-op, established in 1976.

**HAITIAN ART COMPANY, 605 Simonton St., Ste. A, Key West, FL 33040; (305) 296-8932; haitian-art-co.com.** Bold, wild colors and primitive designs mark the artistic offerings of Haiti, displayed in the multiple rooms of the

# Close- up

# Art Here, Art There, Art Everywhere

The Florida Keys Council of the Arts created Art in Public Places to visually maintain the character, identity, and history of our island community. This public display of creative talent charges no admission fees for events. Some works are permanently mounted in or on buildings, and the pieces are appropriate for all age groups. Visit artinpublicplaceskw.com for more information.

Haitian Art Company. The intricate paisley-style designs often weave an image of a serpent or wild animal within the overall picture. The work of Haiti is a study of form and color not readily encountered in this country. All pieces are originals.

**HANDS ON,** 1206 Duval St., Key West, FL 33040; (305) 296-7399; hands ongallery.com. The gallery is home to the work of 30-plus artists, each with a unique style dedicated to wearable art. Shop here for handcrafted earrings, bracelets, and beads to accessorize your wearable art, as well as an array of other fine American-made crafts.

★**HARRISON GALLERY,** 825 White St., Key West, FL 33040; (305) 294-0609; harrison-gallery.com. Sculptor Helen Harrison and her husband, Ben, a musician and author, have operated this charming gallery since 1986. Helen's spirit is discovered in a calabash, a palm frond, and a gourd. Her pieces are just glorious! In addition to Helen's own work, changing exhibitions highlight local artists. Open daily.

**ISLAND NEEDLEWORK,** 527 Fleming St., Key West, FL 33040; (305) 296-6091; islandneedlepoint.com. Julie Pischke is one of a handful of needlepoint designers who specialize in tropical designs. Her award-winning creations draw from the colors and textures of her home in the Florida Keys, and she offers her art on pillows, bags, belts, shoes, rugs, and footstools. Julie's bold, colorful, and eclectic motifs befit their inspiration.

**KEY WEST ART CENTER AND GALLERY,** 301 Front St., Key West, FL 33040; (305) 294-1241; keywestartcenter.com. This nonprofit organization is devoted to encouraging local talent by giving artists a canvas for their creativity. Dues and commissions for their works keep this artistic colony thriving. Housed in a historic building that was once a grocery store near the waterfront, the Key West Art Center offers a wide variety of art for sale created by dedicated local artists.

**LUCKY STREET GALLERY, 540 Greene St., Key West, FL 33040; (305) 294-3973; luckystreetgallery.com.** Contemporary fine art of the cutting-edge variety is the focus here. Sculptures by John Martini and the works of famed Key West artists Rick Worth, Lauren McAloon, and Debra Yates have been featured, as well as many others. New shows are staged often and coincide with gallery events.

**SODU GALLERY, 1102B Duval St., Key West, FL 33040; (305) 296-4400; sodugallery.com.** An unrestricted window display showcases amazing local artists, enabling them to display their wares in grand style. Jewelry, acrylics, paintings, and pencil drawings, with painting on furniture, dinnerware, and fabrics, fill the shop with excitement and fun.

**SOUTH POINTE GALLERY, 1201 Duval St., Key West, FL 33040; (305) 295-9354; authenticvintageposters.com.** The owner of South Pointe Gallery travels extensively in pursuit of authentic vintage posters to add to her collection. The striking works are primarily French, with a mix of American, German, and Italian. Decorating with posters is not a unique idea but very appealing due to their bold images and prices that are less expensive than other art forms.

**WYLAND GALLERIES, 102 and 623 Duval St., Key West, FL 33040; (305) 295-5240 and (305) 292-4998; wylandkw.com.** Wyland's world-renowned, life-size whaling wall murals reflect his unshakable commitment to saving the Earth's oceans, and thereby its marine creatures. In 2007 Wyland painted his 95th and final "Whaling Wall" in the US at MM 99.2 in Key Largo. The mural covers 7,500 square feet and wraps completely around a building (a whaling cube). A time-lapse view can be seen at wylandfoundation.org. The Key West galleries showcase Wyland's art, as well as other passionate nature-inspired artists.

# Shopping

So here is the ultimate road map to the shops. We describe our favorite shops by category (Bookstores, Clothing & Jewelry, Home Decor, and Gift & Specialty Shops) and location within each category. Many of our shops are open daily until 9 p.m., especially in Key West, but many close on Sunday. Some close on different days, so it is best to call before venturing out, as hours and days of operation can vary from season to season.

## BOOKSTORES

### Upper Keys

**HOOKED ON BOOKS, MM 81.9 Oceanside, 81909 Overseas Hwy., Islamorada, FL 33036; (305) 517-2602; hookedonbooksfloridakeys.com.** Hooked on Books is filled to the rafters with used books and paperbacks and run by true book lovers who will be happy to help you find anything you're looking for. This shop is perfect for travelers, specializing in books that are by local authors writing about Florida Keys history, fishing, diving, cooking, and landscape. In addition to their extensive Florida and Florida Keys collection, Hooked on Books stocks a large selection of current fiction and nonfiction titles, both new and used, several options for a perfect beachside companion. There is also a children's room with books for all ages.

### Key West

**KEY WEST ISLAND BOOKSTORE, 513½ Fleming St., Key West, FL 33040; (305) 294-2904; kwislandbooks.com.** This shop sells everything from the classics to the bestsellers, along with topical nonfiction and the works of Florida Keys and Key West writers. The store is especially supportive of Florida authors and often hosts book-signing events that generate lots of local excitement and a party atmosphere. Carl Hiaasen, James Hall, Jimmy Buffett, Philip Caputo, James Dickey, and Thomas McGuane have all signed books here. Be sure to check the rare-book room in the back.

## CLOTHING & JEWELRY

### Upper Keys

**BLUE MARLIN JEWELRY, MM 81.9 Oceanside, 81915 Overseas Hwy., Islamorada, FL 33036; (305) 664-8004 or (888) 826-4424; bluemarlinjewelry**

.com. Discover treasure in this interesting jewelry shop. Blue Marlin sports a great selection of gold, sterling silver, or gem-encrusted charms, depicting most of the species of our ecosystem. These pieces are perfect touchstones to bring home and help you recall your time spent at the Keys.

**MILK & HONEY, MM 82.2 Oceanside, 81681 Overseas Hwy., Islamorada FL 33036; (305) 304-9107; facebook.com/milknhoneystore.** This sweet jewelry store sells select designer pieces that will make you feel special. Known for unique styles that are feminine and fun to wear, specializing in boho beach style and street indie-label outfits and accessories for women.

**SANDAL FACTORY OUTLET, MM 102.4 Oceanside, 102411 Overseas Hwy., Key Largo, FL 33037; (305) 453-9644; sandalfactory.com.** The Sandal Factory Outlet allows you to fit yourself. Pick from a copious sea of ladies' sandals—strappy, sporty, and utilitarian. Men and children can be accommodated here, too. You won't find every style in every size, but you can choose from hundreds of designs, and there are always deals offered for the smart shoppers among us.

★**WORLD WIDE SPORTSMAN, Bass Pro Shops, MM 81.5 Bayside, 81576 Overseas Hwy., Islamorada, FL 33036; (305) 664-4615 or (800) 227-7776; basspro.com.** Don't miss a stop at World Wide Sportsman, the massive fishing emporium that is an Islamorada must-see. World Wide showcases a real boat (the *Pilar*) inside its walls, as well as an impressively large marlin statue, perfect for some choice selfies to share. In addition to the other treasures, World Wide is stocked to the rafters with a wide assortment of fishing tackle (see the Outfitters section in the Fishing chapter), and a full line of men's and women's clothing.

## Middle Keys

**BAYSHORE CLOTHING, MM 52 Oceanside, 8911 Overseas Hwy., Marathon FL 33050; (305) 743-8430; facebook.com/BayshoreClothing.** Bayshore caters to men's and women's tropical garment needs, a guaranteed attitude adjustment from the busy workaday world up north. The children's department beckons parents and especially grandparents with a cute selection of swimsuits, warm-weather clothing, and toys.

## Key West

**ABACO GOLD, 418 Front St., Key West, FL 33040; (305) 296-0086; abacogold-keywest.com.** The jewelry line here is exclusive—like no other in the Florida Keys, or elsewhere for that matter. Abaco Gold specializes in unique nautical designs featuring mermaids, dolphins, and tropical themes. They also have an entire collection designed just for dog lovers!

★**ASSORTMENT, INC.,** 514 Fleming St., Key West, FL 33040; (305) 294-4066. This chic men's clothing store, just a few steps off Duval Street, carries the latest in men's casual fashions with a dressy flair. Handsome jackets, shirts, slacks, and shoes are tastefully displayed. Polo by Ralph Lauren, Barry Bricken, and Cole Haan shoes are just a few of the lines you'll find here. Assortment, Inc. also offers great-looking gifts and accessories for that special guy in your life.

★**BESAME MUCHO,** 315 Petronia St., Key West, FL 33040; (305) 294-1928; besamemucho.net. Step into this tastefully decorated shop, and you will feel as though you have stepped back in time. The shelves are filled with items that look as though they belong on a romantic movie set, circa 1940. Take your time to examine their unique assortment of charming objects that inspire feelings of "Old World simplicity."

**BIRKENSTOCK OF OLD TOWN,** 612 Duval St., Key West, FL 33040; (305) 294-8318 or (800) 330-2475 (orders); birkenstore.com. With sandals being essential apparel for island life, it makes good sense for Birkenstock to have a large, full-service store right in the middle of it all. Although Birkenstocks don't come cheap, the shoes are exceptionally durable and comfortable. You can sometimes get a pretty good deal here on discontinued styles. This store also does in-house repairs.

**BLUE BOUTIQUE,** 718 Caroline St., Key West, FL 33040; (305) 292-5172; blueislandstore.com. Shop here for classic linen skirts, tops, jackets, pants, and dresses that will look just as appropriate on Fifth Avenue as they do on Duval Street. Be sure to check out the accessories here, too. The brilliant colors are a perfect complement to the easy-fitting, understated styles. Men's fashions are available, too!

**COMMOTION (LOCAL COLOR),** 800 Caroline St., Key West, FL 33040; (305) 292-3635; localcolorkeywest.com/commotion. Casually elegant island separates that are as fun to wear as they are practical to own await you here. These natural, washable linen and flax fabrics will help you keep your cool—a definite must in the Florida Keys. Best of all, unlike some island designs that look out-of-place outside the tropics, these will look just as great when you get back home.

**FAIRVILLA MEGASTORE,** 520 Front St., Key West, FL 33040; (305) 292-0448; fairvilla.com. When locals are in need of a corset, tutu, or feather boa for one of the numerous events during Fantasy Fest (see the Events chapter), they head to Fairvilla, which also sells intimate apparel, adult DVDs, and more. You must be 18 or over to enter the store.

★**GILDED PEACH INSPIRED STUDIO**, 1114-B Truman Ave., Key West, FL 33040; gildedpeach.com. Owner and jewelry designer Abigail Houff creates one-of-a-kind handcrafted earrings, necklaces, and bracelets using semi-precious stones sourced from all over the world. Her jewelry is extremely popular with locals as it is inspired by the vibrant flora and fauna found on our island.

★**ISLE STYLE SALON, SPA & BOUTIQUE**, 1204 Simonton St., Key West, FL 33040; (305) 292-4000; islestylekeywest.com. Step inside this airy boutique packed with designs from artisans all over the world and meet the owner who is a stylist. The stock changes frequently, so one visit may not fill your shopping bag. Also on the property is a spa where you can get a massage, facial, manicure, and pedicure. So, you can shop till you drop, be revived, and then do it all over again.

**JIMMY BUFFETT'S MARGARITAVILLE RETAIL**, 500 Duval St., Key West, FL 33040; (305) 296-9089 or (800) 262-6835 (mail order); margarita villekeywest.com. Everything here is tuned to one thing: the works of Key West's favorite son, Jimmy Buffett. His CDs are available here, along with tons of shirts, books, photos, and other Parrothead paraphernalia. Spend some time perusing the walls—they're packed with photos and memorabilia related to events in the life of the man from Margaritaville. This place is a must-stop for Buffett fans old and new.

**KINO SANDALS**, 107 Fitzpatrick St., Key West, FL 33040; (305) 294-5044; kinosandalfactory.com. After Roberto and Margarita Lopez emigrated from Cuba, they opened a sandal factory in Key West in 1966. Using his nickname, Kino, for the business, Roberto built a lovely Cuban-style factory that is still in operation today. Here you choose from a variety of leathers and colors for your custom sandals. Prices are extremely reasonable (typically under $15 per pair), and they make a terrific souvenir.

**LILLY PULITZER**, 600 Front St., Key West, FL 33040; (305) 295-0995; lilly pulitzer.com. In 1960 a young socialite, Lilly Pulitzer, opened a juice stand in West Palm Beach. When her uniform (a colorful printed shift dress she wore to hide fruit juice stains) seemed more popular than her juice, the famous "Lillys" were created. Today Lilly Pulitzer shops offer the signature piece in bright and fun prints, in various tantalizing colors. You can also find jewelry, shoes, and a clothing line for children at this chic boutique.

**LIPPY'S HOT HATS OF KEY WEST**, 613 Duval St., Key West, FL 33040; (305) 294-1333; lippyshothatskeywest.com. If you're heading outdoors in Key West, you'd best wear a hat. And you're sure to find a flattering one at this shop devoted entirely to headgear, including everything from canvas caps to straw boaters for both men and women.

★**LOCAL COLOR**, 276 Margaret St., Historic Seaport, Key West, FL 33040; (305) 292-3635; localcolorkeywest.com. This Margaret Street shop is where locals and tourists come to purchase the colorful, comfortable clothing that fits the Key West lifestyle. In addition to casual apparel for men and women, you'll find fun hats, handbags, and beautiful jewelry to complete your island look.

**NEPTUNE DESIGNS**, 301 Duval St., Key West, FL 33040; (305) 294-8131; orchidspecies.com/neptune2.htm. Most of the jewelry filling this shop has an oceanic motif and is wrought in gold or silver. Leaping silver dolphins frolic with golden, gliding sea turtles on necklaces displayed on a black background. Gold mounted treasure coins and Tahitian black pearls are also sold in this fine store that loves to collaborate with patrons to make a special, custom piece.

**RON JON SURF SHOP**, 503 Front St., Key West, FL 33040; (305) 293-8880; ronjons.com. Two stories of the latest beachwear and accessories await you at the Ron Jon Surf Shop Key West location. They carry everything you need to spend a day in the sun, from swimsuits to boogie boards and even skateboards.

---

### "KW" Jewelry

Created in Key West for Key Westers and visitors alike, this jewelry design has made a huge hit with men, women, and kids. The design features the initials "KW" hooked together, with a braided nautical wrap signifying the tribute to Key West and the islands' connection to the sea. For those who wear such pieces, this symbol means they will always return here. A lot of stores carry these items, but to ensure you are getting the real thing, the following list is a good guide: Local Color, 276 Margaret St. (305-292-3635) and 425 Greene St. (305-296-0151); Commotion, 800 Caroline St. (305-292-3364); Lili's, 424 Greene St. (305-292-2343).

---

★**RUBIES & CLAY**, 529 Whitehead St., Key West, FL 33040; (305) 294-5556; rubiesandclay.com. This tiny shop, located down the block from the Mile Marker 0 sign, is packed with fabulous items by Key West's favorite artisans. Must-have items include photography by Rachel Ligon (racheleligon .com) and hand-thrown pottery by fifth-generation Conch Grace Epperly (potterybygrace.com).

**THE SEAM SHOPPE,** 1113 Truman Ave., Key West, FL 33040; (305) 296-9830; tropicalfabricsonline.com. This fabric shop offers a fabulous selection of tropical fabrics for fashion, quilting, and home decor. Patterns include fish, shells, nautical and Hawaiian themes, palm trees, and tropical foliage. You'll find quilt fabrics, batiks, and bark cloth here as well.

**THE SOLE MAN,** 610 Duval St., Key West, FL 33040; (305) 292-2505 or (866) 524-WALK; soleman.com. Everyone who lives here, or visits for any length of time, winds up buying clever, glitzy, fun sandals. The Sole Man has something for every "sole," and you will end up tossing your socks in the back of your drawer or suitcase. Owner John "the Sole Man" Brandolino will be sure to take care of you.

**TIMMY TUXEDOS,** 812 Fleming Sreet, Key West, FL 33040; (305) 294-8897 or (800) 654-2931; timmytuxedos.com. In spite of what you may think about the Keys dress code of flip-flops and T-shirts, we do dress up occasionally, and Timmy's Tuxedos is the only formal attire shop in the Keys. Here you can buy all the "dress-up" garb you need, plus rent jackets and tuxedos. They also carry beautiful Keys prints (some hand-painted!) for ties and cummerbunds, to ensure that your formal gathering has the perfect amount of tropical flair. Call toll-free for more information about these fancy tropical duds.

**WANDERLUST,** 310 Petronia St., Key West, FL 33040; wanderlustkw.com. This beach-chic clothing store carries national lines like Tulle and Level 99 Denim, as well as cute kids' clothing lines like Peppercorn Kids. Great sundresses and one-of-a-kind bags and jewelry are on offer, as well as a small selection of shoes for any occasion. Wanderlust is also home to clothing and accessories by local artists.

## HOME DECOR

### Upper Keys

**THE BANYAN TREE,** MM 81.2 Oceanside, 81197 Overseas Hwy., Islamorada, FL 33036; (305) 664-3433; banyantreegarden.com. A lush, shaded garden courtyard is the cool, unruffled invite greeting you at the Banyan Tree. The proprietors know their stuff with an ever-changing inventory, making the Banyan Tree a real find. An eclectic mix of antiques and contemporary items for home and garden abound.

**THE RAIN BARREL ARTISAN VILLAGE, MM** 86.7 Bayside, 86700 Overseas Hwy., Islamorada, FL 33036; (305) 852-3084; keysdirectory.com/rainbarrel. You can't miss this place! Ready to greet eager shoppers, the famous 30-by-40-foot sculpture of Betsy the Lobster is a great photo opportunity. Inside is a lush, tropical hideaway housing artists and crafters who work in retail shops that are peppered beneath the gumbo-limbos, amid the bougainvillea.

**SEA DRAGON, MM** 82 Oceanside, 82239 Overseas Hwy., Islamorada, FL 33036; (305) 664-0048; seadragonfurniture.com. Billing itself as "exotic island decor," Sea Dragon will help you craft your own Shangri-la. The owners travel to Bali each season to make selections that allow their customers to create a tropical Asian look in their home. Indonesian artwork and teak furniture with unusual pieces make this shop a must-see.

## Middle Keys

★**D'ASIGN SOURCE, MM** 53 Oceanside, 11500 Overseas Hwy., Marathon, FL 33050; (305) 743-7130; dasignsource.com. At D'Asign Source, you'll find the very latest and very best in materials, fixtures, finishes, and designs for home remodeling, building, and furnishing. Even if you aren't in the market for a home makeover, make your way to D'Asign Source's megastore, with home ideas for both indoors and out. Browsing the gigantic showroom is always inspiring.

## Key West

**ARCHEO GALLERY,** 1208 Duval St., Key West, FL 33040; (305) 294-3771; archeogallery.com. Not everyone can trek to Timbuktu, Ouagadougou, Djenne, or Paris, but at this shop you'll be suddenly transported. The owners fly halfway around the world to bring one-of-a-kind rugs, ceremonial pieces, sculptures, and artifacts to their customers.

**COCKTAILS! KEY WEST,** 808 Duval St., Key West, FL 33040; (305) 292-1190; cocktailskeywest.com. This distinctive atelier has all of the accent pieces to fashionably enhance bending your elbow. Hand-painted martini glasses, coasters, towels, cocktail shakers, wine holders, and wall-mounted Key West-themed bottle openers can be found here.

**FUNKY CHICKEN STORE,** 814 Duval St., Key West, FL 33040; (305) 295-9442; funkychickenstore.com. Come here to celebrate the Key West chickens (and roosters). This colorful boutique pays homage to the Key West chickens with paintings and sculptures by local artists, T-shirts, hats, signs, pillows, and even hand-painted "Poultry in Paradise" signs.

SHOPPING

**DUCK AND DOLPHIN ANTIQUES,** 601 Fleming St., Key West, FL 33040; (305) 295-0499. This elegant shop—reminiscent of the antiques shops we've seen in Europe—is filled with ornate furnishings and accent pieces that can only be called *très chic*. You'll find everything from a grand piano to a crystal chandelier. These items are in mint condition, with price tags to match. The staff is friendly and knowledgeable, happy to help find a special piece just for you.

**KEY ACCENTS,** 804 Caroline St., Key West, FL 33040; (305) 293-8555; keyaccents.net. New England in feel but Key West in style, Key Accents is like a breath of fresh air. Nicely displayed inside an old home, articles include furniture, pictures, lamps, and home accessories. The inventory is not large, but the pieces they do offer are an inspiration.

**THE RESTAURANT STORE,** 1111 Eaton St., Key West, FL 33040; (305) 294-7994; keywestchef.com. The Restaurant Store is chock-full of kitchen and cooking gear to feed 5 or 50. You'll discover state-of-the-art utensils, pots and pans, and accessories for culinary aficionados and chefs alike. This store is nirvana for foodies. On Sun in season you can partake in the Key West Artisan Market at this location, sampling good times and good vibes from local artists, chefs, wine experts, beer enthusiasts, and entertainers.

## GIFT & SPECIALTY SHOPS

**Upper Keys**

**ISLAND SMOKE SHOP,** MM 103.5 Bayside, Pink Plaza, 103400 Overseas Hwy., Key Largo, FL 33037; (305) 453-4014 or (800) 680-9701; island

**smokeshop.com.** With more than 1,600 brands and sizes of premium cigars on-site, this is the largest cigar shop in all of South Florida. Showcasing a full line of cigars, lighters, and accessories, it has one of the best selections of pipes in the area, as well as some wonderful house blends of tobacco.

**KEY LIME PRODUCTS AND TROPICAL GIFTS,** MM 95 Oceanside, 95200 Overseas Hwy., Key Largo, FL 33037; (305) 853-0378; keylime products.com. From tangy edibles and thirst-quenching beverages to soothing lotions and luscious bath products, Key Lime Products and Tropical Gifts offers a cornucopia of Florida Keys products. Have no fear about getting this stuff home on the airplane: They ship worldwide, so you can buy full size!

**LARGO CARGO,** MM 103.1 Oceanside, 103101 Overseas Hwy., Key Largo, FL 33037; (305) 451-4242 or (800) 795-8889; largocargo.com. Inside this bright white-and-blue dwelling is some pretty cool stuff for your souvenir collection. They have pirate flags and wind socks with skulls and crossbones, key lime products, tropical apparel, nautical jewelry handcrafted from silver and sea glass, metal sculptures, and the all-time favorite, a message in a bottle.

**PINK JUNKTIQUE,** MM 98 Oceanside, 98275 Overseas Hwy., Key Largo, FL 33037; (305) 853-2620. You can't miss this unusual building going north on the Overseas Highway, as it is hot pink with giant flamingos out front. Inside is an inviting, nostalgic collection of vintage clothing, housewares, bedding, jewelry, and collectibles. The inventory changes constantly, so it is a great place to browse and recall those "happy days" of whatever era you fondly remember.

**SHELL WORLD,** MM 97.5 Bayside, 97600 Overseas Hwy., Key Largo, FL 33037; (305) 852-8245; shellworldflkeys.com. At Shell World, they have your typical clam, oyster, and mussel shells, but they also carry a tremendous variety of other shells from throughout the world. In the aisles throughout the store are conch, abalone, cone, and nautilus shells, as well as wind chimes, jewelry, and flowers made from various shells.

### Marathon

**PIGEON KEY FOUNDATION GIFT SHOP,** MM 47 Oceanside, Pigeon Key Visitor Center, 1 Knights Key Blvd., Marathon, FL 33050; (305) 743-5999; pigeonkey.net. Look for the old red railway car, still sitting on the tracks of Flagler's railroad at MM 47 Oceanside. Hidden unassumingly inside is the Pigeon Key Foundation Gift Shop, which contains numerous Keys memorabilia and gift items. The gift shop, like everything on Pigeon Key, is run by a contingent of loyal volunteers, and all proceeds go to the Pigeon Key Foundation.

## Lower Keys

**LITTLE PALM ISLAND GIFT SHOP,** MM 28.5 Oceanside, 28500 Overseas Hwy., Little Torch Key, FL 33042; (305) 872-2524; littlepalmisland.com/shop. Stop at this mainland substation of Little Palm Island and visit the gift shop. If you go out to Little Palm Island itself, for lunch or dinner or to stay the night, don't miss the island shop. You'll find interesting glassware, sculptures, tote bags, and cookbooks in addition to upscale clothing and straw hats.

> **i** Scan local newspapers and look for yard sales. This is a fun way to get out into the neighborhoods, up and down the Keys, and see how the natives live! The houses and streets of our vacation mecca are beautiful and charming.

## Key West

**DOG 30,** 1025 White St., Key West, FL 33040; (305) 296-4848; facebook.com/dog30kw. Florida Keys residents love their animals, and here at Dog 30 they show how much they care. The owners carry healthy dog and cat food, homemade bakery treats, pet beds, carriers, and even catnip.

**KEY WEST ALOE,** 416 Green St. and 419 Duval St., Key West, FL 33040; (305) 735-4927 and (305) 517-6365; keywestaloe.com. Step into Key West Aloe for a showroom of the only perfumes, skin-care products, and cosmetics to boast a "made in Key West" label. Their products are shipped throughout the world.

**KEY WEST WINERY, INC.,** 103 Simonton St., Key West, FL 33040; (305) 292-1717 or (866) 880-1717; thekeywestwinery.com. This is wine like you've never tasted before: Not one variety is made from grapes! Most of the wines are made from fruits, such as Eleganta, a semisweet red raspberry variety. And 14 Karats, a buttery semidry white wine that is similar to a Chardonnay, is 100 percent carrot and much more flavorful.

**PELICAN POOP SHOPPE,** 314 Simonton St., Key West, FL 33040; (305) 292-9955. This eclectic collection of artwork includes pieces from all over the Caribbean. For a small purchase or a nominal admittance fee, you can tour the private Casa Antigua gardens out back, linked forever to Ernest Hemingway by a quirky twist of fate. He completed *A Farewell to Arms* here while awaiting delivery of his new Ford back in 1928.

**REEF RELIEF ENVIRONMENTAL CENTER & STORE, 631 Greene St., Key West, FL 33040; (305) 294-3100; reefrelief.org.** You can learn about our fragile coral reef here at the Reef Relief Environmental Center. Continuous videos, displays, and free information will heighten your awareness of what you can do to protect North America's only living coral reef. Merchandise on sale includes coral reef books, educational products for both adults and children, and informational videos.

**TOWELS OF KEY WEST, 806 Duval St., Key West, FL 33040; (305) 292-1120; towelsofkeywest.com.** This simple store has been producing towels in all shapes and sizes and for all budgets for over 25 years. Get the best-selling, colorful print terry robe, or immerse yourself in big, warm, oversize, colorful beach and bath towels.

# Appendix:
# Living Here

In this section we feature specific information for residents or those planning to relocate here. Topics include real estate, education, health care, and much more.

# Relocation & Vacation Rentals

Most snowbirds and full-time residents of the Florida Keys (except for the native-born Conchs) first rented homes, condominiums, or mobile homes while on vacation in Paradise. Rentals primarily are classified as short- and long-term. Short-term rental agreements range from a weekend to six months; anything exceeding six months is considered a long-term rental. However, to preserve the integrity of our residential communities, the Monroe County Planning Commission has prohibited short-term rentals of 30 days or less throughout residential areas of unincorporated Monroe County. Incorporated areas such as Islamorada, Layton, Key Colony Beach, Marathon, and Key West can opt for differing regulations. Few short-term rental options are currently available in the Florida Keys, and the competition is fierce for those that are. The best advice we can offer is to work through a rental agent who knows what's legally available, and always book your accommodation early.

## OVERVIEW

Owning a parcel of Paradise in the Florida Keys can be summed up in two words: very expensive. Real estate prices in the Florida Keys depend largely upon access to the water. Direct oceanfront or bayfront property garners the highest prices, followed by property on a canal with an ocean or bay view, and by property on a canal with access to the ocean or bay. Other areas, such as Ocean Reef, Duck Key, and Sunset Key, have special features that make homes desirable—such as gated security, golf courses, swimming pools, strict building covenants, and other community amenities—and owning a home there is pricey indeed.

Some relief is available for certain owners in the form of a homestead exemption. In Florida this exemption allows $25,000 of the assessed value of a house purchased as a primary residence to be exempt from property tax. Real estate taxes in Monroe County are based on a millage rate that changes annually with the county budget and are some of the highest in the state. In addition, besides homeowner's insurance, homeowners must factor in the cost of wind storm and flood insurance to guard against our ever-threatening hurricanes.

Those of us who have chosen to live in the Florida Keys think the price of paradise is worth it. To assist you in your search for a piece of the rock, we provide you with a general overview of the communities of the Florida Keys, as well as the types of homes you'll encounter in our neighborhoods. At the end of the chapter, we include listings of real estate professionals who can assist you in finding a rental property or a home of your own. Look to our Key West section of this chapter for vacation rental and real estate information in our southernmost city.

## RENTAL PROPERTIES

### The Role of Real Estate Agents

Real estate agents handle most short-term rental properties. The exceptions are condominiums that act as hotels and employ on-site managers (see the Accommodations chapter) and homeowners who market rentals on their own. Because of changes in laws as indicated above, the latter choice is becoming more and more scarce.

Depending upon its size and specialty, an agency that handles rentals may list anywhere between 10 and 200-plus short-term rental options. Most large agencies employ sales associates who specialize in short-term rentals. Except for Key West, where agents handle much of the entire island, Florida Keys agents typically specialize within the region of their office (see the Real Estate Companies sections in this chapter).

Finding a rental property through an agency has its advantages. Rental agencies almost always offer descriptions and photographs of available properties and advice on the best option for your needs and desires. Most of them, in fact, maintain websites, which allow you to peruse the options at your leisure and, in most cases, actually see the property you are booking. Agents ensure that a home is clean and that its grounds are maintained.

In order to manage short-term rentals for stays of fewer than 30 days, real estate agencies and/or property owners and managers of condominium complexes must be licensed by the state of Florida. Units rented for fewer than 30 days are considered resort dwellings, and agents and/or owners and managers must therefore abide by a Florida statute that applies to hotels and restaurants. Depending upon the category of accommodation (condominium or single-family home, for instance), safety and health standards set by this statute may require fire extinguishers, electric smoke detectors in sleeping areas, mattress covers on all beds, and deadbolt locks on doors.

### Seasonal Rates

In the wintertime, travelers flock to the Florida Keys seeking respite from the cold and snow. Referred to locally as "snowbirds," these visitors drive rental rates up between the months of Dec and Apr, the high season. Summertime is when diving is typically best (see the Diving & Snorkeling chapter), and it's also the time of year when residents throughout Florida head to the Keys for the relief of the ocean breezes. However, the rest of the mass market moves back home, so rents may be a bit lower than high season during the months of

May through Aug. Sept through Nov is relatively quiet tourism-wise, because autumn is the prime season for hurricanes in the Florida Keys. During this period you'll find reduced rates, and, as long as you keep a watchful eye on the forecasts, you'll be able to enjoy uncrowded shops, attractions, and streets.

## Minimum Stays

Most short-term tenants rent a home or condominium in the Florida Keys for a week to 3 or 4 months. The bulk of the short-term rental market consists of 2-week vacationers, but our islands are also popular with northern residents and retirees who retreat here for the winter. Virtually no private homes are available for rent on a daily basis.

During holidays, such as Christmas and Easter, and special events, including sport lobster season and Fantasy Fest, minimum stays range from 4 days to 2 weeks. Individual property owners establish these policies. Inquire of your rental agent or property owner/manager.

## Options & Restrictions

Owners designate their rental properties as smoking or nonsmoking.

Children are generally welcome, but some condominium complexes restrict the number of children allowed in a single unit. One adults-only facility, Silver Shores, a mobile-home park in Key Largo catering to senior citizens, exists in the Florida Keys.

Condominiums typically do not allow pets, but some single-family homes and mobile-home parks do accept them. An additional security deposit or a fee (sometimes both) is often required. The fee covers the cost of spraying the home for fleas, which ensures accommodations free of pesky insects. Tending to pets outside the rental facility, however, is the owner's responsibility, and fleas can be abundant on hot and humid days.

> **i** In the 1950s Philip Toppino built houses on Summerland Key for avid pilots. The homes sit along the airstrip, and private planes can be parked underneath the houses.

## Reservations & Payment Options

Naturally, the most desirable rental properties tend to book the earliest, and many tenants book the same home for the same weeks year after year. To achieve the greatest selection of rentals, we suggest that you reserve at least 6 months to a year in advance. During holidays the demand for short-term rentals can exhaust the supply. If you plan to travel to the Florida Keys during the high season (Dec through Apr) and holidays (especially Christmas week or during Fantasy Fest), you would be wise to reserve 1 to 2 years in advance.

Payment options vary according to how far in advance you book and when you check in. Typically, an initial deposit of 10 to 25 percent of the total rental cost, made with a personal check or a credit card, will hold a unit. Some agents allow you to pay with cash or credit card upon arrival, provided that you check in during office hours, which vary from agency to agency. Ask about these specifics when you call.

## Security Deposits

Your rental agreement holds you responsible for any damage to the dwelling and its contents. Security deposits provide the homeowner with added protection. As a general rule, count on supplying 50 to 75 percent of one week's rent (slightly more for a monthly rental). Security deposits on large homes with expensive furnishings can be much higher.

## Cancellation Policies

Homeowners set monetary penalties for cancellations anywhere between 30 days in advance of reservations, with a nominal cancellation fee for administrative services, to 60 days in advance, with a full refund. Don't assume that an impending hurricane or other emergency beyond your control will warrant a refund of your payment. In such cases, some homeowners may be generous in providing full or partial refunds or offering credit toward accommodations at a future date—but don't bank on it. Generally, you forfeit your deposit when weather emergencies cancel your vacation plans.

Refund policies are negotiated among the tenant, real estate agency, and property owner, and usually are not included in lease agreements.

## REAL ESTATE: COMMUNITY PROFILES

### Upper Keys

*Key Largo*

Key Largo is popular with divers interested in the abundant reefs within John Pennekamp Coral Reef State Park and the Florida Keys National Marine Sanctuary. And because Key Largo is within 20 miles of the mainland, property here often is in great demand by weekday commuters and South Floridians purchasing weekend retreats. In real estate terms, Key Largo generally includes the exclusive, members-only Ocean Reef subdivision at the extreme northeast edge and encompasses all land southwest to Tavernier.

## Ocean Reef

A luxury subdivision in North Key Largo, Ocean Reef is a private, all-inclusive gated community of large single-family homes, condominiums, and town houses. Properties here attract buyers seeking privacy, exclusivity, and the opportunity to fish, dive, snorkel, swim, shop, and dine out without ever leaving the complex. This community has three golf courses, a marina, and other amenities open only to residents.

## Tavernier

Toward the southern end of Key Largo is Tavernier, one of the Florida Keys' oldest settlements. Some Tavernier homes date from the early farming settlements at the turn of the last century. Plantation Key (its northern end also maintains a Tavernier postal designation) has a wide range of real estate opportunities, with single-family subdivisions primarily bayside. The Snake Creek Drawbridge makes Plantation Key an ideal homesite for owners of large yachts and sailboats.

## Islamorada

Islamorada stretches from Plantation Key to Lower Matecumbe. Lot sizes in Islamorada typically are larger than those in other areas of the Florida Keys, a factor intended to attract builders of large, impressive homes. Upper Matecumbe Key is the heart of Islamorada, commercially developed but with homes tucked along the waterfront in quiet residential areas. Lower Matecumbe Key is Islamorada's predominantly residential island, with a bike path, tennis club, and private beach.

## Layton

The late Del Layton, a Miami grocery store owner, developed tiny Layton into a subdivision in the 1950s. Later he incorporated it as the Florida Keys' smallest city. Except for several oceanfront homes, all single-family residences in Layton are on oceanside canals, with the nearby Channel 5 Bridge allowing access to the bay. Fifteen miles from Marathon and Islamorada, Layton is largely a community of retirees.

## Middle Keys

### Duck Key

Duck Key is composed of five islands connected by white Venetian-style bridges. A series of flow-through canals encircle each island, ensuring that nearly half the homes or lots offer canal-front dockage or open-water views. The uniquely situated islands allow direct access to both the ocean and the Gulf of Mexico. The Duck Key Property Owners Association, an active group, maintains rights-of-way and public-area plantings, has established distinctive signage, and sponsors social events throughout the year. Duck Key Club, a private swim and tennis club, is located on Center Island and also sponsors myriad social activities for its members. Residents pay a small out-of-pocket tax to employ a private security firm to supplement county services. Hawk's Cay Resort is on the first island, Indies Island, which is zoned differently from the rest. The other four islands—Center, Plantation, Harbour, and Yacht Club—are designated for single-family residential housing only. All homes must be of concrete-block-style (CBS) construction.

### Grassy Key

Grassy Key, a sleepy, rural island with a few oceanfront bungalow courts and several restaurants, is distanced from Marathon by preservation lands. With no canals on Grassy Key, there is no pricing middle ground. The area has single-family homes on dry lots or waterfront estates along the Gulf of Mexico and the Atlantic. Grassy Key is now a part of incorporated Marathon.

### Key Colony Beach

Incorporated in 1957, Key Colony Beach—a 285-acre peninsular finger surrounded by incorporated Marathon—developed its property with a row of condominiums directly on the Atlantic and single-family homes built on a series of canals. Key Colony Beach employs its own police and enforces its own signage and zoning ordinances. Accessed by a causeway from US 1, Key Colony Beach has a post office and a few small shops and restaurants.

### Marathon

Marathon was heavily developed in the 1950s, when dredging was relatively commonplace. This area probably has more canals and waterways—and thus more canal-front properties—than any other region of Monroe County. However, with no active zoning ordinances for all these years, in some neighborhoods it is not uncommon to find a run-down mobile home situated next to an upscale canal-front dwelling. Marathon was incorporated in 1999 and now has its own mayor and city commission, as well as the ability to levy citywide property taxes. Marathon is the commercial hub of the Florida Keys, featuring supermarkets, a movie theater, Home Depot, Office Depot, Kmart, and other shops and restaurants.

## Lower Keys

### Big Pine Key

This rural, semi-isolated island has acres of open space and limited development potential. Home to the National Key Deer Refuge, the island is popular with many Key West and Marathon workday commuters. Big Pine Key probably offers the best value for the money in affordable housing.

### Little Torch & Ramrod Keys

Little Torch Key and Ramrod Key have a rural feeling, with homes on both the Atlantic and the Gulf of Mexico as well as on dry lots.

### Summerland, Cudjoe & Sugarloaf Keys

Heading closer to Key West and into the more-exclusive subdivisions of Summerland, Cudjoe, and Sugarloaf Keys, you'll find luxurious properties. Summerland features a number of waterfront homes, along with a small airstrip that allows residents to park their private airplanes directly beneath their homes.

### Baypoint, Shark Key, Big Coppitt & Key Haven

Shark Key is a gated community developed with strict architectural guidelines. The large open-water lots on Shark Key are beautifully landscaped, and the houses set on them typically are very expensive. Baypoint, Big Coppitt, and Key Haven are in demand for their convenient location, only minutes from Key West.

## Key West

### Old Town

Settled in the early to late 1800s and the early 1900s, Old Town is characterized by large wood-frame houses of distinctive architectural styles. Typically built by shipbuilders and carpenters for New England sea captains, many of these homes feature Bahamian and New England influences and high ceilings. Several historic district homes are now exquisite guesthouses (see the Accommodations chapter).

In addition to its obvious aesthetic qualities, Old Town is desirable because it is within walking distance of just about everything Key West has to offer, including shops, restaurants, nightlife, and galleries. Among the community's residents are a large number of artists and writers.

Toward the southern end of Whitehead Street and west of Duval on Petronia Street, about a block from the Ernest Hemingway Home and Museum, lies Bahama Village. This community now is undergoing gentrification, as home buyers purchase and renovate existing properties here.

One of Key West's more recent developments in Old Town is Truman Annex, where private homes, town houses, and condominiums all boast features of Key West's distinctive architecture. This self-contained development once was an extension of the island's Bahama Village section, and later a portion of the Key West naval base. Truman Annex was constructed and renovated according to a unified plan reminiscent of Old Town but with more green space and winding streets. Because of the charm that this gated development exhibits, even the hubbub created by large cruise ships entering the nearby harbor does not affect its pricey real estate values. Condominiums in the Harbour Place complex of Truman Annex are almost directly on the water and run well into seven figures. Single-family homes are in the multimillion-dollar price range.

### Midtown & New Town

Stretching from White Street all the way east to Kennedy Boulevard, Midtown boasts a mix of wood-frame and concrete-block ground-level homes built in the late 1950s and 1960s. New Town, developed a bit later, spreads out along N. Roosevelt Boulevard and is largely commercial on its perimeter.

Recently completed in the Midtown area is Roosevelt Annex, a gated community of 25 single-family homes and town houses fronting the Gulf of Mexico on the former county fairgrounds along N. Roosevelt Boulevard. Billed as the last developable site in Key West with open-water views, Roosevelt Annex was constructed by the developer of Truman Annex and the Key West Golf Club.

The Key West Golf Club community, on Stock Island, looks a lot like Truman Annex. Here, single-family homes, town houses, and condominiums display elements of Conch-style architecture. Each residence overlooks the Florida Keys' only 18-hole public golf course, along with surrounding lakes and ponds. If you are not in the market to buy at this time, a variety of long-term rental options are available. All residents have free access to tennis courts, nature walks, several swimming pools, and, of course, golf.

### Sunset Key

If you would truly like to live on a secluded island—but not too far from civilization—consider a home on Sunset Key. Formerly known as Tank Island (the navy once stored its fuel in huge tanks here), Sunset Key is just a stone's throw across the harbor from Mallory Square. About half of the island is devoted to guest cottages and a beachfront restaurant-bar operated by the Westin Key West Resort and Marina (see the Accommodations chapter); the rest is reserved for single-family homes. Interior building lots begin at $1.5 million. In addition to fabulous open-water sunset views, homeowners on Sunset Key enjoy such amenities as a health club, pool, tennis courts, and putting green. Their cars, however, must remain behind at the Westin parking garage on Key West; only golf carts and bicycles are permitted on Sunset Key. Regular ferry service is available from the Westin Marina.

## KINDS OF PROPERTIES

### Condominiums

Condominiums are scattered throughout the Upper and Middle Keys, and many home buyers find them to be a low-maintenance way to keep up a part-time residence. For full-time residents, condos commonly offer amenities not always available in a single-family home, such as swimming pools, fitness facilities, saunas, hot tubs, boat dockage, and covered parking.

During our peak tourist season (generally Dec through Apr), condominiums often are teeming with activity, affording residents the opportunity to meet renters from across the country. When the low season rolls around and occupancy typically drops to 30 percent or less at any given time, full-time residents have the facilities nearly all to themselves. If you plan to become a full-time Florida Keys resident in a condominium, be sure to check on whether the complex you have your eye on maintains an active rental program. You may not enjoy living alongside transient residents.

What you'll pay for a condo depends on the size of the unit, its location, and its view. You also need to factor monthly maintenance fees into the overall cost; these increase with unit sizes and cover maintenance of the common area, a reserve account for future major repairs, and insurance for damage by flood, wind, storm, peril, and salt air. (See the Close-up in this chapter.)

## Mobile Homes

First the good news: A mobile home is the least-expensive real estate you can buy in the Florida Keys. The bad news? Most vulnerable to hurricane damage, mobile homes are the first properties ordered for evacuation during severe-storm watches in the Florida Keys.

Zoning ordinances restrict mobile homes to specific communities. Often the least-expensive mobile homes are those that have existed in residential subdivisions since before zoning ordinances were established. These mobile homes, which have individual septic tanks, lack the recreational and service-oriented amenities typically offered in mobile-home communities here.

Buyers who purchase property in a mobile-home community pay more but frequently enjoy a clubhouse atmosphere complete with a swimming pool, shuffleboard court, boat ramp, dockage, on-site manager, sewage treatment, and a convenience store. The price of any mobile home increases with a concrete or wood-frame addition, an elevated Florida room, built-up gravel roof, poured concrete slab, and other features.

## Single-Family Homes

Dry-lot homes—those not fronting a water view or canal—are the least-expensive single-family home option in the Keys. Canal-front homes generally sell for much more, with homes on the open water usually in the millions. Because many real estate purchases here are made by boaters, homes that sit closer to a bridge—providing access to both the ocean and the bay—sell more quickly.

Since 1975 the county has required that most homes be constructed of concrete block, be positioned on stilts, and have hurricane shutters. Non-conforming structures built before the 1975 ordinance took effect have been

# Close-up

## Hot—It's Not

Key Wester and famed playwright Tennessee Williams's *Cat on a Hot Tin Roof* is a slinky, sensual, artistic play and movie. In the real world of tin roofs, the title could not be further from the truth.

Thomas Jefferson was an advocate of tin roofs and used one for his home, Monticello (construction began in 1768 and ended in 1809). Prior to tin roofs, copper was imported from England until the end of the 18th century, when rolling sheet metal was developed in America. Corrugated, stiffened sheets allowed greater span over lighter framework, thus decreasing installation time and labor. In 1857 one of the first metal roofs in the South was used on the US Mint in New Orleans. In the late 19th century, patterned tin roofs were all the rage, as they are today.

The durability of these roofs proves they hold up during hurricanes. Heat from the sun reflects off the metal, and lightning discharges over the metal, thus helping to prevent the spread of fires. Long used on barns and rural outbuildings, they hold an authentic simplistic charm of another era. The resurgence of metal roofing in newer homes is on the increase due to attractive designs, the distinctive look that is more compatible with historic neighborhoods, and the fact that the metals may be recycled.

Wend through the streets of Old Town in Key West on foot or trolley, cast your eyes skyward, over the delicious cakelike, gingerbread-trimmed, historic homes, and marvel at the icing of tin on the roofs of these beautiful ladies. The Tennessee Williams home on Duncan Street still sports a metal roof and is as charming today as when the famous owner was in residence in this southernmost city. Tin roofs on vintage homes are "hot" commodities in the ever-sizzling South Florida real estate market.

grandfathered, but if 50 percent or more of the dollar value of a nonconforming use structure is destroyed and requires rebuilding, new zoning laws and building restrictions apply.

Much of a buyer's decision to purchase a home in the Florida Keys depends upon the structure's ability to withstand a hurricane. Concrete-block-style (CBS) homes are considered more solid than those made of wood. Most are elevated on stilts to avoid potential flooding. CBS stilt homes typically cost more than ground-level CBS homes of comparable sizes. CBS homes typically command higher prices than all-wood frame structures.

A large percentage of Lower Keys homes are factory-built, wood-frame modulars. Because they are constructed under controlled circumstances and designed to withstand 135-mph winds, some homeowners believe they're stronger than wood-frame homes built on the site.

If you are considering buying a home in the Florida Keys, landscaping also may influence your decision. Some buyers prefer intricate vegetation, which requires costly irrigation, while others want low-maintenance xeriscaping (landscaping using indigenous plantings that require no irrigation).

## REAL ESTATE COMPANIES

Though all Florida Keys agents share a multiple listing service (MLS) with properties available throughout Monroe County, each agency tends to specialize in its own territory. We describe some of the largest agencies for sales and rentals in the section that follows. This is not meant to be a comprehensive listing by any means. For a complete list, consult the Yellow Pages for the appropriate communities, or pick up copies of the many real estate guides available free of charge at supermarkets and other locations throughout Monroe County.

### Upper Keys

**AMERICAN CARIBBEAN REAL ESTATE INC.,** MM 81.8 Bayside, 81800 Overseas Hwy., Islamorada, FL 33036; (305) 664-4966; american caribbean.com. American Caribbean handles more than 100 properties for sale or rent from Duck Key to Key Largo.

**FREEWHEELER REALTY,** MM 98.5 Bayside, 98500 Overseas Hwy., Key Largo, FL 33037; (305) 852-4400 or (877) 852-4450; freewheeler-realty .com. Freewheeler deals in property management, rentals, and sales for homes, condos, villas, and efficiencies on the beach, bay, and canal. Another location is at MM 86 Bayside in Islamorada (305-664-4444 or 866-664-2075).

i As you drive along our residential streets, our neighborhoods look like any small town. But every once in a while you see a house or building that is completely entombed in a red-and-yellow circus-like tent. These are signs that the exterminators are at work! In the tropical Florida Keys, we have all sorts of critters that a can of bug spray just won't eradicate.

**MARR PROPERTIES, MM** 100 Bayside, 999000 Overseas Hwy., Key Largo, FL 33037; (305) 451-4078 or (800) 277-3728; floridakeysproperties .com. Serving the Keys since 1965, this office offers sales of commercial and residential properties and knowledge of the upper Keys real estate market.

## Middle Keys

**AMERICAN CARIBBEAN REAL ESTATE INC., MM** 52 Oceanside, 9141 Overseas Hwy., Marathon, FL 33050; (305) 743-7636 or (800) 940-7636; acresales.com. American Caribbean specializes in Middle Keys sales and rental properties from Duck Key to Key Largo.

**COLDWELL BANKER SCHMITT REAL ESTATE, MM** 52.5 Bayside, 11100 Overseas Hwy., Marathon, FL 33050; (305) 743-5181 or (800) 366-5181; realestatefloridakeys.com. Sales and vacation rentals in the Middle Keys are the focus at this office of a firm that covers the real estate market from one end of the Keys to the other.

**RE/MAX KEY TO THE KEYS, MM** 49.5 Bayside, 4680 Overseas Hwy., Marathon, FL 33050; (305) 743-2300 or (800) 743-2301; wilkinsonteam .com. Agents handle sales and rental properties from Long Key to Big Coppitt.

**WATERFRONT SPECIALISTS, MM** 54 Oceanside, 80th Street Station, Ste. 1, Marathon, FL 33050; (305) 743-0644 or (800) 342-6398; waterfront specialists.com. Despite its name, this agency can direct you to sales and rental opportunities both on and off the water.

## Lower Keys

**ACTION KEYS REALTY, INC., MM** 24.8 Oceanside, 24814 Overseas Hwy., Summerland Key, FL 33042; (305) 745-1323 or (800) 874-1323; actionkeysrealty.com. In addition to residential sales throughout the Lower Keys, this agency handles vacation rentals, primarily on Summerland, Ramrod, and Little Torch Keys.

## PRIVATE ISLANDS, HOMES & HIDEAWAYS

Picture yourself in the following locations, and soon you will know the meaning of "lost in paradise." Vacationing at its finest, these properties will leave you incredulous: You were where? On an island? Out in the middle of the ocean? On a helicopter pad? Aboard a private skiff? Only one word can sum it up: fabulous.

## Upper Keys

**ALLIGATOR REEF,** MM 86 Bayside, Islamorada, FL; (305) 393-3343 or (866) 664-2075; alligatorreef.net. Need 10 bedrooms, 4 kitchens, 2 heated pools, 8 bathrooms, and accommodations for 25 people? Then Alligator Reef compound is for you! With an observation deck overlooking the Atlantic Ocean, you can relax or enjoy all of the amenities on the property. Go kayaking, play Ping-Pong, swim, or swing in the hammocks. Do it all, or do nothing—this getaway packs a true "tropical punch."

**TERRA'S KEY,** MM 79.3 Oceanside, Islamorada, FL; (305) 664-2361 or (877) 412-7339; terraskey.com. Located off Islamorada is Terra's Key (also known as Tea Table Key). This sun-drenched 7-acre private island is connected to US 1 by a causeway. Five bedrooms, 6 bathrooms, a tennis court, a heated pool with a wet bar, and inspiring vistas of the Atlantic Ocean make this a setting for a vacation you will never forget.

## Middle Keys

**EAST SISTER ROCK ISLAND AND SOMBRERO ROCK HOUSE,** MM 50 Oceanside, Marathon, FL; (305) 796-8439; floridaisland.com. Piloting your own 21-foot Carolina skiff to and from the mainland of Marathon, you travel to your island in the sun, East Sister Rock Island. Completely surrounded by a moat, the house sits on a coral reef. A 12-foot veranda swings around the 5,000-square-foot home. This is a diver's and snorkeler's haven. If that isn't your bag, you can swim in the pool, or a bigger "pool"—the Atlantic Ocean! If the skiff is too slow for your entrance—or exit—there is a helicopter pad on the grounds.

## Key West

Despite the fact that Key West is heavily developed, with both old and new homes on generally small lots throughout the city, real estate agents report that the demand for homes far outstrips the island's supply. Also, while waterfront property is a prime attraction for home buyers throughout the rest of the Florida Keys, it is rarely found in Key West, because commercial development lines all waterfront areas. Nevertheless, real estate in the southernmost city is expensive.

The island of Key West is an incorporated city governed by local elected representatives as well as by Monroe County. Consequently, the property tax structure here includes both city and county government expenses. Key West has its own land-use plan with zoning ordinances, permitting units, density requirements, and building height and setback minimums. Within the historic district of Old Town, another layer of control and review exists. The Historical Architecture Review Commission (HARC) reviews applications for improvements and new construction. Established in 1986, HARC works to ensure the integrity of the historic district.

Key West offers a selection of styles in single-family homes, town houses, and condominiums. The island has few mobile-home parks, and the only mobile-home communities here are small and hidden away. There are also several on Stock Island.

Town houses, typically adjoining structures with a common wall, allow homeowners to own the ground beneath them. The center of the common wall is the dividing line, and party wall agreements determine who maintains responsibility in cases of repair or destruction.

If you wish to purchase beachfront housing, a condominium is without a doubt the way to go. Along the south side of Key West are several multi-story beachfront condominiums with elevators, enclosed parking, pools, tennis courts, and hot tubs.

The majority of single-family homes in Key West are in areas known as Old Town, Midtown, and New Town, and real estate agents further break two of these regions into "old" and "new" Old Town and "old" and "new" New Town. Boundaries are roughly established, with some overflow, and within all Key West areas you'll discover a diverse array of properties dating from between the early 1800s and the late 1900s.

Convenience to the water or to touristy Duval Street is not usually a factor in the cost of Key West property. Rather, prices generally depend on the size and condition of the house, its lot, and its location. The island itself is only 2 miles long by 4 miles wide, so beaches and harbors are never far away. Some home buyers seek property as far from the busy roadways and attractions as possible.

**BASCOM GROOMS REAL ESTATE,** 1716 N. Roosevelt Blvd., Key West, FL 33040; (305) 295-7511 or (888) 565-7150; bascomgrooms.com. In addition to residential sales, this agency handles commercial properties and vacation rentals.

**BEACH CLUB BROKERS INC.,** 1075 Duval St., Ste. C-11; (305) 294-8433 or (800) 545-9655; kwreal.com. Specializing in the sale, purchase, and management of local and international property, Beach Club Brokers also has a separate rental division, Rent Key West Vacations (see separate listing).

**BERKSHIRE HATHAWAY KNIGHT & GARDNER REALTY,** 336 Duval St., Key West, FL 33040; (305) 294-5155 or (800) 843-9276; keysrealestate .com. This group concentrates its efforts on the purchase, sale, rental, or lease of properties and boat slips from Key West to Marathon.

**CENTURY 21 ALL KEYS,** 1720 N. Roosevelt Blvd., Key West, FL 33040; (305) 294-4200; c21allkeys.com. Century 21 deals with real estate sales and rentals in our southernmost city.

★CENTURY 21 SCHWARTZ, 211 Simonton St., Key West, FL 33040; (305) 766-0585; c21schwartz.com. Regularly featured on HGTV, these agents will work with you, whatever your home-buying needs.

COMPASS REALTY, 201 Front St., Ste. 101, Key West, FL 33040; (305) 292-1881 or (800) 884-7368; compass-realty.com. Compass Realty sells property throughout Key West but also focuses on the sale and rental of Truman Annex properties, as well as those in the Key West Golf Club and Roosevelt Annex communities.

ISLAND GROUP REALTY, 2409 N. Roosevelt Blvd., Ste. 10, Key West, FL 33040; (305) 295-7110 or (800) 225-4277; isellkw.com. This real estate company offers any of the services you might need for relocating to the Florida Keys. Whether your needs are residential, commercial, or rental, the sales associates at Island Group Realty can assist with your request.

KEY WEST REALTY INC., 1109 Duval St., Key West, FL 33040; (305) 294-3064; keywestrealty.com. This agency is very heavily into real estate sales in Key West.

RENT KEY WEST VACATIONS, INC., 1075 Duval St., Ste. C-11, Key West, FL 33040; (305) 294-0990 or (800) 833-7368; rentkeywest.com. This agency handles rentals exclusively. Rent Key West offers extensive listings, with properties ranging from studio apartments to four-bedroom homes.

TRUMAN & COMPANY, 1205 Truman Ave., Key West, FL 33040; (305) 292-2244; trumanandcompany.com. Most of the principals in this company are longtime residents and provide firsthand knowledge when it comes to the unique residential and commercial aspects of buying and selling property in the Florida Keys.

VACATION KEY WEST, 100 Grinnell St., Key West, FL 33040; (305) 295-9500 or (800) 595-5397; vacationkw.com. This agency will help you choose a great location for a few days or for an extended visit here in the tropics. They can place you in a historic inn, romantic hideaway, condo, or cottage.

VACATION HOMES OF KEY WEST, 507 Whitehead St., Key West, FL 33040; (305) 294-7358 or (800) 404-2802; vacationhomesofkeywest.com. They will help you rent your vacation home: a Duval Street penthouse, an authentic historic home, a modern island villa, a romantic Caribbean cottage, or even an oceanfront luxury condo.

# Health Care

We have included information on health-care options, ranging from full-service hospitals and specialty care providers for patients in need of cancer or dialysis treatments to physical therapy clinics and mental health services. And don't miss the information on veterinary options. We care about Spot and Fluffy, too!

Please be reminded, however, that this is not intended to be a comprehensive listing of all possible health services. The Florida Keys and Key West are served by physicians in nearly every specialty, as well as by osteopaths, chiropractors, podiatrists, dentists, and optometrists. So if, while visiting our islands, you should develop a sudden toothache from downing one too many frozen coladas or drop a contact lens somewhere in the sand, don't despair. One of our many health-care providers will be available to help you, even on short notice. Ask your hotel concierge for a referral to the appropriate specialist, or consult the Yellow Pages.

And should your situation call for medical expertise that is not available in the Florida Keys, rest assured that you will still be able to receive state-of-the-art treatment in a timely manner. The University of Miami's renowned Jackson Memorial Medical Center, as well as other mainland hospitals and trauma facilities, are just a helicopter ride away.

## OVERVIEW

This chapter lists health-care options by category in alphabetical order by location from the Upper Keys down to Key West.

## ACUTE-CARE CENTERS

### Upper Keys

**THE GOOD HEALTH CLINIC, MM 91.5 Oceanside, 91555 Overseas Hwy., Tavernier, FL 33070; (305) 853-1788.** This Upper Keys clinic opened for the specialized and primary care of the uninsured population. The facility offers X-rays, general orthopedic surgery, and the services of doctors in Miami who specialize in hematology, oncology, back surgery, ophthalmology, and more. Local doctors associated with the clinic include dermatologists, mental health practitioners, pediatricians, and optometrists.

★**MARINERS HOSPITAL, MM 91.5 Bayside, 91500 Overseas Hwy., Tavernier, FL 33070; (305) 434-3000; baptisthealth.net.** Mariners Hospital, established as a nine-bed physicians' clinic in 1959, today is a state-of-the-art hospital facility. Among the services provided here are 24-hour emergency care, surgery (including outpatient), respiratory therapy, pulmonary rehabilitation, cardiac rehabilitation, and radiology (including MRI, CT scans, and mammography). Mariners maintains a sleep diagnostic center, laboratory, and pharmacy, and has a hyperbaric, or decompression, chamber. The hospital has a helicopter pad for transfer of severe cases to mainland hospitals. Mariners Hospital is a part of Baptist Health South Florida, a nonprofit health-care organization. Mariners also maintains and operates a state-of-the-art physical therapy center in a separate location at MM 100.3 Bayside, Key Largo, (305) 451-4398.

## Middle Keys

**FISHERMEN'S COMMUNITY HOSPITAL, MM 48.7 Oceanside, 3301 Overseas Hwy., Marathon, FL; (305) 743-5533; fishermenshospital.com.** The medical staff at Fishermen's offer care in the areas of cardiology, cardiac rehabilitation, family practice, general surgery, gynecology, oncology, internal medicine, neurology, pathology, radiology, rheumatology, and plastic/reconstructive surgery. A CT scanner, known as a helical scanner, provides three-dimensional images with extraordinary clarity. Emergency service and same-day surgery also are available.

A helicopter pad allows for emergency chopper services, and a hyperbaric emergency response team is on call for divers. Fishermen's Overnight Guest program provides testing and presurgery (the night prior to surgery) room and board. Also licensed to provide home health care, Fishermen's accepts most forms of insurance. Other hospital resources include a certified diabetes educator and nutritional support services.

## Lower Keys

**BIG PINE MEDICAL AND MINOR EMERGENCY CENTER, MM 30 Oceanside, 2966 Overseas Hwy., Big Pine Key, FL 33043; (305) 872-3321; bigpinemedical.com.** This emergency-care center, conveniently located on Big Pine Key, treats minor illnesses and emergencies (broken bones, cuts, insect bites, and so on). Although appointments are encouraged, walk-ins are welcome. The clinic is generally open Mon through Fri from 8 a.m. to 5 p.m. and some Sat mornings. However, hours may vary with the season and patient demand, so it is best to phone ahead.

## Key West

**BODY OWNERS, 5450 MacDonald Ave., Stock Island, FL 33040; (305) 294-8866; keywestphysicaltherapy.com.** The knowledgeable staff and compassionate care make this physical therapy and wellness center a popular one with patients and physicians. Everyone goes out of their way to make sure your therapy sessions are comfortable and informative. They offer sessions for children with special needs as well.

**KEY WEST URGENT CARE,** 1503 Government Rd., Key West, FL 33040; (305) 295-7550; keywesturgentcare.com. Not feeling so hot? This is the place to go, no appointment necessary. Treatment for minor illnesses and injuries is available Mon through Fri, from 8 a.m. to 3 p.m., and credit cards are accepted. Some local insurance plans may also be accepted.

**LOWER KEYS MEDICAL CENTER,** 5900 Junior College Rd., Stock Island, FL 33040; (305) 294-5531; lkmc.com. This accredited primary-care facility is the only hospital in the Florida Keys to offer maternity services. Lower Florida Keys Health System maintains a 24-hour emergency room, a clinical lab, and a heliport. Added services include pediatrics, inpatient and outpatient psychotherapy, physical therapy, radiation therapy, chemotherapy, and cardiovascular and ambulatory care. The hospital offers substance-abuse assistance and comprehensive wellness programs.

**21ST CENTURY ONCOLOGY OF KEY WEST,** 3426 N. Roosevelt Blvd., Key West, FL 33040; (305) 296-0021; 21concologykeywest.com. This health-care treatment center provides a full spectrum of radiation therapy services to cancer patients. The center offers conventional external beam treatments and advanced services such as prostate seed implants, 3-D conformed treatment planning, intensity modulated radiation, and image-guided radiotherapy.

**SELECT PHYSICAL THERAPY,** 3156 Northside Dr., Key West, FL 33040; (305) 292-1805; novacare.com. Select Physical Therapy maintains a network of therapists throughout the Florida Keys, specializing in physical, speech, and occupational therapy. Some locations also offer orthopedist, family physician, and internist referrals.

**TRUMAN MEDICAL,** 540 Truman Ave., Key West, FL 33040; (305) 296-4399; trumanmedical.org. This walk-in-only clinic will see patients from 9 a.m. to 4:30 p.m. Mon through Fri and 9:30 a.m. to noon on Sat. Truman Medical is closed on Sun.

## MOBILE MEDICAL CARE

### RURAL HEALTH NETWORK OF MONROE COUNTY

Key West and Lower Keys, (305) 292-6422

Marathon and Middle Keys, (305) 289-8915

**Tavernier and Upper Keys, (305) 735-4218**

rhnmc.org

The Rural Health Network was established to provide primary medical care and dental services to the uninsured and underinsured residents of and visitors to Monroe County. Two fully equipped RVs travel up and down the Keys to provide medical services to folks who are uninsured and might not otherwise seek primary-care treatment. A combined effort of the Monroe County Health Department, the three Keys hospitals, the Health Foundation of South Florida, Catholic Charities of the Archdiocese of Miami, HUD, FEMA, HRSA, and the Florida Keys Area Health Education Center in conjunction with the University of Miami, this mobile medical service covers Key Largo to Key West.

The vans are equipped like doctors' offices. Each has two small examination rooms and a cab that doubles as a triage area, and is staffed by a registered nurse, a nurse practitioner, and a health educator, as well as nursing and medical students. Patients needing care beyond the scope of the Medi-Van staff may be referred to specialists and area hospitals. Appointments are available and walk-ins are welcome. The Medi-Vans charge a co-pay for their services.

## HOME HEALTH SERVICES

**VISITING NURSE ASSOCIATION AND HOSPICE OF THE FLORIDA KEYS,** 1319 William St., Key West, FL 33040; (305) 294-8812 and 92001 Overseas Hwy., Tavernier FL 33070; (305) 852-7887; hospicevna .com. Hospice provides care for terminally ill patients with six months or less to live. Services are provided in private homes and nursing homes throughout the Keys by a staff of registered nurses, patient-care managers, and social workers. Certified nursing assistants tend to personal needs such as bathing, grooming, and bedding. All home-care patients must be referred to the agency by a physician. Comfort Care, which is private-duty nursing care, is also available. Hospice's purpose is to ensure patients' comfort so that the last days of their lives are quality ones.

Within this same nonprofit organization, the Visiting Nurse Association (VNA) provides more-aggressive home care for patients still undergoing various treatments or who need blood tests or care for wounds. This service also is provided upon a physician's request. Both Hospice and VNA are on call 24 hours a day, 7 days a week. Medicare and Medicaid are accepted.

HEALTH CARE

## MEDICAL/HOSPITAL EQUIPMENT

**CORAL MEDICAL HOME EQUIPMENT,** MM 88 Oceanside, 87899 Overseas Hwy., Islamorada, FL 33036; (305) 852-4393; coralmedical.com. This long-established Keys business gives customers first-rate delivery of their medical equipment needs, including 24-hour emergency service, home IV provisions, respiratory and oxygen supplies, and the usual variety of crutches, walkers, and various medical apparatuses.

## ALTERNATIVE HEALTH CARE

Many of the people who reside full-time in the Florida Keys are laid-back types who were drawn to our islands by a desire to pursue a less-than-conventional lifestyle. In many cases their approach to health care is as nontraditional as their approach to life.

The Florida Keys, and Key West in particular, boast a wealth of options in the alternative health-care category. These include everything from yoga classes and massage therapy on the beach to acupuncture, homeopathic medicine, organic foods, and herbal remedies.

### Emergency Numbers

While we sincerely hope you won't ever need to use the following telephone numbers, it is a good idea to keep this information in a convenient place.

| | |
|---|---|
| • Police, Fire, or Rescue | 911 |
| • Florida Poison Information Center | (800) 222-1222 |
| • US Coast Guard Marine and Air Emergency channel 16 | (305) 295-9700 or CG/VH |
| • Florida Marine Patrol of the FWCC | *FMP or (800) DIAL FMP |
| • Florida Highway Patrol | *FHP or (800) 240-0453 |
| • Monroe County Emergency Management | (305) 289-6018 |
| • Hurricane Preparedness | (800) 427-8340 |
| • Emergency Information Hotline | (800) 955-5504 |

**ISLAND DOLPHIN CARE, 150 Lorelane Place, Key Largo, FL 33037; (305) 451-5884; islanddolphincare.org.** Island Dolphin Care specializes in working with special-needs children interacting with dolphins. This not-for-profit facility provides assisted therapy to children with critical illnesses, disabilities, and special needs who come from all over the world.

## VETERINARY SERVICES

Your four-legged friends and "family" sometimes need health care, too. These pet clinics cater to their needs from the top of the Keys to Key West.

### Upper Keys

**ANIMAL CARE CLINIC, MM 100.6 Bayside, 100660 Overseas Hwy., Key Largo, FL 33037; (305) 453-0044; animalcareclinickeylargo.com.** Boarding and grooming are small parts of the operation at Animal Care Clinic. The clinic maintains oxygen-intensive critical-care units and offers surgery, lab testing, X-rays, EKG, and ultrasound dentistry, as well as emergency on-call service, 24 hours a day, 7 days a week.

### Middle Keys

**KEYS ANIMAL HOSPITAL, MM 52.5 Bayside, 11425 Overseas Hwy., Marathon, FL 33050; (305) 743-6250; keysanimalhospital.com.** This veterinary hospital has been serving Marathon since 1974. They offer 24-hour emergency service and air-conditioned boarding facilities for your pets, along with separate areas for cats, small dogs, and large dogs.

★**MARATHON VETERINARY HOSPITAL, MM 52.5 Oceanside, 5001 Overseas Hwy., Marathon, FL 33050; (305) 743-7099 or (800) 832-7694; marathonvet.com.** Pet owners in Key West have been known to drive the hour it takes to get here for an appointment. The doctors here are that good. Marathon Veterinary Hospital offers full services, including 24-hour emergency care, for dogs, cats, and all exotics. You do not have to be a client to be seen for an emergency.

### Lower Keys

**CRUZ ANIMAL HOSPITAL, MM 27 Bayside, 27063 Overseas Hwy., Ramrod Key, FL 33042; (305) 872-2559; cruzanimalhospital.com.** Cruz Animal Hospital offers a variety of medical services for virtually all pets, plus 24-hour emergency service. Military and senior citizen discounts are available.

### Real Playboy Bunnies

*Sylvilagus palustris hefneri* is not the name of a *Playboy* centerfold, but it is the name of a marsh rabbit found on Big Pine Key in 1980. Hugh Hefner, founder and editor of *Playboy* magazine, funded a study that identified the species as endangered. In 2007 feral cats were killing the marsh rabbits, and Hef once again stepped in and donated funds to Stand Up For Animals to capture the cats and to ensure they would not be euthanized.

## Key West

**ISLAND PAWS OF KEY WEST,** (305) 859-0005; islandpawshousecalls .com. Island Paws of Key West will make the trek to you and your pet, as they make veterinary house calls in the lower Keys.

**LOWER KEYS ANIMAL CLINIC,** 1456 Kennedy Dr., Key West, FL 33040; (305) 294-6335. This facility treats small exotics but mostly sees cats and dogs. The staff offers regular checkups, surgery, dentistry, vaccinations, X-rays, and general medical treatment for pets.

# Education & Child Care

The Florida Keys and Key West are served by public and private schools, pre-schools, and a community college. Thanks to a visiting institute and college degree programs at the Boca Chica Naval Air Station in the Lower Keys, students can earn bachelor's, master's, and even doctoral degrees without ever leaving our islands. In addition, several institutions of higher education in Miami are within commuting distance. Also included in this chapter is a comprehensive look at the child-care scene in the Florida Keys and Key West. We explore traditional child-care services, along with other handy (sometimes vacation-saving) options such as drop-in care, babysitting, sick-child and respite care, family child-care homes, and public after-school programs.

## EDUCATION

### Public Schools

The Monroe County School District oversees schools from Key Largo to Key West, including three high schools. Some elementary and middle schools within our county occupy the same building; other facilities are shared by middle and high schools. Stretching more than 100 miles, traversing 42 bridges, with more than 8,000 students attending 17 schools and centers in its jurisdiction, the Florida Keys is a unique and stimulating classroom setting.

The school system operates on a school year that runs from late Aug through early June. An elected board headed by an elected superintendent, who oversees five district representatives, governs our public schools. Board members serve four-year terms. School funding comes from Monroe County property taxes. For more information on Monroe County Public Schools, go to keysschools.com.

### Charter School

**BIG PINE ACADEMY, MM 30.2 Oceanside, 30220 Overseas Hwy., Big Pine Key, FL 33043; (305) 872-1266; bigpineacademy.com.** This small charter school on Big Pine Key is for preschool through seventh grade. Their curriculum is designed to ensure a safe and nurturing school environment teaching basic skills that enrich and challenge children's lives and prepare them for their next grade levels.

## Private Schools

Private schools typically offer smaller student-teacher ratios and a variety of learning curricula. The following list includes private schools operating in the Florida Keys and Key West.

**THE BASILICA SCHOOL OF ST. MARY STAR OF THE SEA,** 700 Truman Ave., Key West, FL 33040; (305) 294-1031; basilicaschoolkeywest.com. The Basilica School follows a prekindergarten through eighth-grade curriculum and is fully accredited by the Florida Catholic Conference Accreditation Program. The school's mission is to provide opportunities for all Lower Keys families to experience a high-quality Catholic education.

**GRACE LUTHERAN SCHOOL,** 2713 Flagler Ave., Key West, FL 33040; (305) 296-8262; glskw.org. Established in 1952 and designed for prekindergarten through eighth graders, Grace Lutheran offers computers and teaches Spanish in all but prekindergarten classes. During "God Time," students learn about Christian ideals and how to live them.

**ISLAND CHRISTIAN SCHOOL,** MM 83.4 Bayside, 83400 Overseas Hwy., Islamorada, FL 33036; (305) 664-2781; islandchristian.org. Established in 1974 by a group of parents from Island Community Church, Island Christian began with 54 students. As grade levels were added and the school became accredited, enrollment increased to 300. Island Christian today teaches prekindergarten through high school students in a traditional college-preparatory curriculum that incorporates the Abeka and Bob Jones Christian teachings. The school offers a full interscholastic sports program to junior and senior high school students.

**KEY WEST MONTESSORI CHARTER SCHOOL,** 1400 United St., Key West, FL 33040; (305) 294-4910; keywestmontessori.com. The Key West Montessori Charter School is a nonprofit, public school teaching children in kindergarten through middle school. The school utilizes the work of Maria Montessori, who developed a method of educating children focusing on the child as the foundation for learning.

**MONTESSORI ISLAND SCHOOL,** MM 92 Oceanside, 92295 Overseas Hwy., Tavernier, FL 33070; (305) 852-3438; montessoriislandschool.com. Montessori Island School offers guidance for infants and toddlers up to prekindergarten in a natural setting. There is no air-conditioning in the building, and the use of natural light brings the environment closer to the classroom.

**TREASURE VILLAGE MONTESSORI SCHOOL,** MM 86.7 Oceanside, 86731 Overseas Hwy., Islamorada, FL 33036; (305) 852-3482; treasure villagemontessori.com. Montessori schools across the country work on the principle of self-pacing for children. This Montessori school, established in 1996, works on the same idea of purposeful action. The school provides education for preschool through eighth grade with Montessori-certified teachers.

## I Spy . . .

In 2004 two students doing a moth survey in the Key West Tropical Forest & Botanical Gardens (see the Attractions chapter) looked up in an Arjuna almond tree, *Terminalia arjuna*, the only one of its kind in the garden, and discovered a *Phyllops falcatus*, better known as the Cuban fig-eating bat, or white-shouldered bat. This was an exciting discovery because these bats have only been known to exist in Cuba, Hispaniola, and on Grand Cayman. The appearance of the Cuban fig-eating bat is the first recorded in Florida and the first in the US.

### Additional Educational Opportunities

Residents and visitors to the Florida Keys may participate in a number of hands-on educational opportunities, such as those listed below.

**MARINELAB, MARINE RESOURCES DEVELOPMENT FOUNDATION**, 51 Shoreland Dr., Key Largo, FL 33037; (305) 451-1139 or (800) 741-1139; mrdf.org. Since 1972, the nonprofit Marine Resources Development Foundation (MRDF) has offered students an in-depth introduction to the ecology of the Keys. The MRDF provides customized programs for students, who learn about sea life in the Emerald Lagoon or explore the MarineLab Undersea Laboratory. Customized programs also include scuba certification, coral reef ecology, mangrove ecology, and a trip to the Everglades.

**SEACAMP**, 1300 Big Pine Ave., Big Pine Key, FL 33043; (305) 872-2331 or (877) 732-2267; seacamp.org. This scuba and marine science camp for children ages 12 through 17 has been in Big Pine Key since 1966. Children from across the world sign up for Seacamp's 18-day program to experience scuba diving, sailing, snorkeling, and sailboarding. Marine science classes teach about such subjects as exploring the seas, animal behavior, and Keys critters. Scuba certification is available.

### Higher Education

**FLORIDA KEYS COMMUNITY COLLEGE**, 5901 W. College Rd., Stock Island, FL 33040; (305) 296-9081; fkcc.edu. When Florida Keys Community College (FKCC) began operation in the fall of 1965, it became the first institution of higher education in the Florida Keys. Today FKCC offers associate of science and associate of arts degree programs in such fields as business administration, computer programming and analysis, nursing, multimedia technology, and marine environmental technology.

FKCC's performing and visual arts programs are enhanced by the college's Tennessee Williams Fine Arts Center (see the Entertainment chapter). Its marine environmental technology and dive programs are especially popular. In addition to its main campus on Stock Island, Florida Keys Community College also offers a limited number of classes at two other Keys locations: the Middle Keys Center at 900 Sombrero Beach Rd., MM 50, Marathon, (305) 743-2133; and the Upper Keys Center at MM 89.9, Tavernier, (305) 852-8007.

## LIBRARIES

### MONROE COUNTY PUBLIC LIBRARY

Key Largo, MM 101.4 Oceanside, (305) 451-2396

Islamorada, MM 81.5 Bayside, (305) 664-4645

Marathon, MM 48.5 Oceanside, (305) 743-5156

Big Pine, MM 31 Bayside, (305) 289-6303

Key West, 700 Fleming St., (305) 292-3595

keyslibraries.org

Each library offers a free paperback exchange and an ongoing book sale, with most titles less than $5. The libraries host numerous kid-friendly events and readings throughout the year. Call ahead or check the website for specifics.

## CHILD CARE

The problem of finding good, competent child care is compounded here by a shortage of available providers at any cost. According to the National Association for the Education of Young Children, child care is the fourth-largest item in the family budget after food, housing, and taxes. Infant care (birth to age 1) and weekend and evening care are in particularly short supply in Monroe County, which encompasses the Keys. Day-to-day child care in the county generally falls into two categories: center-based care and family child-care homes. In this section we provide information on types of child-care programs and contacts for centers that serve the Florida Keys and Key West.

**WESLEY HOUSE FAMILY SERVICES,** Coordinating Agency, 1304 Truman Ave., Key West, FL 33040; (305) 809-5000; wesleyhouse.org. With offices in Key West and serving all of the Florida Keys, Wesley House assists families in making the best of a difficult situation. (Wesley House is a national division agency of the United Methodist Church and a United Way of Monroe County agency.) The Wesley House Resource & Referral Network (WHR&RN) is perhaps the most important resource in the Keys for parents looking for appropriate, quality child care. WHR&RN acts as a link between families and the child-care services they seek. It can recommend affordable child care for children up to 5 years old and after-school and summer care for children up to 12 years old. Families may access services at three locations in the Florida Keys: 175 Wrenn St., Tavernier, (305) 853-3518; 2796 Overseas Hwy., Marathon, (305) 289-2675; and 1304 Truman Ave., Key West, (305) 809-5000.

WHR&RN offers other assistance in the forms of subsidized child care, scholarships, and help in obtaining legal aid, medical aid, food stamps, and other services. The network conducts classes for parents in money management, parenting skills, nutrition, and handling everyday pressures. It provides personal help for families with at-risk children, assisting them in filling out paperwork to meet eligibility requirements. Wesley House also offers transportation to and from child-care centers for children in at-risk situations. It will also provide referrals for families needing sick care or in-home nursing specialists. Some child-care centers offer drop-in care.

## Baby Chicks Rental

It's hard to travel on a plane (or in a car, for that matter) and bring along cribs, strollers, high chairs, and all the gear for the little one. By calling the owner of this come-to-your-door baby equipment rental business, you can travel with just your luggage and baby! Call (305) 879-3340 or visit baby chicksrental.com for more information.

### Types of Programs
This section describes the center- and home-based child-care options available to parents in Monroe County.

#### *Child-Care/Preschool Centers*
The minimum state licensing requirements dictate that a child-care center must hold a valid license from the Health and Rehabilitative Services (HRS)

Department of the State of Florida. The license must be posted in a conspicuous place within the center.

The center must adhere to the number of children for which it is licensed, and it must maintain the minimum staff-to-child ratio for each age level: younger than age 1, 1 teacher for every 4 children; age 1, 1 to 6; age 2, 1 to 11; age 3, 1 to 15; age 4, 1 to 20; and age 5, 1 to 25. We stress that this is the minimum ratio, which may not be sufficient to give your child the level of care you desire.

Licensing standards mandate health and safety requirements and staff training requirements. These include child abuse and neglect training, a 20-hour child-care training course, a 10-hour specialized training module, and 8 hours of in-service training annually. In addition, there must be one CPR- and first-aid-certified person on-site during business hours. Some centers are prepared to accept infants; others are not.

Some child-care centers are exempt from HRS licensing. They are accredited and monitored by religious agencies, the school board, or the military. Contact Wesley House (see listing under Resources) for a list of HRS-licensed and license-exempt child-care/preschool centers in the Florida Keys and Key West. Unfortunately, no child-care centers are open weekends or evenings in the Keys.

## Aquarius Install Project

In June 2011 Teens4Oceans brought a 20-person group—composed of student representatives, parents, and dive instructors—down to Key Largo, Florida, to complete the Aquarius Install Project, installing cameras on the Aquarius Reef Base. Teens4Oceans uses these cameras as lenses into the ocean, allowing them to produce unique educational materials for students of all ages, and empowering students and teens to be good stewards of the oceans through science, research, and philanthropy. Visit teens4oceans.org for more information.

### Family Child-Care Homes

Family child-care is considered by the State of Florida to encompass home-based child care with five or fewer preschool-age children from more than one family unrelated to the caregiver. Any preschool children living in the home must be included in the maximum number of children allowed. The adult who provides the child care is usually referred to as a family child-care home operator.

Some counties in Florida require that family child-care homes be licensed. Monroe Country, which includes the Florida Keys, requires only registration with the Department of Health and Rehabilitative Services. Every adult in the household must be screened. Registration requires no on-site inspection of the home for minimum health, safety, and sanitation standards, however. Nor is there a requirement that the family child-care operator have CPR or first-aid training.

Military programs are exempt from this registration. They have their own accreditation procedures and are available only to family members of military personnel.

Wesley House offers and actively recruits for a 3-hour course covering basic health and safety issues to persons who wish to operate registered family child-care homes.

### Public After-School Programs

Many public schools in the Florida Keys and Key West run their own after-hours programs for school-age children from 2:15 to 5:30 p.m. and also on school holidays and summer weekdays. Most schools charge for this service.

Contacts at the schools are: Key Largo Elementary School, MM 104.8, Key Largo, (305) 453-1255; Plantation Key School, 100 Lake Rd., Tavernier, (305) 853-3281; Switlik Elementary, MM 48.8 Bayside, 33rd St., Marathon, (305) 289-2490; Big Pine Key Neighborhood School, Palomino Horse Trail, Big Pine Key, (305) 872-1266; Sugarloaf Elementary/Middle School, 255 Crane Rd., Sugarloaf Key, (305) 745-3282; Poinciana Elementary School, 1407 Kennedy Dr., Key West, (305) 293-1630; Sigsbee Elementary, Sigsbee Naval Base, Key West, (305) 294-1861 (military families only); Gerald Adams Elementary School, 5855 W. Junior College Rd., Key West, (305) 293-1609.

### Babysitting

Personal knowledge of the person you choose to care for your child in your absence is the best of all possible worlds, but it isn't always a reality. If you are a visitor to the Florida Keys or a newly relocated resident, you may have to take a leap of faith and entrust your child to someone you do not know. Therefore, you should check references. For referrals, contact Wesley House (see listing under Resources) or ask the concierge at your hotel.

You can also contact local chambers of commerce, which often keep lists of local residents who babysit: Key Largo, (305) 451-1414 or (800) 822-1088; Islamorada, (305) 664-4503 or (800) 322-5397; Marathon, (305) 743-5417 or (800) 262-7284; Lower Keys, (305) 872-2411 or (800) 872-3722; and Key West, (305) 294-2587 or (800) 527-8539. Be sure to ask by what criteria these referrals have been checked for more insight as to who may best suit your needs.

# Media

Even after Henry Flagler's extension of the Florida East Coast Railroad provided Florida Keys residents access to the mainland, communications on our islands were limited. To receive local news and news outside the South Florida area, residents relied on radio broadcasts from Miami, sporadic postal service, and what was probably their most effective and timely means of dispatch: word of mouth, or what is jokingly referred to as "the Conch telegraph."

Today two dailies and a contingent of weeklies and free papers tie the Keys together. Both AM and FM radio stations are still restricted by wattage, and residents must subscribe to satellite or cable service to get television reception.

## NEWSPAPERS

In addition to home delivery, our newspapers are often sold in curbside vending racks, grocery stores, pharmacies, convenience stores, and bookstores. A handful of shops carry national and international newspapers. Because the Florida Keys are considered a remote distribution site, some national newspapers, such as the *New York Times,* are sold at a higher newsstand price. A rule of thumb: Get to the newsstand early. The farther you travel from the mainland, the more quickly the out-of-town papers sell out.

> **i** Prior to 1917 the Florida Keys were a much more peaceful place. It was in that year that the first long-distance phone connection linked the Keys to Miami.

### Dailies

**KEY WEST CITIZEN,** 3420 Northside Dr., Key West, FL 33040; (305) 292-7777; keysnews.com. In 1904 a small weekly newspaper known as the *Citizen* appeared on the newspaper scene in Key West; it was later consolidated with the 1899 *Inter-Ocean* to form the *Key West Citizen.* Cooke Communications now owns the *Key West Citizen,* along with weekly *Solares Hill* (now published in the Sunday edition of the *Citizen*), the *Free Press* community newspapers, and the Florida Keys News Service.

The *Citizen's* editorial focus is primarily on features. *Paradise,* which appears in Thursday's edition, is a comprehensive compendium of what's currently happening in the theaters and at the clubs and galleries around town. Free copies of

*Paradise* are available at newsstands, hotels, guesthouses, restaurants, and other businesses throughout Key West. The *Citizen* also publishes "The Menu," a free quarterly guide containing menus from many area restaurants.

## Hidden Talent

Everyone knows Jimmy Buffett can sing, but did you know he also wrote three books that made the *New York Times* bestseller list? Three of his books were fiction: *Tales from Margaritaville*, *Where is Joe Merchant?*, and *Swine Not*. His nonfiction book is titled *A Pirate Looks at Fifty*. Buffett is one of only six authors in the list's history to have number-one titles in both fiction and nonfiction. The others were Ernest Hemingway, Dr. Seuss, Mitch Albom, William Styron, and John Steinbeck. Wanna bet those five couldn't sing?

### Weeklies & Biweeklies

**CONCH COLOR,** 314 Simonton St., Key West, FL 33040; (305) 294-7566; conchcolor.com. Publisher and editor Tom Oosterhoudt's *Conch Color* showcases the exciting and entertaining life in the Keys. Tom is everywhere and is invited to everything that is anything. He has taken this lifestyle and turned it into a fun and colorful photographic chronicle. The paper is published weekly, covers Marathon to Key West, is free, and can be picked up at most commercial locations.

**FLORIDA KEYS *KEYNOTER,*** MM 48.6 Oceanside, 3015 Overseas Hwy., Marathon, FL 33050; (305) 743-5551

**KEY WEST *KEYNOTER,*** 2720A N. Roosevelt Blvd., Key West, FL 33040; (305) 296-6989; keysnet.com. The *Keynoter* is Monroe County's second-oldest publication. Known for its in-depth coverage of the Keys' political scene, once a week the *Keynoter* also features "L' Attitudes," an arts and entertainment section that includes complete TV listings for the area, special features, and upcoming Keys events. The *Keynoter* is published each Wed and Sat and is widely available in shops, newsstands, and curbside racks throughout the Keys.

i Handy websites for visitors and locals: general information, fla-keys.com; cities: islamorada.fl.us, key westcity.com, keycolonybeach.net, and ci.marathon.fl.us.

## Radio

Radio reception in the Florida Keys is heavily influenced by factors such as weather and distance from the transmitter. Clear skies and sunshine will optimize good reception; luckily, we have plenty of both most of the time. Some of our more-popular radio stations include:

WEOW Today's Hits, 92.7
Key-Z FM, 93.5
Conch Country, 98.7
Sun Classic Rock, 99.5
US-1 Radio, 104.1
Island, 107.1

## Television

Florida Keys residents must pay for cable TV service in order to receive network channels. Our cable provider is Comcast, (866) 288-3444.

In addition to national programming, local-origination programming is offered on channels 5, 24, and 75 through 79. This public service programming includes live coverage of city commission and local political meetings, as well as real estate listings and local-interest shows on a variety of topics, such as health care and fishing. Channel 5 also offers interesting and informative infomercials during the day and evening, highlighting many of the Keys attractions found in this book.

Satellite communication is an alternative to cable service. Check the Yellow Pages for companies offering satellite dishes and service.

# Index